THE PHILOSOPHY OF DISCOURSE

THE PHILOSOPHY OF DISCOURSE
THE RHETORICAL TURN IN TWENTIETH-CENTURY THOUGHT

Volume 2

Edited by

Chip Sills

Assistant Professor of Philosophy
Department of History
United States Naval Academy

George H. Jensen

Associate Professor
Department of English
Southwest Missouri State University

BOYNTON/COOK PUBLISHERS
HEINEMANN
Portsmouth, NH

Boynton/Cook Publishers, Inc.
A Subsidiary of
Heinemann Educational Books, Inc.
361 Hanover Street, Portsmouth, NH 03801
Offices and agents throughout the world

Chapter 1 incorporates material by Dr. James A. Boon previously published in "Claude
Lévi-Strauss" (Chapter 9 of *The Return of Grand Theory to the Human Sciences*,
Quentin Skinner, ed., Cambridge University Press, 1985) and *Other Tribes, Other
Scribes: Symbolic Anthropology in the Comparative Study of Cultures, Histories,
Religions, and Texts* (Cambridge University Press, 1982). The incorporated material is
reprinted with the permission of the publisher.

Library of Congress Cataloging-in-Publication Data
The Philosophy of discourse: the rhetorical turn in twentieth-century
    thought/edited by Chip Sills, George H. Jensen.
        p.   cm.
    Includes bibliographical references.
    ISBN 0−86709−286−6 (v. 1). −ISBN 0−86709−287−4 (v. 2)
    I. Sills, Chip. II. Jensen, George H.
B804.P536 1992
149′.94−dc20   91−14249
                                                                        CIP

Cover designed by T. Watson Bogaard.
Printed in the United States of America.
92 93 94 95 96   9 8 7 6 5 4 3 2 1

Contents

7   Gadamer's Hermeneutics: Prejudice, Dialogue, and Edification
Georgia Warnke   188

Myth, History, and Discourse   *209*

Introduction
George H. Jensen   211

8   Ernst Cassirer and the Philosophy of Symbolic Forms
C. H. Knoblauch   215

Feminism   *233*

9   The Woman Question — And Some Answers
Angelika Bammer   235

Contributors   *265*

Preface

The twentieth century has seen a protean development of the notion of "discourse." A number of challenging and contradictory discursive theories have been elaborated, attacked, and defended. These developments are stimulating but somewhat overwhelming, because of the wealth of the material and the lack of any attempt at a unitary accounting. The large number of critical vocabularies and styles descendant from the various paradigms unfortunately discourages many from entering what often seems a bewildering series of arcane debates.

The present work is an attempt to offer a useful introduction to a number of contemporary discursive models. The wealth of material has required that the work be presented in two volumes, and even so the editors have been forced to limit coverage to a representative collection of themes and persons. Volume 1 contains sections devoted to the philosophy of science, pragmatism, the Frankfurt School, the Bakhtin Circle, and the revival of rhetoric. Volume 2 contains sections devoted to structuralism and poststructuralism, hermeneutics, Cassirer, and feminism. Although most readers will probably find both volumes necessary for a more thorough introduction to the philosophy of discourse, the work has been designed so that either volume can be studied independently. The general introduction appears in both volumes.

Each volume presents chapters that concentrate, for the most part, on the work of individual figures, such as Lévi-Strauss, Foucault, or Rorty. Two of the chapters, the ones on philosophy of science and feminism, are more general, covering a group of theorists. Most chapters are elements of larger thematic sections, each of which is preceded by a general introduction. For example, the section on the Frankfurt School in Volume 1 begins with a general introduction, followed by chapters on Adorno and Habermas. By working from the introductory material to the chapters, the reader should be able to develop a broad overview of the "rhetorical turn."

This overview cannot claim to be comprehensive. Even with the expansion of this project into a second volume, we could not include a chapter on every noteworthy twentieth-century thinker who commented on the nature of discourse. Most readers will believe that some important figure has been unaccountably left out, while some lesser figure has been included. Such criticism is to be expected. In our defense, we say only that we struggled long and hard with the issue. It is difficult to select a limited number of important and representative figures, and we acknowledge that some important ones—Emilio Betti, Roland Barthes, Paul Ricoeur, Antonio Gramsci, Michael Oakeshott, Susanne K. Langer, Roman Jakobson, and James Hillman, to name a few— have been excluded. We have tried to fill in some gaps with our introductory sections.

Even though it was impossible to exhaust the richness of the "rhetorical turn," we have included enough important figures to provide the reader with a sense of this important conversation. That it is a conversation will become evident upon reading and rereading the work. The chapter on Rorty will help the reader better understand the chapter on Gadamer, and the chapter on Heidegger will help to comprehend Rorty.

It is our hope that the two volumes of *The Philosophy of Discourse* will be useful to the reader who has little prior knowledge of the "rhetorical turn," yet still be instructive for those who are actually participating in this conversation. The volumes should provide a much-needed general orientation that can serve as an entrée for more specialized study of individual figures.

Acknowledgments

These volumes could not have been completed without the help of many people. We would like to express our appreciation to our authors, many of whom told us, "This is the hardest thing I have ever written." We appreciate their willingness to cut massive rough drafts and clarify difficult concepts.

We wish to thank those who suggested authors for individual chapters: Hans Kellner (Michigan State University), Robert Detweiler (Emory University), Richard Rorty (University of Virginia), Allan Megill (University of Iowa), Robert Paul (Emory University), Martin Jay (University of California—Berkeley), Ian Hacking (University of California—Santa Cruz), and Ben W. McClelland (University of Mississippi).

We also wish to thank those who generously agreed to supplement our knowledge by reading and critiquing rough drafts: Ron Jackson (Emory University), Kathryn Kirkpatrick (Emory University), Janet Summers (University of North Carolina—Greensboro), Walter Adamson (Emory University), Sheryl Gowen (Georgia State University), and Chris Zervos (Purdue University—Calumet).

For his general support, we wish to thank Donald McCloskey (University of Iowa).

For their patience and support, we wish to thank our respective wives and children.

THE PHILOSOPHY OF DISCOURSE

General Introduction

Chip Sills

To speak of the "rhetorical turn" in contemporary discourse is to risk
further eroding an already well-worn turn of phrase by creating yet
another variant. There are no shortages of "turns" proposed, discovered,
announced, and disseminated in the contemporary discursive jungle.
Richard Rorty started it all with his influential *Linguistic Turn*, a
collection of essays in the tradition of recent linguistic analysis, in
1967. Rorty's Introduction to this work stressed the tension between
the modernist quest for a neutral methodology and the specific substantive assumptions — such as methodological nominalism — endemic to
linguistic philosophy.[1] Since then, patient readers have received numerous updates. Geoffrey Hartmann, for instance, posited a "hermeneutic
turn" initiated by Hegel.[2] Since the exploitation of charming and
world-disclosing turns of phrase is a fundamental element in any rhetoric,
it was only a matter of time before the self-reflexive mania of contemporary intellectual culture hit upon the strategem of turning the
various devices of rhetorical practice on the rhetoric of modernity
itself. The resulting "rhetorical turn" was heralded by the editors of
The Rhetoric of the Human Sciences, which announced itself as a
preliminary report of this movement.[3]

It is tempting to characterize the rhetorical turn as the "big picture,"
as the synthetic entity that includes and continues the twentieth-century
emphasis on language in a more comprehensive mode. From this point
of view, the rhetorical emphasis on the pragmatics of communication
completes the more formalist inquiries of linguistic and hermeneutic
analysis and *Verstehen*, which then appear as but partial manifestations.
But the self-consciousness implied in the rhetorical turn also implies
the ironic reminder that such a characterization is itself the instantiation
of a strategy — often called "Hegelian" — that can be seen as a rhetorical

1

gambit, one that has come under heavy criticism. Let us begin, then, to introduce this newcomer by adopting the strategy of simply examining the constituent terms of the phrase: "rhetoric" and "turn." The account that follows will hopscotch around vast cultural icons and clichés, giving only preliminary and contentious indications of one way to view the rhetorical turn, but I may crave indulgence from the reader, for any statement of introduction announces by its title that it is only a fragment, indicating a greater account to follow.

Rhetoric is an ancient discipline currently experiencing a phoenixlike rebirth. Not so long ago, the term "rhetoric" was perhaps most often associated with empty verbiage and long lists of obscure terms whose purpose was to provide names for formally distinguishing various poetic operations, for naming the parts of a discourse, for classifying the elements of persuasion, for classifying genres or prescribing which moves were appropriate to those genres. "Rhetoric" was also supposed to prescribe appropriate mechanisms for composing and delivering speeches. But the current rebirth of intense interest in rhetorical concerns is perhaps best understood as a recrudescence of the ancient warfare waged for millennia between philosophy and rhetoric.

A good case could be made for the proposition that Western philosophy first took form as an effort to distinguish itself from rhetoric. There is no question that Socrates himself was popularly considered by many of his contemporaries to be a sophist, a master of rhetoric who attracted an admiring entourage of listeners and codisputants. But Socrates was a rhetorician with a difference — he showed a sustained and subtle interest in exploring the limits of rhetorical principles in the pursuit of truth. In the process, he succeeded in initiating a problematic separation of the philosophical project — said to be an inquiry after truth — from that of rhetoric — said to be a discipline that explores the dynamics of persuasion as the manipulation of opinion. Plato's *Gorgias* has Socrates analyzing rhetoric as a rather disreputable enterprise, essentially a subdivision of the art of pandering.[4] But Plato was evidently dissatisfied with this somewhat dismissive judgment and returned to the problem of properly relating philosophy and rhetoric in the *Phaedrus*. This dialogue begins with a humorous restatement of the earlier position, dramatically realized by Lysias's speech in favor of giving love to the nonlover — the theme of the speech itself is already a very specific and open instance of pandering, in the most obvious and provocative sense. The lustful nonlover has commissioned a speech from Lysias to win the favor of some attractive young man, and Lysias has graciously complied. But Socrates does not take the opportunity thus offered to repeat the charges made in the *Gorgias*. Instead, he first meets Phaedrus's challenge to outdo Lysias's effort with a speech of his own, directed towards the same thesis: it is better to give one's love to a person who is not in love with you. His *daimon* then warns him that he has blasphemed love, and Socrates makes amends with the famous speech about love as a form of divine madness, with the power to lead both lover and beloved towards the truth — which is seen explicitly as a divine realm. He then goes on to consider more closely the relations of philosophy and rhetoric, arguing that philosophy and "true rhetoric" are inextricably linked. We are invited to interpret his recantation of his earlier speech as also being a recantation of his earlier dismissal of rhetoric. Philosophy, in employing the dialectical method, both ensures that its results are true and embodies the rhetorical approach best calculated to achieve adherence to the truth found. So truth and persuasion are joined for Socrates; philosophy and rhetoric are synthesized.

This uneasy synthesis was not maintained, however, and for good reason. Philosophy in general has upheld the distinction between opinion (*doxa*) and truth (*episteme*), and sophists/rhetoricians have in general denied that this distinction can be given any nondogmatic or trans-contextual validity. As Blumenberg points out, "Rhetoric belongs to a syndrome of skeptical assumptions."[5] Since the truth that philosophy seeks is *universal*, the devotees of rhetoric have marked their disagreement with this project by deploying the skeptical tropes that oppose the assertion of universal truths by pointing out the equal plausibility of differing "truths," or arguing that philosophical pretensions to absolute truth invariably involve arbitrary assumptions (the trope of hypothesis), an infinite regress in justification, or begging the question (the trope of circular reasoning). All this achieved canonical expression by the second century A.D. in the work of Sextus Empiricus.[6] In fact, however, the skeptical approach shows the *necessity* of the opposition between philosophy and rhetoric, as much as it undermines the positive assertion of any specific version of philosophical truth, for Sextus Empiricus reduces the problem of justified knowledge to the following dilemma: every object of apprehension seems to be apprehended either through itself — immediately — or through something else — via mediation. But nothing, evidently, is apprehended through itself, because everything is (potentially, at least) an object of controversy. And if something is taken to be apprehended through something else, then the tropes of hypothesis, infinite regress, and circularity see to it that no certainty is available here, either. Philosophy, in the widest sense, tends to choose the first alternative, and seeks a truth that is self-grounding. This is the motivation for the endless philosophical quests for "presuppositionlessness" and "neutral methodology." Rhetoric, on the other hand, is inherently other-oriented, and provisionally adopts whatever is at hand in order to develop its persuasive strategies. The skeptical dilemma is more damaging to philosophy, inasmuch as philosophy maintains its project of seeking truth. Rhetoric, by adopting a more modest criterion of practical persuasion via opinion, seems more at home in a skeptical environment, and confines itself to analyses of the media by which persuasion is effected. Rorty's more recent outlook begins to look like the reprise of a viewpoint formulated eighteen centuries ago.

The skeptic's use of the word "trope" (often misleadingly translated as "mode") provides the best opportunity for examining the second term of our title: "turn." For a trope is, among other things, a turning, as when we refer to the phototropism of plants (turning to the light) or even simply the "tropics" (where the sun annually "turns" at the solstices). Troping also variously implies movement, change, innovation, stratagem, adaptation, transfer, difference, exclusion, inclusion, merger, and identity.[7] The rhetorical turn can thus be viewed as yet another attempt to renew the creative tension between philosophy and rhetoric, involving all the tropal dimensions listed above. If the synthesis of philosophy and rhetoric has proved problematic, so has the effort to keep the disciplines separate. Philosophy of rhetoric, the effort to achieve systematic and comprehensive understanding of the proper use of rhetorical terms and procedures, has frequently shown a telos towards first principles, while no philosophy has ever been able to completely dispense with the apparatus of persuasion. In this regard, the above-mentioned tendency for philosophy to experiment with various attempts to achieve a "neutral" *methodical* explication of its theses (thus claiming not to rely on any rhetorical presuppositions) seems remarkable, and indeed constitutive of much of what has been termed "philosophy." From Spinoza's method of deduction from definition and axiom to more recent positivist flirtation with mathematicological formalism, to the various strategies anthologized in Rorty's collection, philosophy in the age of modern science has shown a recurring tendency to claim the rhetorical higher ground of a neutral truth-securing method. In the wake of Goedel's theorems, however, which are arguably only the restatement of the skeptical objections of Sextus Empiricus in mathematical form, this claim looks more and more threadbare.[8] Odd as it may seem, even mathematics arguably has rhetorical elements in its procedures.[9]

The contemporary recrudescence of rhetorical interest can be seen, then, in the context of the decline of the fortunes of scientific philosophy, which developed itself amid the most extreme and strenuous efforts to positively banish all rhetorical elements from its presentation. Paul De Man has collected representative statements from early modern philosophers, documenting their uniform hostility to rhetoric. Descartes, Locke, Hobbes, Condillac, and Kant all made efforts to distinguish rhetoric from proper philosophical procedure.[10] Reading through these manifestos, one cannot escape a certain feeling of irony: in the midst of proclaiming a skeptical assault upon the religious, political, and philosophical legacy of the past, these thinkers uniformly belittle the discipline of rhetoric, which our analysis thus far has shown to be most congenial with skeptical assumptions. The discrepancy coalesces around the issue of science. Mathematicological procedures find their intuitive justification in the fact that they prove so valuable in extending the limits of mechanistic natural science. Other attempts to ground natural philosophy in such a way as to justify the success of Newtonian mechanics show a similar ambivalence about skepticism: one was *not* permitted to be skeptical about the Newtonian world-picture. When Bishop Berkeley, in correspondence with Samuel Johnson, cited logical reasons for doubting crucial elements of Newton's account, Johnson's reply was a blank incredulity that Newton could be wrong.[11] And, in general, early modern philosophy is often taught as an attempt to establish a mode of knowing certainty that could maintain itself in the face of skeptical considerations. From this point of view, the rhetorical turn could be seen as the development of tendencies present at the outset in modern philosophy. Still, compared with the place of honor held by rhetoric in the medieval intellectual world, the decisive rejection of rhetoric in the early modern period must be considered one of its defining characteristics, and the rhetorical turn of today appears as a "return of the repressed."

The *locus classicus* of the confrontation of skepticism and scientific philosophy has long been held to be the critical philosophy of Immanuel Kant. Kant's problem was to somehow guarantee the rational acceptability of the Newtonian world-picture in the face of Hume's skeptical objections. The everyday world of sense-perception seemed to depict a world of real objects, extended in space and enduring in time, a world that seemed to follow Newton's laws of motion and gravitation. Yet our perceptions were not immediately revelatory of these objects, but depended on our own sensory apparatus, which organized the "signals" arriving from the real objects into "ideas" (this, at least, was the view of thinkers as disparate as Locke, Leibniz, Berkeley, and Hume).[12] It is only with these "ideas" that we are in immediate contact. Kant's ingenious solution was to deny (along with the skeptical tradition) that we have any knowledge of "things in themselves" apart from our perception of them, while at the same time arguing that the "objectivity" we seek (so our knowledge can be actually true) is available on *this* side of the phenomena, so to speak, as a rationally deducible set of categories of understanding that guarantee the possibility of any experience whatsoever. Any possible experience is organized automatically by the categories of our "transcendental unity of apperception." These categories, happily enough, fit Newtonian conceptions very neatly. Kant's philosophy may owe some of its enduring appeal, despite its difficulties, to its proposed arrangement of skepticism, experience, and truth. Precisely some such arrangement was required as an ideological justification of physical science, which claims a skeptical methodology (it purports not to rely on political, philosophical, or religious dogma, and it experiments, or subjects its hypotheses to skeptical testing) while at the same time making claims to truth and basing its justification on the commonplace experiences of a technological society.[13]

It is not widely appreciated how deeply Hegel's critique of Kantian philosophy and the Newtonian science that formed its motivation was informed by (1) Hegel's abiding concern with confronting and answering the objections of the ancient skeptics to objective knowing, and (2) his realization that this concern required "a new concept of science."[14] At issue is a "method" that is viewed as integral to, rather than externally imposed upon, the subject matter. Hegel's work, while acknowledged as immensely seminal, is rarely taken seriously on its own terms. The rhetoric of "absolute knowing" is typically viewed with incredulity (and often, faint condescension) as a last-gasp effort at a final metaphysics of Being (in the Aristotelian tradition) or Consciousness (in the Cartesian tradition). The fact that neither of these interpretations bears serious scrutiny is a measure of the sorry state of Hegel scholarship in contemporary academic culture. Even while the breathtaking events in the Soviet Union and Eastern Europe are being heralded as "Hegel's revenge," few observers are aware that a real confrontation with Hegel's contribution to philosophy requires a recognition of how his reconception of philosophic "science" involves a subtle and searching treatment of the relations of philosophy and rhetoric.[15] The most promising new directions in Hegel interpretation are redirecting attention to the importance of rhetorical considerations in Hegel's notion of *Bildung*, to the key role that the tropes of ancient skepticism played in Hegel's overall view of opposition and negation in the advancement of knowledge, and to a more nuanced appreciation of the rhetoric of "absolute knowing."[16] The absence of reference implied in the term "absolute" warns us not to take *anything* as a fixed and final reference-point for the construction of a comprehensive view of the world. But, paradoxically, we cannot make *any* beginning without incurring some debt of reference, some acknowledgment that something appears to be the case. At issue is whether it is useful to proceed along the assumption that what appears is in some sense, finally, conducive to a comprehensive account about all that is the case. Here Hegel and pragmatism (which has taken of late an openly rhetorical turn) are in agreement. At the very least, thought after Hegel should know enough to think "rhetoric" every time we hear the word "method"!

With Hegel, the transition from modernism to postmodernism is already in question. This can be scrutinized in terms of the issue of foundationalism. It seems to us that "modernist" foundationalism is different from traditional foundationalism in an important way that needs to be elucidated. In brief, the difference is that the modernist foundational project proceeds *after* a radical skeptical gesture that makes (or seeks or claims to make) traditional *metaphysical* foundationalism impossible. Modernist theory no longer looks for an "objective" reality behind the appearances, but seeks through various methodological strategies (tending always toward positivism, which is most clear and intransigent about this dismissal of metaphysics) to "found" certain knowledge on *this* side of the appearances. Alternatively, "certainty" and "truth" themselves are scrapped as viable strategies for organizing knowledge, and one resigns oneself to some version of probabilism. Postmodernism, viewed most broadly as the acceptance of this situation, is then the final blow against *any* project of foundations. If Hegel, for instance, is seen as identifying speculative reason as the "absolute" foundation for reality, then his project comes under postmodern attack. But the very peculiarity of Hegel's vision is that the "absolute" becomes determinate, intelligible, only through the comprehensive inspection and critique of all foundational schemes. In this sense, Hegel's work has served as a strategic resource for many subsequent antifoundational projects.[17] And the postmodern attack on foundations has itself bifurcated into two general tendencies: one that keeps vigilant watch on any attempt to reestablish foundations of any sort, and another that takes the inability to establish any *single* foundation as a license to use any and all foundational discourses as seems convenient.

Hegel was, if never really refuted, certainly bypassed and ignored. Marx, of course, genuinely attempted to overcome Hegel dialectically.[18] But the subsequent development of Western ideology, including Marxism, owed less to any sense of "dialectics" than to triumphant scientism, which developed from neo-Kantianism to logical positivism. The separation of fact and value and the acknowledgment of physical science as the paradigm of genuine knowing have served as almost unchallenged arbiters of rational discourse until recently.[19] The rhetorical turn can be seen as the attempt to undermine the hegemony of positivism via a reconsideration of rhetoric. The Marxist variants of the rhetorical turn have had to fight a war on two fronts: in addition to criticizing discourse — including positivism — as the ideology of the (bourgeois) rulers, the more intelligent (and democratic) Marxist critics have always had to bear with the atrocities being committed daily in the name of "Marxism." Writing in the spring of 1990, when practical revulsion against the pretensions of Marxist hegemony has swept so much of the communist world, it seems difficult to credit the long and sympathetic hearing that Marxist ideology has received (and continues to receive) in the Western Academy. But surely one advantage Marxism accorded to theorists of discourse was its proposal to analyze discourse as ideology: as the rationalization of a complex historical configuration of interests, divided conveniently into the thought that rationalized the proprietors and the thought that gave marching orders to those indentured to struggle against the proprietors in the name of the coming socialist configuration. That most Marxist theorists were in no sense proletarians has always given the role of Marxist theoretician (beginning with Marx) an odd redolence of uninvited pretender, a role seemingly congenial to academics and intellectuals generally.

The rhetorical resources subsumed under Paul Ricoeur's "hermeneutics of suspicion" have thus played an ambivalent role in introducing the rhetorical turn. Nietzsche and Freud, besides Marx the most brilliant and compelling practitioners of the genre, have also played the role of radical critic, only to find their insights codified and institutionalized. Nietzsche, master of rhetoric that he was, ambiguously combined a form of fatalistic positivism (the "eternal return") with a straightforward attack upon the Western project of metaphysical truth and an unparalleled awareness of the protean powers of language to construct alternative realities. By radically distinguishing between "life" and "language," however, Nietzsche trades on just those metaphysical oppositions that he wishes to overcome.[20] Yet Nietzsche's incomparable rhetorical power, together with his uncompromising hostility to bourgeois culture, has attracted many who wanted an alternative to Marxism that embodies a stance intransigeantly opposed to the culture of modern liberal capitalism. Nietzsche has had a well-documented influence on many thinkers of this century, including several dealt with in these volumes. Heidegger, Foucault, and Derrida, at least, owe enormous debts to Nietzsche's example. The idea that discourse should be considered finally an art form, a spontaneous creation of the will to power, continues to have great appeal to many.

The final hermeneut of suspicion, Freud, also had an influential contribution to the interpretation of signs, and deserves mention as an introducer of the contemporary rhetorical turn. Freud first gained wide acceptance for his work with *The Interpretation of Dreams*, and the psychoanalytic art/science/therapy he founded is based upon a regressive hermeneutic analysis of neurotic *symptoms* disclosive of a dynamically repressed unconscious life.[21] Where Marx had interpreted human culture as formed by the antagonistic impulses of class struggle, and Nietzsche had analyzed culture as will to power, Freud saw an immortal battle between life and death instincts within the individual, and a constitutive struggle between the conflicting demands of instinct and communal life. Freud's interpretive discourse also implied an interpretation of discourse: the motivations and discursive counters of our conversations were to be understood as sublimated reenactments of primal scenes whose fantasy-memories formed the unconscious parameters of our possible experience.

All three of the hermeneuts of suspicion were modernist in opposing classical transcendence: the traditional Judeo-Christian interpretation that the ultimate purpose of discourse was the task of reconciling revealed truth with the experiences of finite life. Yet even the radical immanentism of these modernist critics maintained various covert ties to transcendence. Marx's classless utopia, Nietzsche's superman, and Freud's not-so-surreptitious self-identification with Moses all betokened an inability to rest easy in contemporary Western culture. It may be that the relatively uncritical view each of them took towards natural science is symptomatic of this inconsistency. Since the nineteenth century, as the first chapter of this work attests, science has lost much of its lustre as the one "natural" explanation of the way things are, and has come to disclose many of the same inconsistencies and intractable difficulties that have characterized other disciplines of knowing.

The fact that Freud's name is often immediately linked with that of Jung, as a fellow pioneer of depth psychology, brings out some of the pathos of the transition from the modern to the postmodern. Where Freud was forthright in his opposition to any future for religious "illusion," Jung thought he discerned in the traumas of irreligious modernity the outlines of a psychological quest for wholeness deserving of respect and requiring an imaginative reconstruction. Where one tendency of postmodernity follows Freud in denying recognition to any further traffic with the absolute, another follows Jung in countering that any and all such traffic is justified by psychological necessity. Where Freud, like an Old Testament prophet, places an interdict on any further theology — a gesture that makes any religion in effect a form of idolatry — Jung responds that precisely our lack of a culturally reinforced faith makes the equal access to any and all modalities and symbols of faith permissible.[22] It is noteworthy that further development of archetypal psychology since Jung's death has included its own "rhetorical turn": James Hillman closes his *Re-Visioning Psychology* with a call for a return to Renaissance rhetoric and neo-Platonist panpsychological consciousness.[23]

Another avenue to the contemporary rhetorical turn is twentieth-century semiotic theory, which can be viewed as having a twofold origin in the work of Charles S. Peirce and Ferdinand de Saussure. Peirce's contribution is dealt with in the chapter contributed by Peter Skagestad, so I will not comment on it here. Saussure contributed an

influential analysis of the semiotic dynamics of language that is still
being exploited and debated. Briefly, Saussure argued that the *sign*
could be understood only when analyzed into its component parts:
signifier (the perceptible sign itself, the word or gesture or mark) and
signified (the concept intended).[24] The analysis has spawned a great
interpretive and critical literature. Saussure claimed that the signifier
had a "horizontal" relationship of *signification* — it indicated a "lack"
or relationship to its concept, only accessible via other signs — as well
as a "vertical" relationship — its *reference* or denotation of some aspect
of experience. Poststructuralist semiotics has characteristically denied
access to the vertical dimension, by arguing that it doesn't exist or
cannot be known via signification. The play of surfaces is all we have;
the illusion of depth characteristic of Western thought since Heracleitus is
denied. The post-Hegelian war against comprehension is being fought
on every front.

These comments may serve to place the rhetorical turn in some
preliminary context. Perhaps they are best summarized by the statement
that we are now more willing than before to realize that whenever we
speak of "discourse," we are ineluctably on rhetorical terrain.

Notes

1. Richard Rorty, ed., *The Linguistic Turn: Recent Essays in Philosophical
Method* (Chicago: Univ. of Chicago, 1967). Rorty defines "methodological
nominalism" thus: "The view that all questions which philosophers have asked
about concepts, subsistent universals, or 'natures' which (a) cannot be answered
by empirical inquiry concerning the behavior or properties of particulars subsumed under such concepts, universals, or natures, and which (b) can be
answered in *some* way, can be answered by answering questions about the use
of linguistic expressions, and in no other way." (p. 11)

2. Geoffrey Hartmann, *The Fate of Reading and Other Essays* (Chicago:
Univ. of Chicago, 1975), p. 120.

3. John S. Nelson, Allan Megill, and Donald N. McCloskey, *The Rhetoric
of the Human Sciences: Language and Argument in Scholarship and Public
Affairs* (Madison: Univ. of Wisconsin, 1987).

4. Here I am following the discussion of Walter Hamilton in his Introduction to his translation of the *Phaedrus, Phaedrus and Letters VII and VIII*
(Hammondsworth, Middlesex: Penguin, 1985), pp. 7–18.

5. Hans Blumenberg, "An Anthropological Approach to Rhetoric," in
Kenneth Baynes, James Bohman, and Thomas McCarthy, eds., *Philosophy:
End or Transformation* (Cambridge, Mass.: MIT, 1987), pp. 429–58.

6. Sextus Empiricus, *Outlines of Pyrrhonism*, trans. R. G. Bury (London:
Heinemann, 1976).

7. The literature on tropes is immense and growing. See, for starters,
Mark Johnson, ed., *Philosophical Perspectives on Metaphor* (Minneapolis:

Univ. of Minnesota, 1981); Kenneth Burke, "The Four Master-Tropes," Appendix D of *A Grammar of Motives* (New York: Prentice-Hall, 1945), pp. 503–17; Hayden White, *Metahistory* (Baltimore: Johns Hopkins Univ., 1973) and *Tropics of Discourse* (Baltimore: Johns Hopkins Univ., 1978); and Hans Kellner, *Language and Historical Representation: Getting the Story Crooked*, part III (Madison: Univ. of Wisconsin, 1989), pp. 189–264; for a more inclusive bibliography, see Chip Sills, *The Myth of Reason: Is Hegel's 'Logic' a Speculative Tropology?* 1988 diss. Emory University.

8. See John Kadvany, "Reflections on the Legacy of Kurt Goedel: Mathematics, Skepticism, Postmodernism," *Philosophical Forum*, 20 (Spring 1989), pp. 161–81.

9. This has been argued by Philip Davis and Reuben Hersh in Nelson, et al., *Rhetoric of the Human Sciences* (Madison: Univ. of Wisconsin, 1987), pp. 53–68.

10. Paul De Man, "The Epistemology of Metaphor," in Sheldon Sacks, ed., *On Metaphor* (Chicago: Univ. of Chicago, 1979), pp. 11–28. De Man treats Locke, Condillac, and Kant, but similar statements by Descartes and Hobbes are well known. One noteworthy exception to this hostility to rhetoric is the great Neapolitan philosopher and rhetorician Giambattista Vico, whose recent vogue is itself a symptom of the rhetorical turn.

11. George Berkeley, *Principles, Dialogues, and Correspondence*, ed. Colin Turbayne (New York: Library of Liberal Arts, 1965), pp. 215–42.

12. The "common sense" philosophy of Thomas Reid, now enjoying a bit of a renaissance, was noteworthy in its insistance that we *do*, for all practical purposes, immediately perceive external objects. Reid thus denies the premise that makes skepticism seem invincible—the premise that all we have to deal with immediately are the *appearances* of external objects. See his *Inquiry Into the Human Mind on the Principles of Common Sense* (1764).

13. It is of course a matter of controversy within the scientific community whether or not science makes any metaphysical claims to truth. Many, if not most scientific practitioners, conditioned by positivist protocols, would deny that the "truths" of science have any more than a pragmatic standing. But the rhetorical situation is quite different. Science is widely held by many of its practitioners and by virtually all contemporary official organs of authoritative discourse to be *the* authoritative discourse—the paradigm of what truth means.

14. Michael Forster's *Hegel and Skepticism* (Cambridge, Mass.: Harvard Univ., 1989) is a welcome recent exception to the habitual minimizing of this aspect of Hegel's project. Hegel makes the claim for a "new form of science" in several places. See, for example, *Science of Logic*, trans. A. V. Miller (New York: Humanities Press, 1969), pp. 27ff. and 53ff.; *Philosophy of Right*, trans. T. M. Knox (Oxford: Oxford Univ., 1967), pp. 1–2.

15. See John H. Smith, *The Spirit and Its Letter: Traces of Rhetoric in Hegel's Philosophy of 'Bildung'* (Cornell: Cornell Univ., 1988). While Smith is agnostic at best about the continuing value of Hegel's speculative philosophy, his study broaches in a serious and scholarly way the issues of philosophy and rhetoric in Hegel's work.

16. In addition to the works of Forster and Smith, see Chip Sills, "Is Hegel's *Logic* a Speculative Tropology?" *Owl of Minerva*, 21:1 (Fall 1989), pp. 21–40.

17. See, for instance, Henry Sussman, *The Hegelian Aftermath* (Baltimore: Johns Hopkins Univ., 1982), for an exploration of post-Hegelian philosophy and literature as selective exploitation of various Hegelian tropes. Exploration of Hegel as an antifoundational thinker has been undertaken by William Maker in "Reason and Modernity," *Philosophical Forum*, 18:4 (Summer 1987), pp. 275–303; and by Richard Dien Winfield in "The Route to Foundation-Free Systematic Philosophy," *Philosophical Forum*, 15:3 (Spring 1984), pp. 323–43.

18. See Richard Bernstein's *Praxis and Action* (Philadelphia: Univ. of Pennsylvania, 1971), especially Part I, for a reasoned defense of this reading.

19. Gillian Rose, in *Hegel Contra Sociology* (London: Athlone, 1981), offers a succinct summary of the continuing and pervasive influence of neo-Kantian assumptions in contemporary thought.

20. This argument is made forcefully in Stephen Houlgate, *Hegel, Nietzsche, and the Criticism of Metaphysics* (Cambridge: Cambridge Univ., 1986).

21. Sigmund Freud, *The Interpretation of Dreams*, trans. J. Strachey (New York: Avon, 1968).

22. This opposition, together with the analysis of the culture taking shape under its pressures, is given brilliant exposition in Philip Rieff's *Triumph of the Therapeutic: The Uses of Faith After Freud* (Chicago: Univ. of Chicago, 1987); the 1987 edition contains a new Preface by the author. See also Peter Homans, *Jung in Context* (Chicago: Univ. of Chicago, 1980), for a complementary discussion.

23. James Hillman, *Re-Visioning Psychology* (New York: Harper Colophon, 1975).

24. See Ferdinand de Saussure, *Course in General Linguistics*, trans. W. Baskin (New York: McGraw-Hill, 1959); also Oswald Ducrot and Tzvetan Todorov, eds., *Encyclopedic Dictionary of the Sciences of Language*, trans. C. Porter (Baltimore: Johns Hopkins Univ., 1983), pp. 95–105, which contains useful bibliographies. Perhaps the most trenchant and accessible introduction to contemporary semiotics, including Saussure's contribution, is Walker Percy's "A Semiotic Primer of the Self" in *Lost in the Cosmos*, (New York: Washington Square, 1984), pp. 86–126. Percy refuses to grant the postmodern ontological distinction between "signified" and "referent" that underwrites so much of contemporary semiotic discourse; his realism in this regard is refreshing; while undoubtedly unsatisfactory to many, it enables semiotic discourse to escape the nominalistic quandaries of contemporary theory. See also his "The Divided Creature," *Wilson Quarterly*, 13:3 (Summer 1989), pp. 77–87.

Structuralism and Poststructuralism

Introduction

George H. Jensen

In *Course in General Linguistics* (1916), Saussure argued that language "is a system of signs" and that it is this system of signs that should be the object of a linguist's study. He continued:

> If we are to discover the true nature of language we must learn what it has in common with all other semiological systems; linguistic forces that seem very important at first glance (e.g., the role of the vocal apparatus) will receive only secondary consideration if they serve only to set language apart from the other systems. This procedure will do more than to clarify the linguistic problem. By studying rites, customs, etc. as signs, I believe that we shall throw new light on the facts and point up the need for including them in a science of semiology and explaining them by its laws.[1]

It is interesting that, here, in Saussure's seminal work, we find the theoretical foundation of Parisian structuralism (that culture and other subjects could be studied as a system of signs),[2] for the theory traveled from Geneva (where Saussure lectured) to Moscow (where it influenced Jakobson and other Russian Formalists) to Prague (where Jakobson refined structural linguistics) and then to New York before Claude Lévi-Strauss saw it as the solution to a perplexing intellectual problem.

Lévi-Strauss first encountered the problem when he began to teach at the University of São Paulo in 1934. There he had the opportunity to study the Brazilian Indians and consider questions about the meaning and significance of kinship patterns. In "The Lessons of Linguistics" (a preface to Jakobson's *Six Lectures on Sound and Meaning*, 1976), Lévi-Strauss recalled how anthropologists were then floundering in their attempts to explain kinship patterns; he wrote that "they could not grasp the rationale for phenomena, they were condemned to the futile task of seeking things behind the things, in the vain hope of attaining more manageable facts than the empirical data on which their analyses were stumbling."[3]

From 1942–1943, as Lévi-Strauss was attempting to make sense of his fieldwork in São Paulo, Jakobson introduced him to structural linguistics, both the seminal theory of Saussure and his own refinement of it. During that academic year, Jakobson and Lévi-Strauss were both teaching at École Libre des Hautes Études in New York. Jakobson was lecturing on linguistics; Lévi-Strauss on kinship systems. The two attended each other's lectures, which eventually led to Lévi-Strauss's application of linguistic theory to an object of study other than language or literature. As Lévi-Strauss wrote: "However irregular may be such notions as those of the phoneme and the incest taboo, my conception of the latter was ultimately inspired by the role that linguists have assigned to the former. Like a phoneme [the smallest unit of sound in a language], a device having no meaning of its own but helping to form meanings, the incest taboo struck me as a link between two domains."[4] The details of Lévi-Strauss's theory will be explained in the following chapter; here, however, a general description of the brand of structuralism that it inspired is in order.

Parisian structuralism, as conceived by Lévi-Strauss, was seen as being revolutionary because it applied the theory and methodology of structural linguistics to the study of domains that were not then viewed as language systems. The Russian Formalists and the Prague structuralists had already refined Saussure's linguistic theory and showed that it could yield fascinating insights if applied to the study of literature. For example, Jakobson used binary oppositions (e.g., voiced versus voiceless phonemes) to study the structure of Czech verse.[5] Lévi-Strauss extended the application of Saussure's theory by applying it — as Saussure had already anticipated — to the study of kinship patterns, myth, magic, or culture in general. For example, he used binary oppositions like cooked/uncooked to study cultural variations in eating.[6]

The move was radical and had a dramatic effect on twentieth-century thought: it extended the notion of "text." Lévi-Strauss studied kinship patterns as if they were a manifestation or performance of language (*parole*) that is governed by a system of signs (*langue*) to uncover its underlying structure, its grammar. At the same time that he expanded the boundaries of *parole* to include kinship patterns, dance, and magic, he distilled *langue* into a structure that was both universal and subconscious, into what might be called the structure of the mind.[7] As *langue* could account for a wide range of variety in *parole* in Saussure's linguistics, the structure of myth could account for cultural variations in particular myths.

That Parisian structuralists studied culture, psychology, mathematics, biology, and other topics as if they were a language is certainly its most salient feature, but some other contrasts and affinities should be mentioned. Parisian structuralism ignored the attempts of Prague structuralists to integrate the synchronic and diachronic, returning to a more purely Saussurean focus on the synchronic. This, some feel, was their greatest error. Contrary to Saussure, or at least traditional interpretations of Saussure, the Parisian structuralists agreed with Jakobson that the nature of the sign is not entirely arbitrary.[8] This is what made their work so enticing. The structuralists moved, in what at times seemed to be anthropological legerdemain, from a fragmentary record (say, the partial and contradictory record of a primitive myth) to an understanding of the deep structure of the myth and back to fragmentary record with missing pieces in hand. Or, they could use the deep structure of a myth from one culture to fill in the gaps of a partial myth from another.[9]

Parisian structuralism met with a wide and generally enthusiastic acceptance because it was, initially, seen as an alternative to the subjectivism of phenomenology, a "scientific" method that could fulfill modernism's need for a foundation without resorting to naive positivism.[10] Its enormous influence, however, began to wane about the time of the 1968 student protests, a period when the fortunes of a number of French intellectuals dramatically shifted.[11] Structuralism simply seemed too apolitical to an intensely radicalized community of professors and students. It was also about this time that limitations inherent in structuralism's promise were recognized. The movement was criticized on various fronts for being too mechanical, for ignoring history, for delivering metaphysics in the guise of science, and for crushing difference with the weight of universal structures. It was during this period of turmoil that French intellectuals began a shift from structuralism to poststructuralism, which was part of the global shift in intellectual thought from modernism to postmodernism.[12]

What emerged from the shift away from structuralism is difficult to define clearly, in part because poststructuralists wished to move away from the kind of rational, orderly, patterned thought that makes tidy conceptual boundaries possible.

We could say that poststructuralism is essentially a brand of postmodernism that is directed against the scientific, rational, univocal attempt of structuralism to establish a foundation for the human sciences, but that "reaction" against structuralism takes many forms. The postmodernists are difficult to pin down, and they would have it no other way. We could also say that poststructuralism, like postmodernism in general, holds that any attempt to ground knowledge is not only futile, it is potentially dangerous. For example, some poststructuralists regard Lévi-Strauss's seemingly benign use of binary oppositions as a form of philosophical totalitarianism. As Claire Parnet wrote in a dialogue with Gilles Deleuze:

It is wrong to say that the binary machine exists only for reasons of convenience. It is said that "the base 2" is the easiest. But in fact the binary machine is an important component of apparatuses of power. So many dichotomies will be established that there will be enough for everyone to be pinned to the wall, sunk in a hole.[13]

Binary oppositions, which Lévi-Strauss viewed as a method for uncovering the structure of the mind, if not reality, become a machine of totalitarian oppression. The poststructuralists' reactions to other forms of established order is similar—at times, rather predictable—but it is rarely boring. With one impressive intellectual tour de force after another, they dismantle any and every rational system—historical epochs, genres, science, and univocal interpretations—and revel in the "difference" that Lévi-Strauss, in their view, worked so hard to theorize away.

As we will see in the chapters that follow, the poststructuralists have shaken the very roots of Western thought and opened the way for radical reformulations of a variety of disciplines. "No correct ideas, just ideas," say Deleuze and Parnet.[14] But more intellectuals are feeling that poststructuralism (and postmodernism in general) has taken us on an exciting journey that has left us in the middle of the desert without a canteen or compass.[15] How can we even say that "there are no univocal statements" without making a univocal statement? And what will life be like when we have no means of distinguishing the "correct ideas" from the "incorrect ideas," when we accept any ideas? As the poststructuralists were in the heat of critiquing the project of structuralism, they seemed to raise an equally perplexing problem about their own project: where do we go from here?[16]

Notes

1. Ferdinand de Saussure, *Course in General Linguistics*, eds. Charles Bally and Albert Sechehaye in collaboration with Albert Riedlinger, trans. Wade Baskin (New York: McGraw-Hill, 1916, 1959), p. 17. Although Saussure is listed as the author of this work, it is actually the editors' compilation from Saussure's unpublished papers and their notes of his lectures. Marc Angenot has argued that it is Saussure, or at least his terminology, that holds together the chaotic discourse among French intellectuals since Lévi-Strauss. Even though, Angenot feels, structuralists and poststructuralists did not come to grips with Saussure as a system, they did regard his terminology as a "password" or "commonplace" that created a sense of unity among thinkers who were pursuing divergent agenda. See "Structuralism as Syncretism: Institutional Distortions of Saussure," in *The Structural Allegory: Reconstructive Encounters with the New French Thought*, ed. John Fekete (Minneapolis: Univ. of Minnesota, 1984), pp. 150–63.

2. We are here using the term "Parisian structuralism" to denote the

structuralism that was inspired by Lévi-Strauss and was generally considered to begin with the publication of his *Tristes tropiques* (Paris: Plon, 1955). Although many scholars simply use the term "structuralism" to refer to the work of Lévi-Strauss and his followers, we prefer "Parisian structuralism" because it allows us to distinguish it more precisely from Prague structuralism and other brands of structuralism.

3. Lévi-Strauss, "The Lessons of Linguistics," in *The View from Afar*, trans. Joachim Neugroschel and Phoebe Hoss (New York: Basic, 1983, 1985), pp. 139–40.

4. Ibid., p. 142.

5. For a discussion of this aspect of Jakobson's work with poetics, see his and Krystyna Pomorska's "The Role of Consonants in the Discovery of Phonemic Oppositions," in *Dialogues*, trans. Christian Hubert (Cambridge: MIT, 1983), pp. 27–34.

6. Lévi-Strauss, *The Raw and the Cooked*, trans. John and Doreen Weightman (New York: Harper & Row, 1964, 1968), passim.

7. Lévi-Strauss's view of structures is essentially Kantian. We find, thus, the same patterns again and again because the organization of our mind leads us to perceive reality in a certain way. Not all structuralists, however, view "structure" in precisely this way. For Piaget, structures seem more external, although not necessarily concrete. See his *Structuralism*, ed. and trans. Chaninah Maschler (New York: Harper and Row, 1968), pp. 3–10.

8. Lévi-Strauss, "The Lessons," p. 142.

9. For an interesting discussion of the power of the structural analysis of myth, see Dan Sperber, *Rethinking Symbolism*, trans. Alice L. Morton (Cambridge: Cambridge Univ., 1974, 1975), pp. 60–63.

10. Jean Hyppolite, Preface to *Studies in Marx and Hegel* (New York: Basic, 1955, 1969), pp. vii–viii.

11. Edith Kurzweil, *The Age of Structuralism: Lévi-Strauss to Foucault* (New York: Columbia Univ., 1980), p. 28. For a more extended discussion of the effects of the May 1968 riots on the French intellectual community, see Pierre Bourdieu's *Homo academicus*, trans. Peter Collier (Stanford: Stanford Univ., 1984, 1988), pp. 159–93.

12. Although the shift from structuralism to poststructuralism might seem abrupt in this brief description of its history, it was fairly gradual. Indeed, the careers of several key thinkers—including Roland Barthes, Jacques Lacan, and Michel Foucault—straddle the paradigm shift. For example, Foucault's early works, especially *The Archeology of Knowledge*, employ a structuralist language that is absent in later works. See Paul Rabinow and Hubert L. Dreyfus's *Michel Foucault: Beyond Structuralism and Hermeneutics*, 2d ed. (Chicago: Univ. of Chicago, 1982, 1983), passim, and John O'Neill's "Breaking the Signs: Roland Barthes and the Literary Body," in *The Structural Allegory: Reconstructive Encounters with the New French Thought*, pp. 183–200.

13. Gilles Deleuze and Claire Parnet, *Dialogues*, trans. Hugh Tomlinson and Barbara Habberjam (New York: Columbia Univ., 1977), p. 21.

14. Ibid., p. 9.

15. For example, see Carl Rapp's "Coming Out into the Corridor: Postmodern Fantasies of Pluralism," *The Georgia Review*, 41 (1987), pp. 533—52, and P. Steven Sangren's "Rhetoric and the Authority of Ethnography: 'Postmodernism' and the Social Production of Texts," *Current Anthropology*, 29 (1988), pp. 405—33.

16. It could be argued that for some poststructuralists, Marxism becomes the implicit and unacknowledged foundation for making ethical judgments, which is odd given Marx's claims that his theory was scientific. Some interesting answers—or alternatives—to the poststructuralist critique of structuralism (or the postmodernist critique of modernism) are William Maker's "Reason and the Problem of Modernity," *The Philosophical Forum*, 18 (1987), pp. 275—303; Laura Nader's "Post-Interpretative Anthropology," *Anthropological Quarterly*, 61 (1988), pp. 149—59; Bradd Shore's "Interpretation Under Fire," *Anthropological Quarterly*, 61 (1988), pp. 161—76; and Pierre Bourdieu's *Outline of a Theory of Practice*, trans. Richard Nice (Cambridge: Cambridge Univ., 1972, 1977).

1

The Reticulated Corpus of Claude Lévi-Strauss

James A. Boon

Is mine the only voice to bear witness to the impossibility of escapism?

Tristes tropiques

Claude Lévi-Strauss's discourse: world-weary, yet enchanted by evidence of remotest human differences; dubious of progress, yet skeptical of regaining anything lost; devoted to the systematic analysis of all social, religious, economic, and artistic order; and capable of a sustained prose of classical balance, baroque counterpoise, and stately pace, marked by open-ended ironic returns. These qualities are most evident in *Tristes tropiques*, Lévi-Strauss's retrospect on a career already *en marche* and his prospectus for the program of life's work to which he had become resigned and which earned him a professorship of anthropology at the Collège de France since 1960, and election to the Académie Française in 1973.[1]

Tristes tropiques was an autobiography dissolving its "self" in the act of discovering a cross-cultural, transhistorical "language," a method. It was a quest *en texte* that metaphorically figured the world's forms, experienced across its tribal vestiges, its colonial margins, and its wartime outcasts in their degraded circumstances. *Tristes tropiques* was the news — not from nowhere but from everywhere — that there was no "news," only repeated transformations. Its narrator — first a voluntary exile, then a forced one — constructed chapters, each in a contrasting tonality, that moved transfiguringly from jaded interwar Europeans, to bustling New World cities hollowly echoing Old World aspirations, to

21

dispirited settlements remaining from colonial boomtowns of yore, to not-quite-lost tribesmen descended from large-scale pre-Columbian cultures. It was a book of recollections in which fragmentation and refugeedom took over. *Tristes tropiques* revealed a world without destiny, without ultimate aim, a world of remnants, only remnants. Historical consciousness, an ideology favoring certain privileged societies, alone pretended otherwise.

Tristes tropiques renounced "seeking in vain to recreate a lost local colour with the help of fragments and debris."[2] Manifestly, it was the travel book to end all travel books, literally. Towards putting "an end to journeying," it mocked its own mission:

> Then, insidiously, illusion began to lay its snares. I wished I had lived in the days of *real* journeys, when it was possible to see the full splendour of a spectacle that had not yet been blighted, polluted, and spoilt.... Once embarked upon, this guessing game can continue indefinitely. When was the best time to see India? At what period would the study of the Brazilian savages have afforded the purest satisfaction, and revealed them in their least adulterated state? Would it have been better to arrive in Rio in the eighteenth century with Bougainville, or in the sixteenth with Léry and Thevet? For every five years I move back in time, I am able to save a custom, gain a ceremony or share in another belief. But I know the texts too well not to realize that, by going back a century, I am at the same time forgoing data and lines of inquiry which would offer intellectual enrichment. And so I am caught within a circle from which there is no escape: the less human societies were able to communicate with each other and therefore to corrupt each other through contact, the less their respective emissaries were able to perceive the wealth and significance of their diversity. In short, I have only two possibilities: either I can be like some traveller of the olden days, who was faced with a stupendous spectacle, all, or almost all, of which eluded him, or worse still, filled him with scorn and disgust; or I can be a modern traveller, chasing after the vestiges of a vanished reality. I lose on both counts.... (TT, 33)

Degradation is the condition of understanding. *Tristes tropiques* stands in the great Ruskinesque tradition of transvaluing decay. Out of ruins it garnered, if not hope, at least meaning, or signification. This lyric, mordant, enigmatic composition, this opera seria in prose, is properly accompanied less by commentary than by a descant.

In tones of Rousseauan regret rather than Nietzschean *ressentiment*, Lévi-Strauss resigned himself to the universe of message, only message. What communicates is already corrupted; no pristine purity can speak. Epistemologically and methodologically, one "knows" not in isolation or directly but only thanks to the mediation of contrastive others. The circle and cycle through history from culture to culture is full and closed. In this tragicomedy there is no exit, only transpositions of equivalent terms: theme through variations, the same song in different keys plus occasional improvisations, over and over and over and over and over again.

Tristes tropiques portrayed all cultures — the narrator's own foremost among them — as failures in destiny's eyes. Yet it celebrated how every culture elaborates value out of precisely what another culture has rejected. Lévi-Strauss approaches human forms as languagelike social facts, consensual values, dialectical selections. One summary statement in *The Way of Masks*, written twenty years after *Tristes tropiques*, argues against interpreting any forms, including artistic creations, simply by what they represent in themselves or by their aesthetic or ritual use:

> A mask does not exist in isolation; it supposes other real or potential masks always by its side, masks that might have been chosen in its stead and substituted for it.... A mask is not primarily what it represents but what it transforms, that is to say, what it chooses *not* to represent. Like a myth, a mask denies as much as it affirms. It is not made solely of what it says or thinks it is saying, but of what it excludes.
>
> Is this not the case for any work of art? ... Contemporary styles do not ignore one another. Even among peoples called primitive, a certain familiarity is established in the course of wars followed by pillage, intertribal ceremonies, marriages, markets, occasional commercial exchanges. The originality of each style [and each culture], therefore, does not preclude borrowings; it stems from a conscious or unconscious wish to declare itself different; to choose from among all the possibilities some that the art of neighboring peoples has rejected. This is also true of successive styles [from one period to another].[3]

Tristes tropiques had construed societies, cultures, and historical periods on the whole as dialectical in just this way: significant for what they suppress as well as evince, each style saying something "which the preceding style was not saying but was silently inviting the new style to enunciate" (WM, 144). As in Freud, and perhaps Marx (or Hegel), everything possible is already prefigured, covertly.

Tristes tropiques, then, presumed to embody — critics would say to expropriate — the ethnological calling, declaring it the guilty conscience of Europe's excessiveness, a guilt that the rest of the world is fated to share:

> Western Europe may have produced anthropologists precisely because it was a prey to strong feelings of remorse, which forced it to compare its image with those of different societies in the hope that they would show the same defects or would help to explain how its own defects had developed within it. But even if it is true that comparison between

our society and all the rest [*toutes les autres*] whether past or present, undermines the basis of our society, other societies will suffer the same fate. (TT, 443)

It was and is a book of its culture (France, the West) and against it; a book of its century (the twentieth) and against it; and against, as well, those few other centuries of the West's political mission to dominate the world's differences. Lévi-Strauss ingeniously, perhaps winkingly, matches formulas for distinguishing temporal eras to formulas for distinguishing Amazonian societies, in a book designed to convert both cultures and histories into a catalogue of variations:

> The Nambikwara had taken me back to the Stone Age and the Tupi-Kawahib to the sixteenth century; here [among rubber-producers in the *seringal*] I felt I was in the eighteenth century, as one imagines it must have been in the little West Indian ports or along the coast. I had crossed a continent. But the rapidly approaching end of my journey was being brought home to me in the first place by this ascent through layers of time. (TT, 423)

Background

Lévi-Strauss's narrative ascent through time by crossing cultures itself emerged in time: it was written in 1954–55. The book's success in France may be explained by the expanded horizons it offered readers after their wartime claustrophobia, by restoring to comparative studies, ethnology, and worldwide discovery literature inflections from French moral philosophy. Lévi-Strauss had already produced a study of Nambikwara social organization, based on his ethnographic expeditions in the mid-1930s in Brazil's Amazon basin when he was teaching sociology at the University of São Paulo. He had achieved professional prominence from incisive articles on social structure, linguistic models of cultural phenomena, and difficult issues in comparative method (collected in 1958 in *Structural Anthropology*). Deported from Vichy, France, with other Jewish intellectuals, he had spent time at the New School for Social Research with fellow refugees in New York, where Franz Boas's ethnographic collections were displayed in the American Museum of Natural History. Lévi-Strauss worked with surrealist André Breton, befriended linguist Roman Jakobson, and after the war served as French cultural attaché. Back in France he worked for the Musée de l'Homme and taught comparative tribal religions at the École Pratique des Hautes Études. In late 1953, still a "simple director of studies at the École," he was offered a full professorship with tenure at Harvard University by the late Talcott Parsons, but declined, unwilling to "lead to the end of his career an expatriot's life."[4]

In 1949 Lévi-Strauss had completed his monumental volume on varieties of exchange systems implicit in different societies' marriage and descent rules. *The Elementary Structures of Kinship* eventually gained controversial renown as a landmark in the general theory of social structure; it remains ardently debated today. In good anthropological fashion the work emphasized societies lacking both centralized agencies of legitimate force and market-based redistribution, where kinship was the encompassing order and/or the template of polity. *Elementary Structures* established Lévi-Strauss as a major heir to Émile Durkheim's work on social solidarity, the division of labor, and primitive religion and to Marcel Mauss's sensitive analyses of nonrationalized systems of ritualized economic exchange. He drew on American anthropology, such as Robert Lowie's systematic comparisons of variant social organization and kinship nomenclatures; and he developed, critically, efforts by such British structural-functionalists as A. R. Radcliffe-Brown to refine abstractions of rules implicit in fields of social relations. Following many leads in Dutch, British, American, and French anthropology, *Elementary Structures* emphasized the importance of an apparent ethnographic curiosity: certain societies make their broadest divisions *by definition* reliant on each other for basic social needs. Here base units (those engaged in production) are socially incomplete, dependent on partner units to reproduce themselves. The most striking cases are organized like multiparty systems constituted in and of the fact that one party must find its spouses among another party. Such societies cannot be construed as an amalgamation of even ideally independent units. Both competition and cooperation are institutionalized across exchange relations; one unit's rival is also its benefactor: those who take are, directly or indirectly through the workings of the whole system of exchanges, those who provide. This paradox forms part of an unprettified "reciprocity" that Lévi-Strauss has called "the essence of social life." Both anti-Hobbes and nonutilitarian (since there is no way totally to divorce self-interest from social interest), this image of solidarity has fundamental implications for political theory and the philosophy of social practice. Lévi-Strauss's *Elementary Structures* effectively posed something like a "social unconscious" lurking behind all varieties of human public and private life: the "need" to relate somewhat "out" (nonincestuously), but not too far out, not randomly.

One theme has remained primary in all Lévi-Strauss's works, including his magnum opus on mythology: cultures encode proprieties by imagining their transgressions. Both marriage systems and mythic systems are about proper communication—a kind of combined ethics and aesthetics—balanced against certain threats and risks. The ultimate threat against orderly communication is noncirculation (incest in the realm of social exchange; silence or nonquestions and nonanswers in the realm of language). The more immediate risk to balanced order is nonreturn on an investment: for example, no spouse received in return by a social unit that gives up an offspring as another's spouse, or no answer returned on a question posed. Throughout his work, Lévi-Strauss draws parallels among ritual recognition of nature's alternation of seasons, the circulation of spouses in society, and the exchange of words in conversation: three realms of proper "periodicity" in the perpetuated give-and-take called "culture." Catherine Clément has handily summarized his views on the "incorrect distance" myths envision in counterdistinction to desirable equilibrium, first citing Lévi-Strauss's central discussion of incest and riddles, a leitmotif in his work on mythic logics:

> "Like a solved riddle, incest brings together terms that are supposed to remain separate: son and mother or brother and sister, as does the answer when, against all expectation, it links up with its corresponding question...." The prohibition of incest has an ecological moral. The consequences of incest, of solving the riddle, are decay and flood. By contrast the consequences of estrangement, of chastity, of leaving the answer without a question, is sterility (animal and vegetable). As always in myths there are two opposing dangers: the danger of too much and the danger of not enough, the danger of excess and the danger of lack. "To the two prospects that may beguile his imagination—the prospect of eternal summer or an eternal winter, the one profligate to the point of corruption, the other pure to the point of sterility—man must resolve himself to prefer the balance and periodicity of the alternation of seasons...."[5]

Since *Tristes tropiques*, Lévi-Strauss has continued his detailed analyses of kinship and marriage, ritual and social classifications, and particularly myths in which communication balance-against-excess predominates. Two additional collections of essays have appeared— *Structural Anthropology II* and, more recently, *Le Regard éloigné*, which defends an ethic and aesthetic of mutual distancing, and *Paroles données*, with summaries of his courses from 1951 to 1982 at the École Pratique des Hautes Études and the Collège de France. But his major work has been a succession of interrelated volumes, each in its way an expansion on different implications of *Tristes tropiques*: *Totemism*, *The Savage Mind*, the four volumes of *Mythologiques*, plus *The Way of the Masks*, *The Jealous Potter*, and related studies. Principal predecessors to this corpus remain Durkheim and Mauss, particularly their classic essay on primitive classification, and the works of Franz Boas on Northwest Coast Indian cultures; but Lévi-Strauss has seasoned his accounts with dazzling insights from hosts of social theorists, philosophers, scientists, and literary figures. In all his works he empathizes more with the systems he analyzes than with their enactors. Critics unsympathetic to this characteristic analytic remove in linguistics, musicology, iconography, and similar endeavors consider Lévi-Strauss's work to be overly intellectual, cold, aloof, even sterile. Moreover, his organization of studies around an encyclopedic range of variations has run counter to the "ethnographer" centered works and professional identity that gained ascendency in British and American anthropology through the influence of Bronislaw Malinowski, Margaret Mead, and many others.

Lévi-Strauss's life's work has unfolded with uncommon consistency and extraordinary controversiality. He has combined *tour de force* reviews of world ethnographic evidence with polemics designed to make tribal studies, comparative ethnology, and mythological analysis play second fiddle to no discipline. He has challenged and responded to challenges from social theorists, existentialists, phenomenologists, psychologists, functionalists, formalists, various fellow anthropologists, and many sentimentalists both past and present. Reactions, both friendly and hostile, to Lévi-Strauss have been complicated by difficulties in translation, by possible misunderstandings on the part of commentators who have explicated his views (particularly, in Britain, Rodney Needham and Edmund Leach), and by internecine wars among French intelligentsia, launched by the celebrated dispute between the Sartre of *Critique de la raison dialectique* and the Lévi-Strauss of *La Pensée sauvage*. Lévi-Strauss has seemed almost to invite controversy, perhaps because rival approaches are, like contrasting styles and cultures, another source of differences and therefore grist for structuralism which, without oppositions systematically to analyze, would have nothing to say.[6]

The year 1968 was pivotal in political perceptions of methods and −isms. Structuralists − a label resisted by most scholars so designated, including Lévi-Strauss − stress systematic order in various dialectic rhythms, promote analytic rigor, and equate the manifest (including manifestos) with the superficial, insisting that profound values (including truths) are inevitably concealed. The political context of 1968 intensified alarm about whether structuralism was compatible with various Marxisms and whether it ultimately drained the "human" out of humanism. Anything devoted to "order," even covert marginalized orders of the social and linguistic unconscious, tended to be indicted as part of the establishment's will to oppress − and repress. As Clément artfully writes in her narrative recall of psychologist Jacques Lacan and other so-called structuralists: everything was "swept away in May 1968 in favor of a return to history, to events, to randomness."[7] Because it was precisely any positive, absolute sense of history, events, and even randomness that Lévi-Strauss had set critically in question, the consequences of 1968 for the reception of his works were extreme. Thus, structuralism, variously defined vis-à-vis Marxism, literary formalism, and other movements, has been "under suspicion" at least since 1968. By now, however, those challenging it are in turn suspect; so the cycles continue. As usual, many foes have actually internalized certain structuralist assumptions. We are all, as the saying goes, structuralists nowadays.

Several broad components of Lévi-Strauss's approach — very different from the structuralisms of Piaget, Chomsky, Dumézil, and others — should be mentioned before sketching some intricacies of his work. Like Boas, Edward Sapir, and other predecessors, he was stimulated by modern linguistic convictions that every language is both a self-sufficient communication system and a variation on more abstract principles, ultimately on "language" in general. He incorporated many ideas and methods from Ferdinand de Saussure's models of languages as systems of signifiers-signifieds, Roman Jakobson's poetics of message making, and other structural linguistics, adapting them to studies of social system, ritual, and mythic data. His structuralism is characterized by a doubled trajectory of obsessive attention to ethnographic detail (everything a potential "sign"), plus bolder generalization, even grand universals, about human rules such as the incest taboo. For example, all societies restrict allowed sexual partners and back up these rules with other classifications; the more interesting point, however, is that all societies (universalization) do so variably (significant differences).

Lévi-Strauss employs technical terms, such as the Saussurian distinctions of *langue* (the systematic basis of a language act's communicability) versus *parole* (the continuously altering language acts themselves). A related distinction opposes synchronic analysis (abstracting a system, a *langue*, as if it were timeless) to diachronic analysis where temporal duration is factored in. ("Diachrony," which must be understood in counterdistinction to "synchrony," should not be confused with "history.") Also important are notions of "binary oppositions" and "distinctive features" that effect selective connections of relationships across different sectors of rule and meaning. These important analytic devices enable structuralism to approach everything in experience as "matter for" communication codes. Such codes interrelate values and practice; they establish terms of exchange among different social divisions and cultural categories; and they constrain the possibilities of translation across languages and cultures. In the extreme structuralism equates life, or knowledge of it, with language (or with structuralism's disputed view of language). It is intent on how things signify, on the way societies produce meaning, not truth. Meanings produced are conventionally called "cultures."

Lévi-Strauss developed his method explicitly against functionalist notions of societies as ideally stable isolates whose different parts interlock and reinforce each other in machinelike or organismlike fashion. He has rejected some views of Durkheim and certain followers who made metaphors of organicism and mechanism central in conceptualizing societies. Yet he has praised Durkheim's emphasis on contradictions that sustain social and cultural divisions; here Durkheim foreshadowed structuralism. Standard functionalist theories consider contradictions in any systems as potential obstacles to its proper functioning, which must be corrected, repaired, purged, or cured. This is a therapeutic model in which contradiction is not so much integrated as released and tensions felt by the actors thus eased. In contrast, structuralist theories consider contradiction unavoidable; this much they share with various schools of dialectic, including Hegelian and Marxist ones. Systems, such as sets of mythic variants, operate not despite contradiction but by means of it (an example will be given below). Systems exist *for* differential communication, not for stability. In the advanced structuralism of Lévi-Strauss's *Mythologiques*, one need imagine no social stability nor even equilibrium. Rather, one traces cultural codes that achieve relative and transient order out of relative randomness through continuous adjustments, shifts, and ongoing fluctuations. Although Lévi-Strauss has questioned the adequacy of conventional causal models in theories of change (compare Michel Foucault), he has not, as is often charged, ignored history. Indeed, *Structural Anthropology* began with a chapter declaring ethnology and the historiography of founders of the *Annales* school to be ideal alliance partners. He has, however, proposed that "history," like everything else, can only be known and transmitted through codes of contrasts. History is not a privileged form of consciousness and offers no exclusive access to either truth or freedom. For Lévi-Strauss, time, like space, exists at the human level *for variation*.[8]

Elements of Lévi-Strauss's Discourse

Lévi-Strauss seldom converts his investigations into conventional didactic formats. Instead, he writes retrospects of his discovery process. His books are kaleidoscopic extensions of their subject matter; they contain spirited puns and unremittingly erudite allusions. This serious playfulness has made Lévi-Strauss notorious among literal-minded readers suspicious of *doubles entendres* (his *entendres* may be even trebled or quadrupled, although he avoids graphic antics and "letterplay" favored by poststructuralists writing in the wake of Mallarmé). His works have been declared harder to pin down than the myths they analyze. They sustain, with added precision, the play of contrastive relations across sensory orders that myths, ritual, and social regulations are shown to contain.

Readers of the French editions of Lévi-Strauss receive fairer warning of his quality of mind and prose. The self-conscious titles are matched by emblematic covers devised to expand the arguments' relevance. Translation kills the puns; and original cover illustrations have been removed in English versions. The most notorious example is *La Pensée sauvage* (both "savage thought" and "wild pansy"), whose original floral cover illustrated an appendix (both deleted in *The Savage Mind*) offering European examples of concrete symbols for abstract classifications, complementing the book's elucidation of tribal logics and practice. For reasons equally obscure, complex cover illustrations of *Mythologiques*, Lévi-Strauss's four-volume study of myth, have been removed from English editions. We thus lose this level of demonstration along with the rhyme that orchestrates the tetralogy's titles into a cycle (Lévi-Strauss compares them to Wagner's *Ring*). Upon completing the path-breaking series, he claimed that he had always intended that the uncultured *cru* of *Le Cru et le cuit* (*The Raw and the Cooked*) would modulate into variant cooking customs, then dress codes, winding eventually back to the natural *nu* of *L'Homme nu* (*The Naked Man*). He thus wrapped up, between *le cru* and *le nu*, over two thousand pages interrelating tribal techniques and ethics in areas of cooking, food production and preparation, hunting, warfare, domestic consumption, menstruation, age grading, costume creation and exchange, and related cultural arts. The entire set of *Mythologiques'* titles bears scrutiny: one is a juxtaposed opposition (*Le Cru et le cuit*): one names a transforming process linking honey (beyond the raw) to ashes (beyond the cooked) (*Du Miel aux cendres*); one is a classic just-so formula (*L'Origine des manières de table);* and the last is a modified noun, in fact *the* modified noun (*L'Homme nu*). Each title's form encapsulates distinctive mythic operations and narrative emphases. *Mythologiques* is simultaneously an elaborately contextualized comparative analysis of select components of New World aboriginals and an intricate typology of different myths, different modes of ordering variants, plus critiques of the history of reductive explanations of mythology and related cultural forms.

The volumes' most sustained generalization is that myth is to semantics or meaning (*sens*) as music is to sound (*sons*), and that complementary spheres of human order are myth, music, math, and language, four autonomous varieties of "metacodes" or codes of codes. Music thus joins a series of metaphors that Lévi-Strauss has developed for structuralist analysis itself. Over the years he has also likened structuralism to mathematics (algebraic models), language (linguistic models), and myth (structuralism as the "myth of mythology," exponential to myth as myth is exponential to language). When Lévi-Strauss analogizes myth and music (one bundles semantic features, the other sonic features), he characteristically develops the point by reversing the equation:

> Myth coded in sounds in place of words, the musical work affords a table of decodings [*une grille de déchiffrement*], a matrix of relationships that filter and organize lived experience, substitutes itself for that experience and procures the beneficent illusion that contradictions can be surmounted and difficulties resolved.[9]

Lévi-Strauss views all cultural forms as "necessary illusions," systems of signification substituted for experiences that cannot be communicated, cannot be "known," directly, however they are lived.

Musical analogies work at many different levels in *Mythologiques*. For example, the striking "Overture" to *The Raw and the Cooked* includes a musicological parallel for its implicit typology of narrative forms and the pattern of emergence, development, and eventual exhaustion detected in cycles of myths. Lévi-Strauss contrasts dominant tendencies in Bach and Stravinsky (whose works emphasized what he calls "code"), Beethoven and Ravel (who emphasized "message"), and Wagner and Debussy (who emphasized "myth"). Works of the first pair tend "to expound and to comment on the rules of a particular musical discourse; the second group tell a tale; the third group code their messages by means of elements that already partake of the nature of narrative."[10] Lévi-Strauss then winks at his own analogy in a witty footnote (mysteriously deleted from the first English translation of the "Overture" in *Yale French Studies* that influenced many critics before they ever saw the volume):

> Needless to say, I took the first six names that came to mind. But this was perhaps not entirely an effect of chance, since it turns out that when one lists these composers in chronological order [Bach, Beethoven, Wagner, Debussy, Ravel, Stravinsky], the special functions to which they relate form a closed cycle [code, message, myth, message, code], as if to demonstrate that in the space of two centuries tonal music has exhausted its internal possibilities of renewal. (RC, 30)

Both playfully and profoundly, Lévi-Strauss views everything as pulsating cycles coding both affect and intellect, a rhythm repeated in his works' organization.[11]

Such reverberations in his books (Lévi-Strauss has called them "the negative of a symphony") pertain not just to the macrodimension of his corpus—frustrating to many, exhilarating to some—but to the microlevel as well. To illustrate well-known difficulties, I shall summarize several paragraphs from *The Savage Mind*[12] that typify most pages of his score of books. Densely woven data is laced with methodological guidelines, provisos, theoretical tenets, and assessments of rich New World variations in ritual taboos (particularly varieties of isolation during menstruation), posed against the West's movement toward conformity. This comparative theme of *Mythologiques* was rehearsed in *The Savage Mind* in an analysis first developed for a course in 1959–60 (PD, 268–72).

The ostensible subject is eagle hunting among North American aboriginal Hidatsa, who credit supernatural animals with teaching their men its special techniques. A long-standing ethnographic question has been attested by several investigators: Was this culture hero the black bear or the wolverine (Latin name provided)? Lévi-Strauss considers the identification vital for interpreting Hidatsa hunting. Lacking direct evidence, he reviews the etymology of the Indian name for "wolverine" and the folklore of neighboring tribes where it is reputed for gluttony and cunning in craftily avoiding being trapped; wolverines steal both trapped animals and the traps themselves. Lévi-Strauss then turns to the Hidatsa context: hunters here hide in pits waiting for eagles to take the bait. (He reserves additional vital facts for later: that the bait must be bloody and that the eagles themselves are strangled bloodlessly.) Hidatsa eagles hunters thus assume the location reserved in all other kinds of hunting for the trapped animal. Simultaneously hunter and hunted, the eagle hunter embodies a contradiction. Lévi-Strauss compares his paradoxical quality to the contradictory reputation of the wolverine: both hunter and hunted, unfearing of traps, trapping the trapped in turn.

We recall that for Lévi-Strauss the basic logical process behind myth (and ritual, which relates to myth dialectically) is to *convert* contradictions, not so much to solve them as to surmount them (or "motivate" them in the Saussurian sense) by restating their components in other terms. Lévi-Strauss suggests a totemic equivalence between the eagle hunter and the wolverine: wolverine is to Hidatsa nature as eagle hunter is to Hidatsa culture. He demonstrates an analogy between the contradictions each represents. "Analogies of contradictory relationships," by the way, is one bare-bones definition of "*pensée sauvage.*"

Lévi-Strauss next broaches explicit hunting cosmology. Eagle hunting's special style ritually conjoins the distant extremes of the Hidatsa cosmos: *subterranean* hunters capture an *aerial* quarry, portrayed in myths as soaring the highest. Many obscurities in ritual and practice can now be clarified. Myths narrated during hunting expeditions portray wildcats and racoons as culture heroes who bestow arrows and are forbidden as eagle bait. Eagle hunting is unique in eliminating intermediaries between hunter and game: eagles must be killed without arrows, and animals associated with arrows may not be used to lure eagles. More is afoot here than protecting valued plumage from bloodstains. A classification of hunting styles, creatures, and tools emerges. Lévi-Strauss could have set it out didactically; instead he coaxes it from data during the course of his prose. He might well have provided a diagram of pluses and minuses as an alternative projection of the same data, but in this case he did not.

Lévi-Strauss next reveals what may be the guiding anomaly of this entire analysis, although he does not here say so (I surmise as much from the way *Mythologiques* eventually developed; one can never know for sure in a structuralist study whether "leads" were there at the start or discovered retrospectively). Contrary to all other Hidatsa hunting, and to most hunting rituals everywhere, menstruating women are considered beneficial rather than unauspicious in capturing eagles. Menstrual blood is both a metaphor for blood and organic decay (like bait) and a part (a metonym) of the ritual materials. One Hidatsa word means both a lover's embrace and the grasping of bait by eagles. Lévi-Strauss relates these points to Amerindian ideas of excessive unions, where components ordinarily separated by proper periodicities are dangerously conjoined. Eagle hunting and intercourse during menstruation are conceptualized in parallel, both tied to complex codes of orderly succession versus putrefaction and rot — another fundamental topic of *Mythologiques*.

At this juncture Lévi-Strauss's analysis accelerates its pace and increases its sweep. It happens that eagle hunting is an indicator of differences between hunter-gatherers' and agriculturalists' ideologies of pollution. By construing "eagle" not referentially but operationally as "bloodless game lured in the presence of menstrual blood," interesting comparisons can be made with prominent Pueblo mythology. Lévi-Strauss investigates not what eagles mean to Pueblos but how whatever eagles might mean to Pueblos can clarify whatever eagles might mean to Hidatsa. His analyses remain equally removed — *éloigné* — from any particular case (including Hidatsa); they are essentially comparative. Because the Pueblo myths equate an eagle-girl protagonist and a ghost wife, Lévi-Strauss leaps to South American evidence also devoted to ghost wives, thus clarifying certain historical and geographical issues, without necessarily claiming that all the myths were borrowed from a common northern source. He concludes with his famous kind of disclaimer: "The most that can be said ... is that analogous logical structures can be constructed by means of different lexical resources. It is not the elements themselves but only the relations between them which are constant" (SM, 53).

This kind of essayette represents, I suggest, the "atom" of all Lévi-Strauss's work. Both their advantages and their limitations can be better appreciated if one concentrates on the strategies and logic of such paragraphs, rather than seeking some surefire Gallic gimmick, as so many commentators on his method have done. The pages are vintage Lévi-Strauss; no detail of evidence can be ignored; what is trivial in one case may be paramount in another (more echoes of Freud), whether myth to myth or culture to culture (different levels of transformed selections). Moreover, one never knows what contents will signify, until one proceeds empirically.

Furthest Reticulations of a Varying and Vast Corpus

In *Le Totemisme aujourd'hui* Lévi-Strauss traced tribal modes of transforming natural surroundings, social relations, ritual, and myth into reciprocal codes that convert different levels of continuity into interrelated discontinuities:

> Totemism as a system is introduced as *what remains* of a diminished totality, a fact which may be a way of expressing that the terms of the system are significant only if they are *separated* from each other, since they alone remain to equip a semantic field which was previously better supplied and into which a discontinuity has been introduced. Finally the two [totemic] myths suggest that direct contact . . . , i.e., a relation of contiguity, is contrary to the spirit of the institution: the totem becomes such only on condition that it first be set apart.[13]

Moreover, like such totemic operations, the book *Totemism* dismantles the conditions of possibility of hypostatizing its own topic. Similarly, *The Savage Mind* imploded the notion of any discrete preliterate mode of meaning by collapsing historical understanding itself into oppositional structures.

Principles outlined in *Totemism* and *The Savage Mind* continue through *Mythologiques*. Ranging across the universe of Amerindian tribal values, the books gain critical leverage against standardized uniformity engendered in Western political, economic, and historical supremacy. In continuity with both Durkheimian sociology and Boasian ethnology, Lévi-Strauss remains prodifference, provariegation over monoculture, prospices over bland cuisine, procold societies over hot states, while perfectly aware that most trends are running against him and, more importantly, against *them*. He criticizes Western science and philosophy for abetting forces of centralization and standardization that level differences. Paradoxically, however, he also congratulates the human sciences for coming to understand the significance of tribal and archaic codes, at last recognizing that Western reason and rationality is itself just one variation in the human field of differential knowledge.

Thus tribal-style logics ultimately win out in Lévi-Strauss's sense of the history of ideas in the human sciences.

Mythologiques analyzes at a distance the mythic motifs that have been exchanged among groups with different social organizations and languages or maintained by two once-identical groups as their social organizations and languages diverge (or, if we follow his implications to the limit, perhaps social organization and languages have been exchanged across myths). He maps the patterns of principles behind differences the myths assume, as when one variant presents a set of elements in an inverse relation to the same set of elements in another variant. He calls what he maps "structure." As some portion of a myth is borrowed, transformations occur; or if a group splits, its once coterminous mythic corpus is differentiated in dialectic with the now-different ethnographic conditions and historical events. The most general principle behind the studies is that "matter is the instrument, not the object of signification. In order that it yield to this role, it is first necessary to impoverish it: retaining from it only a small number of elements suitable for expressing contrasts and for forming pairs of oppositions" (*Le Cru et le cuit*, 346–47). His vast empirical demonstrations disclose codes of interrelationships across different orders of experience — as when myths depict the dawn of cooking and dining customs as norms or when concepts of cyclical time are symbolized by female biological cycles and solar and seasonal phenomena. Different societies can be culturally contrasted according to the different orders selected. Lévi-Strauss thus considers New World Indian myth as a continually selecting and reselecting totality but never a synthesized whole:

> From the start, then, I ask the historian to look upon Indian America as a kind of Middle Ages which lacked a Rome: a confused mass that emerged from a long-established doubtless very loosely textured syncretism, which for many centuries had contained at one and the same time centers of advanced civilization and savage peoples, centralizing tendencies and disruptive forces ... [The set of myths], such as the one studied here, owes its character to the fact that in a sense it became crystallized in an already established semantic environment, whose elements had been used in all kinds of combinations — not so much, I suppose, in a spirit of imitation but rather to allow small but numerous communities to express their different originalities by manipulating the resources of a dialectical system of contrasts and correlations within the framework of a common conception of the world. (RC, 8)

Only by moving across groups and languages, as the myths themselves have, can we discern the principles of order that set societies apart from each other while leaving them interrelatable. As Lévi-Strauss concludes:

Rarely seized upon at their origin and in a state of vitality, these relationships of opposition between myths emerge vigorously from a comparative analysis. If thus the philological study of myths does not constitute an indispensable preliminary approach, the reason for this lies in what one might call myths' diacritical nature. Each of the myths' transformations results from a dialectical opposition to another transformation, and their essence resides in the irreducible fact of translation *by* and *for* opposition. Considered from an empirical point of view, every myth is at once pristine [*primitif*] in relation to itself, and derived in relation to other myths; it is situated not *in* a language and *in* a culture or sub-culture, but at the point of articulation of cultures with other languages and other cultures. Myth is thus never in its language [*de sa langue*], it is a perspective on *another language* . . . (*L'Homme nu*, 577)

This inherently comparative locus of myths highlights the inadequacy of functionalist views of social cohesion:

One of the most pernicious notions bequeathed us by functionalism — one which still holds many ethnologists under its sway — is the notion of isolated tribes [*peuplades*], closed in on themselves, each living on its own account a particular experience of mythic, ritual, or aesthetic order. One thereby fails to understand that before the colonial era and the destructive effects from afar exercised (even in the most remote regions) by the Western world with its pathogenic germs and exported goods, these more numerous populations were also more interlocking [*coude à coude*]. With a few exceptions nothing that transpired in one went unnoticed by its neighbors, and the modalities by which each explained itself and represented its universe were elaborated in a dialogue, uninterrupted and vehement.[14]

Lévi-Strauss's rejection of functionalism is particularly vivid in *The Origin of Table Manners*, the third and pivotal book in the four-volume *Mythologiques*. Indian populations never developed a permanent centralized state and lacked a standardized writing system; thus their myths emerge from various circumstances of language, environment, and social organization. Yet Lévi-Strauss seeks to understand myths and their contexts according to a total system of implicit meanings and not with an eye to any particular tribe, place, or time. He both detects the rules that transform one tribal myth to another and suggests translations of myths into our own logical ethical, philosophical, and scientific paradigms.

Because myths are basically "in between," they are ideal subjects for the structuralism Lévi-Strauss has championed in cultural anthropology. Myths establish connections between the different ways tribes acquire, prepare, and consume foodstuffs (hence "table manners") and how they organize diverse aspects of their languages, rituals, social structures, ecologies, music, and beliefs. The details of myths sound to us unseemly; for example, Plains Indian styles of trophy ornamentation: scalps, porcupine quillwork (the typical female craft), or human pubic hair.[15] Indeed many myths recall those Arapaho tales that "from a certain distance ... appear rather like a cross between a picturesque and exotic Book of Genesis and a decorous version of *The Story of O*" (OTM, 227). But for Lévi-Strauss myths employ such contents to relate codes to codes: astronomical cycles, menstrual cycles, and seasonal cycles; social cycles; and so forth. Myths signify signification. Their fractured metaphors and unexpected relationships — whether pubic hair trophies or swallowed chickadee songs — form part of mythologics in the same way that phonetic sounds are part of languages or "scaled" tones composed music.

Lévi-Strauss demonstrates that the ethical concerns of North American Indians focused on "good little girls." Different tribes obliged their daughters to dine, converse, groom, court, and yes, menstruate, in strikingly different fashion, because social harmony and balance depended on the distinctive etiquette of daughters. This basic assumption of Indian societies (often made up of intermarrying clans) explains the elaboration, diversity, and seeming arbitrariness of customary restrictions of women:

> When a young Indian woman from the Chaco or the surrounding areas first began to menstruate, she was laced up in a hammock and remained suspended.... Throughout the west and north-west of North America, a girl menstruating for the first time was not allowed to touch the ground with her feet, nor to look at the sun.... The Algonquin of the Great Lakes area merely required her to keep her eyes lowered. Any contact between her hands and her body or domestic utensils would have been fatal. Among several Athapaskan tribes, she wore mittens, used a scratcher for her head and back, and sometimes even for her eyelids, drank through a tube and picked up her food with a sharpened bone (unless some other girl was given the task of putting the pieces into her mouth one by one).... Menstruating girls could drink neither hot nor cold beverages, only tepid ones. Their solid food also had to be lukewarm; it could not be raw (in the case of the Eskimo who often ate their food raw), nor undercooked in the case of the Shuswap, nor fresh in the case of other tribes; nor boiled, in the case of the Cheyenne. The Klikitat, for their part, forbade the eating of rancid food. (OTM, 500−1)

Lévi-Strauss contrasts tribal codes to our own rites of passage and dietary customs that have been homogenized, standardized, and seem universally imperative:

> We have changed our table manners then, and adopted others, the norm of which at least has been generalized throughout the Western world, where different ways of chewing no longer denote national or local traditions; they are merely either good or bad. In other words, and

> contrary to what we have observed in exotic societies, eating habits for Westerners no longer constitute a *free code*: we opt for some habits and prohibit others, and we conform to the first order to transmit a *compulsory message*. (OTM, 499)

The "free code" of tribal cooking customs and table manners complements the code of menstrual seclusion, providing that girls behave themselves. In fact, menstruating daughters are highly regulated and as crucial to a tribe's well-being as its warrior sons; for example: "The menstruating girl can drink neither hot nor cold liquids for the same reason that she is not allowed to eat fresh or tainted food. She is subject to a violent internal commotion, which would become even more violent if her organism ingested solids or liquids that were, in one sense or another, strongly marked."

Table Manners provides unprecedented perspectives on gerontology, sex-role dichotomy, and ideals of socialization, all woven into meaningful relationships by myths. Just to suggest Lévi-Strauss's complex summary:

> The myths use the theme of ageing ... to introduce a fundamental category, that of periodicity, which modulates human existence by assigning it a certain duration, and by establishing, within this duration, the major physiological rhythms which have their seat in the female organism. We have also learned from other myths that the education of girls is mainly achieved by the mental and biological interiorization of periodicity.
>
> We now see that the absence of mediatory utensils such as combs, head—scratchers, mittens, and forks between the subject and her body causes the hair to turn white, the skin to wrinkle, etc. (OTM, 506)

In the concerted universe of tribal myths, old age, mortality, war rules, menstrual cycles, and domestic technology are culturally as interconnected as the natural fact of night following day ... following night. *Table Manners* pursues a theme begun in *Tristes tropiques* (ch. 23): "According to the myths discussed in this volume, it was boys in South America and girls in North America who, at the onset of puberty, were the first repositories of these rules of good behavior." If females are "natural" from the vantage of North America, males are natural in South America. Lévi-Strauss underscores the variance recognized by the myths themselves, where women and men appear (for the purposes of meaningful codes) transformations of each other. This variance also allows Lévi-Strauss to place North America together with European moral philosophy. The musical epigraphs of *The Raw and the Cooked* are replaced in *Table Manners* with ethical epigraphs—in turn replaced in *L'Homme nu* (1971) with metaepigraphs—epigraphs on the nature and purpose of epigraphs. North American Indian etiquette is paralleled by excerpts from Erasmus, Montaigne, Chateaubriand, and particularly Rousseau, whose *Emile* likewise situated the well-being of civil society in the manners of regulated, that is to say educated daughters.

Finally, besides male/female, senility/youth, and sex/death, *Table Manners* also considers less grandiose issues, like chickadees. To take one of the many comic mythic images Lévi-Strauss investigates, members of the Ojibwa tribe believed that "there will be a storm if the chickadee swallows the last syllable of its song: "*Gi-ga-be; gi-ga-be; gi-ga-me*." Obviously, the swallowed syllable involves the *m*/*b* distinction of the phonological spectrum. But to understand how the chickadee's oral apparatus symbolizes units of time as well as language, we must turn to the more elaborate views of the Shoshones. Did you know that chickadees have barbed tongues? Traditional Shoshones could hardly forget it:

> The chickadee is usually non-migrant. But its tongue is barbed with filaments, of which — according to the Shoshone — there are six: one falls off each month and grows again six months later, so that it is possible to tell, by capturing a chickadee, which month in winter or in summer it is. This is why it is wrong to kill chickadees.... The belief is sufficiently widespread to be also found among the Mandan and the Hidatsa, who reckon the months of the year from the Chickadee's tongue. (OTM, 236)

That chickadee tongues can symbolize different months explains their relevance to thunderstorms. Similarly, the entire volume explores relations among temporal, natural, and cultural cycles: seasonal change, menstruation, solar and lunar phenomena, the ritual organization of hunting and warfare, and ultimately the Amerindian logic that relates scalped men to menstruating women.

Lévi-Strauss thus modulates the shriller issues of our "human condition" with the softer obsessions of Ojibwas. This fact helps explain his rejection of existentialism, expressed forcibly in *Tristes tropiques*, *The Savage Mind*, and *L'Homme nu*. He thinks that a self-centered existentialism arose from an arrogant humanism that assumed tribal orders were isolated and closed, when in fact the West itself was becoming a "reservation," trapped in the conformity of standardized *compulsory message*.

The famous *finale* of *Mythologiques*'s last volume, *L'Homme nu*, evokes the professed twilight (sunset) of Lévi-Strauss's *oeuvre*; it converts his scholarly opponents plus his own rejoinders into fragments arranged in a confessedly extravagant display. *Tristes tropiques* — narrative prelude to *Mythologiques*'s discursive "twilight of man" — had retained a forgetting raconteur as its ostensible center and authority, yet one displaced with each successive episode. The narrator is rendered literally unreliable in the play-within-the-story, "The Apotheosis of Augustus," (ch. 37), an allegory begging to be construed as representational of the very book that includes it. The discourse of *Tristes tropiques* emerges from the process of forgetting ("Forgetfulness has done its task . . ., fifteen years have lapsed"). The text offers from the start "the opposite of a voyage," all departures having "blended together in my memory" (TT, 54–55). This discourse of forgetting, the sunset of Lévi-Strauss's voyages, recognizes itself, or its equivalent, in nature's own memory: repeating catalogues of celestial fragments at dusk. In the celebrated sunset chapter:

> Daybreak is a prelude, the close of day an overture which occurs at the end instead of the beginning, as in the old operas. . . . Sunset is quite a different matter; it is a complete performance with a beginning, a middle and an end. . . . Dawn is only the beginning of the day; twilight is a repetition of it. . . . The operations of consciousness can also be read in these fluffy constellations. . . . Remembering is one of man's great pleasures, but not in so far as memory operates literally, since few individuals would agree to relive the fatigues and sufferings that they nevertheless delight in recalling. Memory is life itself, but of a different quality. And so, it is when the sun declines towards the polished surface of calm water, like alms bestowed by some heavenly miser, or when its disc outlines mountain summits like a hard, jagged leaf. . . . (TT, 56–57)

Lévi-Strauss implicates his own discourse's metaphoric extravagances along with the solar extravagances, both of which pale and gain significance, "since the insignificance of external events in no way justified any extravagant atmospheric display" (TT, 57). Can these sunset-memory extravagances be distinguished from tribal mythic extravagances? This is the ambiguity of *Tristes tropiques*'s mythlike discourse, deepened into the subsequent texts of Lévi-Strauss's corpus.[16]

The finale of *Mythologiques* returns to the *je*-eclipsing mode of Jean-Jacques Rousseau initiated in *Tristes tropiques*, thereby placing several thousand pages of path-breaking analysis of tribal codes into quotation marks, communications that in becoming so can only be alienated from a presumed author:

> The preceding reflections (of the finale) do not constitute a thesis. Still less do they claim to sketch a philosophy, and I hope that they will be taken for what they are: a free reverie, not devoid of confusion and errors, to which the subject abandons himself during the brief moment when, delivered from his task, he does not yet know into what it will come about for him to be dissolved anew. Casting an ultimate retrospective glance on the work of eight years soon guaranteed to become for me as foreign as if it had been the work of an other. (*L'Homme nu*, 619)

And in the subsequent, antipenultimate paragraph of the entire *Mythologiques* series, we discover that we have never left the sunset chapter of *Tristes tropiques*:

> Arrived at the evening of my career, the last image myths leave me — and through them the supreme myth related by the history of humanity, the history also of the universe in whose midst the other unfolds — thus rejoins the intuition which, at my beginnings and as I related in *Tristes tropiques*, made me seek in the phases of a setting sun, awaited since the installation of a celestial scenery which complicates itself progressively to the point of becoming undone and abolished into the annihilation of night, the model of facts that I was later going to study and of problems that I would have to resolve on mythology: vast and complex construction, it too iridescent with a thousand hues, which deploys itself under the gaze of the analyst, slowly fades and closes up, engulfing itself in the distance as if it had never existed. (*L'Homme nu*, 619–21)

Lévi-Strauss often concludes his books with a nod to the nothingness (*rien*) prevalent in existentialist values that he has rejected yet whose anxiety of the void he shares. He describes both his own studies and cultures themselves as means of setting in abeyance not *anomie* but *ennui*. He often *also* concludes his books (many have multiple endings) with mysterious hints of communication between the human and non-human worlds: knowing glances exchanged with a cat, conversations with hermetic lilies, genetic and topological codes interrelating all forms of life and structure, including human consciousness. Somewhere between the extremes of not being and being (Lévi-Strauss theatrically invokes at the end of *L'Homme nu* Hamlet's false alternatives) — and somewhere within the full circle of relentless transformations without progress — pulse the variational forms that Lévi-Strauss's works pursue and in whose nature they participate. In this human condition of permuting messages, there is endless additional information, but never the total picture and no news. Lévi-Strauss's method promises neither escape to freedom nor even autonomy; such states themselves are deemed relative to one's position in a system. There is in his exquisite resignation no escapism. "Only communicate."

Notes

1. Lévi-Strauss's career has been an interdisciplinary phenomenon; books about his work — and particularly the literature for, against, and ambivalent about so-called structuralism — would fill a good-sized library. Many sources are listed in my *From Symbolism to Structuralism: Lévi-Strauss in a Literary Tradition* (Oxford: Oxford Univ., 1972); *Other Tribes, Other Scribes* (Cambridge: Cambridge Univ., 1982); "Structuralism Routinized, Structuralism

Fractured," *American Ethnologist*, 11 (1984), pp. 807–12; and *Affinities and Extremes* (Chicago: Chicago Univ., 1990).

2. *Tristes tropiques* (Paris: Plon, 1955; 2d ed. 1973); trans. John and Doreen Weightman (New York: Atheneum, 1977), p. 33. References to TT are to the 1977 English translation.

3. *La Voie des masques* (Geneva: Skira, 1972; 2d ed., Paris: Plon, 1979); trans. Sylvia Modelski as *The Way of the Masks* (Seattle: Univ. of Washington, 1982), p. 144. References to WM are to the 1982 English translation.

4. *Paroles données* (Paris: Plon, 1984); trans. by Roy Willis as *Anthropology and Myth: Lectures 1951–1982* (Oxford: Basil Blackwell, 1987), p. 258. This and latter references to PD are to the French edition.

5. Catherine Clément, *Vies et légendes de Jacques Lacan* (Paris: B. Grasset, 1981); trans. as *The Lives and Legends of Jacques Lacan* (New York: Columbia Univ., 1983), pp. 134–35.

6. Helpful reviews of technical concepts in structuralism, semiotics, and related "sciences of language" are provided in *Dictionnaire encyclopedique des sciences du langage*, eds. Oswald Ducrot and Tzvetan Todorov (Paris: Seuil, 1972); trans. as *Encyclopedic Dictionary of the Sciences of Language* (Baltimore: Johns Hopkins Univ., 1979). Constructive discussions of poststructuralist and deconstructionist (particularly Derrida's) responses to and critiques of structuralism are compiled in *Textual Strategies: Perspectives in Post-Structural Criticism*, ed. Josue Harari (Ithaca: Cornell Univ., 1979). For some unfortunate aspects of Derrida's "take" on Lévi-Strauss, see my *Other Tribes, Other Scribes* (pp. 278–79) and *Affinities and Extremes* (p. 210).

7. Clément, p. 133.

8. For more discussions of many issues in kinship analysis, structuralist Marxism, and challenges to positivism, see *Structural Sociology*, ed. Ino Rossi (New York: Columbia Univ., 1982) and *The Logic of Culture: Advances in Structural Theory and Method*, ed. Ino Rossi (South Hadley, Mass.: Bergin & Garvey, 1982). For more information on semiotics, see Milton Singer's *Man's Glassy Essence: Explorations in Semiotic Anthropology* (Bloomington, Ind.: Indiana Univ., 1984). Interesting essays that extend Lévi-Strauss's ideas into classics, intellectual history, and comparative religion appear in *La Fonctione symbolique*, eds. Michel Izard and Pierre Smith (Paris: Gallimard, 1979); trans. by John Leavitt as *Between Belief and Transgression: Structuralist Essays in Religion, History, and Myth* (Chicago: Chicago Univ., 1982).

9. *Mythologiques: L'Homme nu* (Paris: Plon, 1971); trans. by John and Doreen Weightman as *The Naked Man* (Chicago: Chicago Univ., 1981), pp. 590–91. Quotations from *L'Homme nu*, the fourth volume of *Mythologiques*, are my translations; references are to the original French edition.

10. *Mythologiques: Le Cru et le cuit* (Paris: Plon, 1964); trans. by John and Doreen Weightman as *The Raw and the Cooked* (New York: Harper & Row, 1969), p. 30. Quotations to *Le Cru et le cuit*, the first volume of *Mythologiques*, are my translations; references are to the original French edition. References to RC are to the English translation.

11. For a fuller discussion of musical and musicological analogies at work in Lévi-Strauss — including continual intertextual resonances with the works of Wagner, Debussy, and Ravel, as well as literary "musicalists" such as Proust — see my *From Symbolism to Structuralism* and "Lévi-Strauss, Wagner, Romanticism: A Reading-back," in *History of Anthropology: Romantic Motives*, vol. 6, ed. G. W. Stocking (Madison: Univ. of Wisconsin, 1989).

12. *La Pensée sauvage* (Paris: Plon, 1962); trans. as *The Savage Mind* (Chicago: Chicago Univ., 1966), pp. 49–54. References to SM are to the English translation.

13. *Le Totemisme aujourd'hui* (Paris: Plon, 1962); trans. by Rodney Needham as *Totemism* (Boston: Beacon, 1963), p. 26.

14. *La Voie des masques*, vol. 2, pp. 118–19. My translation.

15. *Mythologiques: L'Origine des manières de table* (Paris: Plon, 1968); trans. by John and Doreen Weightman as *The Origin of Table Manners* (New York: Harper & Row, 1978), p. 404. Future references to OTM are to this, the English translation of the third volume of *Mythologiques*.

16. Intense reverberations linking *Tristes tropiques*, *Mythologiques*, and indeed *The Elementary Structures of Kinship* are traced in greater detail in chapter 7 of my *Other Tribes, Other Scribes* and in "Lévi-Strauss, Wagner, Romanticism: A Reading-back." *Other Tribes, Other Scribes* also outlines differences and affinities between Lévi-Strauss and M. Merleau-Ponty, C. Geertz, and V. Turner (see pp. 281, 137–47); see also Geertz's *Works and Lives* (Stanford: Stanford Univ., 1987). On Merleau-Ponty and Lévi-Strauss, see my *From Symbolism to Structuralism*.

2

Jacques Lacan
Speaking the Truth

Thomas DiPiero

In 1968, the year that tumultuous events rattled France's political and intellectual arenas and radically altered the nation's conservative university system, there appeared a new journal called *Scilicet*. Devoted to the teachings of Jacques Lacan and the École freudienne de Paris, which he had founded four years earlier, *Scilicet* addressed its readers on the cover of each issue, assuring them just beneath the title that "you can know what the École freudienne de Paris thinks about it." The strangely equivocal slogan, which expresses both a condescending self-assurance of readers' pressing desire to know what the École thinks as well as a generous willingness to allow them admission to the recondite in-group it represents, in many ways figures the Lacanian philosophy of psychoanalysis. While on the one hand it posits a mastery of knowledge attainable through the intersubjective dialogue the "you" establishes, on the other hand it sustains the hermetic and inaccessible nature of that knowledge by relating it to an unidentified "it" to which it applies.[1]

The difficult and esoteric character of Lacan's writing has been its hallmark since at least as far back as the 1966 publication of his *Écrits*. Jacques Brosse, reviewing the work in *Arts*, complained that "the work is oppressive because of its thorny impenetrability. Lacan no doubt wants to screen his reading public.... One fears that masochistic intellectual snobs might, in the face of such aggressive obscurity, proclaim the work a great success without having read it."[2] The notorious inscrutability of Lacan's writing, however, does not simply mark the analyst's jealous defense of his intellectual property. Rather, the difficulty it poses readers contributes to the formation of a specific philosophy and practice of both teaching and analysis that put the student or analysand in what Lacan called the Promethean necessity to take knowledge from the master in a dialectical struggle of power and desire. Lacan continually maintained that the knowledge the analyst has or represents is illusory — analysts are "supposed to know" in the sense that analysands come to them in the belief that they can learn from another what is wrong with them and that this other knows the truth of their problems and can cure them. However, Lacan maintained that the analyst effectively knows nothing about the analysand and only occupies a functional position in an intersubjective dialectic. That is, through the course of analysis, the analysand speaks about his or her desire but must learn that the position from which he or she speaks, a position traditionally represented by the subject pronoun "I," is displaced from the true center of being. By speaking to the analyst as a nonindividuated other who frustrates his or her attempt to relate to another surface ego, the subject discovers that the conscious, speaking subject cannot articulate unconscious desire. That desire occupies another scene and has its own means of expression, and it is the object of analysis to separate a subject's unconscious *moi* from the surface ego.

Lacan pioneered analytic techniques designed to facilitate analysands' discovery of their unconscious subjective individuation, and his techniques earned him the censure of the International Psychoanalytic Association. Lacan taught that the analyst should remain silent, refusing to interpret the subject's speech. He maintained that the analyst should rarely answer the analysand directly and even then not in any forthright fashion that would provide a response to his or her articulated question. Lacan himself frequently paced about the room during analytic sessions and even counted his money while his analysands spoke. The logic dictating such behavior derives from the fact that the analyst has a function in analysis, but not an identity. That is, to answer the analysand's direct requests would be to acknowledge the ascendancy of the speaking subject, the surface ego one generally associates with an interlocutor in a normal conversation. The goal of analysis is to unleash the unconscious structures of an analysand's discourse, and this can be accomplished only by frustrating standard avenues of speech. Lacan frequently compared his role in analysis to the dummy in bridge who, once he puts his cards on the table, can only watch in silence as his partner in the match makes choices and selects paths for proceeding. The analyst, as the subject presumed to know, must wait impassively until the analysand recognizes the fact that he or she is not speaking to another ego, but is, in fact, speaking to an individualized or personalized other which he or she has constructed through the course of analysis. Lacan frequently claimed that the unconscious is the desire of the other, and in analysis the analyst comes to figure that other for the analysand.

As the slogan embossed on each issue of *Scilicet* suggests, there exists in a specific but unnamed site a particular knowledge to which one can and may accede, but only through the exertion of a great deal of effort. Lacan attempted to control the intellectual effort required to understand his work, contending that his writing is marked by a "kind of tightening up that I like in order to leave the reader no other way out than the way in, which I prefer to be difficult."[3] In other words, Lacan strived to put his reader in the transferential necessity of presuming that the text holds great theoretical secrets that he or she needs to unlock. His writing, with its densely encoded theoretical jargon and its hermetic and unattributed references to ancient and modern philosophies and letters, keeps his reader in the subordinate position of the disciple attempting to accede to mastery. Despite Lacan's repeated claim that the master's position is untenable, however, the seemingly aggressive and pointless obscurity of his prose might attest to his vehement attempt to occupy that position as well as to his dogged refusal to transfer it to another.

Lacan's rise to celebrity status in the mid-1960s was accompanied by incessant criticism and personal attack. In one somewhat trenchant criticism of the controversial figure who revolutionized psychoanalysis and its teaching, Lacan is censured for never abandoning the position of the master. "Lacan accomplished the *tour de force* of never appearing, in public or in private, as anything but the analyst," François Roustang writes, "or more subtly of making sure that all the personal traits exposed to us fell under the constituted figure of the analyst."[4] Lacan's control of the transfer of psychoanalytic knowledge overflowed into his administrative capacities as well as into his personal life. The polemical and charismatic figure remained in control precisely because he commanded the fashion in which his followers identified with him and transferred their professional and personal feelings onto him. Lacan never ceased to be criticized for his teaching and for his analytic practices as well as for his personal conduct — some found him to be outlandishly boorish and others were persuaded that he was, in fact, psychotic. Lacan had only friends or foes — no one who had met him or read his work seems to have remained indifferent to either his theories or his style. Lacanianism was consequently not only an intellectual phenomenon that swept the French academy in the 1960s and 1970s, but something of a sociological one as well. By ceaselessly embodying the figure of the charismatic master in control of the dissemination of truth, Lacan the man was and is inseparable from the philosophy and practice he taught.

Jacques-Marie Emile Lacan was born of middle-class parents in Paris on April 13, 1901.[5] Jacques-Marie and his two siblings—both of whom, curiously enough, were born on Christmas Day—were born near the Place de la Bastille, but the family later moved to the rue du Montparnasse in Paris's sixth arrondissement. Displaying at an early age a gift for the German language, Lacan became interested in philosophy, particularly the writings of Spinoza and later Kant and, despite his father's protests, the study of medicine. He renounced Christianity at an early age, even though his mother was a staunch believer, and during his youth he was briefly involved with the right-wing group, Action française. Upon receiving his *baccaulauréat* he moved out of his parents' apartment to take a maid's room in Montmartre, where he began a series of romantic involvements that would later interest his critics. Elizabeth Roudinesco describes Lacan's life as a young adult as follows:

> In his amorous relationships he was quite frankly something of a libertine and he resembled a noble under the Regency much more than he did a nineteeth-century intellectual. He always had numerous mistresses. Lacan preferred androgynous women with narrow hips, small breasts and long legs. An outrageous flirt, he dressed like a dandy and quickly spent the little bit of money that his parents gave him. Lacan scorned the middle class in which he was born and wished to gain fame, fortune and distinction. (Vol. 2, 119)

Lacan received a traditional medical training. Between 1926 and 1930 he published a handful of articles in collaboration with Heuyer, Courtois, Meignant, and others on neurological disorders, hallucinatory delirium, and general paralysis.[6] In 1928 he began to train at an institution for the criminally insane with Gaëtan Gatian de Clérambault, a noted psychiatrist whose revolutionary work on erotomania and paranoia tremendously influenced Lacan's thinking and whom he would later call his only master in psychiatry.[7] Clérambault studied paranoids who believed that their own obsessive objects, usually famous people, were in love with them, and he attempted to provide an ordered classificatory system for the various psychoses he observed. Clérambault believed that psychoses were predominantly constitutional in nature; this position separated him from early theorists like Kraepelin, who posited that psychoses developed from internal causes, and his insistence on the systematic and structural classification of disorders affiliated him with Bleuler, the Swiss psychiatrist who had earlier attempted to link paranoid disorders with subjects' use of language.[8]

By the early 1930s Lacan had begun to study Freud and he had met André Breton and had interviewed Salvador Dali about his theory of hallucination, paranoia, and interpretation. It was also during this period that Lacan began his observation of Aimée, a patient in Sainte-Anne Hospital who was incarcerated for having attempted to stab a famous actress whom she believed was persecuting her. In his doctoral thesis in medicine, Lacan wrote that

> Aimée's delirium almost completely represents the gamut of paranoid themes; themes of persecution and of grandeur tightly intermingle. The former express themselves in ideas of jealousy, prejudice, and in typical delirious interpretations.... The latter come through as dreams of escape to a better life, as vague intuitions of having to fill a great social mission, or as reforming idealisms: in short, as a systematized erotomania centred on a royal character.[9]

Lacan's work on Aimée's case accomplished an amalgamation of psychiatry with Freudian psychoanalysis. Integrating Bleuler's theories of schizophrenia with Freud's interpretation of dreams, Lacan wrote that "dream images have a *signifying* effect whose value ... for disclosing psychogenetic mechanisms we can no longer deny" (*De la psychose*, 210). Lacan's study of Aimée was significant primarily because he emphasized the relationship between traumatic events in the patient's life and internal psychic conflicts related to her desire for self-punishment; this latter phenomenon, he theorized, was determined by a fixation in the genital stage in the evolutionary development of her personality. The third section of Lacan's thesis is devoted to establishing a methodology for the science of personality and a critical assessment of narcissism, the ego-ideal and the *moi*, the locus of a subject's unconscious identifications. Commenting on the significance of his work for the development of psychoanalysis, Lacan observed, "My work is original in that it is the first, at least in France, to attempt an exhaustive interpretation of the mental phenomena of a typical delirium as a function of the subject's concrete history, reconstituted as completely as possible by direct analytical investigation."[10]

Lacan's thesis did not immediately cause a stir in the psychoanalytic world, primarily because the senior members of the Société psychoanalytique de Paris had all done their analyses either with Freud or his direct disciples and consequently held to a rigid dogmatism that put little stock in theoretical revision. Lacan's greatest notoriety arose initially among the young surrealists and Marxists who viewed his work as ideologically opposed to the idealism of contemporary psychiatry. For example, in *La Critique sociale* Jean Bernier praised Lacan's implicit radicalism of "illustrating the Marxist conception of human personality" and for showing that in all of the human sciences "historical materialism declared war on bourgeois civilization."[11] David Macey points out the liberating goals psychoanalysis and surrealism seemed to share because of their common interest in freeing sexuality from the constraints that a Victorian industrial society had imposed, and he calls attention to the use both made of automatic writing.[12] Surrealists employed automatic writing based on dream images and snatches of discourse culled from a variety of sources as a means of poetic production. The works so produced contested the representational nature of language and privileged not its referentiality but its effects. Lacan once noted, in fact, "I feel a great personal connection with Surrealist painting."[13]

Dali had written about his theories of automatic writing and the revolutionary sort of literary criticism it might produce in an article entitled "L'Âne pourri" ("The Rotten Ass"). Wishing to sound the death knell for the conception of reality as rational, present, and universal, Dali wrote that paranoia, a sort of frenetic and raving interpretation of the world, had a great deal to offer literary production and criticism:

> It is through a strictly paranoid process that it has become possible to produce a double image, that is, the representation of an object which, without the least anatomical or figurative dimension, is at the same time the representation of another object; this representation is also stripped of any sort of deformation or abnormality which might reveal a formal structure.[14]

A quarter of a century later, Lacan penned a startlingly similar formulation concerning the nature of the work of art and he theorized its significance for psychoanalysis:

> Of course, works of art imitate the objects that they represent but their goal is not simply to represent them. In providing the imitation of an object, they make this object into something else. Thus, they only pretend to imitate. The object is inaugurated into a particular relationship with the Thing, whose purpose is at once to surround and confine, to presentify and to absentify (*présentifier et absentifier*).[15]

Representation in Lacan's view not only makes absent things present but more crucially it creates a cavity or emptiness around the objects it depicts. The Thing, that portion of reality that undergoes and endures the play of signifiers that combine to depict it, nevertheless radically resists complete representation. The Thing is that which is never available in and of itself and Lacan compares its coming into being as such to a vase on a potter's wheel. As the potter molds the lump of clay into a vessel capable of containing something, he or she is first and foremost circumscribing an emptiness whose purpose is ultimately to be filled. Language has the potential to fill the emptiness — at least partially — constituted by the inability to achieve a direct adequation with the totality of the real, but subjects whose consciousness is determined by language are consequently split and incorporate into themselves the lack that the Thing represents.

Lacan's interests in the surrealist project for exploring representation's effects and in language's capacity to hollow out of the real an emptiness that is by definition excluded from language later evolved into a direct confrontation with linguistics. With varying degrees of scientific specificity, Lacan elaborated on concepts developed by, among others, Ferdinand de Saussure, Noam Chomsky, and Roman Jakobson. From Saussure's *Course in General Linguistics* Lacan borrowed the concept of linguistic value, the differential and relational construction of signification and the materiality of the signifier.[16] Saussure posited that language's role was to provide a material link between thought and sound. The signifier or sound image (*image acoustique*) is arbitrary in the sense that there is no inherent connection between it and the concept it represents and its value is "purely negative and differential" (*Course*, 119). That is, signifiers in discourse only function through their relation to and difference from other signifiers. Signifiers form chains of association that play off of one another.

Lacan interrogated the negative and differential relationship among signifiers to arrive at a somewhat radical notion of linguistic meaning or sense for psychoanalysis. Elaborating theories that Freud had developed, particularly in *The Interpretation of Dreams* (ch. 6, sec. C) concerning the means of representation dreams employ, he theorized that the play of signification arises specifically when there is "a lack of taxematic material for the representation of such logical articulations as causality, contradiction, [and] hypothesis ..."[17] The unconscious resorts to a quilted amalgamation of signifiers that fails to produce meaning in any customary sense of the word in order to express repressed wishes and desires, an amalgamation which, for however incomprehensible it may be, "follows the laws of the signifier" ("Agency of the Letter," 161). Following Jakobson, Lacan repudiated Chomsky's attempt to associate agrammatical sentences with breakdowns in meaning. He maintained that collections of signifiers not only can produce sense for a given subject, but that they cannot fail to do so; analysis forces the subject to consider the unconscious's eruptions into consciousness and to confront the unconscious identifications and incorporations layered beneath the surface ego.

By the 1950s Lacan was already speaking of a Copernican revolution of knowledge, heralded in by Freud, that had as a result the discovery that "the very centre of the human being was no longer to be found at the place assigned to it by a whole humanist tradition."[18] That place was the autonomous human subject, displaced from its traditional self-conscious position as the agent and source of all knowledge. As an early proponent of what would later be called structuralism — despite the fact that Lacan only ever makes passing reference to the structuralist movement — Lacan spurned the *cogito* of Cartesian philosophy and held that the thinking or speaking "I" is not in the last instance the author of logic and reason because individuals are born into a ready-made linguistic order, an order that controls and limits the human capacity to reason. Consequently, when Lacan refers to the subject, he invokes not only the individual who speaks, who utters the pronoun "I" as the subject of the verb, but the individual who is subject to language and its maneuvers. Because at any given moment language has both a diachronic, historical dimension in which are encoded a host of social forces underpinning its development, as well as a synchronic, incommutable one composed of grammatical structures and the relationships among signifiers,[19] human subjects are spoken by structures and forces over which they have no control. Lacan thus postulated that the subject is both ex-centric and ex-sistent — that is, removed from the center and the complete control from which it presumes to speak, displaced from the omphalos of being represented by the presence of the spoken word.[20]

In 1933, at about the same time that Lacan began his investigation of surrealism and automatic writing, Alexandre Kojève initiated his seminars on Hegel's *Phenomenology of the Mind* at Paris's École Pratique des Hautes Etudes. Every week Kojève delivered his reading of the *Phenomenology*, walking his students through the text and commenting on its principal theoretical components. The seminars became a major intellectual event in Paris, attended by such luminaries as Raymond Queneau, Georges Bataille, Pierre Klossowski, Maurice Merleau-Ponty, and André Breton, and they had an incalculable influence on the still unknown Jacques Lacan. Lacan put Kojève's Hegel to work for psychoanalytic theory, drawing in particular on the concepts of the master/slave dialectic, negativity, and desire as the desire for recognition.

Commenting on Chapter 4 of the *Phenomenology*, Kojève explained that human desire does not bear on an entity existing in the real and natural world but on the abstraction of another human desire. Desire, he argued, is the presence of an absence, and one desires because of an internal lack: "Hegel shows that Desire that bears on another Desire is necessarily the Desire of *Recognition* which — by opposing the Master to the Slave — engenders *History* and moves it (for as long as it is not definitively suppressed by Satisfaction)."[21] Lacan explained the human dialectic of desire by demonstrating that desire is always unconscious, that its object is forever occulted and unavailable, and that the desiring subject stands apart from the surface ego. "Man's desire is the *désir de l'Autre* (the desire of the Other)," Lacan writes, "in which the *de* provides what grammarians call the 'subjective determination,' namely that it is *qua* Other that he desires...."[22] In two texts fundamental to his theory of psychoanalysis, "The Mirror Stage" (first published in 1936 and later modified) and "The Signification of the Phallus" (1958), Lacan appropriates the Hegelian dialectic of desire and uses it to postulate the subject's accession to language and consequently to the corpus of intersubjective and social relations that he or she will encounter through life.[23]

The mirror stage is a protracted period in an infant's life during which its own specific subjectivity emerges as a series of relationships. Like the negative and differential affiliations among signifiers that characterize Saussure's linguistics and to which the mirror stage owes something of a debt, the intersubjective relationships responsible for the formation of the "I" do not construct a positive identity in a Cartesian sense but a subjective function. In the first six months of life the infant, without speech, is physically uncoordinated and completely dependent. Lacking any recognizable individuality, the infant is empty and psychically undifferentiated. Its perceptions of self, like Condillac's statue, are nearly identical with the effects the outside world has upon its senses. Whatever images or objects it seizes upon will become objects of identification and it will incorporate or introject them. The physically immature infant consequently has no sense of self because it is not aware of its being as an integrated individual; it conceives of itself only as fragments and pieces—an arm here, a head there.[24] These disjointed parts of the body provide the infant with the sense of a fragmented, nonintegral body.

At about the age of six months the infant, having acquired greater physical strength, can move itself about more and in general control more of its movements. It is no longer the purely passive recipient of its mother's attentions but instead participates more actively in the mother/infant dyad.[25] It also learns to recognize images or representations of itself. Since the infant's perceptions of self come to it from without—that is, from its sensory perceptions of the external world which circumscribes it—it identifies with the image it sees and assumes the specular image it perceives in the mirror. Lacan calls the infant's identification with its own specular image a "jubilant assumption."

> This jubilant assumption of his specular image by the child at the *infans* stage, still sunk in his motor incapacity and nursling dependencies, would seem to exhibit in an exemplary situation the symbolic matrix in which the *I* is precipitated in a primordial form, before it is objectified in the dialectic of identification with the other, and before language restores to it, in the universal, its function as subject. (EE 2)

The theory that the infant assumes an external, specular image is crucial to Lacanian psychoanalysis and to the concept of the ex-centric subject. The image the infant receives comes to it as a *Gestalt*, that is, as an integral image exterior to it but nevertheless capable of constituting or imposing on the infant a unity that contrasts with the fragmentary image of self that it has. This image "symbolizes the mental permanence of the *I*, at the same time as it prefigures its alienating destination" (EE 2). That is, the locus of subjectivity, the perception of self as an integrated, self-conscious totality that will later take up its lodging in the ego as the subject speaks about itself, imposes itself on the child and ultimately splits it off from the fragments of identification it experiences within. The ego or the autonomy of consciousness, consequently, is constituted by an illusion of self-sufficiency that Lacan labels misrecognition (*méconnaissance*). The mirror stage establishes a differential relationship—and not an identity—between the subject and its physical and psychic reality.

By eighteen months of age, the child has mastered many of its motor functions and the closing moments of the stage—which, incidentally, Lacan always refers to as a drama—set in. The end of the mirror stage, which is linked to the onslaught of the Oedipal moment, involves a radical split effected in the child's subjectivity; the split occurs both in the child's sense of unity and oneness with the mother and in its sense of self-unity. The child acknowledges its differentiation from the mother primarily in the latter's desire. That is, the mother had been the custodian of the infant's needs, but now her desire is elsewhere. She desires something that is not part of the infant/mother dyad, and that something is located on the side of the father. The child grasps the fact that it neither is nor has what the mother desires. The possibility of satisfaction in the form of total union or plenitude is abolished with the appearance of this third term—the father—and the mother represents for the child a primal loss or the fundamental impossibility of complete satisfaction. The child consequently experiences a feeling of emptiness and radical disjunction that Lacan calls castration. It will be perpetually disarticulated from the objects of its desire, and what the father has that the mother is presumed to desire will become a privileged signifier that Lacan calls the phallus. The presence of the father, who serves as an interdiction to the child not to enjoy complete possession of the mother, is the introduction of a third term in the heretofore child/mother duality, and it is the introduction of this third term that constitutes entry into language: the possibility, indeed the necessity of representing—as in a drama—one's desires. It is important to realize that desires can only be represented, as in the metonymic flow of the signifying chain, and that it will remain impossible to articulate the object of one's desire, which is by definition inaccessible and insatiable.

Lacan theorized along with Freud that unconscious desires result from repression. Freud had argued in *Totem and Taboo* (1912) and *Civilization and Its Discontents* (1930) that the counterpressures that civilization places on human instincts trace back to an unconscious guilt emanating from prohibitions on incest and murder. He postulated that the threat of castration associated with incest and violence toward the father lay at the heart of repression. Lacan endeavored to show that castration, the anxiety surrounding which Freud had exploited in stipulating the manner in which the sexes negotiate their respective gendered positions, is an effect of language with little or no relationship to real physical disfiguration. That is, since an already-constituted language speaks through the human subject ("in man and through man *it* speaks [*ça parle*],"[26]) truth is located in the discourse of a radical Other in relationship to which the subject must find its place. The "it" (*ça*) in this formulation refers to the unconscious subject that speaks a truth of which the conscious subject remains unaware because it fails to recognize or properly interpret its signifiers. The phallus represents the totality of integrated being, a fictional state presumed to exist before recourse to language created a split in the subject that consequently rendered him or her incapable of articulating desire.

The phallus, one of the concepts most frequently attacked in Lacanian psychoanalysis because of Lacan's seemingly uncritical acceptance and perpetuation of an oppressive patriarchal order, has no physical existence. It is not a penis. The phallus "is the signifier intended to designate as a whole the effects of the signified, in that the signifier conditions them by its presence as a signifier" (EE, 285). That the phallus is a pure signifier — one, that is, with no signified, strictly speaking, except in the domain of the imaginary totality from which language has split the subject — is crucial because as a presence it signifies both a primal loss and a totality that is always elsewhere. That is, the phallus designates a plenitude that the subject lacks and that is consequently elsewhere; the lack it demarcates in the subject heralds the Oedipal drama structured around the father's interdiction of pleasure (Law) and the resultant entry into language as the only means available for expressing desire and consequently establishing an identity or a self. The play of presence and absence constitutes the subject as alienated from itself, since the symbolic order to which it has recourse after the separation that castration and the Oedipal drama institute is structured around a primal repression (*Urverdrängung* in Freudian psychology) or renunciation of its most elemental desires.

The alienated subject is consequently determined by and through language and Lacan employs the phallic signifier to articulate the dialectic of desire. Since the phallus is a signifier that is always elsewhere, the subject only has access to it by invoking an Other and by expressing his or her demand for recognition. In the Oedipal situation, the child demands recognition from the mother in the form of love; it wishes to be the phallus in order to satisfy the mother whose desire it perceives to extend beyond their intersubjective dyad. Lacan uses the ambiguous phrase "the desire of the mother *is* the phallus" (EE 289) to point out that desire is always located in another scene, that it is alienated from the subject and that for as much as the mother's desire is *for* the phallus, the child desires the mother *as* the phallus—that is, as the possibility of satiation of its own desire. The desire *of* the mother and *for* the mother are consequently both located outside the dyad linking the two subjects. "The subject takes consciousness of its desire," Lacan wrote, "through the intermediary of the image of the other which gives him the illusion of his own mastery."[27] Desire, Lacan never tired of saying, is the desire of the Other.

The culmination of the Oedipal moment arises with the introduction of the father into the mother/child dyad. It is the father who is presumed to have the phallus that constitutes and structures both the mother's and the child's desire and it is consequently the father[28] from whom originates the threat of castration and the concomitant splitting of the subject. Despite some claims to the contrary, Lacan underscores the paternal *function*—and not an essentially and inherently male identity—with which the phallus is endowed. He maintains that the Oedipal triangle is not a father/mother/child triangle, but a (father) phallus/mother/child one. The father's function is to hold the ensemble together; his function can only be construed as "a series of signifying connotations that give him his existence and his consistency which are far from being interchangeable with the genital function...."[29] The phallus is, however, ineluctably masculine to the extent that it gauges authority as it manifests itself in Western patriarchy. Lacan insisted on the descriptive and historical nature of his account of desire and the phallus: "The Oedipus complex occupies a privileged position, in the current state of our culture, in Western civilization" (*Les écrits techniques*, 222). Finally, Ragland-Sullivan points out that in Lacanian psychoanalysis, "the phallic refers to a secondary identification with social power" (*Jacques Lacan*, 299).[30]

Social power and the ideology that underpins it derive from a specific and systematic regulation of symbols and conventions. The collection of signifiers that mediate between people and the real world is what Lacan referred to as the Symbolic order ("it seems that the symbolic is that which delivers to us the world's system. It is because man has words that he knows things" [*Les Psychoses*, 199]). The Imaginary order, by contrast, is outside the domain of ordinary language and consists of images and erotic attachments incorporated but not articulated through the Symbolic order. Incorporation of objects and identification with the mother, two processes characterized by dual relationships, take place at the Imaginary level, and because imaginary identification is always illusory, *méconnaissance* (misrecognition) distinguishes this order. The collection of incorporated images gives the subject an illusory image of self; consequently, the Imaginary order delineates the subject's narcissistic identification with its ego. The Real, finally, which Lacan defined in counterdistinction to the always-shifting terrain of the Imaginary and the Symbolic, is "that which is always in the same place";[31] it is everything that resists symbolization and is always prior to and outside of any sort of repression.

The subject, then, is always split, radically inaccessible to itself, and the split is occasioned by the introduction of the third term—the father—into the child/mother duality. The phallus is the privileged signifier bringing about castration separation. The cast of characters in the mirror-stage drama has filled out to include child, mother, and father, but there is a final, less specific character whose function is nevertheless crucial in Lacanian analysis for the individuation of the subject—the Other. Throughout his theoretical writings Lacan distinguishes two sorts of others: "an other with a capital *O*, and an other with a little *o*, which is the *moi*. The *Other* is the one that operates in the function of speech. The subject is separated from Others, the real Others, by the wall of language."[32] The *O*ther in general refers to an individual who, in dialogue with the subject, returns to it its objectivity—the subject, that is, becomes the discursive and specular object of the interlocutor and consequently sees itself being seen: it objectifies itself. The *o*ther, however, is the subject's *moi*, composed of the incorporated images and objects from its premirror state. What composes the *moi* are presymbolic and consequently unarticulated images that form a nexus of identification constituting the seat of the subject's unconscious desires. Because these identifications were formed prior to language, the *moi* is unavailable for conscious reflection; nevertheless, it makes itself heard in breaks and eruptions in speech akin to the infamous Freudian slip. Consequently the discourse of the other is that unconscious play of language separate from the subject's ego and responsible for the radical split in subjectivity.

If the subject is split, however, one element in Lacanian theory can never be split or differentiated. That element is the letter. The letter is the impact or consequence language brings to bear on the subject. The letter is a localized signifier designating what Ragland-Sullivan identifies as privileged zones on the child's body that come to be distinguished over and against adjacent zones because of their relative importance in infancy (*Jacques Lacan*, 20). Marked as different and significant, these zones, which take on importance because of the attention both the child and its mother pay to them, become the source of erotogenic impulses later in life. Anika Lemaire provides the most cogent way of conceiving the letter's significance and impact for the subject. Paraphrasing Serge Leclaire, she points out that the letter

> is in fact inseparable from a sensory experience of difference. As an erotogenic zone opens up under the effect of some experience or

other, a mark, a letter is at the same time inscribed in the unconscious as an abstract signifier designating the palpable gap which marks the limits of the erotogenic zone.[33]

In order to see how the letter functions as a signifier in the domain of intersubjectivity and the dialectic of desire, it will be helpful to review one of Lacan's most famous readings, that of Edgar A. Poe's "The Purloined Letter."

Originally delivered as part of the famous seminars and serving as the introductory piece in the French edition of the *Écrits*,[34] this interpretation of Poe's tale illustrates how the signifying chain confers identity on a specific subject with respect to the place that subject holds in the chain. Lacan claims that there are four characters in the tale's first scene: the king, the queen, the minister, and the letter — and not the person who sent it. The letter is a radical signifier because it is a symbol of pure displacement; whoever touches it is drawn into the play of signifiers. In the scene in which the minister makes off with the letter, we know that the letter in question is sitting on the table. We do not know whether it contains words of love or words of treason but in any event — since it is a communication addressed by someone to another it constitutes a sort of pact. The letter is sitting on the table, there, in plain sight, but lying there on the table it does not have its proper value because it has its proper value only with respect to what it threatens: the royal marriage or the security of the state. What is above all important here is that the letter doesn't have the same sense wherever it happens to be. As soon as it passes into the minister's pocket, it is no longer what it was. It is no longer a love letter, or a letter written in confidence: it is evidence. The minister may well intend to use it to blackmail the queen — this is what we expect — but he is only empowered as long as the queen knows that he has it. She does know, of course, for she has been watching the minister all along, but she cannot say anything about it since the king so far has no idea what is going on. The minister has the letter, but in order to get what he wants — in order to get all the mileage he can out of it — he cannot talk about it. If he reveals what it contains he no longer has any power over the queen. In possession of the letter, he also has to keep quiet about it.

The minister's possession of the letter and his inability to talk about it puts him in what Lacan calls a narcissistic relationship with the queen because neither of them can speak of the letter — she because it would be tantamount to showing it to the king and he because speaking about it would render him impotent with respect to the queen.

The police perform a detailed search of the minister's house but they are unable to find the letter. Dupin, however, finds it easily, since it is hiding in plain sight. If Dupin is so readily able to cop the letter, why is it that the cops were unable to do so? Because the stolen letter had become a hidden letter, but it wasn't hidden where and how they thought. That is, the police had a description of the letter — it had a red seal and a particular inscription — but the minister altered the letter's appearance. Of course, the letter had a text, but the police were not given the text of the letter. The letter was, in fact, in plain sight. It wasn't hidden — only the truth of the letter was.

The police couldn't find the letter, Lacan claims, precisely because they are agents of an authority that resides solely in symbols. Part of their symbolic authority involves convincing people that their authority comes from force, and the police seem to believe it, too, but this is why they can't find the letter: force is part of the nonsymbolic real, but since a letter is always in flight, always going somewhere, it *isn't* anywhere. The police, agents of authority, could not find the letter because for agents of authority, truth is hidden, inaccessible — they're only interested in reality. Agents of authority have no relationship to truth.

The scene in which Dupin steals the letter from the minister is a repetition of the first scene. The significant differences Lacan establishes concern exact referentiality and truth. That is, the narrator's account of the dialogue between the prefect of police and Dupin concerns the minute details of the police search: sticking needles into cushions, removing table tops, etc. In addition, the prefect's discourse also reports the queen's description of the scene of the crime — the minister's stealing the letter. There are several filtered layers of discourse in this dialogue, in that the queen tells the prefect what happened, who in turn tells Dupin, and this is relayed to us in the third person narrator's discourse — the story's *récit*. What is important in all of these levels of language is the revelation of *what happened* — that is, the exact transmission of a series of events in the real world. The dialogue between Dupin and the narrator, on the other hand, in which the former tells the latter how he knew where the letter was, deals not with reality but with the revelation of hidden truth. That is, referentiality is no longer a question; what is important is the role a subject plays when he or she is inhabited by the signifier. In this case, the letter, whose contents we never learn, becomes a pure signifier. What the letter says is far less significant than the intersubjective position its possession inscribes on the possessor. The last thing we need to examine, then, is how the position or possession of the letter defines subjectivity and what this means for Lacanian analysis.

Lacan indicts Dupin for his participation in the little drama, showing that through his own possession of the letter he occupies the place formerly held by the queen and the minister. Lacan shows that the subject who presumes to be free of the ruses of the signifying chain is merely deluding itself. Slipping from the position of the exterior third party to the position of one engaging in a dual, narcissistic relationship, the subject is always constituted by the machinations of the signifying chain. And the signifier, the indivisible marker and articulation of difference, separates the subject from its desire in one and the same gesture of articulating it.[35]

Consequently, the letter is a material signifier that signifies the subject's place in a specific symbolic order. It is indivisible because its words — the substance of what it says — matter less than the position its possession bestows upon the holder. Like the phallus, which is the signifier of identity and oneness but in and of itself nothing, the letter is a place holder, the site of an articulation of difference the possession of which confers identity. Barbara Johnson writes that the letter "is a *difference*. It is known only in its effects. The signifier is an articulation in a chain, not an identifiable unit."[36] The letter contributes to bestowing on the subject *l'être* (the being) of his or her social existence and place in the symbolic order. What the subject must learn to do — and this is the principal goal of analysis — is to discern the ex-centricity of its subjectivity: to recognize that the position from which it speaks is defined for it through language. The analysand must assume the mastery he or she presumes the analyst represents by recognizing that there is no guarantee of a secure and unequivocal interpretation of symptoms. When the subject speaks, it is spoken and consequently constituted through language and through the unconscious desires that break into discourse. The other in analysis is consequently not the analyst but the subject's unconscious, and analysis is complete when the subject can negotiate the difference between the Other's desire — that of the analyst, of the interlocutor — and the other's desire — that of its unconscious, which, following the laws of the signifier, inscribes identity on the speaking subject.

This is what constitutes the dialectic of mastery and desire in the analytic situation. Through analysis of the *lettre* and of *l'être*, the subject learns to be *m'être*, a pun Lacan used rhyming the French word for master (*maître*) with a neologism suggesting the ascendency of one's own being (an invented reflexive verb joining the reflexive particle *me* with the infinitive of the verb "to be": *être*).[37] The subject, in other words, must take mastery from the analyst. He or she must renounce the belief in the analyst's possession of stable truth and the concomitant power to requite the loss experienced through castration separation. At the same time, the subject must eschew the attempt to conform to the Other's desire. Lacan describes the end of analysis and the assuming of "*m'êtrise*" as follows:

> What takes place occurs between the subject's *moi* ... and others. The course of analysis marks the progressive displacement of this relation ... as part of the transference which occurs there where the subject does not recognize himself.... Analysis consists of having the

subject become conscious of his relations not with the analyst's *moi*
but with all those Others who are his real respondants and whom he
has not recognized. The subject must progressively discover to which
Other he is really addressing himself without knowing it and he must
progressively assume transferential relations in the place where he is
and where he did not at first know he was. ("Introduction du grand
Autre," 288)

The subject achieves "*m'êtrise*" upon the recognition that there is no
subject of desire that is not an alienated desire. As a particular effect
of the signifying chain, the subject is split off from its desire and it
achieves mastery with the recognition that language "sutures" it to the
gaps inherent in language, gaps inaugurated as both the cause and
effect of access to language.[38] That is, the passage to the Symbolic
order from an Imaginary and narcissistic relationship to its own ego,
characterized by misrecognition of external objects as constitutive of
self, inaugurates the primal loss for which words stand in as imperfect
restitution. Mastery is the abjuration of being's plenitude and the
reconciliation with the Symbolic order—cultural as well as linguistic—
that gives the subject identity.

The manner in which one takes one's place in the Symbolic order
is crucial for the establishment of gender identification, and this aspect
of Lacanian psychoanalysis has had far-reaching effects for contemporary feminist analyses. Briefly, gender identity results from the child's
imaginary identification with the supposed possessor of the phallus.
Since the father intervenes at a crucial moment in the mirror stage and
breaks the Imaginary and dual relationship between child and mother
(whose desire is consequently perceived to extend outside the pair they
form), his intervention is perceived as a prohibition stemming from a
cultural law. It should be noted here that Lacan's theory of gender
identification derives not from a biological essentialism but from a
cultural injunction. As Jacqueline Rose writes, it is "not that anatomical
difference *is* sexual difference . . . but that anatomical difference comes
to *figure* sexual difference, that is, it becomes the sole representative of
what that difference is allowed to be."[39] Lacan stressed not the ascendency of the visual and the present often ascribed to Freud's account
of feminine sexuality, castration, and the possession of a penis, but the
manner in which signifiers connoting gender identity preexist the subject's assumption of a role. His emphasis on the culturally ascribed
aspect of gender identification consequently relegates it not to an
Imaginary essence but to the Symbolic order itself.

In "Agency of the Letter in the Unconscious," Lacan states this
case by referring to the twin doors of public restrooms, each with the
word "Ladies" or "Gentlemen" written above it. Comparing the rest-
room doors to the algorithm of the sign (S/s), Lacan notes that the

gendered signifiers, which apparently relate to the same signified (the door), only take on meaning in relation to one another. The cultural aspect of gender identification lies in the fact that

> the image of twin doors [symbolizes], through the solitary confinement offered Western Man for the satisfaction of his natural needs away from home, the imperative that he seems to share with the great majority of primitive communities by which his public life is subjected to the laws of urinary segregation. ("Agency of the Letter," 151)

Emphasizing the social imperative to take a gendered identity ("away from home") and the fact that public life is structured around these neat distinctions, Lacan identifies the formation of sexuality within the subject's unconscious and the concomitant gender identification that results from it as fundamental to and inherent in the construction of subjectivity.

Lacan furthermore maintained that *man* and *woman* are "only signifiers completely tied to reigning linguistic use"[40] and that engendered subjects consequently align themselves with a specific, socially encoded sexual identity. Woman in a patriarchal culture "is introduced in the symbolic pact of marriage as an object of exchange ... among fundamentally androcentric lineages."[41] Consequently, although both sexes are subject to the laws of the signifier, the woman takes her place on the side of the nonphallic "not-all."[42] As the site of nonphallic lack she signifies male desire; she becomes the Other, the illusory object embodying the lack that castration separation produced in him, the origin and representation of his desire. Woman is, as Rose has written, "the place onto which lack is projected, and through which it is simultaneously disavowed ..." (Introduction to vol. 2, 48), which is why Lacan chooses to put the definite article under erasure in his reference to "The woman."[43]

Lacan always claimed to advocate a strict adherence to Freud's philosophy of psychoanalysis, but despite this assertion the International Psychoanalytic Association barred him from its ranks in 1963, effectively forbidding him from teaching and conducting training analyses. At issue were the short analytic sessions Lacan practiced, frequently dismissing analysands after only a few minutes, and his ostensible manipulation of the psychoanalytic transference. As Roustang pointed out, Lacan never seemed willing to abandon the untenable position of the master; he strived to maintain the illusion that he was the only psychoanalytic theoretician, and he exercised what many considered to be a sort of intellectual terrorism over his students. In the first issue of *Scilicet*, for example, Lacan generously wrote that "*Scilicet* is not closed to anyone," but then added the somewhat menacing statement, "but whoever does not publish here can never be recognized as one of my students."[44] In addition, only Lacan had the right to sign his name to his articles in *Scilicet* — all other pieces were anonymous. Lacan succeeded in bullying his friends and associates into taking him out to dinner and performing services for him — often at considerable personal expense — that went well beyond the call of duty. Yet here was a man who held a generation of scholars and analysts in thrall with his seductive intimation that he knew the truth and could bequeath it to his favorites. Catherine Clément wrote that she attended Lacan's seminars for years without understanding a thing, which prompted Jane Gallop to wonder, "why would anyone listen for several years to something she could not understand?"[45]

The answer appears fairly clear, even if the means through which Lacan accomplished the feat remain clouded. Lacan spoke the truth and he spoke for the truth. One of his favorite exercises, inscribed in "The Freudian Thing," was to speak as the other, the unidentified "it" that speaks the truth of the human subject: "Hommes, écoutez, je vous en donne le secret. Moi, la vérité, je parle" (Men, listen: I will give you the secret. I, the truth, I speak). His most enthusiastic followers recognized the didactic intent of this drill; nevertheless there appeared to be a lingering suspicion that everything that came out of the master's mouth was, in fact, *the* truth. Lacan's citations of poets and philosophers have frequently been re-cited as emanating from the analyst himself: for example, the aphorism that "the mirror would do well to reflect a little more before returning our image to us" ("The Freudian Thing," 138) has more than once been cited as originating from Lacan himself, although it issued some thirty years earlier from Jean Cocteau in "Le Sang d'un poète." Perhaps Lacan's apparent mastery of truth stems from the difficulty with which one can accede to his thought. Or, perhaps his rise to unprecedented celebrity status in Parisian intellectual circles can be attributed to the phenomenon of transference. Inhabiting an uncertain world in which the subject was universally acknowledged as the postexistential and passive receptacle of language and other social forces, people seemed to desire to hear the truth speak one last time.

Notes

1. The French slogan reads, "Tu peux savoir ce qu'en pense l'École freudienne de Paris." All translations in this article, unless otherwise specified, are my own.

2. *Arts*, December 14, 1966. Cited by Elizabeth Roudinesco, *La Bataille de cent ans: Histoire de la psychanalyse en France* (Paris: Seuil, 1986, 2 vols.), vol. 2, 423.

3. "The Agency of the Letter in the Unconscious or Reason Since Freud," in *Écrits, A Selection*, trans. Alan Sheridan (New York: Norton, 1977), p. 146 (hereafter referred to as EE).

4. François Roustang, *Lacan: De l'équivoque à l'impasse* (Paris: Minuit, 1986), p. 14.

5. Details of Lacan's early years are sketchy and difficult to obtain. The biographical information here draws primarily from the following sources: Elizabeth Roudinesco, *La Bataille de cent ans*; Stuart Schneiderman, *Jacques Lacan: The Death of an Intellectual Hero* (Cambridge: Harvard Univ., 1983); Catherine Clément, *Vies et légendes de Jacques Lacan* (Paris: Grasset, 1981); François Roustang, *Lacan*; David Macey, *Lacan in Contexts* (London; Verso, 1988).

6. Joël Dor has published a nearly complete bibliography of all of Lacan's publications, arranged both chronologically and alphabetically. See his *Bibliographie des travaux de Jacques Lacan* (Paris: Intereditions, 1983).

7. In "De nos antécédents," *Écrits* (Paris: Seuil, 1966), p. 65 (hereafter referred to as E).

8. See Eugen Bleuler and C. G. Jung, *Komplexe und Krankheitsursachen bei Dementia Praecox*, Zentralblatt für Nervenheilkunde und Psychiatrie, 31, no. 19, 1908. See also Roudinesco, vol. 1, pp. 115ff.

9. *De la psychose paranoïaque dans ses rapports avec la personalité* (Paris: Seuil, 1980), pp. 158–59.

10. "Exposé général de nos travaux scientifiques," in *De la psychose*, 2d ed. (Paris: Seuil, 1975), p. 401.

11. Cited by Roudinesco, vol. 2, p. 130. Bernier continues: "Of course, Dr. Lacan seems ... yet far from suspecting where his theories can and must lead him."

12. David Macey, *Lacan in Contexts*, pp. 47–55.

13. Discussion following "Of Structure as an Inmixing of an Otherness Prerequisite to Any Subject Whatever," in *The Structuralist Controversy*, eds. Richard Macksey and Eugenio Donato (Baltimore: Johns Hopkins Univ., 1970), p. 197.

14. "L'Âne pourri," *Le Surréalisme au service de la révolution*, July 1, 1930, p. 10. Cited by Roudinesco, vol. 2, p. 125.

15. Seminar of February 10, 1960, *Le Séminaire VII: L'Éthique de la psychanalyse* (Paris: Seuil, 1986), p. 169.

16. See Ferdinand de Saussure, *Course in General Linguistics*, trans. Wade Baskin (New York: McGraw-Hill, 1966), pp. 101–39.

17. "Agency of the Letter," EE, p. 161.

18. "The Freudian Thing, or the Meaning of the Return to Freud in Psychoanalysis," EE, p. 114. This essay is a revised version of a lecture pronounced in Vienna in 1955.

19. Saussure qualifies the possibility of an ahistorical, synchronic state of language by arguing that "in practice a language-state is not a point but rather

a certain span of time during which the sum of the modifications that have supervened is minimal. The span may cover ten years, a generation, a century, or even more." *Course in General Linguistics*, p. 101.

20. Jacques Derrida argues the same point from the perspective of Western philosophy and its privileging of the *logos* in *De la grammatologie* (Paris: Minuit, 1967), English trans. Gayatri Spivak (Baltimore: Johns Hopkins Univ., 1976).

21. Alexandre Kojève, *Introduction à la lecture de Hegel*, ed. Raymond Queneau (Paris: Gallimard, 1947), p. 368.

22. "Subversion of the subject and dialectic of desire," EE, p. 312.

23. On Lacan's debt to Hegelian philosophy, see Edward Casey and J. Melvin Woody, "Hegel, Heidegger, Lacan: The Dialectic of Desire," *Interpreting Lacan*, eds. Joseph Smith and William Kerrigan (New Haven: Yale Univ., 1983), and Alain Juranville, *Lacan et la philosophie* (Paris: Presses universitaires de France, 1984), Deuxième partie.

24. Ellie Ragland-Sullivan points out that some parts of the body, however, in particular the erotogenic zones that Freud identified — the mouth, the anus, the genitals — become charged with meaning because they are privileged or differentiated through the roles they play in early infancy. "Because they are distinguished as 'different' or meaningful," she writes, "they later play a key role in drive and sexual desire. From such a perspective, sexual pleasure is not inherent in body parts or in hormones per se." *Lacan and the Philosophy of Psychoanalysis* (Urbana: Univ. of Illinois, 1987), p. 20.

25. It is important to point out here that the term "mother" does not necessarily denote the gender of the caretaker. As is generally the case with the principal components of Lacan's theories, relationships and functions play a more crucial role than identities. Consequently, the "mother" is a function, a position in the duel relationship between caretaker and infant, but I will continue to refer to her as "she" as a matter of convenience and convention.

26. "The Signification of the Phallus," EE, p. 284.

27. Seminar of April 7, 1954, "Zeitlich-Entwickelungsgeschichte," *Le Séminaire I: Les Écrits techniques de Freud* (Paris: Seuil, 1975), p. 178.

28. Just as the mother fills a role, as elaborated above, it is important to recognize here that the father fills a function and is not possessed of a specific identity.

29. "Le phallus et le météore," seminar of July 4, 1956 in *Le Séminaire III: Les Psychoses* (Paris: Seuil, 1981), p. 359.

30. See also "On the Possible Treatment of Psychosis," EE, especially p. 298.

31. Seminar of December 16, 1959, "*Das Ding* (II)," *Le Séminaire VII*, p. 85.

32. Seminar of May 25, 1955, "Introduction du grand Autre," *Le Séminaire II: Le Moi dans la théorie de Freud et dans la technique de la psychanalyse* (Paris: Seuil, 1978), pp. 276, 286.

33. Anika Lemaire, *Jacques Lacan*, trans. David Macey (London: Routledge and Kegan Paul, 1979), p. 146.

34. April 26, 1955 in *Le Séminaire II*, pp. 225–40.

35. A game Lacan proposes illustrates in similar fashion the phenomenon of thinking oneself in another position. A game of wits is proposed to three prisoners, and the one who solves it will be freed. They are shown 5 disks, three of which are white and two of which are black. Each has one affixed to his back, and the one who discovers the color of his disk will be freed. Each has a white disk placed on his back and the one who is freed discovers the color of his disk by reasoning in the position of the two others: if his disk is black, one of the two others sees one black and one white disk. Consequently, one of them would already have guessed the color of his disk. Since this is not the case, he reasons, his disk must be white. See *Le Séminaire II*, pp. 332ff.

36. "The Frame of References," *The Purloined Poe: Lacan, Derrida, and Psychoanalytic Reading*, eds. John Muller and William Richardson (Baltimore: Johns Hopkins Univ., 1988), p. 242. Johnson's article, which initially appeared in *Yale French Studies* nos. 55–56, is a response both to Lacan's seminar on the Purloined Letter and to Jacques Derrida's "Le Facteur de la vérité," which originally appeared in *Poetique* (1975) and is reprinted in the *Purloined Poe*.

37. Seminar of February 13, 1973, "Aristote et Freud: L'Autre satisfaction," *Le Séminaire XX: Encore* (Paris: Seuil, 1975), p. 53.

38. On the notion of "suture," see Jacques-Alain Miller, "La Suture," *Cahiers pour l'analyse*, 1, January–February, 1966.

39. "Introduction—II," *Feminine Sexuality: Jacques Lacan and the École Freudienne*, eds. Rose and Juliet Mitchel (New York: Pantheon, 1982), p. 42.

40. Seminar of January 9, 1973, "La Fonction de l'écrit," *Le Séminaire XX*, p. 36.

41. "Sosie," seminar of June 8, 1955, *Le Séminaire II*, p. 304.

42. Seminar of February 20, 1973, "Dieu et la jouissance de la femme," *Le Séminaire XX*, p. 68.

43. For a provocative critique of Lacan's theory of femininity, see Jane Gallop, *The Daughter's Seduction* (Ithaca: Cornell Univ., 1982).

44. *Scilicet*, 1, p. 11.

45. Catherine Clément's remarks are in *L'Arc*, 58, p. 33. Gallop's response is in *The Daughter's Seduction*, p. 37.

3

The Derridean Turn

Martin Donougho

Nous sommes embarqués
Pascal

Had this essay a Derridean title, it might well be something along the lines of "Derrida's Invoice." And there would follow a lengthy footnote remarking on the disparate meanings set to work: the "envoi" or destination of the communication sent on its way (*voie*), the plural form of which gives the English "invoice"; the actual contents of the message Derrida is sending us; the gridlike listing of the items sent and the debt incurred; a circulation of commodities, values, or investments within the restricted economy it denotes; an accounting of what we owe Derrida—our debt, our guilty implication—of what he owes the tradition, or simply of what he charges for a lecture; the substitution for and absence of Derrida's own voice, or what is supposed to be such; and not least, an ambiguity of the syntax, with its naughty suggestion that Derrida is "on," that he is a performer, a star turn— and so on.[1]

But I shall resist all such wordplay. There are enough people as it is only too ready to dismiss Derrida as a mere rhetorician, litterateur, poseur, or worse; as someone who at any rate does not seem to know one end of an argument from another, yet another of those Continental polluters of reason, or whatever. Would it be useless to point out that such exclusionary tactics are themselves rhetorical in nature, presupposing a certain purity of philosophical medium, genre, or thematics,

I should like to thank Eve Bannet and Eric Folley for their genially sceptical comments on a preliminary draft.

the decorum of which is just what Derrida wishes to question? More to the point, would it be equally useless to ask Derrida to declare what his own philosophical position amounts to or how it may be justified? As Derrida himself might reply: Perhaps.

Here is a paradox at the threshold of any such enquiry: If Derrida teaches us that reading or writing texts (whether philosophical, legal, literary or whichever) is not a matter of determining a univocal meaning but consists rather of a potentially endless disseminating activity, how can we lay down the law as to what he (or at least his text) means once and for all? In particular, if what Derrida practices is less "explication" than "implication de texte," where does that ever end? Aren't we led down the garden path, or even down "an infinite regress ... of enabling interpretations," each text pointing to the syntactic instability intrinsic to some object text, yet itself unstable by the same token?[2] Some may feel unfairly victimized by this challenge. John Searle, stung by an earlier brush with Derrida, cited Michel Foucault's accusation of "obscurantisme terroriste": the text "is written so obscurely that you can't figure out exactly what the thesis is (hence *obcurantisme*), and when one criticizes it, the author says, 'Vous m'avez mal compris; vous êtes idiot' (hence *terroriste*)."[3] But how — the objection goes — can Derrida claim to be *misread* when there is by his own admission no possibility of a *proper* reading?

Even so, Derrida himself has on occasion left some fairly direct indicators as to what he means, notably in the volume of interviews entitled *Positions*.[4] In effect, he declares (in the third interview dating from 1971), he will take *no* position, philosophical or political, will posit (Hegel's *setzen*) nothing, but will rather take position*s* — the "s" being the disseminating letter par excellence. Unable *not* to interpret (since everything is interpretion, as Nietzsche said), he will propose multiple readings rather than police what meaning may or may not properly be upheld, or else will adopt an "a-thetic," nonpositional approach, an approach that addresses but never arrives at its topic or its audience. As for method, "pas de méthode" he will proclaim: both "no method" and a tentative procedural "step" (*pas*), thus conflating imperative and descriptive modes.[5] Can we even say that he is a philosopher? "I'm not happy with the term 'philosopher,'"[6] he has said. Are his texts rather to be understood as literary? "I will say that my texts belong neither to the 'philosophical' register nor to the 'literary' register," we read[7] (though what are we to make of the gesture of "I will say that ..."? Does it add anything to what he "says"?).

If, then, we are to look for what he has to say about language, equally we have to look out for the language in which he says it. To attend both to his thematics and to his formal procedures, and do so without violating the rules (however provisional) of his own practice, calls for ventriloquism of a high order. As a prospective explainer of Derrida's thought, I have to declare a certain impurity of motive: I must claim a distance from Derrida that properly should be that of a page; must be serious and yet be "beside myself" with a kind of Nietzschean laughter; must interpret from somewhere for someone (for you, dear reader!), etc. At the same time, if Derrida *is* professing or recommending some theory of language, that does of itself lodge a claim to a determinate meaning and validity (or "decidability" as he terms it). We may at least proceed on such faith.

A second, related paradox: if we could give a complete account of Derrida's mode or genre of discourse, where can that account be located with respect to the discourse itself? That is, can Derrida give an account of his *own* procedure, and if so, what sort of account would it be? (It is a special case of the general problem of determination of meaning; philosophical systems have always claimed to be able to reflect on their own status.) The astonishing things is that Derrida attempts such a self-accounting, even while admitting its necessary failure. By means of what has been well called "the veil of displacement," he appeals to various "undecidables"—a locution drawn informally from Gödel's theorem, which holds that the meaning of a proposition within a system cannot be determined with both completeness and consistency.[8] Such "undecidables" would comprise a series of concepts (or rather "nonconcepts") which serve provisionally to unlock the potential for meaning in his chosen texts. If I mention a few items from this changing lexicon—e.g., *différance*, mark, spacing, hymen, trait, graft, grid, supplement, fold, hinge, economy, reserve, (archi)writing, double session/science, play, inscription, decentering, general text, *mise-en-abyme*—it is in order to remark the instability of each, the way each demarcates a sphere of operation while at the same time threatening to pass beyond it.

Can we take such constructs as more than provisional, that is, as laying down, what a Kantian tradition of transcendental philosophizing would term "the conditions of possibility" for a certain discourse? Rodolphe Gasché dubs them "infrastructures," by which he means to secure "a middle-ground between the structural plurality of Derrida's philosophy—a plurality that makes it possible to elevate any final essence of his work into its true meaning—and the strict [philosophical] criteria to which any interpretation of his work must yield if it is to be about that work and not merely a private fantasy."[9] I shall return to the question later. But for the moment it is enough that these provisionary features can serve as orienting devices in mapping out the Derridean landscape.

A third paradox, the terms of which take up the other two: if there are problems (1) with determining a text's meaning, and (2) with self-reflexively determining one's own meaning, it is equally difficult (3) to ascribe responsibility for a text—to give a proper meaning a proper name, we might say. What Derrida on occasion terms "deconstruction" consists usually of taking on such eminent authorities as Aristotle, Hegel, Husserl, or Heidegger, and tracing in their writings effects at odds with the mechanism producing them; *what* they state is found by inspection not to square with the performative *act* of stating it. For example, Husserl is shown to display a longing for stable presence beyond the voice that announces such stability; and that is at odds with the tendency towards an anonymous writing already at work in the textual production itself. The text—Husserl—is thus found to turn against itself. At the same time the very act of locating such "double writing" must also appeal to an authoritative source—Edmund Husserl "par lui même"—to set the oppositional drama in motion. It is not as though Derrida was at first oblivious to this problem, but it is one he comes more and more to face explicitly. As we read in one of his later works, *The Post Card* (1980):

> What happens when acts or performances (discourse or writing, ana-lysis or description, etc.) form part of the objects they designate? when they can give themselves as examples of that which they speak or write? There is certainly no gain in self-reflexive transparency— on the contrary. An account is no longer possible, nor a simple report (*compte rendu*), and the borders of the whole (*ensemble*) are no longer either closed or open. Their trait divides itself, and its inter-weavings (*entrelacements*) can no longer be disentangled.[10]

How can an author—Freud, Derrida—"inscribe himself"? How can s/he take up position? We may detect in Derrida's styles a shift from a "logic of positionality" (to give it a name) towards a "logic of the beyond," or rather, of the "step beyond" (*pas au-delà*), from "thetic" to "a-thetic" speculation, from opposition to circulation, in what Gregory Ulmer calls our "post-age."[11] Derrida's "missives" (in quotes, for they are not *really* postcards, are they?) never arrive at their destination, but are always returned to sender. The spirit of his meaning comes down to a letter. There is no "bottom line" to his accounting, to his account; at the end of the day, the teller never balances his books.

But then, neither can we, prospective interpreters of Derrida. Some (like Rorty) have divided Derrida's career into a systematic, philosophical phase, and a playful, literary tendency. Derrida himself, in his belated doctoral defense (June 1980)—published as "The Time of a Thesis: Punctuations"—[12] divided his career in three, based upon his changing attitude to educational institutions and to the "thesis" in particular. The initial period up to 1968 was (he says) followed by an "a-thetic" and even "anti-thetic" phase, and then—in 1980—by a return to the thesis. Ten years later, the observer is tempted to trace Derrida's involvement with political and ethical questions to such a "positionality." But it is unclear whether that is so, or indeed which genealogical narrative could fit such a protean figure. "The Derridean Turn" — The Turn of (*chez*) *Derrida*": but there are many turns possible; he is polytropological.

Which ushers in a last, if minor, paradox: we — at least I — refer to someone called Jacques Derrida, a man born just outside of Algiers in 1930 to assimilated Jewish parents, educated at the École Normale-Supérieure, actively teaching in Paris, the United States, and elsewhere, involved in educational reform both in schools and universities, married, a pipesmoker, and by all accounts a very modest, likable person. Yet here is an author who writes of the disappearance (if not death) of the subject, and never tires of playing upon the conventions of signing a piece, of naming its author. The man dissolves into the moniker. Derrida himself becomes an effect of (his) language. The same goes, of course, for his audience, for you and me: we too risk becoming figments of his discourse. Some philosophers of language, especially those within the orbit of hermeneutics, would stress its relation to subjective experience. By contrast, Derrida along with Foucault and other structuralists or poststructuralists, tend towards an impersonal mode, in line with their thematics of impersonality. I shall continue to speak of Derrida, of his career, his intentions, and so on. Whether there are problems with his understanding of the subject as a discursive effect is a question to take up later.

So much by way of introduction — save to add that Derrida is well aware of the crucial role played by prefaces, marginal discourses, parerga, frames, thresholds, foyers, and so on, all of which are supposed outside the text and yet operate as its organizing center.[13] But again, enough! All this fiddle is just what Derrida's critics object to. Has Derrida anything more to say?

Derrida and the Linguistic Turn

"He do the Police in different voices."[14]

A provisional way to locate Derrida's thinking is to ask where it fits into "the linguistic turn," conveniently summarized in Ian Hacking's lively book, *Why Does Language Matter to Philosophy?*[15] Hacking anatomizes modern philosophy into (1) the "heyday of ideas," where words stand for entities in the mind, (2) the "heyday of meanings," where words signify logical rather than psychological items, and (3) the "heyday of sentences" — "Words, words, words," to cite *Hamlet* — for which there is no appeal outside language itself for the interpretation of meaning. This last phase is "the epochal regime of quotation marks"

(Derrida notes in *Spurs*),[16] the epoch of *epochè*, so to speak. It is exemplified by such figures as Quine, T. S. Kuhn, Feyerabend, and Davidson, though Hacking allows that it is possible to substitute others, such as Foucault or Derrida. For they too renounce the apparent security of a "transcendental signified" (i.e., a fixed order of meaning independent of, yet accessible through, language). Hacking discusses a central problem — central for Derrida also — that of the "indeterminacy of translation." Suppose that someone, say in a foreign culture, utters a string of words the meaning of which is not obvious: how can we ensure we have successfully interpreted them, even after questions and empirical tests have run their course? Quine holds that the conventions of language are in principle insufficient to determine meaning. Others (e.g., Feyerabend) would hold that, on the contrary, the fit is too loose, and the sentence could mean several things (though not just anything). Davidson holds, perhaps, that the fit is "exactly right": the meaning is neither under- nor overdetermined.[17]

Derrida belongs wholeheartedly to Feyerabend's camp, though not for the same reasons. His primary argument seems to run as follows: because a given utterance cannot determine implicitly and in advance the infinitely many contexts in which it might enter, it cannot (or we cannot) lay claim to a univocal or "proper" meaning. Does the argument then commit Derrida to saying that "no statement ever has a determinate meaning," as Alexander Nehamas thinks?[18] And if Derrida is right that "[w]riting is read, and 'in the last analysis' does not give rise to a hermeneutic deciphering, to the decoding of a meaning or truth," what does he think he is doing (Robert Scholes asks) when he writes about how this or that philosopher is to be read?[19] Is Derrida a bomb-throwing textual anarchist?

First, even if (*pace* Quine) there were insufficient evidence to decide on "the" meaning, it would not follow that a sentence has no meaning. It certainly does not follow from a *surfeit* of possible meanings that there is no meaning at all — though we might be encouraged by its undecidability to multiply our construals in protean fashion, almost to the point of nonsense. It is not that there is no truth, but that there is *too much*: "truth is plural" (*Spurs*, 103). Much of Derrida's effort is accordingly directed to exploring the limits of construal, to the articulating and joining together of all manner of readings — that is the point of the exercise. He does not reconstruct but "deconstructs" meaning, by demonstrating the looseness of the syntactic mechanisms that are supposed to produce it. For there is no final authority: "Everything becomes possible against the language-police" he tells Searle (whose speech-act theory assumes a universal "background" or set of conventions and shared beliefs to police the meaning).[20] Which is not to say there is *no* authority and *no* police: only that some police are polite and open, while others are more political and even violent in protecting their property. Nor is it to suppose that anything is allowed, in some "pluralist" fashion:

> I am not a pluralist, and I would never say that every interpretation is equal, but I do not select. The interpretations select themselves. I am a Nietzschean in this sense.... I would not say that some interpretations are truer than others. I would say that some are more powerful than others. The hierarchy is between forces and not between true and false.[21]

It might seem, accordingly, that for Derrida meaning is after all contextual, a function of the shared predicament of speaker and audience. Yet that too is inexact. Pragmatists like Richard Rorty and hermeneuticists like Hans-Georg Gadamer have indeed sought to claim Derrida as one of their own. And it is true that, for example, Gadamer and Derrida share a great deal: they are antifoundationalist, emphasize a kind of "linguisticality," they think of subjectivity as emerging eventlike from an unthematized stratum. But as the recent "improbable debate" between them showed, Derrida resists the invitation to a common ground, and does not accept Gadamer's imputation of a shared "good will" to understand and be understood (for otherwise why should Derrida communicate or interpret at all? — an argument already heard).[22] Without going into the intricacies of Gadamer's own position, why does Derrida not embrace this particular "principle of charity"?

Two reasons suggest themselves. Briefly, on the one hand, the invitation asks too much of language, namely, that the participants can be inscribed without remainder in a common discourse, that the mechanism of interpretation and self-interpretation work smoothly; Derrida by contrast would stress the elements that lead to miscommunication and opacity — play in the machine, or at least in its application. On the other hand, it ignores the rhetorical force of linguistic utterance, the element of "forced" or "bad" usage. Interpretation is hierarchical — Derrida's Nietzscheanism would say. From his standpoint (if he can be said to have one), the invitation to agree might be seen as a trap; he could choose only *not* to engage in conversation. The best-willed encounter proves treacherous: charity begins at home, *chez lui*, we might say, rather than with the other. "My friends, there are no friends!" as Montaigne put it, a clause quoted by Derrida in another "encounter," this time with Thomas McCarthy.[23] In a nutshell, Gadamer thinks that in context otherness can be understood, Derrida that context entails dispersion and disparity, can never be taken neat. Instead of stressing the pragmatics of the situation, or the "application" of interpretive judgment, Derrida will recommend what he has dubbed "program(ma)tology": the continual reinscribing of context into text, a thematization of the meaning of the situation. Characteristically, Derrida's "position" is to stand *between* rival allegiances: on the one hand, to the ideal of deciding the meaning of objective events—either through eidetic reduction or structuralist decoding; on the other, to applying interpretive judgment in a pragmatically defined context—an inferential rather than coding model of communication.[24]

Derrida: Phenomenology, Foucault, Structuralism

"A place for the genuine."[25]

Whether the line of thought just sketched disqualifies Derrida from entering into controversies (how could he argue *against* another possible interpretation?) is moot. For the moment let me turn to some particular consequences of Derrida's linguistic focus. The epochal shift from "meanings" to "sentences" captures quite well two of Derrida's early concerns through the 1960s: his critique of the phenomenology of Edmund Husserl and his critique of formalism in the guise of semiology (Ferdinand de Saussure) and structuralism (Claude Lévi-Strauss). Both concerns, incidentally, helped Derrida become known across the Atlantic: essays on Husserl were translated in the early 1970s and found a ready audience, and his previous 1966 address to a conference on structuralism held at Johns Hopkins was an important event, especially for North American literary criticism.[26]

Phenomenology

Derrida's first published work was in fact a book-length introduction to Husserl's *Origin of Geometry*, and he has continued to write a great deal on the idea of phenomenology. Derrida gives close and "rigorous" readings of the various texts of the master, readings the following summary must drastically foreshorten. Husserl's *epochè* or "bracketing" of the existential and psychological context attempts to uncover a realm of essential "meaning"—an intelligible or spiritual ideality, a "pure meaning, or a pure signified" as Derrida puts it (*Positions*, 31). For Husserl this was prelinguistic, a pure intentional act performed by consciousness. At the same time, Husserl was puzzled by the way the intuition was always "interwoven" with the conditions of its expression via language and signification. Derrida considers first the role of language here as supposedly the mere externalization of an inner meaning, where the latter is thought of as somehow immediately and intuitively present to itself; and second, the role of Husserl's own language, notably his metaphor of weaving (in Latin, *textere*). That allows Derrida to reverse the privilege accorded the "inner" and essential, and so declare it no more than an effect of linguistic "text-ure." Husserl's text is shown to undermine its claims through its own linguistic devices: it "deconstructs" itself from within, so to speak, by its very reliance on a language it had deemed ancillary to pure intuition. Derrida's tack is thus to replace (1) the paradigm of knowledge as "seeing" by one of "reading," and (2) an emphasis on (self) presence by one on deferral and displacement.

The same goes for Husserl's much-disputed thesis of a "transcendental ego" supposedly constitutive of objective meanings, as well as for his theory of "internal time consciousness": in both cases the ego's "presence to self" is shown to be mediated by language. Consciousness of temporal flux supposes a unified state that can never actually be achieved. Indeed, the "experience" (literally, "going through") of time provides a paradigm of the actual process that goes on in Husserl's own writing; the experience of the present is continually being deferred, the moment of self-presence put off, by the very textual means that are to mimic it. Ultimately it can only be thought, in a kind of Kantian "regulative Idea." As Derrida phrases the result: "Husserl's premises should sanction our saying exactly the contrary" (*Speech and Phenomena*, 96). Reading the text produces a countertext within its own boundaries.

Foucault

Derrida's critique aligns Husserl's project with an entire history of attempts to found philosophy on rock, beyond mere language, deep within our consciousness, a place of sheer self-presence. The project is as old as the history of metaphysics. In 1963, at approximately the time he was grappling with Husserl, Derrida also delivered a lecture on Michel Foucault's *Histoire de la folie* (1961), entitled "Cogito and the History of Madness."[27] It is worth a brief look not only because this was to be their only public debate, but also because the critique of Descartes' "cogito" is similar to that of the "transcendental ego." Derrida argues that Descartes proceeds to try to make the cogito reasonable by reflecting on and temporalizing it, talking about it even though it is accessible only through intuition ("'I am, I exist' is true whenever I think it"—you either see it or you do not). But Derrida's main focus is on the role of madness, which Descartes hypothesizes in the First Meditation, only to drop for no very good reason. Foucault had wanted to argue that philosophy in the sixteenth century constituted itself (as "classical reason") precisely by excluding madness, whereas in medieval times there had been no such distinction. Derrida objects that this is to construct a myth of origin (medieval unity) from which the classical age descended; that it supposes madness to have always had the same determinate meaning; and that Foucault fails to go back to the Greek logos or reason, in the history of whose exclusionary tactics classical reason forms just one episode. Foucault makes rational the exclusion of madness, he puts it within a certain frame, and thus repeats that very gesture of exclusion in lifting it out of the larger history of which it is a part. There is madness in the method of metaphysical reason. In reply Foucault does not address these larger issues, but finishes with a portrait of Derrida that out of decorum I will put in the endnotes.[28] The only interesting question, apart from how Derrida paints Foucault into the metaphysics of presence, is how Foucault might paint his way out!

Structuralism

The structuralist project — regarding all cultural phenomena *as if* they were elements of language — seems at first blush to epitomize the "heyday of sentences." It abstracts from any historical or psychological context and attends to the logical grammar or syntax in which any meaning or message is embedded. Yet it has a foot also in the "heyday of meanings" inasmuch as it relies on the total system of coding operations for disambiguating utterances. Meaning is a matter of coding and decoding. Derrida's critique exploits the split between these allegiances.

Structuralism takes its inspiration from Saussure's posthumously edited *Course in General Linguistics*, which outlines several strategic oppositions: between *langue* and *parole*, general code and individual message; between paradigmatic (or "associative") and syntagmatic relations, the first concerning substitutional equivalents, the second sequential possibilities; between synchronic and diachronic axes; and between the signifier and the signified, which together make up the sign. The linguistic sign as such is arbitrary, unmotivated. The very principle of significance is a differential one. As Saussure puts it: "*In the language [la langue] itself, there are only differences.... *In a language there are only differences, *and no positive terms*."[29] Lévi-Strauss then applied some of these ideas to anthropology, first to kinship systems, and then to myth. In his wake literary theorists and others applied the model throughout the cultural field. "Meaning" is now located at the pole of the "signified" and is considered inseparable from its opposite, the signifier, for each becomes a term within a differential relation. The semiologist is interested less in the semantic content or substance as such (the thought expressed, the gift exchanged, the thematics of a literary work, etc.) than in the virtual structure of which they are (at various levels, from word through sentence to discourse) the instances.

Yet it was precisely the structuralists' lingering attachment to the (supposedly) extralinguistic that came under fire in Derrida's 1966 paper — an intervention which, it has been said, shot down the structuralist project before it had even gotten off the ground, at least in North America and in departments of literature. It remains one of the most direct routes into Derrida's ways of thinking. Derrida first notes that structure is as old as science or philosophy itself, its distinctive feature being an organizing "center" (or first principle) that makes possible the "play" of constituent elements and closes off the system from other possible systems. Such a "center," it appears, is the hallmark of (Western) metaphysics. And the paradox of metaphysics is that the center (ground, origin, etc.) lies outside the structure proper, for it could not otherwise make the structure intelligible. Moreover, it signals a desire for foundation or authority, for a full "presence" beyond the structured play. The history of metaphysics indeed amounts to no more than a series of names or metaphors for the center. Following Heidegger, Derrida calls it "Being as presence" and its figuration "logocentrism." With the coming of structuralism, a rupture with this history threatened. Derrida calls it

> the moment when language invaded the universal problematic, the moment when, in the absence of a center or origin, everything became discourse ... that is to say, a system in which the central signified, the origin or transcendental signified, is never absolutely present outside a system of differences. (*Writing and Difference*, 280)

Like Foucault (in *The Order of Things*) Derrida finds other discourses likewise shaking the foundations: Nietzsche's attack on metaphysics and his reduction of truth to metaphor and the will to power; Freud's displacement of consciousness' self-presence; but especially Heidegger's "undoing" (*Destruktion*) of tradition, which interprets Being as presence. Yet all, from Nietzsche to Saussure and Lévi-Strauss, remain bound by the very metaphysical dialect they wished to purify.

Saussure, for example, betrays his differential view of language and the inseparability of signifier and signified, Derrida alleges (*Of Grammatology* enters into detail). He falls back into isolating the signified as an intellectual substance independent of the sign that embeds it, thus explaining identity of meaning through various formulations. He holds to a systematicity or total structure beyond the differential play contained in it. Last, while emphasizing the arbitrariness of signs, Saussure occasionally privileges its phonic basis — the voice is self-possessed, whereas writing records that which is already present (compare Husserl's "inner voice" of intuition).

Lévi-Strauss fares little better. For even while dissolving the metaphysical language of a positivistic science, he also appeals to its authority. He compares the myth maker to a *bricoleur* (someone who knocks together gadgets from odds and ends); his own "mythologiques" are like *bricolage* too, as they borrow randomly from the past. But if *all* social science is *bricolage*, then the very idea begins to lose its meaning, for it can exist only at the margin of science and engineering. Lévi-Strauss wants to have it both ways: to subvert an order of discourse on which he relies, and to practice differential *bricolage* while exhibiting a nostalgia for some original *pensée sauvage*. Such a play is allowed only by the absence of a center and an "overabundance" of the signifier, a movement Derrida calls "supplementarity" (in *Of Grammatology* there is a long analysis of the ways in which the supplement organizes Rousseau's discourse and his writing).[30] Moreover, this scientific dream of a unified theory, homogeneous and stable, while aiming to neutralize time and history, Derrida remarks, in fact serves by its very insistence on origin or totality only to foreground the sheer flux of time, the discontinuities and dispersions of history.

Despite this recidivism, Lévi-Strauss (like Saussure and Husserl) is said to exhibit a "countertext," a shift towards "decentering" and the "play of difference" (not "free" play, a common misquote or distortion). Indeed, Derrida counsels a surrender "to *genetic* indetermination, to the *seminal* adventure of the trace" (*Writing and Difference*, 292) — full entry into the "heyday of sentences" so to speak. There is no foundation outside differential play, no positive terms, no origin, only *talk* of such. Derrida proposes the replacing of "sign" by "mark" or "trace" so as to make clear the fact that it cannot claim full presence, that it exists only as a momentary effect of difference. A mark can be re-marked, reiterated; but the user cannot step outside to check on consistency of meaning.

There is one more twist in store for us. We seem to have been promised a kind of Barthesian "jouissance" or Nietzschean affirmation without limits; once God the center is dead, anything is allowed. But just as we cannot step out of language as such, so we cannot step out of the language of metaphysics: "the passage beyond philosophy does not consist in turning the page of philosophy (which usually amounts to philosophizing badly), but in continuing to read philosophers *in a certain way*" (*Writing and Difference*, 288). Derrida now draws a conclusion whose ambivalent tone will reecho through his work. I quote at length:

> There are thus two interpretations of interpretation, of structure, of sign, of play. The one seeks to decipher, dreams of deciphering a truth or an origin which escapes play and the order of the sign, and which lives the necessity of interpretation as an exile. The other, which is no longer turned toward the origin, affirms play and tries to pass beyond man and humanism, the name of man by the name of that being who, throughout the history of metaphysics or of onto-theology [Heidegger's term for metaphysics] — in other words through-out his entire history — has dreamed of full presence, the reassuring foundation, the origin and the end of play.

There seems no third way; but Derrida comments: "For my part, although these two interpretations must acknowledge and accentuate their difference and define their irreducibility, I do not believe that today there is any question of *choosing...*" (*Writing and Difference*, 292−93). Instead we should wait on events, meanwhile trying to think of how the two horns of the dilemma are (differentially) related, preparing ourselves for a "monstrous birth."[31]

Difficult though it is to interpret these dark sayings, let me venture a few remarks. First, the later Heidegger is Derrida's *maître à penser* here, for he was the first to diagnose the sickness of logocentrism, while also falling victim to it in supposing he could name what was beyond Being-as-presence: he too remained caught in the toils of his words and gestures.[32] Derrida himself named what was to come "grammatology" (after the *grammé*, or "trace") and by implication claimed to practice it; yet he soon gave up on such extravagant gestures. Second, philosophizing becomes, if not impossible, at least an eccentric and improper activity. It can survive (in his book) only as the attempt to think philosophy *otherwise*, as "philosophy beside itself" (to cite one of the best introductions to Derrida), as "invention of the other."[33] "I try to keep myself at the *limit* of philosophical discourse" by practicing a "double play" (*Positions*, 6) − for a limit is both inside and outside. "My central question is: from what site or non-site [*non-lieu*] can philosophy as such appear to itself as other to itself, so that it can interrogate and reflect upon itself in an originary manner?"[34] One site is the literary mode of writing, which Derrida uses within his texts so as to throw them out-of-kilter (the relation of philosophy with literature is something I shall come back to). Another derives from Derrida's (non)method, and in fact "deconstruction" and *différance* will turn out to inhabit the dilemma given above, shuttling and weaving between the extremes of faithful enclosure and violent escape. Philosophy at Derrida's hands will take on a certain apocalyptic or prophetic tone, annoying to some; though whether his whole approach, or its best side, should be typed as "oracular" (Rorty) is an issue I shall defer for the moment.

One last remark − again to come back to − and that concerns the status of subjectivity. On one side of the dilemma, the self exists, and indeed may act as an organizing center of philosophical discourse (as with Descartes' cogito or Kant's transcendental ego). On the other side, the self has been decentered, disappears into a Nietzschean play of forces. Meanwhile Derrida plays with rhetorical and tropological effects of apostrophe ("dear reader") and irony ("dear reader"), as if to preserve rather than dissolve selfhood. And he declares "I have never said that the subject should be dispensed with. Only that it should be deconstructed. To deconstruct the subject does not mean to deny its existence"; it simply tries to resituate it.[35] But where does that leave us? or Derrida?

Derrida's Abecedary

"My ambition is to say in ten sentences what others say in entire books — what others do *not* say in entire books" (Nietzsche: *Twilight of the Idols*).

Since a few steps have already been taken towards characterizing Derrida's *pas de méthode*, perhaps we can take some more. For this purpose I select some "keywords," if there could be such, in Derrida's lexicon; they serve only to mark his procedures, to constitute the "folds" in his own writing.

Deconstruction

This is the most notorious of Derrida's neologisms. He himself has remarked that "it is a word I never liked and one whose fortune has disagreeably surprised me,"[36] though he continues to use it frequently. In particular, its appropriation by literary critics as a tool or principle for textual exegesis has been sharply attacked, both formally (e.g., Gasché's wholesale critique) and more rhetorically (it says the same thing, no matter what text is under analysis: it always tells a story of failure, like some barroom bore, as Terry Eagleton puts it).[37] Derrida in fact has applied deconstructive techniques solely to philosophical texts, and his approaches to literary writing tend to be quite different. The term itself is borrowed from Heidegger's *Destruktion*, or the dismantling of metaphysics; the German lacks the purely negative sense of French or English "destruction." Derrida claims to have found the word already in Littré, which gives the following meanings: (1) to disassemble, e.g., a machine, for transport elsewhere; (2) grammatically, to render verse as prose, by suppressing meter, etc.[38] Derrida adds that the term was first used in the heyday of structuralism, and should be understood in that light. Lastly, if metaphysics is to be dismantled, ready for removal, this carries the proviso that the slate can never be wiped clean, the old words simply crossed out. Deconstruction plays a double game, then, at once inside and outside the texture of metaphysics, a duplicity caught in the following extended passage:

> Very schematically: an opposition of metaphysical concepts (for example, speech/writing, presence/absence, etc.) is never the face-to-face of two terms, but a hierarchy and an order of subordination. Deconstruction cannot limit itself or proceed immediately to a neutralization: it must, by means of a double gesture, a double science, a double writing, practice an *overturning* of the classical opposition *and*

a general *displacement* of the system. It is only on this condition that deconstruction will provide itself the means with which to *intervene* in the field of oppositions that it criticizes, which is also a field of nondiscursive forces.... Deconstruction does not consist in passing from one concept to another, but in overturning and displacing a conceptual order, as well as the nonconceptual order with which the conceptual order is articulated.[39]

To unfold this a little, deconstruction first locates an opposition, in which one of the terms is subordinate and often hidden within the margin of the unthought. It must then engage polemically with the dominant term, rather than taking a neutral, detached stance (Gasché links such disengagement with Romantic irony and its latter-day adherents among literary deconstructors).[40] Derrida calls this the moment of "overturning"; for example, "writing" would be foregrounded at the expense of speech. Equally important, however, is its complementary moment of "displacement," "spacing" (*espacement*), demarcation, or marking an interval; for example, by grafting on the host text a foreign text, genre, or troping manoeuvre. Since the interpreter can neither remain within nor escape from the old order, she will stretch the boundaries of logocentrism to breaking point. Lastly, only so can interpretation "intervene" (politically? ethically?) in the nondiscursive order "with which the conceptual order is articulated" as Derrida phrases it. Intervention is, literally, a "coming between," while articulation is both a joining and a separating. One supposes that Derrida cagily wishes to hold all these possible meanings open. In *Positions*, for example, pushed by his Maoist interrogators to declare his hand, he notes that the interval or "between"

> can only be marked in what I would call a *grouped* textual field: in the last analysis it is impossible to *point* it out, for a unilinear text, or a punctual *position*, an operation signed by a single author, are all by definition incapable of practicing this interval. (*Positions*, 42)

Différance

This second nonconcept captures the paradoxical side to Derrida's practice. We have already had occasion to speak of difference, and indeed of "difference," but always as something determinate. The difference from *différance* is unspeakable — the "a" sounds the same as "e" to the phonocentric mind. More to the point, the concept itself is indeterminable: "If there were a definition of *différance*, it would be precisely the limit, the interruption, the destruction of the Hegelian *relève* [the author's punning translation of Hegel's *Aufhebung*, or "sublation," that is, both negation and preservation] *wherever* it operates" (*Positions*, 40–41) — no relief in sight, one might say. Perhaps, though, a detour via Hegel is not necessary to capture something of its tone. It does not name anything: the game of the name, then, as much as the name of the game, it obeys a few provisional rules. The following summary is drawn from the essay entitled "Différance" (1968) and from remarks in *Positions*:

- The "a" indicates a missing presence, for it can never be heard, yet conditions the term's operation.

- The suffix "−ance" also indicates a verbal state undecided as between active and passive, somewhat like the middle voice in ancient Greek.

- Etymologically, the Latin *differe* means the following: differentiate, differ with someone, defer to, and defer (in the sense of delay, put off, temporize, reprieve) — as well as something Derrida does not mention, that is, defame and distort (and he does that too). Thus it points to an orientation by origin or first principle, which, however, can never appear; difference is always secondary, a substitution or simulacrum. The sense of relay, detour, temporizing, etc., captures the dispersion, for example, of Husserl's internal time consciousness, never able to unify itself into a living, punctual present.

- As such it describes the working of any system, of any "economy" of meaning, always a structure of nontotalizable differences.

- More than the differentiated elements, then, *différance* signifies the medium of the "same" (not the already determinate "identity") with respect to which the elements appear.

- Hence, it is the production of different marks, effects, traces; Derrida mentions here Nietzsche's thinking of force as always differentiating, Freud's theory of selfhood as self-differing, Heidegger's "ontological difference" (the gulf between Being and beings).

- *Pace* Heidegger, Derrida says that *différance names* the unfolding of difference, while avoiding the implication that there *is* anything corresponding to the name. Hence it might escape even the ontological difference, pointing to an Other that cannot be thought (Derrida has been influenced very much by Levinas's critique of Heidegger).

Hegel too has a theory of difference; his most general term for the latter is "negation." In "differing" from Hegel, Derrida also draws on some of his ideas — indeed, his own term may well come initially from the Logic. Derrida mentions some comments that Alexandre Koyré made on Hegel's Jena system, and notably the characterization of time given there as a "differential relation" (*differente Beziehung*).[41] The odd thing about Hegel's neologism is that it too wavers between active and passive, differentiating and differentiated, thereby putting in question any putative foundational structure — a dynamism that is precisely what Derrida prizes. I might add that the odd formula occurs prior to that point, in the Jena *Logic* itself, and is used to "name" the paradoxical dialectic of the "limit" (*Grenze*), which is to determine finitude and thinghood. Here is the heart of Hegel's dialectic, and of his own distancing from a Romantic irony of self-reflexion, the moment (as Derrida would see it) of maximum risk, when the other is at once named, hence subordinated, and yet allowed its radical alterity. If Hegel runs this risk, he does so in order to recover selfhood and self-presence *in* the other, setting up what Derrida terms a "restricted economy" of controlled differences, one in which the subject can make a return of his investment, can speculate, etc.[42] Derrida refuses this option (if it can be called that) and indefinitely defers the return to self, remaining in the very limit that would mark out the economy. It goes without saying that he refuses the alternative: the claim to live in some "general" economy of otherness as such, where all relations are external — a force field in which no point is not alien.

Another example of Derrida's closeness to Hegel may be found in the section of the *Phenomenology of Spirit* that deals with "force and the expression of forces," a section that takes off from the attempt at saying what a "thing" might be, how it is determined and limited. Such a thing enters into (causal) relations with other things, is determined as what it is by determining other things, and vice versa. This Leibnizian-Kantian insight does not, however, resolve the question of how the determining force is both active and passive — Hegel speaks of "soliciting" and "being solicited by" the other force. Derrida picks up on this notion, typically inserting a bit of etymological play:

> It is the domination of beings that *différance* everywhere comes to solicit, in the sense that *sollicitare*, in old Latin, means to shake as a whole, to make tremble in entirety. Therefore it is the determination of Being as presence or as beingness [thingness] that is interrogated by the thought of *différance*. . . . It is not a present being. (*Margins*, 21)

Hegel proceeds to resolve these differences, via an astonishing tactic, the supposition of "the inverted world," or rather two such "worlds," the first that of law, the second that of "pure change" — almost like the Derridean "overturning," although the inversion ushers the reader into the peaceable kingdom of Kantian subjectivity rather than into the instabilities of Derrida's "double science."

Derrida thus takes his leave of Hegel precisely at this point of no return (in fairness, for Hegel, too, the Kantian totalization is, in turn, undermined). Yet the terms of this refusal are Hegelian, and — with the possible exception of Heidegger — Hegel is the figure Derrida is closest to, the angel with whom he must always wrestle. Above all, it is the Hegelian model of reflexion that Derrida has to avoid: as he characterizes that model in a lovely image, "Philosophy [is] incapable of inscribing (comprehending [Hegel's *begreifen*]) what is outside it otherwise than through the appropriating assimilation of a negative image of it, and dissemination is written on the back—the *tain*—of that mirror."[43] It is understandable how he could say: "We will never be finished with the reading or rereading of Hegel, and in a certain way, I do nothing other than attempt to explain myself on this point" (*Positions*, 77). If Derrida's texts "tremble" and "make tremble" at the edge between texts from the past and present circumstances, it is the Hegelian book that occupies much of Derrida's shelf space (too much for his own good?).

Writing

Much has already been said on how this term (*écriture*) folds into Derrida's own writing. It should be clear, in the first place, that it does not signal a kind of reversal of phonocentric bias, so as to privilege writing over speech, absence and loss over presence, abyss over ground (a kind of existential pathos Derrida resists). Nor, on the other hand, would he abolish the hierarchy altogether. Certainly the bias exists, and Derrida expends much effort showing its subtleties. In the essay called "Plato's Pharmacy," writing is both scapegoat (*pharmakon*) and poison (*pharmakos*), yet becomes part of the economy of thinking, too.[44] Plato stigmatizes writing as bad, but some writing is invisibly demarcated as good; for example, when the Idea is somehow "inscribed" on the mind, on memory. For Derrida, writing is an instance of the anonymity and materiality of language in general. Like Barthes' "writerly" text, it lies beyond—or rather, at the margins of—the opposition between speaking and writing. Reading thus becomes (re)writing, a disseminating activity that consistently follows the logic of the supplement.

In the second place, we find Derrida gesturing to what he calls "the general text." By that phrase he names the continual possibility of an overflow beyond the generic or contextual bounds of particular texts, texts that operate by an internal logic, economy or mechanism whose rationale can be measured and figured out. The general text is no regulative idea—as it were "in the limit"—functioning so as to stabilize and hold in reserve the "limited economy" of the text at issue. Rather it marks the moment of excess, the border that both demarcates and escapes specific meaning. We have already seen how Derrida wields it against Foucault's thematizing of the history of madness: "A writing that exceeds, by questioning, the values 'origin,' 'reason,' and 'history' could not be contained within the metaphysical closure of an archaeology" (*Writing and Difference*, 36). Relative to a limited discourse, Derrida calls "text"

> that which "practically" inscribes and overflows the limits of such a discourse. *There is* such a general text everywhere that (that is, everywhere) this discourse and its order (essence, sense, truth, meaning, consciousness, ideality, etc.) are *overflowed*, that is, everywhere that their authority is put back into the position of a *mark* in a chain that this authority intrinsically and illusorily believes it wishes to, and does in fact, govern. (*Positions*, 59–60)

Writing and inscription convey (in the third place) the idea of spacing, displacement; this is part of the deconstructive strategy, as was seen. Derrida will utilize typography, margins, diagrams, etc., to disrupt the supposed immateriality of thought. It is as if his text comprises a series of footnotes to itself—but then, so does the text of philosophy proper. This kind of double reading can be enacted before our very eyes, as in the article "The Double Session," which juxtaposes Plato and Mallarmé in alarming ways, or as in *Glas*, perhaps Derrida's most eccentric experiment in book form—a mix of Hegel and Genet on either side of the page, interwoven with critical commentary.[45] Even his own texts may be broken up, interleaved, hinged, and articulated in various ways. Thus we find Derrida using the device of grafting one text onto another, so that although the first seems to hold sway, the other also manages to escape and resist. Derrida often employs the trope called "chiasmus" (from the Greek *chi* or *X*), not only to recall Heidegger's "crossing out" of bad old words, or his "Fourfold," but also to suggest the systematic reversal of terms in differential relationships.

Marginal Thinking (or Parerga and Paralipomena)

Taking his cue from the later Heidegger play on the "frame" (*das Gestell*) to characterize technology, Derrida never tires of exposing the limits of/to a given text (including the texts of painting)—limits that allow it to mean or "re-present" (*vor-stellen*) in the first place. In the text called "Parergon" (from *The Truth in Painting*), for instance, he continually draws attention to the many ways in which Kant's discourse on beauty depends on exclusion (of the ugly, the useful, the sublime, and so on). His own texts often resemble *parerga*, commentaries upon a host text simultaneously from within and at one remove (the opposition "inside/outside" having been dissolved). Another metaphor sometimes put to work along the same lines is that of the *mise-en-abyme* (or *abîme*), the primary force of which comes from the heraldic device of placing one escutcheon within another, and yet (since it is one and the same shield) outside it at the same time. J. Hillis Miller dubs it the "Quaker Oats box" effect: we see on the box a picture of someone holding a box, on which is a picture ... and so on, into the abyss. Just as "there is" the general text (everywhere and nowhere), so "*[t]here is* frame, but the frame does not exist."[46] Derrida criticizes Lacan's reading of Poe's "The Purloined Letter" precisely because Lacan, usually so alert to tacit cues in enunciation, manages to neutralize the frame and find inside it an Oedipal scene. He notes:

> But a text never entitles itself, never writes: I, the text, write, or write myself. It causes to be said, it lets be said, or rather it leads to being said, "I, the truth, speak." I am always (I am still following) [*Je suis toujours*] the letter that never arrives at itself [*s'arrive*].[47]

Metaphor

It is widely thought that Derrida wants to reduce philosophy to metaphor, as if to reverse the hierarchy of abstract concept over aesthetic figure. But that is as false an imputation as its complement, that he wishes to found a science or philosophy of metaphor, a *metaphorology* (in the manner, say, of Hans Blumenberg).[48] The first suggestion is exposed at the outset of Derrida's 1971 article "White Mythology: Metaphor in the Text of Philosophy," where he presents the story of philosophy as the displacement of some original meaning into metaphor, followed by a forgetting that metaphysical language was ever metaphorical to begin with—a double effacement of meaning, which produces a kind of "white mythology."[49] Nietzsche has a well-known version of the same tale:

> What then is truth? A mobile army of metaphors, metonymies, anthropomorphisms: in short, a sum of human relations which became poetically and rhetorically intensified, metamorphosed, adorned, and after long usage, seem to a nation fixed, canonic and binding; truths are illusions of which one has forgotten that they *are* illusions; worn-out metaphors which have become powerless to affect the senses and now are no longer of account as coins but merely as metal.[50]

Far from reversing the story, so as to remind philosophers that they have been speaking poetry all along, Derrida wants to expose this "originary metaphor" as myth. Philosophy's "sublation" (or *relève*) of metaphor is itself a metaphorical turning. "Plus de métaphore," as one of the sections is headed, meaning at once the "no more metaphor" effected by philosophical literalness, and the "excess of metaphor" brought into play by this excluding gesture.

Derrida has often been accused of reducing everything to metaphor. Yet that construal is as illusory as its opposite, that nothing is metaphorical, properly speaking. (Donald Davidson might serve to represent the latter position, when he contrasts metaphorical *use* — in pragmatics or rhetoric — to literal *meaning*.)[51] These two extremes ignore the margins. Thus if "everything becomes metaphorical, there is no longer any literal meaning and, hence, no longer any meaning either" (*Dissemination*, 258). On the other hand, the very concept of "metaphor," in seeking a philosophical control over such "improper" meaning, will always have a blindspot to its own metaphoricity — a symptom we may trace from Aristotle down to Davidson. Metaphor will always be in "retreat" (*retrait*); to catch it is to lose it.

Derrida's essay, then, explores what Gasché terms "quasimetaphoricity," that is, metaphor signifying a *mise-en-abyme* of the philosophical concept of metaphor, of the metaphors *for* philosophical metaphor. One such is the circulatory metaphor of truth as coin.[52] Another is the cluster around truth as light, as sun, with metaphor as its heliotrope, ever turned towards the sun while being no more than the turning, tropic movement itself (*Margins*, 250). There is no escape from metaphor, any more than from the language of metaphysics. At the same time, Derrida wants to deconstruct both. In his hands metaphor can no longer be contrasted with the literal or "proper," for the latter is always contaminated (the logic of the supplement again). Entire discursive economies will accordingly be subjected to a kind of hyper-inflation of meaning, exposed to a general metaphoricity, which Derrida would prefer to call "catachresis" — bad or forced usage (since all metaphor is bad). Derrida recommends wholesale *im*propriety, especially in regard to meaning and mimesis; he makes doubtful connections, mixes in barbarisms and anachronisms, plays at the dangerous edge of things.

Coming to Terms: Questions for Derrida

"The road of excess leads to the palace of wisdom" (William Blake, "Proverbs of Hell").

By way of conclusion let me raise a number of questions which may serve to situate Derrida in some critical contexts:

Derrida and the Scene of Writing

To many it has appeared scandalous that Derrida should spend as much time writing about literature as on philosophy; that he should be hired by departments not of philosophy but of literature (or yet worse, comparative literature); that even when he attends to philosophical texts he proceeds as a literary critic would, examining rhetorical devices and tropological procedures, or even as a literary practitioner himself, playfully and with no pretence to accuracy. Others — Richard Rorty, for example — actually prefer the literary mode they see Derrida adopting in the 1970s. Hence Rorty's suggestion that Derrida really takes "philosophy as a kind of writing," that is, as some literary or rhetorical exercise.[53] It is not merely that "garden path utterances" — their ambiguity or opacity leads us to defer semantic closure — offer belated rewards — for example, "aesthetic" pleasure in the sweet smoke of rhetoric. They are valued also for cutting loose any transcendental moorings language might aspire to, and allowing us to float with the pragmatist current.

Is it fair to describe Derrida as "literary" — not "merely" but with commendation? We already know enough to say, not quite. For on the one hand, by his own admission (in a 1983 interview),

> my "first" inclination wasn't really toward philosophy, but rather toward literature, no, toward something that literature accommodates more easily than philosophy. I feel as if I've been involved, for twenty years, in a long detour, in order to get back to this something, this idiomatic writing whose purity I know to be inaccessible, but which I continue, nonetheless, to dream about.[54]

However we might characterize this "something" — this property you can never appropriate, especially not in philosophical lingo —, it is hardly to be found in Literature (with a capital *L*): literature as genre or circumscribed register, placed by philosophical categories (aesthetic, rhetorical, critical), accorded values such as meaning, content, form, etc. (*Positions*, 69), studied by philology or a "science" of literature. For the same reason Derrida doubts whether "deconstruction can function as a literary *method* as such"[55] since both method and the "literary" register are bracketed wholesale. Literature was always in the shadow of Philosophy, we might say. By a familiar chiasmus Derrida deconstructs both. Like structuralism in regard to language, literary formalism both submits texts to a limited economy ("literariness," the aesthetic or self-referential function) and releases the potential of writing, the texture of figures and tropes. While such effects are more evident in literature (or what we call such), they can be put to work in philosophy too. By setting "philosophical" and "literary" registers at odds, Derrida undermines the two at once. *Glas*, for example, becomes an extended catachresis, violent writing, a monstrous mutation (Kearney, 122): "I think that a text like *Glas* is neither philosophic nor poetic. It circulates between these two genres, trying meanwhile to produce another text which would be of another genre or without genre."[56] Such a general-cum-generic text is the impossible dream Derrida wants to liberate in his readings. But note, once again, that it is not the same as literature, any more than "quasimetaphoricity" is metaphor. Derrida admires Valéry's attempt to render philosophy "an affair of form," writing which has forgotten that it is writing; but the task of reading philosophy as a kind of literary writing is not his own.[57]

Derrida's Politics of Responsibility

Rhetoric has often been attacked on the grounds that it opts for words over things. In much the same way Derrida has been criticized for ivory-tower textualism, even linguistic solipsism. And although he protests against such a misconstrual, still it has seemed to some that his verbal distinctions are mere pussy footing around the real (political or ethical) issues. Again, despite his recent interest in racism, apartheid, and nuclear deterrence, or his involvement with educational reform and with the philosophical curriculum, he has been assailed for lacking a social theory. Is Derrida — despite or just because of his protestations — guilty of a kind of textual idealism, especially when he says (in a notorious phrase) "il n'y a pas de hors texte"?[58] And where does that put him/us? Does Derrida have a political position, and if so, can he justify it? Is there a "politics of deconstruction," or are the effects of Derrida's ministrations a "deconstruction of politics"?[59]

We read in "Parergon" of "the necessity of a deconstruction":

> Following the consistency of its logic, it attacks not only the internal edifice, both semantic and formal, of philosophemes, but also what one would be wrong to assign to it as the external housing, its extrinsic conditions of practice: the historical forms of its pedagogy, the social, economic or political structures of this pedagogical institution. It is because deconstruction interferes with solid structures, "material" institutions, and not only with discourses or signifying representations, that it is always distinct from an analysis or a "critique." (*The Truth in Painting*, 19)

Or again, Derrida assures us:

> It is totally false to suggest that deconstruction is a suspension of reference. Deconstruction is always deeply concerned with the "other" of language. I never cease to be surprised by critics who see my work as a declaration that there is nothing beyond language, that we are imprisoned within language; it is in fact saying the exact opposite. (Kearney, 123)

It is a seeking for an other beyond language, which summons language — though of course that cannot be named (as "Being" or "God"). But how are we to take this assurance? I suggest two paths to follow.

We should note, first of all, that the sentence "there is nothing outside the text" itself has a border, the context (or the type of which it is a token) in which it is uttered and attains a meaning. To take it "as such" is precisely to commit the fault it describes, leaving inside/outside as oppositional terms. "Nothing outside the text" implies for Derrida "nothing outside the context." And while Derrida would bracket reality (reference) or meaning (the signified) at least insofar as they are thought of as independent essences to which language somehow attaches, it is not as though he remains "on the inside": he plays on the very border between inside/outside.

To put it another way, his texts "solicit" and are "solicited by" what he calls the "other" to language. Recalling Hegel's thematization of the expression of forces, we might speak of the force of language, that which can never be expressed by language but serves instead violently and thoroughly to shake it up. As Derrida puts it (*Margins*, 27): "Force is the other of language without which language could not be what it is." An utterance inscribes both the subject who speaks and the context within which she speaks into what is said, and so "trembles" between language and its other (call it for the nonce the "nondiscursive"). Thus in "The Ends of Man" (1972; published in *Margins*) a prefatory "exergue" recalls that it was delivered at an "international" conference, and was composed at the time of the Vietnam peace talks, and later of the 1968 events, all of which are expected to resonate through the text itself. Or again, "The University in the Eyes of its Pupils" comprises an address given at Cornell University which seeks to inscribe the circumstances of its utterance into what it means to say; Derrida is throughout "responsible" to the pragmatics of the predicament. Neither pragmatics, nor semantics, the text may be described as "programmatological," to employ one of Derrida's neologisms: it exists and signifies in a context implying rules of discourse but no ultimate metacontextuality or metadiscursivity.

What is Derrida's own attitude towards these "rules" or "norms"? When asked by Richard Kearney whether he could endorse a radical political praxis, he replied that "the available codes for taking a political stance are not at all adequate to the radicality of deconstruction"; a fact which has given the impression that "deconstruction is opposed to politics or is at best apolitical" (Kearney, 119–20). If "programmatology" intervenes at all, it cannot do so directly, then, but only implicitly, and by displaying the forces at work in a given normative discourse. This attempt may be seen in Derrida's more recent "political" pieces, such as "The Laws of Reflection: Nelson Mandela, in Admiration."[60] Here Derrida draws attention to the very norms by which Mandela is branded an "outlaw," the dialectic by which "democracy" and "law" expose their own limits. Yet in mapping out the force field that normative language exerts, Derrida (or his own language) scrupulously avoids any endorsement of the positions at issue.

There is a more directly ethical intervention that deconstruction performs, in Derrida's view. The force in the notion of "otherness" comes in part from Emmanuel Levinas, and leads Derrida to speak of a response to its "call." This "apocalyptic tone"[61] derives from the double movement we have seen already in deconstruction: attending the end of metaphysics (of "onto-theology") and awaiting the monstrous event of a new, unrestricted economy of meaning. Derrida speaks also (in the context of his friend de Man's concern with "allegory" or "other-language") of language as "invention of the other," a breaking with the conventions that always rule any contextual utterance.[62] And this playing with and against the grain of given codes is precisely what allows the invocation of and by the other. In *The Post Card*, Derrida plays variations on this gesture through such devices as apostrophe to the addressee of his communications, postals that never finally arrive at their destination (insofar as the other can be inscribed within the postcard, (s/he is no longer other). Where does that leave us or him? Certainly not as mere effects of language, however much we/he might appear to be inscribed, but as the other to which language remains "solicitous." A precarious occasion for community and commitment, no doubt, but one Derrida is anxious not to close off.

I have so far presented two modes of intervention, which we can label *programmatology* and *allocution*. Derrida will monitor the activities of the Language Police, and he will respond to the call of the Other. But does either succeed in getting him out of the ivory tower? There are several reasons for doubting it.

First, we may well ask (with Thomas McCarthy) what the practical *effect* of deconstruction amounts to. For all that Derrida announces a positive, reconstructive moment on the other side of the "undoing" of philosophy, his actual practice is colored by a certain iconoclastic, defeatist, naysaying quality. Derrida is a sceptic, and that too is a position. One of Derrida's admirers, Gregory Ulmer, has indeed suggested that deconstruction be supplemented by the pedagogy of "applied grammatology," rightly pointing out that "deconstruction" operates only on *philosophical* texts, whereas Derrida's way with literary texts is "economimesis," a writerly dissemination more appropriate to our computerized world. And Derrida has often enough pointed out that deconstruction is neither monolithic nor a method — not the putative "deconstructionism" of McCarthy's thoroughgoing attack. But whatever we call them (careful to avoid preemptive classification), his various engagements with ethical and political issues remain ghostly; his "grammar of response" invokes but does not enter the force field of normative discourse. McCarthy alleges that when Derrida discusses Nelson Mandela or nuclear deterrence, for example, he is inconsistent in appealing to the very norms he would suspend.[63] Even if the charge fails to stick, for Derrida avoids all such "appeal," his own texts seem parasitic upon the normative charge inherent to talk of "law" or "friendship" and so on — talk that Derrida seems to respect, while admitting that it is always contextual and historicized.[64]

But one could go further and suggest — in the second place — that Derrida fights shy of context and pragmatic commitment because he remains too philosophical "in the last analysis" (as Derrida would put it). Peter Dews presents this objection most trenchantly when he writes "the question of the meaning of objectivity is considered *de jure* prior to any objective enquiry . . ."[65] Dews goes on to compare Derrida's response to Husserlian phenomenology with Merleau-Ponty's or Adorno's: it was not like theirs "to move 'downstream' towards an account of subjectivity as emerging from and entwined with the natural and historical world, but rather to move 'upstream', in a quest for the ground of transcendental consciousness itself."[66] History is elided into "historicity," politics (*la politique*) into "the political" (*le politique*), as Nancy Fraser puts it. The critic might be tempted to broaden this objection by saying that we should treat linguistic idealizations as presuppositions of communicative interaction (Habermas, McCarthy) rather than as a structural lure to be resisted, if only because a fastidious attitude towards the impurity of context opens the door not just to a harmless quietism but also to the less fastidious forces of reaction. In any event, the argument runs (in parallel with Gadamer's), the looseness of our vocabulary, its indeterminacy "in the last analysis," is always resolved and concretized in practice. Such a broadening goes too far, however. It is unclear why one should prefer one to the other: we cannot urge a pragmatic attitude on pragmatic or prudential grounds. Nor can we justify our move downstream into history by claiming that the move is made willy-nilly. Derrida admits that the move is made, but, as he writes apropos the revelations about his friend de Man's wartime record, "through the indelible wound, one must still analyze and seek to understand."[67] Understanding comes not by being severe or indulgent in judging de Man's personal complicity, but through generic talk about the meaning of "allegory" and "friendship," or (in Heidegger's case) the implicatures of terms like "spirit" (*Geist*). To some this looks like a whitewash, a refusal to admit the facts. Yet the strength of Derrida's fastidious nonposition is precisely that it attempts to suspend itself *between* meanings and facts, and does not try to escape the implications of either. "My friends, there are no friends!" — the quote from Montaigne, which Derrida used in the debate with McCarthy — comes close to being what we might call a citation from the heart, given the scandal about de Man then brewing.

One last shot across Derrida's bow: for even if Derrida escapes linguistic idealism through such deferral and dissemination, might he not still be deemed guilty of a kind of "semanticism," because he inscribes pragmatics, if not into universal pragmatics, à la Searle or

Habermas, into the semantics of the *word*? Both Rorty and Gadamer level this kind of charge. Contexts, that is, involve judgments and propositions rather than just meanings; but Derrida remains "subpropositional" (as Rorty would say, citing Ernst Tugendhat), in this respect much like Hegel, even though he eschews any final *Aufhebung*. "We think in names," Derrida quotes Hegel as saying. Isn't that his problem?

Derrida again might reply, *Nomen est omen*. For, (1) his interventions are typically in response to a situation in which justice and fault are at issue, in which we too are called to account, stand before the law or a faculty of judgment. In any case, (2) he considers precisely the implications of the venue for decision, the context-boundedness of the speech act, what it means to say what is said. Prag(ram)matology wants to have it both ways, forever panting, forever free.

Argumentative versus World-Disclosing Philosophy

My last question devolves perhaps upon the first two, and once more it is Rorty who has put it most forcefully. He first reports a quarrel "between those of us who read Derrida on Plato, Hegel and Heidegger in the same way as we read Bloom or Cavell on Emerson or Freud — in order to see these authors transfigured, beaten into fascinating new shapes — and those who read Derrida to get ammunition, and a strategy, for the struggle to bring about social change."[68] Rorty suggests that Derrida is better read as a freewheeling textualist than as proposing arguments for supporting some radical praxis. Should Derrida be understood (despite his protestations) as arbitrary, self-willed, merely playful, or is he a species of "rigorous" thinker? Is his procedure (as Habermas says of Heidegger) oracular, "world-disclosive," or is it rather "argumentative," problem-solving (like Aristotle or Russell)? Does he indulge in what he himself dubs "mystagoguery" (*The Post Card*, 8), or is he more in the business of transcendental philosophy, laying down conditions of possibility for certain vocabularies?

In Rorty's (hardly disinterested) view, Derrida's chief use has lain in dissolving old vocabularies and coming up with novel ways to talk about other philosophers: "It is precisely *Aufhebung* that Derrida is so good at," *not* argument. Where arguments are in evidence, they are often poor; Derrida tends to rely on the rhetorical ploy (which Searle says is borrowed from logical positivism) of claiming that unless a distinction can be made rigorous and precise it isn't really a distinction at all. Rorty values what he sees as a shift from an earlier pretence at rigor towards a more playful and "literary" manner, one that treats language no longer as a putatively universal medium but instead as a practical set of tools. Derrida becomes a nominalist by default.

Of course, by Derrida's own lights, writing is always something read, and an author's history of reception or effect can outrun any "proper" or "original" meaning. Perhaps Rorty's is after all the most useful way to take him. On the other hand, there is no need for Derrida (or us) to take a position in this exclusive disjunction, which has the appearance of a double bind: either way he stands to lose. Is Derrida, then, a transcendental philosopher? No, if that means appeal to universal conditions for the use of linguistic medium or tools, rules for "iterability" and so on. And no, if it means subscribing to some "logic of positionality," Kantian or Hegelian; epistemology is expressly displaced by the epistolary, an accounting that never ends. Conversely then, does he escape theory altogether, so that everything is contextual and for the nonce? No, if that means abandoning the claim to rigor (e.g., consistency between constative and performative functions), without which his paradoxes would be unthinkable. Far from borrowing a ploy from logical positivism, it is rather taken from Hegel's dialectic, and depends for its cogency on some version of discursive implicature: the speech act appeals to an enabling limitation elided or taken for granted in *what* is said by the act. And again no, if it is supposed that the prophetic *tone* of his "postcard apocalypse" (*The Post Card*, 13) commits him to an oracular role.

Is he then, and finally, the joker in the pack, thumbing his nose at any philosophical propriety, performing a wholesale *Verflüssigung*? No, if that means that play is not serious, or that there is nothing at stake (*en jeu*). We might see Derrida as trying to renew a procedure of topical "invention." The rhetorical and dialectical tradition set great store by *inventio*, i.e., finding the right topics to begin debate. In "Psyché, invention de l'autre," Derrida appeals to *ars inveniendi*, the art of judging what cannot be prejudged, that which is to come (*l'avenir*). He suggests that in modern times two modes of invention have become authorized: "We invent, on the one hand, *stories* (fictive or fabulous accounts [*récits*]) and on the other, *machines*, technical devices [*dispositifs*], in the broadest sense of the word ..."[69] By implication he remains on the side of the fabulist rather than the mechanic beholden to *techne*. For their part, baroque rhetoricians labeled the art of invention *ingegno*, and saw it personified in the juggler. Accordingly let us call Derrida a juggler in just this sense, as he struggles to keep several topics aloft simultaneously, always and wittily alert to the dangers of dropping them, as well as to the pressing contingencies of circumstance.

Post Script

Much remains to be said, if not written. And if I began with a paradox—how to introduce Derrida—it is only fitting to end with another—how to end. How should I close this potted account of his thinking? For there is no end of Derrida; he is always a "step beyond" the demand for a last word — to understand *that* is to go some way to catching his drift. At the same time, if we are in no position to bring down a decision, we can at least situate him in the turn (or return) to rhetoric in North American philosophy. Where that turn has often tended towards formalism (*elocutio*), at one extreme, or towards the pragmatics of speech act theory, at the other, Derrida has sought to suspend his texts *between* those positions. But on the question of whether this calculated trope of nonpositionality can succeed, or whether it founders on one or other alternative, the jury remains out.

Notes

1. See his "Envois," in *The Post Card: From Socrates to Freud and Beyond*, translated by Alan Bass (Chicago: Univ. of Chicago, 1980, 1987), pp. 1–256, and p. xxi in the Glossary.

2. See Carl Rapp, "Coming Out into the Corridor: Postmodern Fantasies of Pluralism," in *The Georgia Review*, 41:3 (1987), pp. 533–52, at 542–43; Rapp thinks there must be *at some point* a "literal" or "naive" reading to make deconstructive claims even meaningful.

3. *The New York Review of Books*, October 27, 1983, p. 77: "You've misunderstood me; you're stupid!" Derrida's 1971 text, "Signature Event Context," was translated in *Glyph*, 1 (1977), pp. 172–97, and followed by Searle's magisterial rebuke, "Reiterating the Difference: Reply to Derrida," pp. 198–208. Derrida replied with "limited Inc." in *Glyph*, 2. His part in this (non)encounter was reprinted, with an important afterword, as *Limited Inc.* (Evanston: Northwestern Univ., 1988). The objection that an author cannot simultaneously claim that all texts are indeterminate in meaning and yet that his own have been misunderstood — in short, people living in *Glas* houses shouldn't throw stones — is found also in John Ellis, *Against Deconstruction* (Princeton: Princeton Univ., 1989), pp. 13f. Derrida's appeal is said to rest ultimately not on logical but on rhetorical and psychological grounds (p. 151); he encourages a fast and loose play with linguistic distinctions.

4. Published in French in 1972; trans. (Chicago: Univ. of Chicago, 1981).

5. It conflates the axis of succession and the axis of simultaneity as well, so as to upset the priority of the latter. Saussure comments on this very ambiguity. See *Course in General Linguistics* (1916), trans. Roy Harris (London: Duckworth, 1983), p. 90: "Diachronic identities and synchronic identities are two very different things. Historically, the French negative particle *pas* is the same as the noun *pas* ('pace'), whereas in modern French these two units are entirely separate. Realizing these facts should be sufficient to bring home the necessity of not confusing the two points of view."

6. "Dialogue with Jacques Derrida," in Richard Kearney, *Dialogues with Contemporary Thinkers* (Manchester: Manchester Univ., 1984), pp. 105–26, on p. 108. He adds (p. 114) "Now, less than ever, do I know what philosophy is."

7. *Positions*, p. 71: the sense of bracketing or quotation at one remove is reinforced by the quotation marks.

8. The phrase "veil of displacement" is taken from Eve Tavor Bannet, *Structuralism and the Logic of Dissent: Barthes, Derrida, Foucault, Lacan* (Urbana: Univ. of Illinois, 1989) pp. 219f. Julia Kristeva made the appeal to Gödel in order to explain how the meaning of a text devolves upon an infinite "intertextuality." It should be added that for Derrida, undecidability applies not to the proposition so much as to the syntax connecting its constituent words; the meaning of *concepts* and *terms* is what is self-contradictory, and hence undecidable. The "undecidables" spoken of here cannot be tied down to one sense or use; they slip and slide in ways that escape code or regulation. In "Afterword: Toward an Ethic of Discussion" (in *Limited Inc*, pp. 111–60, at p. 116) Derrida distinguishes two further meanings for "undecidable": one opposing any binary opposition—we cannot decide between the terms—and one that brings in an "ethico-political" decision in a quasijuridical context or "venue—a decision cannot be "brought down."

9. *The Tain of the Mirror: Derrida and the Philosophy of Reflection* (Cambridge: Harvard Univ., 1986), p. 8. The most thorough and systematic study of Derrida going, its very systematicity tends to beg the question whether this is the best approach to its subject. In the passage quoted, for instance, it is unclear whether the posited middle ground is Derrida's or Gasché's.

10. *The Post Card*, p. 391. I follow for the most part the translation by Samuel Weber in "Reading and Writing—*chez* Derrida," now in his *Institution and Interpretation* (Minneapolis: Univ. of Minnesota, 1987), pp. 85–101, at p. 94. Weber raises with special acuity the problem of the *chez* in (or with) Derrida. What constitutes the "domestic economy" of Derrida's textual production? "Return to sender" is hardly a return to self.

11. Cf. Ulmer's *Applied Grammatology: Post(e)-Pedagogy from Jacques Derrida to Josef Beuys* (Baltimore: Johns Hopkins Univ., 1985), which seeks to do justice to this second move, not "deconstruction" but "writing" or "hieroglyphics."

12. *Philosophy in France Today*, ed. Alan Montefiore (Cambridge: Cambridge Univ., 1983), pp. 34–50.

13. For example, see "Outwork" ("Hors livre") in/to *Disseminations* (1972), trans. Barbara Johnson (Chicago: Univ. of Chicago, 1981), pp. 1–59, or "Parergon" (1978), in *The Truth in Painting* (Chicago: Univ. of Chicago, 1987).

14. T. S. Eliot's original epigraph to *The Waste Land* comes from Charles Dickens, *Our Mutual Friend* (Harmondsworth: Penguin, 1971), p. 246. The line is spoken by Mrs Higden, who keeps a "Minding-School," about Sloppy, one of the child-minders. It occurs in a chapter with the very Derridean title "Minders and Re-Minders":

> "For I aint, you must know," said Betty, "much of a hand at reading writing-hand, though I can read my Bible and most print. And I do love a newspaper. You mightn't think it, but Sloppy is a beautiful reader of a newspaper. He do the Police in different voices."

She means the Police Notices—but we can read in the language police just as easily.

15. Published by Cambridge University Press in 1975. I might note that the book was written under a Foucauldian aegis, that is, in the heyday of sentences, thought of as so many discursive formations or *épistémes*. Hacking claims no longer to subscribe to this model, though for the Foucauldian reason that all discourse is interested: he now seeks to write "the history of the present" (see "Two Kinds of 'New Historicism' for Philosophers" in *New Literary History*, 21:2 [1990], pp. 343–64, esp. p. 360).

16. *Spurs: Nietzsche's Styles* (1972), trans. Barbara Harlow (Chicago: Chicago Univ., 1979), p. 107. Cf. "From Restricted to General Economy. A Hegelianism Without Reserve" (1967), in *Writing and Difference* (1967), trans. Alan Bass (Chicago: Univ. of Chicago, 1978), pp. 251–77, p. 268: "We would have to speak of an epochè of the epoch of meaning, of a—written—putting between brackets that suspends the epoch of meaning: the opposite of a phenomeonological epochè, for the latter is carried out in the name and in the sight of meaning."

17. Hacking, pp. 151, 154. On a parallel between Derrida and Davidson, see S. Pradhan, "Minimalist Semantics: Davidson and Derrida on Meaning, Use, and Convention," *Diacritics*, 16:1 (1986), pp. 66–77.

18. "Truth and Consequences: How to Understand Jacques Derrida," *The New Republic* (Octber 5, 1987), pp. 31–36, at p. 35. It may well be that Nehamas does not know how to *read* Derrida, for he quotes "out of context" the following lines from "Envois": "[And you are, my love unique   the proof, the living proof precisely, that] a letter can always not arrive at its destination, and [that] therefore it never arrives" (*The Post Card*, p. 33–Nehamas's omissions in brackets). Is Derrida *really* arguing that miscommunication in principle entails noncommunication in fact, given his elaborate postal framework and his ironic tone? John Ellis (*Against Deconstruction*) construes Derrida's claim in a similar way, viz., because "in the last analysis" there are only differences, as Saussure puts it, it follows that all terms are meaningless. Ellis finds so many obvious misreadings and weak arguments in Derrida's texts that the reader might begin to wonder whether it is not evidence rather of weaknesses in Ellis's ability to read Derrida.

19. Scholes, "Deconstruction and Communication," *Critical Inquiry*, 14:2 (1988), pp. 278–95. The quotation is from *Margins of Philosophy*, trans. Alan Bass (Chicago: Univ. of Chicago, 1972, 1982), p. 307. Scholes counters (p. 281): "It is my contention that 'hermeneutic deciphering' is alive and well in most Derridean practice, though disparaged openly by Derrida himself and his American followers." The gist of Scholes's position is repeated in his *Protocols of Reading* (New Haven: Yale Univ., 1989), ch. 2: "Interpretation: the Question of Protocols."

20. *Limited Inc.*, p. 243.

21. James Kearn and Ken Newton. "An Interview with Jacques Derrida," *The Literary Review*, 14 (April 18–May 1, 1980), p. 21.

22. See *Dialogue and Deconstruction: The Gadamer-Derrida Encounter*,

eds. D. P. Michelfelder & R. E. Palmer (Albany: SUNY, 1989), especially Gadamer's "Text and Interpretation" (1981). The label "improbable debate" echoes Derrida's own comment on the Searle-Derrida encounter (or non-encounter). Other improbable debates — with Davidson, or with Rorty perhaps — are even now going on.

23. Meeting of the Eastern Division of the APA, December 1988. Summaries were published in *The Journal of Philosophy*, 85:12 (1988): Derrida's "The Politics of Friendship," pp. 632–45, and McCarthy's comments, "On the Margins of Politics," pp. 645–48. A revised version of McCarthy's paper is published as "The Politics of the Ineffable: Derrida's Deconstructionism," *The Philosophical Forum*, 21: 1–2 (1989–90), pp. 146–68.

24. This "intersection of a pragmatics and a grammatology" is discussed in "My Chances/*Mes Chances*: A Rendezvous with some Epicurean Stereophonies," *Taking Chances: Derrida, Psychoanalysis, Literature*, eds. J. Smith and W. Kerrigan (Baltimore: Johns Hopkins Univ., 1984), at p. 27. The shift from a "coding" to an "inferential" model of communication — pragmatics rather than syntactics — is advocated by Dan Sperber and Deirdre Wilson in their book *Relevance: Communication and Cognition* (Cambridge, Mass.: Harvard Univ., 1986).

25. "I, too, dislike it: there are things that are important beyond all this fiddle. Reading it, however, with a perfect contempt for it, one discovers in it after all, a place for the genuine" (Marianne Moore, *Poetry* — original version).

26. The main translations are *"Speech and Phenomena" and Other Essays on Husserl's Theory of Signs* (1967), trans. David B. Allison (Evanston, Ill.: Northwestern Univ., 1973) and *Edmund Husserl's "Origin of Geometry": An Introduction* (1962), trans. John P. Leavey (Pittsburgh: Duquesne Univ., 1978). "Structure, Sign and Play in the Discourse of the Human Sciences" was published in the conference proceedings, *The Languages of Criticism and the Sciences of Man: The Structuralist Controversy*, eds. Richard Macksey and Eugenio Donato (Baltimore: Johns Hopkins Univ., 1970), and in *Writing and Difference*, pp. 278–93. It overlaps with much in *Of Grammatology* (1967), trans. Gayatri Spivak (Baltimore: Johns Hopkins Univ., 1976).

27. *Writing and Difference*, pp. 31–63. Foucault replied in the 1972 edition of his book, trans. Geoffrey Bennington, "My Body, This Paper, This Fire," *Oxford Literary Review*, 6:1 (1979), pp. 5–28.

28. Ibid., p. 27: "A system of which Derrida is the most decisive modern representative, in its final glory: the reduction of discursive practices to textual traces; the elision of the events produced therein and the retention only of marks for a reading; the invention of voices behind texts to avoid having to analyse the modes of implication of the subject in discourses; the assigning of the originary as said and unsaid in the text to avoid replacing discursive practices in the field of transformations where they are carried out.... A pedagogy which teaches the pupil that there is nothing outside the text, but that in it, in its gaps, its blanks and its silences, there reigns the reserve of the origin...." A final chapter in Derrida's engagement with "madness": he assisted the architects Bernard Tschumi and Peter Eisenman in the design of

the "Parc de La Villette" (1982–85), an exercise in "deconstructivism" in which variously placed "follies" challenge the idea of architectural reason. See e.g., "Why Peter Eisenman Writes Such Good Books" (1986), in *Restructuring Architectural Theory*, eds. Marco & Catherine Ingrahan (Evanston: Northwestern Univ., 1989), pp. 99–105.

29. F. de Saussure, *Course in General Linguistics* (1916), trans. Roy Harris (London: Duckworth, 1983), p. 118.

30. See Part 2: "Nature, Culture, Writing" (pp. 95–316)—an exegetical tour de force which plays, first, on the ambiguity of "supplement" as between complement, paraphrase, etc., and substitute for an absent original, then links it finally to Rousseau's "dangerous supplement" (his masturbating), and finally to his theory of language.

31. In citing this passage, Ellis (*Against Deconstruction*, p. 60f.) claims that Derrida tends towards the second way—a joyful escape from metaphysics—or at least, that we should not be surprised that his readers have taken him in that way. Perhaps we should not be surprised: but that is neither reason nor justification for such a reading.

32. Derrida's involvement continues, however. See, for example, "*Geschlecht* II: Heidegger's Hand," in *Deconstruction and Philosophy: The Texts of Jacques Derrida*, ed. John Sallis (Chicago: Univ. of Chicago, 1987), pp. 161–96; and *Of Spirit: Heidegger and the Question* (Chicago: Univ. of Chicago, 1987, 1989), Derrida's contribution to a conference on Heidegger's complicity with National Socialism, in which Derrida very subtly uncovers one of the German's "unthoughts," his bond with *Geist* (spirit).

33. Stephen W. Melville, *Philosophy Beside Itself: On Deconstruction and Modernism* (Minneapolis: Univ. of Minnesota, 1986). "Psyché: Invention de l'autre," *Psyché* (Paris: Galilée, 1987), pp. 11–61.

34. Kearney, p. 108.

35. Ibid, p. 125.

36. A parenthesis in "The Time of a Thesis," p. 44.

37. See his "Deconstruction as Criticism," *Glyph*, 6 (1979), pp. 177–216, as well as *The Tain of the Mirror*. The latter contains the fullest treatment of deconstruction, though miming Derrida a little too closely: see Part 2.

38. See "Letter to a Japanese Friend" (1985), in *Derrida and Difference*, eds. D. Wood and R. Bernasconi (Evanston: Northwestern Univ., 1988), pp. 1–8, at p. 2. For the link with Heidegger, see H.-G. Gadamer's "*Destruktion* and Deconstruction," in *Dialogue and Deconstruction*, pp. 102–13, and Robert Bernasconi's careful assessment in his "Seeing Double: *Destruktion* and Deconstruction," Ibid., pp. 233–50.

39. "Signature Event Context," a 1971 "communication" to a conference on communication, in *Margins*, 1972, pp. 307–30, at p. 329. The excerpt is from a section called "Signatures," and occurs just before Derrida appends his own autograph, once within the communication, and again *to* the "communication."

40. *Tain*, pp. 138–40. Gasché points out that Hegel's dialectics (e.g., in

Book 2 of the *Science of Logic*) criticizes Romantic reflexion. So by implication would Derrida, while striving to avoid Hegelian speculation — "spacing" is his substitute. I merely note ("remark") the proximity to Adorno's negative dialectics as it attempts by "mimesis" to engage and escape instrumental reason.

41. See "Difference" in *Margins*, pp. 1–27, at p. 13.

42. See "From Restricted to General Economy," in *Writing and Difference*, pp. 251–77; an essay on Bataille's involvement with the Hegelian discourse.

43. "Outwork," in *Dissemination*, p. 33. Gasché takes the image as the title of his book, which remains one of the best studies of the Derrida's Hegelian legacy. See also Melville, *Philosophy Beside Itself*, and Manfred Frank, *What is Neostructuralism?*, trans. J. Wilke & R. Gray (Minneapolis: Univ. of Minnesota, 1984, 1989), esp. pp. 262–87 for a comparison with Hegelian speculation. John H. Smith takes his epigraph from Frank in his "U-Topian Hegel: Dialectic and its Other in Poststructuralism," *German Quarterly*, 60:2 (Spring 1987), pp. 237–61: "The dialogue with Hegel remains an *ou topos*, a U-topia of Neostructuralism." James L. Marsh briefly compares attitudes on mediation in his "The Play of Difference/Différance in Hegel and Derrida," *The Owl of Minerva*, 21:2 (1990), pp. 145–53.

44. (1968) in *Dissemination*, pp. 61–171.

45. (1970) in *Dissemination*, pp. 173–285; and *Glas*, trans. John P. Leavey (Lincoln: Univ. of Nebraska, 1987).

46. *Truth in Painting*, p. 93.

47. *The Post Card*, p. 486n.

48. See Blumenberg, *Paradigmen zu einer Metaphorologie* (Bonn: Bouvier, 1966).

49. *Margins*, pp. 207–71, at p. 210ff.; this received wisdom is related in Anatole France, *The Garden of Epicurus*.

50. "On Truth and Lies in an Ultramoral Sense," cited by Derrida on p. 217.

51. See *Margins*, p. 228. On Donald Davidson's theory of metaphor as nonexistent, see his "What Metaphors Mean," in *Inquiries into Truth and Interpretation* (Cambridge: Cambridge Univ., 1978, 1984) pp. 245–64.

52. The workings of this particular "restricted economy" of value-language are presented with aplomb in Gregory Jay, "The Value of Deconstruction: Derrida, Saussure, Marx," *Cultural Critique*, 8, (1988, pp. 153–96), and in Chapter 1 of his *America the Scrivener: Deconstruction and the Subject of Literary History*. (Ithaca: Cornell Univ., 1990).

53. See Richard Rorty, "Philosophy as a Kind of Writing" (1978), in *Consequences of Pragmatism* (Oxford: Oxford Univ., 1982). Rorty has continued this line of interpretation in later essays, e.g., "Deconstruction and Circumvention," *Critical Inquiry*, 11 (1984), pp. 1–23; "Two Senses of 'Logocentrism,'" in *Redrawing the Lines...*, ed. Dasenbrock (Lincoln: Univ. of Nebraska, 1989); "Is Derrida a Transcendental Philosopher?" *Yale Journal of Criticism*, 2:2 (1989), pp. 207–17; and "From Ironist Theory to Pragmatic Allusions:

Derrida" in *Contingency, Irony, and Solidarity* (Cambridge: Cambridge Univ., 1989), pp. 122–37.

54. "Interview with *le nouvel observateur*," in *Derrida and Différence*, pp. 71–82, at p. 73. See also "The Time of a Thesis," at p. 37.

55. Kearney, p. 124. Literary critics' tendency to apply "deconstruction" as a "method" has been assailed by Rodolphe Gasché in "Deconstruction as Criticism."

56. "Roundtable on Translation," in *The Ear of the Other: Otobiography, Transference, Translation (Texts and Discussions with Jacques Derrida)*, eds. Claude Levesque and Christie V. McDonald, trans. Peggy Kamuf and Avital Ronell (New York: Schocken, 1985), pp. 91–161, at pp. 140–41.

57. "Qual Quelle: Valéry's Sources" (1971) in *Margins*, pp. 273–306, esp. p. 293: "A task is then prescribed: to study the philosophical text in its formal structure, in its rhetorical organization, in the specificity and diversity of its textual types, in its models of exposition and production — beyond what previously were called genres — and also in the space of its mises en scène, in a syntax which would be not only the articulation of its signifieds, its references to Being or to truth, but also the handling of its proceedings, and of everything invested in them. In a word, the task is to consider philosophy also as a "particular literary genre," drawing upon the resources of language, cultivating, forcing, or making deviate a set of tropic resources older than philosophy itself."

58. This notorious sentence occurs in *Of Grammatology*, p. 158; and in the context of a discussion of Rousseau and "that dangerous supplement" that dare not speak its name, writing/masturbation. In the "Note Against Deconstruction" appended to his *Kenneth Burke and Martin Heidegger* (Gainsville: Univ. of Florida, 1987), pp. 87–105, Samuel Southwell accuses Derrida of linguistic solipsism: Derrida claims a validity for "grammatology" which, just because it can*not* found a new science, forces him to resort to virtuoso mystification.

59. Nancy Fraser, "The French Derrideans: Politicizing Deconstruction or Deconstructing Politics?" *New German Critique*, 33 (1984), pp. 127–54, reprinted in her *Unruly Practices: Power, Discourse, and Gender in Contemporary Social Theory* (Minneapolis: Univ. of Minnesota, 1989), pp. 127–54.

60. In *For Nelson Mandela*, eds. Derrida and Mustapha Tlili (New York: Columbia Univ., 1987), pp. 13–42. See also Leonard Lawlor, "From the Trace to the Law: Derridean Politics," in *Philosophy and Social Criticism*, 15:1 (1989), pp. 1–15; and Bill Martin, "Matrix and Line: Derrida and the Possibilities of Social Theory" (dissertation, Univ. of Kansas, 1990), forthcoming from SUNY Press, Albany.

61. Cf. "Of an Apocalyptic Tone Recently Adopted by Philosophy," (1984), pp. 3–37, which takes up Kant's objection to those who would confuse pure and practical reason.

62. "Psyché: Invention de l'autre," trans. "Psyche: Inventions of the Other," in *Reading de Man Reading*, eds. L Walters & W. Godzich (Minneapolis: Univ. of Minnesota, 1989), pp. 25–65, and *Memoires: For Paul de*

Man (New York: Columbia Univ., 1986), which takes up the topic dear to his friend, the figuring of memory/memoire/memorial. The theme of memory has continued, of course, with the "scandal" of de Man's apparent suppression of his wartime positions—on which more below.

63. "The Politics of the Ineffable," pp. 154–55.

64. McCarthy notes (ibid., 155) how Derrida can speak of—and invoke—"norms of minimal intelligibility," while still claiming these are deconstructible. See Derrida's Afterword to *Limited Inc*, e.g., p. 136: values like "truth" impose themselves "within a context which is extremely vast, old, powerfully established, stabilized or rooted in a network of conventions (for instance, those of language), and yet still remains a context."

65. *Logics of Disintegration: Post-structuralist Thought and the Claims of Critical Theory* (London: Verso, 1987), pp. 1–44, at p. 7. Dews's study is the most penetrating I know.

66. Ibid., p. 19. Dews illuminatingly compares Derrida's critique of Husserl with Schelling's of Fichte (pp. 19–31).

67. "Like the Sound of the Sea Deep Within a Shell: Paul de Man's War," in *Critical Inquiry*, 14:3 (Spring 1988), pp. 590–652. This article occasioned several responses, published in a subsequent issue, along with a reply ("Biodegradables: Seven Diary Fragments," *Critical Inquiry*), which played with the idea of all these texts being so much paper for consumption by history; Derrida begins with quotes and allusions to his own writings, and the "diary" format makes it clear that he is both inside and outside the genre (it's not *really* his own journal, is it?), much as with *The Postcard*. Even so, Derrida has been read as in effect seeking to *defend* de Man's wartime journalism, or at least his silence about it. For a similar engagement with Heidegger, see *Of Spirit*.

68. "Is Derrida a Transcendental Philosopher?" p. 208.

69. "Psyché," p. 21, "Psyche," p. 32.

4

Foucault on Discourse and History
A Style of Delegitimation
Michael S. Roth

At a time when the popular press has joined important figures in the academy in denouncing poststructuralist thinkers for avoiding morality and politics or repressing them for ignoble reasons, one can turn to Michel Foucault's writings for confirmation of the important contribution that poststructuralism has made to our ability to think seriously about our relationship to the past. His work also exemplifies how a rhetorical turn in philosophy and history does not necessarily preclude the development of an informed, critical stance on some of the crucial problems of modernity. Although this essay will be a critical examination of Foucault's use of an analysis of discourse to tell a history of the present, I should preface my remarks by saying that this criticism presupposes the great importance of Foucault's contribution to thinking about history and about politics. Foucault's historical analysis of discursive practices has done more than any contemporary writer to wake those who think about the connection of past and present from their dogmatic slumbers. We must ask, however, where Foucault leaves us when we are thus awoken. Do we, in fact, have any more power to deal with the world around us than we did in our dreams?

Foucault's books tell the story of increasing repression and domination; even when we attempt to be free, he shows how the attempt leads to ever greater constraints. To enter into the work of Michel Foucault is to enter a world of critical pessimism. In this essay I will discuss how his genealogical analysis of discourse in fact creates a pessimism at the expense of criticism, and how his effort at delegitimation undermines the possibility of making history meaningful, which may be essential for any kind of political action or judgment.

I have argued elsewhere that Gilles Deleuze's interpretation of Nietzsche and Foucault's *oeuvre* as a whole should be understood as a reaction against the Hegelian philosophy of history which was so influential in France from the 1930s through the postwar period. In this reaction there is not only a turn away from historical events and toward discourse, there is also a displacement of questions of meaning and direction in favor of an analysis of use or function.[1] Foucault's work illuminates both the powers and the limitations of rejecting the dialectical emplotment of history in favor of the construction of a genealogical history of the present. Foucault's writings are a sustained attempt to find a modern style in which a Nietzschean approach to the past can be coherently and persuasively maintained. And this Nietzschean approach is understood to be in large part charged by anti-Hegelianism:

> In order to liberate difference, we need a thought without contradiction, without dialectic, without negation: a thought which says yes to divergence; an affirmative thought the instrument of which is disjunction; a thought of the multiple — of dispersed and nomadic multiplicity that is not limited or confined by constraints of similarity; ... We must think problematically rather than question and answer dialectically.[2]

Foucault's Nietzscheanism altered as it was confronted with different methodological possibilities and changing political choices. A genealogy of his thought might be developed which connected his work to his biography or which focused on his personal and political commitments to the antipsychiatry, prison reform, and gay rights movements,[3] but here I shall concentrate on how his anti-Hegelian and Nietzschean style of delegitimation develops in his major writings. What Deleuze said of Nietzsche, he might also have said of Foucault: "Anti-Hegelianism traverses his work like a thread of aggressivity."[4]

Foucault, Nietzsche and Interpretation Without End

Michel Foucault's writings on the past and his other political interventions display a sustained attempt to think and apply the lessons of Nietzsche within the contemporary theoretical conjuncture. An important part of this conjuncture has to do with a focus on language in a very broad sense, or on what Foucault preferred to call discourse. His Nietzsche, then, was not so much the theorist of the will to power, but the thinker who examined at what price the subject can speak the truth, and "the relation between 'telling the truth' and forms of reflexivity, of self upon self."[5] And as he emphasized again at the end of his life, he came to this Nietzsche through Heidegger:

> Heidegger was always for me the essential philosopher. I began by reading Hegel then Marx and I started to read Heidegger in 1951 or 1952; and in 1953 or 1952, I no longer remember, I read Nietzsche.... All my philosophic becoming was determined by my reading of Heidegger. But I recognize that it is Nietzsche who took it over ... I tried to read Nietzsche in the 50s, Nietzsche alone meant nothing to me! Whereas Nietzsche and Heidegger, that was *le choc philosophic*![6]

If Heidegger remains an absent target of Foucault's writing, Nietzsche figures prominently in two important texts. By examining them in some detail, we should be able to assess to what extent it is helpful to think of Foucault's *oeuvre* as an example of a French Nietzscheanism, and how that *oeuvre* refigures the connection between history and knowing through an analysis of discourse.

In the Royaumont Colloquium of the summer of 1964, Foucault delivered a lecture on Nietzsche, Marx, and Freud. In this talk he examines what he elsewhere calls a new *episteme*; a new way of knowing and thinking about the world. An episteme, much like a paradigm in a Kuhnian sense, is a strategy of discourse through which we interact with objects and people around us, and with ourselves. The new discursive strategy that he examines in this essay is "interpretation." Of course, interpretation existed well before the nineteenth century, but then it was aimed at the discovery of resemblances. In the nineteenth century, and in particular in the work of Marx, Nietzsche, and Freud, there arises again "the possibility of a hermeneutic."[7] This possibility is based on an awareness of the reflexivity of interpretation, and an increased attention to the meanings of the surface of signs (their interconnections) rather than a probe into their depths (their references).

It is particularly the reflexivity of interpretation — the idea that an interpretation can best be understood by turning interpretive strategies back on the interpretation itself — that leads Foucault to the second major characteristic of nineteenth-century hermeneutics: "Interpretation finally became an infinite task."[8] For these thinkers, the task is infinite because no secure origin or goal acts as a standard for judging meanings.

Foucault notes that for Nietzsche, there is no origin of meaning. As interpretation tries to get beneath signs to something more fundamental than them, it discovers only more interpretations. Meaning comes through the imposition of interpretations.[9] Signs, then, are not prior to interpretations; instead signs are always already the product of interpretations:

> Beginning in the 19th century, beginning from Freud, Marx and Nietzsche, it seems to me that the sign is going to become malevolent;

> I mean that there is in the sign an ambiguous and even suspect means of willing evil, and of *malveiller*. That is insofar as the sign is already an interpretation which does not present itself as such. Signs are interpretations which try to justify themselves, and not the inverse.[10]

In a world without beginnings, without a secure meaning to search out, the goal of interpretation becomes mysterious also. Interpretation for Nietzsche — as for Freud and Marx — is always incomplete, and a total hermeneutic is closer to *l'expérience de la folie* than it is to "absolute knowledge."[11] Dialectical thinking had erred in trying to attribute positive meaning and direction to the play of meaning.[12] In contrast to this appropriation of interpretation for something more secure, and in contrast to the semiologist's faith in the "absolute existence of signs," — and thus a possible systematization of their relationships — Nietzsche, Marx, and Freud leave us with a "hermeneutic which is enveloped on itself," an endless interpretation without foundation and without goal. For Foucault, this legacy defines the current discursive period and, of course, his own interpretation of it:

> The problem of the plurality of interpretations, of the war of interpretations, is, I believe, made strictly possible by the very definition of the interpretation, which goes on to infinity, without there being an absolute point beginning from which it is judged and is decided upon. Thus, the following: the fact that we are destined to be interpreted at the very moment where we interpret; all interpreters must know it. This plethora of interpretations is certainly a trait which profoundly characterizes Western culture now.[13]

Seven years after giving the lecture at Royaumont, Foucault returned to Nietzsche in an essay that would define his historical approach to discursive practices for the rest of his life. In "Nietzsche, la généalogie, l'histoire," Foucault showed what was at stake in adopting a Nietzschean perspective, if not a method, on the past instead of either the traditional historiographical or the "metaphysical" modes of comprehending historical change.

Foucault begins his description of genealogy where his previous discussion of interpretation left off. Genealogy is an examination of the minutiae of history, not of great deeds. It rejects the "metahistorical deployment of ideal significance and of indefinite ideologies" and instead concentrates on the play of interpretations, on primal disparity and not bedrock essence.[14] In fact, Foucault tries to steer genealogy between two dangerous points: Hegelian philosophy of history, and conventional historiography.

The Hegelian philosophy of history — "metaphysics" in Foucault's essay — looks for an essence beneath historical events. Rather than seeking out the meaning that links all events and discourses in a coherent whole, the genealogist recognizes irremediable diversity and discontinuity. Genealogy thus depends on a notion of hermeneutics, because it presupposes the primacy of interpretation over the sign. That is, the genealogist expects that the past will contain only more interpretations, and he or she does not seek out a basic truth or essence to serve as a standard of transhistorical judgment:

> If interpretation were the bringing slowly to light of meaning buried in the origin, then only metaphysics could interpret the becoming of humanity. But if interpretation is the violent or surreptitious appropriation of a system of rules (which in itself has no essential meaning), in order to impose a direction, to bend it to a new will, to force its participation in a different game, and to subject it to secondary rules, then the development of humanity is a series of interpretations.[15]

Whereas the metaphysical (Hegelian) historian searches for a *sens de l'histoire*, the Nietzschean genealogist makes use of a *sens historique*. The division between these two terms is the chasm that for Foucault separates traditional historiography or philosophy and his own work.

The search for a *sens de l'histoire* has been animated by a desire to give meaning and direction to the present by finding its development in the past. In a crucial sense this practice is always one of legitimation. To know the direction of history is to validate a certain contemporary practice, make it "realistic," or "reasonable," or "progressive." The point becomes clear when those in power justify the exercise of their power through an appeal to history, and Hegel himself gave the best example of this in the *Philosophy of Right*. When the State is viewed as highest product of the final stage of history, the appearance of the divine on earth, criticism of it becomes quite literally a form of non-sense.

But the legitimating function of a *sens de l'histoire* is relevant not only to those in power. The same function is operative for those who use history to criticize those in power, of whom Marx is the most obvious example. Marxist theory of history does not so much predict future historical change as justify a certain kind of political action aimed at bringing about these changes.[16] The effort to find a *sens de l'histoire* connects present to past in order to ground judgments and actions. History becomes that place to which one turns for continuity, stability, and the possibility of acting in a meaningful, that is, nonarbitrary way. Without nature or a god to guide us, a *sens de l'histoire* can legitimate an identity as well as a program for change.[17]

Foucault rejects legitimation through history as "metaphysical." The *sens historique* is counterhistorical when compared with the Hegelian approach to the past. Rather than providing stability or continuity, it disconnects the present and its pasts:

> The search for descent [*provenance*] is not the erecting of foundations,
> it disturbs what was previously considered immobile; it fragments
> what was thought unified; it shows the heterogeneity of what was
> imagined consistent with itself.[18]

Nietzschean genealogy sees the "becoming of humanity as a series of
interpretations."[19] Instead of trying to weave together major events
and worldviews into a master narrative of history, it focuses on the
creation of discursive strategies for interacting with oneself and others.
Foucault uses genealogy to uncover the appearance of these strategies
or interpretations and their eclipse. And the question "Interpretations
of what?" is no longer admissible because of his view of language.
Interpretations are primary; there is nothing beneath or behind an
interpretation except another interpretation, and the same holds true
for the work of the genealogist. The reflexive dimension remains crucial
for Foucault. Genealogy cannot take itself for a science that regards
the interpretations of the past from some suprahistorical point of view.
Genealogy affirms itself as another in a series of interpretations, as a
discourse among discourses soon to be revised. The *sens historique* is
nonmetaphysical to the extent that it rejects all absolutes.[20]

In "Nietzsche, la généalogie, l'histoire," Foucault follows Nietzsche
in calling history without absolutes "effective history." At least since
Ranke, historians have taken "metaphysicians" as easy targets for their
empirical wrath, but Foucault is not linking genealogy with traditional
historiography:

> "Effective" history differs from that of the historians in that it does
> not stand on any constant; nothing in man — not even his body — is
> stable enough for recognizing other men and being recognized by
> them.... It is necessary to destroy that which permits the consoling
> play of recognitions. To know, even in the historical order, does not
> signify to "re-find," and above all not to "re-find ourselves." History
> will be "effective" to the extent that it introduces discontinuity into
> our very being. Knowledge is not made for comprehension, it is made
> for cutting.[21]

Effective history will be a "countermemory" teaching us that we live
without foundations, and that the events of our past do not contain the
anticipation of meanings fully realized in the present or the future.[22]
Effective history knows itself to be a partial interpretation in the
service of particular interests in the present; its inquiry includes a
genealogy of itself.[23]

If effective history knows itself to be an interpretation of still other
interpretations that never lead to a stable identity or to comprehension,
why should anyone do this kind of history? Foucault notes that its
reflexive dimension makes genealogy a *carnival concerté*,[24] and that its

first function is to parody those elements in the present that find their legitimation in a proud lineage. The second use of effective history is the "systematic disassociation of our identity":[25] "The purpose of history, directed by genealogy, is not to discover the roots of our identity, but to commit itself, on the contrary, to its dissipation."[26] By dissolving the bases of our identity, effective history undermines the very foundation of our attempts to know ourselves. The genealogist not only asks about the difficulties of knowing a certain object—about the relationship between discourse and "the world"—but also undercuts the subject who would know. This is the third usage of effective history: to destroy the knowing subject by uncovering the hidden vicissitudes of the will to truth. And it is here that Foucault ends his essay, pointing out the way in which a genealogical, Nietzschean history can undermine the security of foundations, continuity, and identity, and place our will to know within the fabric of our desire to interpret.

Foucault's Histories of the Present

Although "Nietzsche, la généalogie l'histoire," marks an important step in Foucault's account of his own work, it is no less a description of what he had already written than a program for what he intended to do. In *Madness and Civilization* and *The Birth of the Clinic*, Foucault's analysis of the discourse of medicine and psychiatry had already privileged the discontinuous and the destabilizing. It has been rightly pointed out that in the former he retained an essentialist notion of the "experience of madness" that remained pure and stable over time, but the work as a whole surely aims to undermine our faith in categories of both mental illness and reason.[27] In the *The Birth of the Clinic*, Foucault describes his project as both historical and critical insofar as it is concerned "with determining the conditions of possibility of medical experience in modern times."[28] But the entire point of determining these possibilities is to bring to mind the opportunities for change. In all of his historical works Foucault situates himself at the beginning of a contemporary shift in the way we interact with the world (episteme, discourse formations, a prioris, paradigms). His histories are effective, insofar as they contribute to hasten this shift by exposing the limits of the present structures of experience.[29]

The Order of Things can be situated in this nascent shift. The book was written when structuralism's critique of historicism and humanism was fashionable, and it contributed to this critique by providing an account of how the notion of "man" became the center of our thinking. The structuralist critique of humanism depended on an analysis of language in which the speaking subject had little or nothing to do with the meaning of what was said. We do not generate the meanings in discourse; we find ourselves always already within a discourse. If "man" or human history was not the origin of meaning, self-consciousness would no longer be the goal of knowing. Heidegger's critique of phenomenology and his notion of man as not the lord of beings but the shepherd of Being was crucial to Foucault's own critique of the human sciences. He not only contributed to the polemic against the "anthropologization" of knowledge, he also pointed to signs of the disappearance of "man" from our thinking and tried to show the transitory nature of "man" so as to hasten that disappearance.[30]

The Order of Things argues that a culture speaks and thinks through different epistemes, and that these epistemes limit the possibilities of perception, cognition and expression. These limitations are unconscious, because they are the very conditions of our discourse. Although Foucault says we are imprisoned within our own language and cannot describe our own episteme, his project is centered on the belief that a new beam of light is beginning to shine into our prison. As a perceiver of this new dawn, as an archaeologist who can place this light in relation to the past and present structures of experience, Foucault appears to have one foot in the modern world and one foot in whatever world will follow.[31]

The genealogist's act of interpretation is an act of will to foster change. The notion of *effective* history becomes more concrete when we see that the desired effect of interpretation is (at least in part) the disintegration of the structures of our discourse, by which Foucault means the dissolution of our contemporary conditions of experience and knowing. Foucault says nothing about the content of change, because for him any future episteme is unknowable. It is perhaps the question why one would choose to foster change about which one knows nothing that leads him to examine in detail the mechanisms by which change takes place. How are different forms of power exercised in various movements for change, and in various resistances to these movements? This examination, although it does not directly answer the question "why one should," does provide a "thicker" interpretation, one which may make action in the present more open to discursive legitimation than it otherwise would be.

Foucault's work always had something to do with power, but with *Discipline and Punish* this concern emerged in the foreground. Whereas previously he had examined the possibilities of knowing and how these were maintained in language, with this book he began to examine the power/knowledge constellation from the perspective of the exercise of power.[32] It is certainly true that the earlier investigations of the possibilities of knowing had much to do with power, especially insofar as the expression of these possibilities in discourse became important for institutions, disciplines, and conceptual change. In *Discipline and Punish* and his later works, Foucault's notion of discourse becomes thicker as it comes to emphasize the operations that depend on (and reinforce) ways of knowing. In a sentence that fits perfectly into his view of Nietzsche's *Généalogie of Morals*, Foucault stresses the connection of knowledge and power:

> We must admit that power produces knowledge ... that power and knowledge directly imply one another; that there is no power relation without the correlative constitution of a field of knowledge, nor any knowledge that does not presuppose and constitute at the same time power relations.[33]

Discipline and Punish not only describes the birth of the prison, it explores the power/knowledge constellation that makes systematic normalization possible.

Foucault's understanding of power has been discussed in great detail elsewhere; here we need note only that he is attaching himself to an interpretation of Nietzsche that underlines the interconnection of the will-to-power and the will-to-truth. Most important, power is viewed not as something that inhibits truth, but as something that produces truth. Thus power is not only repressive, it is creative. And the ability of a discursive strategy for the exercise of power to create truths, or a regime of truth, is the secret to the self-legitimation of the strategy.[34]

Foucault describes *Discipline and Punish* as a "history of the present," and here he means more than just "the history of a paradigm that is about to become outmoded." In this work the development of prisons—of penal "reform"—is linked to mechanisms of power which he clearly thinks need to be resisted now. Resistance to normalization means resistance to the network of power in which the prison has existed. Practical political work for prisoners and against a specific exercise of power has replaced more distant, if still vaguely apocalyptic, references to shifts in the structures of discourse:

> The meaning which bears and determines us has the form of a war rather than that of a language: relations of power, not relations of meaning. History has no "meaning," though this is not to say it is absurd or incoherent. On the contrary it is intelligible and should be susceptible of analysis down to the smallest detail—but this in accordance with the intelligibility of struggles, of strategies and tactics.[35]

The contrast between relations of power and relations of meaning recalls that between *sens historique* and *sens de l'histoire*. The problem with the latter terms in each opposition is that they assume a generalizable, or transcendent function that allows for judgment among particulars. In other words, considerations of meaning and considerations of the *sens de l'histoire* are totalizable. This conclusion is problematic for Foucault because genealogy assumes (and shows) the fragmentation and discontinuity of the past.[36] When Foucault criticizes the search for meaning in history, he is criticizing the notion that there is a uniform meaning or a uniform history, and he aims both at Hegelianism and at semiology:

> Neither the dialectic, as logic of contradictions, nor semiotics, as the structure of communication, can account for the intrinsic intelligibility of conflicts. "Dialectic" is a way of evading the always open and hazardous reality of conflict by reducing it to a Hegelian skeleton, and "semiology" is a way of avoiding its violent, bloody and lethal character by reducing it to the calm Platonic form of language and dialogue.[37]

Semiology is abandoned along with dialectics because both have a pretension to nonlocal knowledge. Foucault sees this pretension as an evasion of the *specific* connections of knowledge and power.[38]

That changes in the past have been fragmentary and discontinuous also shows us something about how our *sens historique* should foster change in the present. Analysis of history, if it is to be "effective" (that is genealogical), must not only examine how power and knowledge are related, but also situate itself in the present in accordance with specific strategies and tactics of resistance, in accordance with another exercise of power. In the 1977 interview from which I have been quoting, Foucault makes clear that the emphasis on specific struggles, strategies, and tactics is a post-1968 phenomenon. One of the lessons of those *événements* is that the state is everywhere but that, in order to combat it without imitating its structure, one has to organize resistance at the micro or local level.[39] In this environment the role of the intellectual also changes. Whereas intellectuals had once spoken in the name of universal values and Truth, they now could speak "within specific sectors, at the precise points where their own conditions of life situate them."[40] The notion of discourse as being fragmentary and heterogeneous and of interpretation as being endless is connected to a view of the intellectual whose interventions have no pretension to totality. The valorization of the specific as opposed to universal intellectual is connected to the dismissal of all attempts at universal history and to an antirepresentational politics that underlines the "indignity of speaking for others."[41]

The problem with this view of the intellectual—and of everyone who speaks—is that it effaces, or accepts the effacement of, public life. According to this view, I cannot speak for you because I do not share the "conditions of life that situate you." The inability to share these conditions undermines one's ability to speak for—or *to*—anybody at all. Foucault has not only dissolved the possibilities for representation, he has also dissolved the possibilities of communication as a form of political participation. Such participation, certainly the heart of any democratic politics, requires that some conditions — Eric Weil called them traditions, or parts of the community that go without saying, Wittgenstein, forms of life — are shared. However, the emphasis Foucault puts on discontinuity, fragmentation and division makes clear that our ability to share such conditions with others is, at best, very limited. Politics is thereby reduced to the pursuit of small, special interests (although since all interests are now "special," the word loses much of its force). There is no General Will to which the intellectual can attach him or herself because there is no longer a public sphere that transcends our specific situations, struggles and strategies; there is, in sum, no longer the possibility of community. Even more strongly, there never has been such a possibility; there has only been the exercise of a specific kind of power in whose interest the illusion of such a possibility functioned. At least this seems to be Foucault's view.[42]

Even in the 1977 interview, however, some doubts emerge. The view of the specificity of intellectuals can become a form of skepticism. We cannot speak for anybody because we can never know what anybody really thinks or wants. Such a skepticism might be theoretically amusing if joined to verbal and textual play, but in political terms it is surely impotent. The specific intellectual has renounced the universal, but what then can be the basis for his or her ability to join with other people, or to teach, learn from, or persuade other people, to work together for change? What, in other words, can serve as the forms of commonality essential for politics? Or does this skepticism entail an anemic view of politics as essentially the pursuit of private interest? Foucault's answer seems to be that our commonality is that we share in the regime of truth production. We are parts of a discourse, of a technology of producing truth; we are enmeshed in "the ensemble of rules according to which the true and the false are separated and specific effects of power attached to the true."[43] The critical intellectual's general task, then, is "that of ascertaining the possibility of constituting a new politics of truth." The point is not to change what people think, but to change the way the "regime" produces truth.[44]

Here we return to the equivalent of the references to the vague shifts in our archive or episteme that animated Foucault's earlier works. The specific intellectual is supposed to work within his or her own situation for change. A university professor, for example, might argue for a democratization of the university or for more equality in hiring; at least these seem to be the kinds of things for which Foucault hoped the intellectual would argue. Of course, there are no transcendent or even general criteria for evaluating arguments for change, and so an intellectual with opposed arguments could be just as specific. "Foucault,"

Paul Veyne tells us, "admits to being incapable of justifying his own preferences; he can appeal to neither a human nature, nor an equivalence to an object. Because knowledge is power, it is imposed and one imposes it."[45] Perhaps this is why Foucault was not satisfied with specificity as a positive political value. In any case, the intellectual is also on a more general level insofar as he or she supports or undermines the regime of truth. There is no way to "emancipate truth from every system of power," just as there was no way to think without discourse or without epistemes or archives. The political task (for those who share Foucault's sympathies) is to "detach the power of truth from the forms of hegemony . . . within which it operates at the present time."[46]

Because we know that truth will always be attached to a system of power, we want to know not only that we are detaching the power of truth but to what new regime we are attaching it. This is the crucial political dilemma of the specific intellectual, but Foucault has nothing specific to say about it. This position recalls his earlier apocalyptic rhetoric, where nothing can be said of the next archive because we can think only within our own archive.[47] The epistemology seems to get in the way of the politics, although one might argue that the failure in political thinking is justified through an epistemology. In any case, it seems that in shifting from large-scale talk about discursive possibilities to more specific local accounts of power, Foucault better positions himself to provide an account of the mechanisms of power and the possibilities for *specific* forms of desirable change. But this is not the case. Instead, the gap separating the present and any goals for change remains supreme. It is a gap of theoretical silence, and it is the gap of politics.[48]

From Discourse to Style

Foucault's understanding of change starts from Nietzschean premises that were important to other French intellectuals in the 1960s and 1970s, but he does not display the faith in Being's progressive selectivity that comforted some of his contemporaries.[49] Foucault does embrace a Nietzsche who endorses the flux of things, who destroys the stable, continuous narrative that legitimates an identity and instead celebrates the blooming, buzzing confusion that might replace it. But he knows that there is no possibility of thinking or living in direct contact with this world of raw Power, Being or Truth. These forces are always already interpreted, always already within the context of a regime. When Foucault talks of change, he is not talking of a liberation from the constraints of discourse; he is talking about the creation of a new discursive regime.

The problem is that there is no indication of what this regime will look like because of the epistemological point that one cannot describe future paradigms, only the present one and those of the past. To call attention to this epistemological point is not enough, however, because it also holds true for the much criticized Hegelian philosophy of history in any of its progressivist versions. One only has to think of the flight at dusk of Hegel's owl of Minerva, or Kojève's notion that we have only dialectical knowledge of the human past. But neither Hegel nor Kojève left politics as simply a gap in theory.

They did not leave such a gap because within the Hegelian model all human change is mediated. Apprehending mediation within this model is equivalent to comprehending the meaning and direction of history. Thus, for Kojève an understanding of the master/slave dialectic is the key for configuring history in such a way as to understand what kind of action is progressive.[50] For Foucault, as we have seen, history has no meaning, and it certainly has no direction. That is, there is no possibility of mediation in Foucault, and this is perhaps the most important aspect of his Nietzschean approach to discourse and history *qua* reaction against Hegelianism. For Nietzsche, as for Foucault, there are events, but these are great irruptions into history. Change is not what we desire, work toward and achieve only out of something that resists our purposeful labor, it is that which happens *between* archives; however, we can understand only that which occurs *within* an archive. Change is not something we intend, it is at best something we can one day (genealogically) map.[51] To borrow a phrase from Charles Taylor, Foucault leaves us with "strategies without projects."[52]

Foucault was sensitive to this criticism of his work. He did not merely mouth the evasion that the ideas of community and the possibility of nonarbitrary, nonprivate action had somehow been deconstructed with the deferral of metanarratives. Instead, he pointed to his political action as that which indicated the direction in which he thought change should occur, and what he was willing to do to further such change.[53] His action was in principle nontotalizable, that is, one could not derive from it the foundation for a theory of progress or progressive action in general. The struggles he wrote about and supported were, in other words, "anarchistic."[54] Perhaps the key issues tying them together were: Who are we? How is it that a form of power "categorizes the individual, marks him by his own individuality, attaches him to his own identity, imposes a law of truth on him which he must recognize and which others have to recognize in him. It is a form of power which makes individuals subjects."[55] If Foucault's work did not indicate the direction of desired change, perhaps it could indicate how we have become subjects who desire to know this direction. Perhaps it could indicate how the connections have been formed between our ways of knowing and our ways of desiring. A critical understanding of these connections might help us to construct not a foundation but a framework for our action in the present. Foucault turned to the history of sexuality for this understanding because this history revealed how we are constituted as subjects.

The three volumes of the *Histoire de la sexualité* have more than one agenda, but the project clearly aims at an understanding of the history of how the subject has been constituted.[56] That is, Foucault wants to show how various "technologies of the self" have created a specific notion of the individual in relation to his or her conduct, desires, and experience. These relations eventually situated sexuality in a moral domain, rather than in a "style of life."[57] The configuration placed sexuality within a network of power and truth which, in its Christian form, made desire not only something to be managed or molded but something to be condemned as inherently evil.

Foucault situates his work in relation to other histories. He does not stress the difference between genealogy and history but instead notes that his essay is a philosophic exercise. At stake, he says, is "knowing to what extent the work of thinking one's own history can liberate thought from what it thinks silently, and to permit it to think otherwise.[58] The idea of thinking in another way he had already raised in the Introduction to Volume 2: "There are moments in life where the question of knowing if one can think otherwise than one thinks and see otherwise than one sees is indispensable for continuing to look and to reflect."[59] How does a study of sexuality among the Greeks and Romans constitute a philosophic exercise? How should it help us to "think otherwise"?

The study of ancient sexuality can be seen as a part of a genealogy of morals. That is, Foucault finds that morality has little to do with following a rule, everything to do with how the self is understood. The difference between pagan and Christian morality is the difference in their strategies for forming an independent and free self.

> The evolution ... from paganism to Christianity does not consist in a progressive interiorization of rule, of act and of responsibility; instead it produces a restructuration of forms of the relation to self and a transformation of practices and techniques on which this relation was based.[60]

Thus for Foucault, the study of ancient sexuality is a philosophic exercise because it shows how we first constitute ourselves as subjects who need rules by which to live. It helps us to think otherwise by calling attention to a way of life not determined or even conditioned by the attempt to follow a rule, one that instead can be described as the cultivation of a style.

Among the Greeks, the same themes of restlessness . . . took form in a reflection which aims neither at a codification of acts, nor at a constitution of an erotic art, but in the establishment of a technique of living. . . . The physical rule [*régime*] of pleasures and the economy it imposes are part of a whole art of the self.[61]

If Foucault's historical studies offered no criteria for evaluating change, they could explore possibilities in the past that might allow us to begin to think, and live, otherwise. They uncover neither models we are to imitate, nor rules we are to try to follow, but innovations that might allow us to create other ways of being. These innovations provide not criteria for prediction — or even production — but material for aesthetic inspiration. The possibilities are not substitutes for lost foundations, nor are they only the objects of nostalgia. Instead they are meant as contradictions to the historical givens that we take as natural or necessary.

We should note, however that the effort to "think otherwise" and to recover an ethics not tied to following a rule is in tension with the understanding of discourse found in Foucault's early works. Recall that he had stressed that an archive or episteme limited the possibilities of discourse and of thought; indeed, that the archive or episteme established the conditions of possibility of discourse and thought.[62] What else could one do within an episteme but follow its rules? But as we have seen, Foucault situated his own work at the limits of our own possibilities of knowing and acting. In the final volumes on the history of sexuality, Foucault wants to expand these limits by imagining other forms of constraint, other regimes. But it should be clear that the project of "thinking otherwise" remains inherently problematical for the genealogist conscious of working within and not just on a history of the present.

If Foucault's work in the 1970s is clearly connected to Nietzsche's *Genealogy of Morals*, the last two volumes of the *History of Sexuality* are more closely tied to Nietzsche's *Birth of Tragedy*. There Nietzsche found in pre-Socratic Greece a time when life was justified as an aesthetic phenomenon, when the cruel bite of scientific Socratic irony had not yet corrupted an aesthetic balance between the Appolonian and the Dionysian. Foucault likewise finds in the Greeks a moment before the constitution of the subject as a moral problem. Here we can perhaps see how Foucault's reading of Nietzsche was mediated by Heidegger, the "essential philosopher."[63] Heidegger's search for a point before the fall is part of a long German fascination with the Greeks. Foucault does not adhere to this tradition completely; he does not search for a romantic origin that must be lamented, recaptured or reiterated.[64] But he does find in the Greeks the notion of morality as a style that might allow us to escape the exigencies involved in establishing universal values through the creation of philosophical criteria legitimated by a notion of the subject.

> A moral experience essentially centered on the subject no longer appears to me to be satisfactory ... The search for styles of existence as different as possible from one another appears to me one of the points on which contemporary research within particular groups can start. The search for a form of morality which would be acceptable to everyone — in the sense that everyone must submit to it — appears catastrophic to me.[65]

Foucault's failure to provide a criterion for judging change should be understood as a refusal. As Habermas has pointed out, Foucault's critique of power depends on criteria from the "analytic of the true" (the Enlightenment tradition) that his criticism undermines.[66] In the terms we have been using, not only does Foucault offer his readers an alternative style, he provides them with a detailed criticism of their values and their limitations. Yet the criticism is attached only to a desire for change, not to an argument for legitimate change.

Deleuze's *Foucault* defends this style of criticism as a Nietzschean mode of the history of the present. He sees Foucault as having written a series of historical ontologies that examine the diverse conditions of power, truth, and the self. But these conditions are never apodictic, they are problematic:[67]

> No solution is transferable from one epoch to another, but there can be encroachments where the penetration of problematic fields which form the "data" of an old problem are reactivated in another.[68]

However, Deleuze recognizes here the same problem that concerns Habermas: How is one to connect the various historical ontologies? How are concerns for change in the present to be connected to historical ontologies? "Finally," Deleuze writes, "it is practice which constitutes the only continuity from past to present, or inversely, the manner in which the present explicates the past."[69]

Once again the absence of a transhistorical criterion to connect the various epochs (clearly what Habermas thinks he can provide) with one another and with the present is filled by appeal to a practice. For Foucault's Greeks, who did not *feel* the absent criterion because they were not looking for it, "style" was the equivalent of "practice." For Deleuze's Nietzsche, the connection was made by a happy reading of the eternal return. The selectivity of the eternal return insured a form of progress that was not dependent on negativity; real (nonreactive) practice presumably gets selected. Present and past are linked by a cycle that forces out those (reactive) elements most deserving of criticism.

At the end of his recent essay, Deleuze rightly brings together the themes of his own interpretation of Nietzsche with his reading of Foucault.[70] In regard to the future, they can "indicate only germs [ébauches], in the embryological sense, not yet functional."[71] And in pages that will be either frightening or invigorating, depending on one's appreciation of science fiction, he speaks of both the difficulty of knowing the future, and the importance of imagining a future in which new forces will be liberated. The liberation of these new forces includes what Foucault called the "death of man," and what Nietzsche named the "superman." In the final sentence of the work, which may recall Heidegger's remark that only a god can save us now, Deleuze adds: "As Foucault would say, the death of man is much less than the disappearance of existing men, and much more than the change of a concept; it is the advent of a new form, neither God nor man, of which one can hope that it will not be worse than its two predecessors."[72] By now, of course, we know that there can be no foundation for this hope. Foucault might have added that what is possible is a style of life in which it could be manifest, but we must recall that his focus on style of life, or on the construction of the subject, is apolitical — or at least a politics reduced to the private. Foucault's earlier work not only dismantled the notion of progress but also undermined the notion of social hope on which his own cultural criticisms fed.[73] In his later turn toward the subject, Foucault finds perhaps a personal hope, an *ethos* that provides a possibility of individual freedom within any regime of discourse. The distance between individual freedom through the construction of a style of life and political freedom may, however, be as great as the distance between epistemes. In any case, it is a distance, according to Foucault, about which we are reduced to silence.

Conclusion

The Nietzschean approach to history through an analysis of discourse insures that politics will occur in a realm that can not be legitimated, because this realm either is that about which nothing can be said or is itself gestured to as the practical connection between ways of thinking and experiencing. The point here is not that an approach to (and emplotment of) historical events in a grand narrative legitimates, while the Nietzschean notion of interpretation critiques. Historicist connections between history and knowing can be an important way of legitimating a critique or validating a form of delegitimation. Perhaps we can conclude that the discursive turn in French thought "represented" by Foucault is a radicalized strategy of delegitimation, because it makes no attempt to save itself from those things which are undermined. But this would be a strange use of the word radical, for the result of the practice can be a return, dizzying but a return nonetheless, to the status quo. I do not question the personal commitment of Foucault to a certain style of politics. However, his inability, or refusal, to justify that politics makes it a *personal* commitment, rather than a commitment that is in principle open to discussion, that is, a political one. As such, it is an option, a style, perhaps, soon to be outmoded.

It may be objected that what counts as political here is foreign to the redefinition of the political for which Foucault deserves partial credit. His effort to think through how we have become subjects who desire certain forms of legitimation indicates that he took seriously the political problem of legitimation even as he tried to historicize it. His last books are an extraordinary attempt to escape these questions. Genuinely bothered by them, and unable to speak to them in a satis-factory way (even for himself), Foucault turned to genealogy for an understanding of their limited significance. Maybe our search for con-nections and criteria is as culture-specific as our sexual practices and our diets. To imagine and reflect on a culture that did not desire these connections and criteria might help us abandon our own search for them.

Foucault's work, like much contemporary history and theory that focuses on discourse as the object of knowledge, leaves us with radical strategies of delegitimation without much attention to the reasons why we might want to use such strategies in relation to specific problems. These reasons cannot be reduced to epistemological issues, and thus the problem of political legitimation is not obviated by recent attempts to move beyond epistemology and foundationalism. New forms of legitimation might consist of narratives linking analyses of injustice with the needs of particular, historically contingent, communities. These forms of legitimation would also be expressions of political identification on the part of intellectuals; neither the forms nor the expressions would be foundational, but instead would be pragmatic. These prag-matic constructions would not depend on the necessity of discovering one's natural community or real comrades. Instead, they would point toward the possibility of acknowledging commonality in the service of particular, contingent, but also vital political goals.

Despite his important political commitments, Foucault never elaborated a way of "thinking otherwise" that went beyond a style of delegitimation. This style (happily) does not provide us with a method of historical analysis, or even with a "philosophy of discourse." Foucault's work does, however, leave us with provocations, suggestions and questions which can stimulate our capacity to work through what is at stake in trying to think and live within discourse and without foundations.

Notes

1. See Michael S. Roth, *Knowing and History: Appropriations of Hegel in 20th Century France* (Ithaca: Cornell Univ., 1988), passim.

2. Foucault, *"Theatrum Philosophicum,"* *Critique*, 282 (1970), p. 899. Modified translation in *Language, Counter-Memory, Practice*, ed. Donald F. Bouchard (Ithaca: Cornell Univ., 1977), pp. 185, 186.

3. A favorite trick of intellectual historians is to see the unity of a life tying together the parts of an *oeuvre*. Although this may sometimes be helpful, there is clearly no good reason for supposing the unity (even the intelligibility) of a life. There are currently a number of projects under way that deal with Foucault's biography: Jerrold Seigel's study of marginality in French intellectual history, and biographies of Foucault by Didier Eribon and James Miller. See also the early intellectual biography by Alan Sheridan, *Michel Foucault: The Will to Truth* (London: Tavistook, 1980).

4. Deleuze, *Nietzsche et la philosophie* (Paris: Presses Universitaires de France, 1962), p. 9.

5. See the interview with Gérard Raulet (first published in 1983) collected in *Michel Foucault: Politics, Philosophy, Culture*, ed. Lawrence D. Kritzman (New York: Routledge, 1988), pp. 30–33.

6. Foucault, "Le retour de la morale," *Les nouvelles* (28 juin–5 juillet 1984), p. 40.

7. Foucault, "Nietzsche, Marx et Freud," in *Nietzsche* (Paris: Les Editions de Minuit, 1967), p. 185. Hereafter NMF.

8. NMF, p. 187.

9. NMF, p. 190.

10. NMF, p. 191.

11. NMF, pp. 188–89. In 1964 Foucault still held fast to the notion of a pure *expérience de la folie*. For a critical appraisal, see Jacques Derrida, "Cogito et histoire de la folie," in *L'Ecriture et la Difference* (Paris: Seuil, 1967) pp. 51–97. Derrida's critique was originally made in a lecture given in 1963. For a historical treatment of Foucault's early views on madness, see Pierre Macherey, "Aux sources de l'*Histoire de la folie*: une rectification à ses limites," in *Critique*, 471–72 (août/septembre 1986), pp. 753–74.

12. NMF, p. 191. See also Foucault's resistance to adding Hegel to the trilogy in the discussion following the article, p. 194.

13. NMF, pp. 195–96.

14. Foucault, "Nietzsche, généalogie et l'histoire," in *Hommage à Jean Hyppolite* (Paris: Press Universitaires de France, 1971), p. 146. Hereafter NGH.

15. NGH, p. 158. Modified English translation from *Language, Counter-Memory, Practice*, pp. 151–52. Hereafter LCP.

16. See Michael S. Roth, Review of Barry Cooper's *The End of History*, in *Political Theory*, 13:1 (1985), pp. 148–52, and Michael S. Roth, *Knowing*

and History, ch. 2 and 5.

17. Thus Dewey can be rightly seen as legitimating hope and solidarity, even if he was a critic of his time. The contrast with Foucault is powerfully drawn by Richard Rorty in "Method, Social Science and Social Hope," in *Consequences of Pragmatism* (Minneapolis: Univ. of Minnesota, 1982), 203–8.

18. NGH, p. 153; LCP, p. 147.

19. NGH, p. 158.

20. NGH, p. 159. The rejection of absolutes is clearly aimed at what Foucault calls the Platonic tradition (nature as absolute), and the Hegelian tradition (end, or *sens*, of history as absolute). It is also aimed at the semiotics to the extent that it strives for a systematic (i.e., more than interpretive) understanding of past interpretations.

21. NGH, p. 160; LCP, pp. 153, 154. For a critique of "continuous history," see Foucault, *The Archaeology of Knowledge*, trans. A. M. Sheridan Smith (New York: Harper & Row, 1972), p. 216.

22. NGH, pp. 167; LCP, p. 162. Hayden White has talked about Foucault's project as a "disremembrance of things past," in "Foucault Decoded: Notes from the Underground," *History and Theory*, 12 (1973), pp. 23–54; reprinted in *Tropics of Discourse: Essays in Cultural Criticism* (Baltimore: Johns Hopkins Univ., 1978), p. 233.

23. LCP, p. 163.

24. NGH, p. 168.

25. NGH, p. 169; LCP, p. 162.

26. NGH, p. 168.

27. See Derrida's critique of Foucault cited above, and Foucault's response, *Histoire de la folie* (Paris: Editions Gallimard, 1972), pp. 583–603. See also the critical commentary on the "nondebate" by Alain Renault and Luc Ferry in *La Pensée 68* (Paris: Editions Gallimard, 1985), pp. 120–29, and the historical essay by Macherey cited above. Georges Canguilhem has underlined the centrality of *Histoire de la folie* in Foucault's *oeuvre* as a whole, "Sur l'*Histoire de la folie* en tant qu'événement," *débat*, 41 (1986), pp. 37–40.

28. Foucault, *The Birth of the Clinic: An Archaeology of Medical Perception*, trans. A. M. Sheridan Smith (New York: Vintage, 1973), p. xix.

29. I am drawing here on the first part of my "Foucault's 'History of the Present,'" *History and Theory*, 20:1 (1981), pp. 32–46. See also the 1984 interview in which Foucault says about his work on the history of prisons: "I wanted to make it [the penitentiary situation] intelligible, and, therefore, criticizable." In *Foucault: Politics, Philosophy, Culture*, p. 101.

30. Foucault, *The Order of Things: An Archaeology of the Human Sciences* (New York: Vintage, 1970), p. 384.

31. Ibid., p. 207. See Roth, "Foucault's 'History of the Present,'" p. 39.

32. Since I am interested here in Foucault as a Nietzschean thinker, I have stressed the role genealogy has played throughout his work, rather than

dividing his work into archaeological and genealogical phases. For a subtle, nuanced discussion using this division, see Paul Rabinow and Hubert L. Dreyfus, *Michel Foucault: Beyond Structuralism and Hermeneutics*, 2d ed. (Chicago: Univ. of Chicago, 1983), especially pp. 104–25. Rabinow and Dreyfus see a clear shift in Foucault's interests away from discourse after May 1968.

33. Foucault, *Surveiller et punir: Naissance de la prison*, (Paris: Editions Gallimard, 1975); trans. by Alan Sheridan as *Discipline and Punish: The Birth of the Prison* (New York: Pantheon, 1977), p. 27.

34. On Foucault's truth/power connection see, for example, Rabinow and Dreyfus, *Michel Foucault*, pp. 126–42, and Larry Shiner, "Reading Foucault: Anti-Method and the Geneaology of Power-Knowledge," *History and Theory*, 21 (1982), pp. 382–98.

35. Foucault, "Truth and Power," in *Power/Knowledge: Selected Interviews and Other Writings*, ed. C. Gordon (New York: Pantheon, 1980), p. 114.

36. In a 1978 interview, Foucault claimed that he aimed to dissolve discontinuities in favor of showing the intelligibility of practices. Here he is simply backing (rightly) away from the paradox of establishing discontinuity as a principle in a philosophy of history. Foucault's work aims to make history's fragmentation and heterogeneity intelligible without appeals to foundations or goals. If one rejects looking for a *sens de l'histoire*, one cannot find this *sens* in discontinuity. See *Foucault: Politics, Philosophy, Culture*, p. 100.

37. Ibid., pp. 114–15.

38. See Remo Bodel, "Foucault: pouvoir, politique et maîtrise de soi," *Critique*, 471–72 (1986), p. 908.

39. Note Deleuze's remark that "we have no need to totalize that which is invariably totalized on the side of power" ("Intellectuals and Power," in LCP, p. 212). In an interview conducted not long before his death, Foucault commented on how the ties between the events of 1968 and Marxism broke the latter's grip on political thinking in France; see *The Foucault Reader*, ed. Paul Rabinow (New York: Pantheon, 1984), pp. 385–86.

40. Foucault, "Truth and Power," p. 126.

41. Deleuze says that Foucault's fundamental lesson was the "indignity of speaking for others," and "the theoretical fact [?] that only those directly concerned can speak in a practical way on their own behalf" ("Intellectuals and Powers," p. 209). See in this regard Mark Poster, *Foucault, Marxism and History: Mode of Production vs. Mode of Information*, pp. 153–57.

42. At the end of his life, Foucault spoke about the rights of persons being "immanent in the discussion." It is important to note, though, that Foucault was talking about discussion at least partly in contradistinction to politics, rather than linking discussion and participation. See *The Foucault Reader*, pp. 381–82.

43. Foucault, "Truth and Power," p. 132.

44. Ibid., p. 133.

45. Veyne admires greatly his friend's "warrior ethic," which includes an

understanding that the enemy has good reasons for fighting, too. "Le dernier Foucault et sa morale," *Critique*, 471–72 (1986), pp. 937–38.

46. Foucault, "Truth and Power," p. 133.

47. See my description of this condition in "The Ironist's Cage," *Political Theory*, 19 (Aug. 1991), pp. 419–32.

48. Ian Hacking points to this same "gap," but does not view it as a weakness in Foucault's work. Hacking claims that Foucault, like Kant, disconnected freedom (and politics) from knowledge, precisely because there are no truths to know about the good life. It is not clear, though, that the fact that there are no truths to know about the good life requires that we undermine our capacity to discuss our projects to construct a better life; that is that we undermine our capacity for political participation. See "Self-improvement," in *Foucault: A Critical Reader*, ed. David C. Hoy (Oxford: Basil Blackwell, 1986), pp. 235–40. I called attention to Foucault's Kant-like position in "Foucault's 'History of the Present'," p. 38.

49. See the critique of Deleuze's reading of Nietzsche in Michael S. Roth, *Knowing and History*, 194–201.

50. See Roth, *Knowing and History*, pp. 94–124, and Roth, "A Problem of Recognition: Alexandre Kojève and the End of History," *History and Theory*, 24 (1985), pp. 293–306.

51. See Deleuze, "Écrivain non: Un nouveau cartographie," *Critique*, 343 (décembre 1975), pp. 1207–27; and *Foucault*, pp. 31–51.

52. Charles Taylor, "Foucault on Freedom and Truth," *Political Theory*, 12:2 (1984), p. 168.

53. Foucault, private communication, 1981. Rabinow and Dreyfus seem to accept this defense; see "Habermas et Foucault: Qu'est-ce-que l'âge d'homme," *Critique*, 471–72 (1986), pp. 857–72; English version, "What Is Maturity? Habermas and Foucault on 'What Is Enlightenment?'" in *Foucault: A Critical Reader*, pp. 109–22. The defense is repeated in the interviews in *The Foucault Reader*, where Foucault goes so far as to say that he "never tried to analyze anything whatsoever from the point of view of politics," p. 385.

54. Foucault, "The Subject and Power," in Rabinow and Dreyfus, *Michel Foucault*, p. 211. Even if he refused to thematize his various political gestures, his appeal to them is an appeal to what he thought was "progressive" at any particular moment. Foucault has been taken to task for his inability to provide a ground for positive action, or for his own critique. See, for example, Michael Walzer, "The Politics of Michel Foucault," in *Foucault: A Critical Reader*, pp. 51–68; Nancy Frazer, "Michel Foucault: A 'Young Conservative'?" *Ethics*, 96 (1985), pp. 165–84; Habermas, *Der philosophische Diskurs der Moderne*, chs. 9 & 10. David Hoy puts these criticisms into an intellectual context in his introduction to *Foucault: A Critical Reader*, pp. 1–25. Foucault "responds" to some of those criticisms in the interviews in the *Foucault Reader* by saying he belongs to no political group.

55. Rabinow and Dreyfus, *Michel Foucault*, p. 212.

56. This part of the agenda only becomes clear in Volumes 2 and 3. Volume 1 is more concerned with showing how the idea of "repression" is

inadequate for making sense of sexuality, in part, because power is creative and not just repressive. See, for example the interview with Foucault, "On the Genealogy of Ethics: An overview of Work in Progress," in Rabinow and Dreyfus, *Michel Foucault*, pp. 229—52.

57. Hayden White has written provocatively on the importance of rhetoric and style in Foucault's work before that work had an explicit concern with style. "Michel Foucault," in *Structuralism and Since* (Oxford: Oxford Univ., 1979), pp. 81–115.

58. Foucault, *Histoire de la sexualité*, 2, *L'usage des plaisirs* (Paris: Editions Gallimard, 1984), p. 15.

59. Ibid., p. 14.

60. Ibid., p. 75.

61. Ibid., pp. 155–56. See also, for example, pp. 30, 106, 107, 111, 133, 224, 248, 275–78; vol. 2, pp. 49, 58, 85, 116, 117, 272–73.

62. Yet another way in which Foucault's project might be seen as a strange historical complement to Kant's. See Roth, "Foucault's 'History of the Present,'" pp. 38–39.

63. Deleuze points out that Foucault's "heraclitism" is more profound than Heidegger's, because he goes on to say—with a discretion that gives a content to his notion of irresponsibility—"phenomenology is too pacific, it has glorified too many things." *Foucault* (Paris: Les Editions de Minuit, 1986), p. 120.

64. As Deleuze nicely puts it, for Foucault there is no Greek miracle, as there is for Heidegger. *Foucault*, p. 121.

65. Foucault, "Le retour de la morale," p. 41.

66. Habermas, "Une flèche dans le coeur du temps présent," *Critique*, 471–72 (1986), p. 799. See also the article by Rabinow and Dreyfus in the same issue, "Habermas et Foucault: Qu'est-ce-que l'âge d'homme," pp. 857–72. English versions of both of these articles are in Hoy's collection. The Habermas page reference in the English edition is 107–8. Foucault, with Habermas in mind, talks of a "consensus model" as a critical principle, but not a "regulatory principle," in *The Foucault Reader*, p. 379.

67. Deleuze, *Foucault*, p. 122.

68. Ibid.

69. Ibid.

70. See Deleuze, *Nietzsche et la philosophie*, and *Nietzsche* (Paris: Presses Universitaires de France, 1967).

71. Deleuze, *Foucault*, p. 139.

72. Ibid., p. 141.

73. See Rorty, "Method, Social Science and Social Hope," 206–8. Habermas's criticism of Foucault, cited above, is also relevant here, although social hope need not be founded on criteria acceptable to the Enlightenment tradition.

5

Lyotard
From Libidinal Aesthetics to Language Games

John Johnston

Jean-Francois Lyotard, born in 1924 in Versailles, belongs to the same brilliant generation of French philosophers and intellectuals that would include Gilles Deleuze, Jacques Derrida, Michel Foucault, Michel Serres, and Jean Baudrillard. It is a generation that rejected Hegelian metaphysics and the phenomenology of Jean-Paul Sartre and Maurice Merleau-Ponty in order to explore a new problematic of concepts derived from the linguistic model of Ferdinand de Saussure and new readings of Nietzsche, Marx, and Freud. "Structuralism" and its self-critical aftermath "poststructuralism" may be the labels under which the diverse writings of this generation are most often grouped, but the individual itinerary or *démarche* that each of these thinkers has followed will usually tell us far more about them than the sometimes misleading attempts to give them a collective identity.

In the case of Lyotard, there is a further danger incurred by this logic of group identification, for since the publication of his book *The Postmodern Condition*, Lyotard has become a nearly obligatory reference in arguments *pro* and *contra* "postmodernism." Though in many ways the least representative of Lyotard's books, this elegant and precise "report on the condition of knowledge in the most highly developed societies" rapidly gained widespread recognition in the English-speaking world by introducing philosophical concepts like "language games" and "metanarratives" into what until then had been a debate about aesthetic criteria and historical periodization.[1] For Lyotard himself the book constituted something of a break with the

125

preceding period of his writing, which had extended roughly from 1968 to 1978, during which he had tried to work out the implications for art, politics and critical theory of his notion of a "libidinal economy," or the transmission and circulation of investments of desire (libido) as "intensities" both within and against the capitalist political economy. Since *The Postmodern Condition*, however, Lyotard has been mainly preoccupied with ethical questions like the problem of injustice, even though, as in the case of his most recent major work, *The Differend*, these questions are posed in the terms of his own highly singular form of discourse analysis.

Indeed, looking over the full spectrum of Lyotard's varied writings, it is apparent that they in no way constitute a unified stream of philosophical reflections posed from within such traditionally defined realms as language, aesthetics, politics, and ethics; instead, they enact a series of theoretical interventions that peremptorily break into and across accepted academic disciplines and genres. In so doing, they do not so much add up collectively to a systematic and coherent philosophy as mark out a trail of thought-events, defining a role for a new "postmodern" philosophy in the process.

The Militant Professor

After completing his university training in philosophy and literature in 1950, Lyotard taught philosophy for two years at a lycée in Constantine, Algeria, where he soon became involved in the movement for Algerian independance. Then, in 1954, he published *La Phénomenologie* in the "Que sais-je" series intended primarily for university students. Hardly a "primer" for initiates, however, this dense first book assesses the contributions of Edmund Husserl and the phenomenological method to the study of psychology, sociology, and history.[2] But rather than settling into a conventional academic career, Lyotard soon turned to radical politics and the life of a militant intellectual. For fifteen years, he will later write, he "neglected all forms of activity and sensibility" other than those directly connected with the cause of "combatting exploitation and alienation."[3] Having joined *Socialism ou Barbarie* ("Either Socialism or Barbarism"), an organization of left-wing workers and intellectuals founded by Cornelius Castoriadis and Claude Lefort expressly in order to critique both the established forms of class struggle and alternatives like anarchism, Trotskyism, and Stalinism, Lyotard "gave up all writing except notes and studies on political topics that were published either in our review or in a mimeographed paper we gave out to workers early in the morning at the gates of factories or on the occasion of demonstrations."[4] In 1964, following a schism within the group, Lyotard joined *Pouvoir Ouvrier* ("Worker Power"), but further dissension led to its dissolution in 1966.

In the following two-year period of "political reclusion" Lyotard wrote *Discours, Figure*, an ambitious philosophical synthesis of linguistic and Freudian theory applied to poetry and visual art that would serve as his doctoral dissertation and, when published in 1971, become a landmark of poststructuralist theory. While teaching philosophy at Nanterre, Lyotard once again engaged in forms of political activism, this time with the *Movement du 22 mars*, which would later become the spontaneist, antiauthoritarian wing of the May 1968 demonstrations. Like most of his generation, Lyotard was profoundly influenced by the events of May, but unlike most of them he felt that all of his work led up to and prepared him for what he described in *Dérive à partir de Marx et Freud* as "not a crisis" but an entry into a "new period of history."[5] In the introduction to this collection of essays written between 1968 and 1971, Lyotard stated that the movement of 1968 "seemed to us to do and say on a grand scale what we had sketched out in miniature in our words and actions as if by anticipation"; at the same time, "it invented yet many more beautiful things we had never thought of."[6] Moreover, the events of May 1968 seem to have brought to a head Lyotard's intellectual itinerary since the 1950s, now leaving him, as the title of the essays suggest, "adrift from Marx and Freud."

In the aftermath of May 1968, Lyotard participated in the large but only partly successful effort to channel the movement's political energies into the French university system. As a professor of philosophy at the newly established and "experimental" University of Paris at Vincennes (later Saint-Denis, after Vincennes was razed by the French government), he published *Des Dispositifs pulsionnels*, a second collection of essays written between 1971 and 1973, and then, in 1974, *Économie libidinale*, a virulently antiacademic book that pushed to its ultimate conclusions his own particular amalgamation of Nietzsche, Marx, and Freud. Though a number of significant short works would follow, in retrospect the second half of the 1970s seems clearly transitional.[7] In fact, the year 1979, when Lyotard published both *The Postmodern Condition* and the extended dialogues with Jean-Loup Thébaud under the title *Au juste*, marks a clean break with the work centered on libidinal aesthetics and politics that had characterized this period of his career.

In the late 1970s Lyotard also began to travel extensively as a visiting professor to many universities abroad: Berkeley, San Diego, Johns Hopkins, and Wisconsin from 1976–78, São Paulo, Siegen (in West Germany), and Montreal from 1978–80. Meanwhile, in France, as director of the Collège International de Philosophie, he worked with GREPH, an organization of professors formed to radically revise the teaching of philosophy in the French lycée. In 1985 he organized *Les Immateriaux*, an internationally acclaimed exposition of "postmodern" art and technology for the Pompidou Art Center in Paris. Lyotard currently holds a distinguished professorship in the Critical Theory Program at the University of California at Irvine.

From Figure to Libidinal Apparatus

Discours, Figure proposes a double critique aimed at phenomenology on the one hand and structuralism on the other. Against the latter's "textualization" of the world, Lyotard argues that "the given is not a text, that there is within it a density, or rather a constitutive difference, which is not to be read but seen: and that this difference, and the immobile mobility which reveals it, is what is continually forgotten in the process of signification."[8] In this sense the book is indeed a defense of the eye, as Lyotard declares at the outset. However, it is not the eye of the phenomenologist that is privileged here, precisely because language does not "translate into available significations a meaning initially captive in the thing and in the world" (DF, 58). Following Saussure and the structural linguistics he inaugurates, Lyotard assumes that language is a quasi-autonomous system of internally differentiated terms which segment and determine meanings that in no way can be said to inhere in a prelinguistic world, concealed somehow in its silent depths, waiting for a speaker to give them utterance. The eye that interests Lyotard, therefore, is that stranger eye, "installed on the edge of discourse" in the primal tearing away of the subject from a world he or she can never fully inhabit again after the entry into language.

With this eye in view (or mind), Lyotard proceeds by playing phenomenology and structuralism off against one another; methodologically, he seeks to "deconstruct" their antithetical assumptions by showing that on both sides there is a necessary reduction of "difference" to an opposition.[9] What is at stake is a reading of poetry and painting that will reveal how they not only resist but disrupt the rational, homogenized space of normal discourse and perception. Lyotard uses the term "figure" to designate these instances of the nondiscursive in poetry and the nonperceptible in painting. But by "figure" Lyotard intends something different from what is usually meant by the terms "figurative" or "figuration." In fact, "figure" in Lyotard's vocabulary has nothing to do with an aesthetics of representation. Instead, it points to an opening both inside and outside of discourse: outside, as a radical exteriority of the visual, which even when transformed into a sign retains a hidden content; inside, as a space within language where the coded intervals of the signifying system are transgressed and an alterity within discourse appears.

Lyotard's version of deconstruction is thus similar to Derridean deconstruction in so far as it opens the text to an "outside." But for Derrida the outside of the text is precisely that which *in* the text makes

self-reflection possible and at the same time limits it.[10] Hence the
importance he accords to the notion of the blindspot. For Lyotard, on
the other hand, the "outside" is what lies beyond the discursive power
of language and which constantly menaces the latter's hegemony. In
fact, reading through *Discours, Figure,* we notice a shift in the connotations of the term "figure" that mirrors its two deconstructive aspects:
in the book's earlier sections the figural is what allows us to distinguish
between the truth [*verité*] and knowledge [*connaissance*], between
orders of visibility which are "seeable" but not "readable"; but in later
sections Lyotard uncovers a "connivance of desire" with the figural
which is now analyzed in relation to the libidinal drives, as the trace or
evidence of a desire that disrupts representation and rational discourse,
or that stirs beneath or within or beyond representation. This transgressive, disordering, and dispersive effect of the figural Lyotard
associates with the unconscious primary processes and the death drive
postulated by Freud.

It is generally well known that phenomenology has never been
able to deal satisfactorily with the unconscious, and least of all with the
"energetic" model of the unconscious that Freud proposes in his essays
on metapsychology. The world spreads its visible face before an observer,
but what lies on the other side of each object or the horizon that
encircles him or her is in no sense "unconscious": It is simply the not-
yet-visible, or the not-visible-from-here. While a shift in perspective
offers a new set of objects (or a new array of their profiles and
therefore a new horizon of visibility), phenomenologists and gestalt
psychologists have had no difficulty showing how easily these divergent
perspectives are brought into rapid accord, and the lived perceptions
of the observer's body synthesized into a continuous, homogeneous
space. A simple lateral motion, however, brings into awareness a
perceptual difference not reduceable to the simple opposition of
the visible and the invisible, an object and its backside or invisible
face. For with a slight twist of the head the assumed orientation of
center-periphery is suddenly destabilized, this homogeneous space
disintegrates, and in the brief moment before it is restabilized and
another center-periphery orientation assumed, we sense a qualitative
difference — not an opposition — between two kinds of perception, one
centered and clearly focused, the other peripheral and diffuse. To
these two qualitatively different kinds of perception correspond two
different experiences of space: the space that appears directly before
us and admits of focus and attentive scrutiny, and the space that eludes
direct vision and spreads out around precisely what we don't look at.

Lyotard argues that these two different kinds of space onto which
our perception thus opens out yield an "alterity" that denies any
simple opposition between the visible and invisible sides of an object in
the perceptual field:

> Spatial difference is still more paradoxical than the gap which "gives"
> the invisibility of the other side of the thing in the gestaltist articulation,
> it is also more rudimentary, it is the ungraspable distance between the
> periphery of the visual field and its focus. This gap gives much more
> than the here and the elsewhere, than the recto and the verso, it gives
> the qualitative discontinuity of the two spaces in their simultaneity,
> the curved, crepuscular, evanescent, lateral space of the first peripheral
> contact with something and the stabilized, constant, central rectangular
> space of the grasp in the foveal zone. This grasp is a taking, a
> prehension, a taking possession, its order is that of the hunter's grip,
> or the worker's or linguist's; the first contact, the entry of something
> at the edge of the field, that's a visual alterity, an invisible of the
> visible; and yet not simply the back of what is grasped face-on in the
> center. This fragile, oblique tact gives the visual event which comes
> before even the outline. (DF, 158)

Furthermore, this "difference" at the interior of the visible is what
makes possible the visual *as* an event. Emerging not out of an opposition
between the visible and the invisible, but out of the "other" of the
visible, so to speak, the visual event cannot be conceived in negative
terms, even though it is neither recognizable nor can it become an
object of knowledge. Precisely how the visual as event eludes attempts
to attribute meaning (or predication) to it involves two distinct kinds of
relationship in Lyotard's account: the first has to do with manner in
which the body or the eye as part of the body inhabits these two
different kinds of space; the second with the kind of relationship with
language that is thereby implied.

In considering centered or focalized space, what matters first and
foremost is the body's mobility, the fact that it moves about and re-
positions itself within a space that remains homogeneous and "readable" in terms of geometrically constant relations. In fact, it is because
the eye can move around, changing angle and/or spatial vantage point,
that the body is felt to be in a space that remains constant. This is the
knowable space of the common or shared world, not exactly the
completely rationalized space of perspective systems, but that in which
visual givens are absorbed and integrated into the synthetic constructions
that make up "visual experience" and which phenomenology convinc-
ingly describes as a form of knowledge. It is within this space, in which
objects are recognized and inscribed in a semantic field, that we give
our focused attention. Now, Lyotard will argue that it is precisely
through the act of attention that language — language understood
in the Saussurian sense of a system of signs based on regulated oppositions — comes to inhabit the space of visual experience:
"attention," he says, "writes space, traces in it lines and triangles; for
its colours are like phonemes, units which work by opposition and not

by motivation" (DF, 155). It is therefore because the visual world can be ordered as a set of oppositions that it makes sense to talk about the "language of painting" or about art as a semiotic system of signs manipulated by the artist. Lyotard himself cites the example of Andre Lhote, who theorizes both a vocabulary and syntax of abstract painting.[11]

In contrast to this focalized space that assumes the body's mobility in the world, the unfocused, "soft" space of peripheral vision is only experienced when the eye is stationary, in a state of immobility. Lyotard thinks that it was precisely this ungraspable sense of space that Cézanne sought to capture while standing immobile for hours before Mont Sainte-Victoire. Not only in the shifting impressions of color and value but in the collapse of space itself as a geometrical organization, the visual reveals itself as pure "donation," an event that cannot be re-cuperated or absorbed into a system of oppositions. Feeling itself is part and parcel of this visual event, not something that could be said to occur later as a "response." For as Lyotard points out, emotion would be impossible "if our bodily hold on the world were not uncertain in its basis, if the possibility of a non-world were not given at the same time as its certainty" (DF, 137). This possibility of a "non-world" is both the condition of the visual as event and its ultimate import. As the "other" or "difference" silently menacing the very possibility that visual experience can have meaning or significance, it guarantees that sensory experience, *pace* Hegel and the dialectic of negation-sublation de-scribed in the first chapter of *The Phenomenology of Mind*, can never be completely raised up and translated into discursive meaning.

There is, then, within visual experience, a difference that is not recognizable, not knowable, that is in effect not readable. And not, paradoxically, because the visual world is inadequately articulated with linguistic expression; in fact, language always already inhabits it, trans-forming its oppositions into signs, which now stand for what henceforth will only have to be recognized and no longer seen. The more legible the world, the harder it is to really see, since we only have to look out at it in order to make our way through it. But in the immobilizing of perception, in those experiences which seem to involve something akin to what the Russian Formalists called the "defamiliarization of percep-tion," this world disintegrates, and the strange, the unrecognizable, and the un- or nonworldly appears.

With certain reservations, the status of discursive language in *Discours, Figure* is roughly analogous to the status of focalized space in the discussion above. Lyotard assumes, as a point of departure, Saussure's theory and the modifications brought to structural linguistics by Roman Jakobson and Emile Benveniste. According to the now-familiar view, Saussure theorized language (*langue*, the system, as opposed to *parole*, the individual speech act) as a synchronic system of signs defined only by their diacritical differences, without any "positive" or self-identical terms. Thus,

> the meaning [*sens*] of a term depends on the presence or absence of a neighboring term. From the system, we arrive at the idea of value, not that of meaning. Thus it will be seen that signification is determined by what surrounds [the term]. The word does not exist without a signified and a signifier: but the signified is only the summary of linguistic value and presupposes the play of terms among themselves.... What is in the world is only ever determined by the concourse of what exists around it, associatively and syntagmatically. (Quoted from Godel, in DF, 97)

In a complex series of critical moves Lyotard proceeds to complicate the Saussurian theory. First, he gives this "flat" space of linguistic value — he calls it the "table of language" — a depth by introducing into consideration the deictic signs (like here, now, I, you) that allow the speaker to position himself or herself along an axis of designation *not* assimilable to the diacritical relations among clustered terms in the closed, linguistic system. Yet Lyotard is not interested in merely playing off a language theory which privileges designation against the Saussurian theory, which privileges signification; he seeks, instead, that space of difference within their opposition and out of which the figural may emerge:

> Signification does not exhaust meaning [*sens*], but signification plus designation doesn't either. We can't remain in the alternative of these two spaces, the space of the system and the space of the subject, between which discourse slides. There is another space, a figural space. It must be supposed as buried; it gives itself neither to be seen nor to be thought. It is indicated in a lateral or fugitive fashion at the heart of discourse and perception as that which troubles them. It is the proper space of desire, the stakes of the struggle that painters and poets never ceased to wage against the return of the Ego and the return of the text. (DF, 135)

This figural space is invisible to the Saussurian linguist, who must take the sign itself as a referent in his own discourse in order to construct the linguistic table. What is thereby repressed is the very act of positioning by which the linguist demonstrates that language is made up of signs, an act which at one stroke also converts everything language designates into objects-as-signs. But, Lyotard argues, as soon as the object designated becomes a sign, it acquires a positionality by which "it conceals a hidden content within its manifest identity, and it reserves another face for another view focused upon it." Lyotard means by this that any designated object caught up in language becomes a multi-dimensional sign inadequately accounted for by the Saussurian "table of language."[12] In the very act of designation the sign acquires a "thickness" or opacity absent from the transparent Saussurian sign, a thickness that can even redound on the word itself in its graphic or scriptive identity. This opacity or thickness in the sign brings about or makes possible an "otherness" of meaning within signification, sometimes disrupting discursive meaning and sometimes playing against it. In Mallarmé's poem *Un Coup de dés jamais n'abolira le hazard*, the words on the page inhabit a graphic space that must also be viewed independently from the reading and that provokes an interaction between sensory and discursive elements. As the reader moves back and forth between reading the words and looking at their visible disposition on the page, rhythmically crossing between intelligible and sensory orders, a figural space emerges.[13]

A poem by e. e. cummings mentioned in passing by Lyotard may provide a more convenient example. In the first eight lines the irregular line spacing and grammatically enjambed syntax open up a space "inhabited" by the figural, a space describable neither in linguistic nor imagistic terms:

> there is a here and
> that here was a
> town (and the town is
> so aged the ocean
> wanders the streets are so
> ancient the houses enter the
>
> people are so feeble the feeble go to
> sleep if the people sit down) . . .
> (Quoted in DF, 319–20)

The lines are enjambed in such a way that the reader is forced to look back again at the normally neutral or invisible graphic space (the disposition of the signifiers on the white page) in an attempt to make sense of the agrammatically run-on assertions that emerge, literally between the parentheses. Here the figural manifests itself as a "deconstruction" of discourse (in Lyotard's sense) through the introduction of elements from an order foreign to discourse (here the activation of the normally inert typographic space) and through the transgression of the norms of discursive syntax.

Following the example of Freud's analysis of the "dreamwork" (in Chapter 6 of *The Interpretation of Dreams*), Lyotard calls this production of a figural sense the poem's "work" [*travail*]:

> Even more than the dream, poetry is interesting not for its content, but for its work. This work does not consist in *externalizing*, in images, forms in which the poet's desire, or ours, is fulfilled once and for all, but in *reversing* the relation of desire to figure, in offering the former, not images in which it will be fulfilled by losing itself, but

forms (here poetic forms) by which it will be reflected as a game, as unbound energy, as process of condensation and displacement, as primary process. Discourse is not poetic because it seduces us, but because, beyond this, it makes us see the *operations* of seduction and the unconscious: lure and truth together, ends and means of desire. (DF, 322)

The example of poetry as a certain kind of "work" performed on normal discourse will allow us now to turn to the central issue in the second half of *Discours, Figure*, namely the relation of the figural to desire. What is clear from the passage above is that the figure does not provide a means for desire's fulfillment; indeed, the figural is not an image allowing the articulation of a phantasy, but assumes for Lyotard a *critical* function by reversing the logic of phantasy in a formalization. But to follow Lyotard's argument here, along this lateral critical tack, we must first consider the significance of negation within discourse.

As Roman Jakobson himself acknowledges, a certain ambiguity in Saussure's notion of value allows structural linguistics to convert differences into oppositions: "All the differences existing between phonemes of a given language can be brought down to binary, simple and indecomposable oppositions between distinctive features. It is therefore possible to break down the phonemes of any language into distinctive features which are themselves indivisible" (Jakobson, quoted by Lyotard DF, 142–43). This binarism, which linguists find operating at every level, from the phonetic to the semantic, in turn supports the forms of propositional negation which for the logician distinguish language as a system of signs from a natural or expressive language. But underlying these forms, Lyotard asserts, is a more fundamental condition of negation posed by the fact of language as a prying loose from the world:

> The No therefore must not be taken only as *the position of exclusion within the system of language*; one can, and it is necessary to, understand it as the position of exclusion *within which all discourse is actualized.* Negation is not only the quality of judgment, it is its possibility; not only a category of discourse, but its place: the speaker has been torn away from that of which he speaks, or that has been torn away from him, and he does not cease, in speaking, to hold it at a distance, as the object of his discourse, in a "vision." (DF, 118, emphases in original)

At this point Lyotard will play Freud against the whole panoply of language theories: Saussure's structuralist account, Merleau-Ponty's phenomenological account, and Gottlob Frege's referential account, by articulating the different forms of negation with what he calls the "negativity of transcendence" theorized by Freud in the essay *Die Verneinung* ("Negation"). Freud's burden in that essay is to explain by what legitimacy he can assert that in his patient's cry "It's *not* my mother" indeed the patient really means "It *is* my mother." In Freud's account the patient's negation is really a de-negation, a denial or disavowal that is at once a repetition of a first and more primal negation, and an acceptance and substitute for its repression. In this way, Freud says, "a repressed thought or image can make its way into consciousness on condition that it is *denied*."[14] But for Freud what is really at issue is the process by which the external, objective world is first constituted for the subject in the dynamic of introjection/rejection (yes/no) enacted by the pleasure-ego and the reality-ego. As a result of the *Entzweiung*, the rupture with the breast and the preworld, the object comes into being and is simultaneously lost, only to be re-presented through the process of phantasy. For Freud, this means that the purpose of reality-testing for the emergent subject is "*not* to discover an object in real perception corresponding to what is imagined, but to re-discover such an object, to convince oneself that it is still there."[15]

Does it therefore follow that language is what holds [*détient*] "this power of rupture with the breast," Lyotard asks (DF, 129)? Is the entry into language, as Jacques Lacan argues, *the* traumatic event, initiating a primal repression that will repeat itself endlessly in the subject's unconscious? Lyotard, following Freud, says no: an ambivalence towards the breast, and towards the mother, comes before language acquisition; what the latter allows is the possibility of appearing as such:

> It is because the infant can avail him/herself of the No of language (*fort*) that the mother's disappearance, her hidden face, its thing-like opacity, can be posed. The quality of negative judgment will be capable of rendering, in the flatness of language, an "equivalent" of the thing. Language does not constitute this opacity, which stems primarily from the alternation of pleasure-unpleasure; but it makes it appear.... The supposed doubling of the pre-world [by language] does not simply open up the distance in which the eye is installed on the edge of discourse. This tearing away produces *in* discourse effects of distortion. A figure is installed in the depths of our speech, which operates as the matrix of these effects; which attacks our words in order to make forms and images with them. (DF, 129)

In short, Lyotard wants to avoid any purely linguistic conception of the unconscious such as Lacan adumbrates, even while asserting that the advent of language necessarily brings about a primal phantasy or matrix-figure that will never cease to disrupt and seek to overturn the order of language. For this reason Lyotard is led to privilege the disruptive aspect of desire, which again, contrary to Lacan's linguistic theory, is seen to operate *on* language rather than merely being articulated within it. As Lyotard states in a chapter entitled "The Dream-work Does Not Think":

> Desire does not speak; it does violence to the order of utterance. This
> violence is primordial: the imaginary fulfillment of desire consists in
> this transgression, which repeats, in the dream work-shop, what
> occurred and continues to occur in the manufacture of the so-called
> primal phantasm. (DF, 239)[16]

Both here and throughout, Lyotard takes advantage of the double
meaning of "desire" in Freud, which designates both wish fulfillment
and the free, unbounded energy of the primary processes.[17] According
to the second sense, desire is a form of libidinal energy that "works"
through ceaseless transformation and metamorphosis, a prime instance
being the "dream-work" that it performs on the "dream-thoughts."
This process, which Freud describes in terms of condensation, displacement, considerations of representability, and secondary revision,
Lyotard will now view as forms of violence "working over" the dream-
thoughts, "compressing the primary text [of the latter], crumpling it
up, folding it, straddling the signs it bears on its surface, fabricating
new units that are not linguistic signs or graphic entities" (DF, 244). In
Lyotard's conception, moreover, the problems raised by the notion of
censorship (how can the censor "know" in advance what to repress or
disguise?) cease to exist: "the disguise does not result from the alleged
deceiving intent of desire; the work itself *is* disguise because it is
violence perpetrated on linguistic space" (DF, 245).

Within this more fully elaborated, Freudian framework the figure
assumes a new complexity: "At the margin of discourse it is the density
within which what I am talking about retires from view; at the heart of
discourse it is its 'form.' Freud himself says as much when he introduces
the term *Phantasie*, which is at once the 'facade' of the dream and a
form forged in its depths. It is a matter of a 'seeing' which has taken
refuge among words, cast out on their own boundaries, irreducible to
saying" (DF, 249). And several pages later, Lyotard states, more
enigmatically, "I am convinced that the figure dwells in discourse like a
phantasm while discourse dwells in the figure like a dream." Such
assertions, in which conceptual oppositions interpenetrate at the level
of statement, as in the penultimate chapter title "Fiscourse, Digure,
Utopia of the Phantasm," underscore Lyotard's insistent attempt to
deconstruct the opposition between discourse and figure by variously
demonstrating how each always inhabits the space of the other, even if
only visible to that "other eye" stationed on the margins of perception
and discourse.

The privilege accorded to art stems from its capacity to make this
deconstruction visible. Evidence of the figural — for what is conventionally or linguistically "unreadable" — is manifest in three distinct
ways. It can be an *image* whose contours are in someway distorted or
ambiguous, or somehow rendered problematic, as in Picasso's drawing

of a sleeping woman which allows several positions of the same body to co-exist at the same time. It can be a *form* which structures the visual but is itself not immediately visible, or only as a "bad" form or gestalt, as in Pollock's drip paintings in which there are no delimiting lines [*traces regulateurs*], where "energy circulates at top speed from one point of the pictorial space to another, prohibiting the eye from resting anywhere, from investing here or there, be it only for a second, its phantasmagoric charge" (DF, 278). Finally, there is the *matrix* that is never visible but whose presence may be inferred as an underlying or primal phantasm which does violence not only to the visual order, but to the intelligibility of every discursive order. Belonging neither to plastic nor textual space, it is difference itself, but without the minimum of opposition necessary for its emergence into the space of discourse, image or form.

This conception of the matrix-figure is derived in large part from Freud's essay "A Child Is Being Beaten," which Lyotard analyzes in some detail. Freud argues that this masturbation fantasy recalled by a patient is a highly revised version of a more primal phantasy which he constructs by hypothesizing an intermediary version. His analysis thus yields three versions, each involving different agents, victims and spectator positions, and hence a multiply distributed subject. Lyotard pushes even further toward an "incompossible multiplicity of versions" which demonstrate that desire is not a legible text, and that it need not disguise itself in order to be represented since it eludes interpretation anyway, due to its "dischronies, polytropisms, and paralogisms." Though it is not directly accessible, the matrix from which the other figures derive as "offshoots" can perhaps be glimpsed through their superimposition, in the confused space in which all three reside together. For the matrix-figure would seem to be the ultimate source from which transgressive desire establishes a "radical connivance" with figurality (DF, 279), repeating itself in the image-figure as an "otherness" at the level of the signified, in the figure-form as an "otherness" at the level of the signifier, with the matrix-figure itself simply designating the ultimate "otherness" of the primal phantasm.

In contradistinction to the artistic techniques analyzed by the Russian Formalists, then, the "figural" only offers itself as a kind of evidence, a manifestation of difference; essentially an "effect," it does not necessarily imply a specific strategy intentionally pursued by the individual artist. Nevertheless, for Lyotard this presence of the figural in the work of art is what insures the work's critical value; it must be distinguished therefore from the merely symptomatic distortions uncovered by typical, run-of-the-mill Freudian analysis. Presumably, in the case of the latter, the work of art functions only as a substitute for an uncontested reality, allowing both artist and viewer to fulfill a more or less interesting desire. If *Discours, Figure* concludes without fully spelling out this distinction, we are left nonetheless with a strong sense of the figural as that which makes a visible "difference" between the two orders of desire: the desire that would fulfill itself in the (dispossessed) space of fantasy, as the eternal repetition of some primal phantasy, and that more disruptive desire through which a kind of reversal (and here Lyotard is vague) short-circuits this repetition in the production of a new visual or poetic event. Essentially opposed to any discursive ordering of desire through the secondary processes, the figural is precisely what resists subsumption into a structure of meaning or representation.

If *Discours, Figure* thus carries us to the threshold of a "libidinal aesthetics," certain problems centering on the critical function of the figure in relation to the artistic transaction, and more generally on the work of art's larger social role, remain unresolved. In several of the essays written from 1968 to 1972 and republished in *Dérive à partir de Marx et Freud* and *Des Dispositifs pulsionnels,* Lyotard addresses both of these concerns, as he moves toward an explicitly "postmodern" critique of representation and a new conception of the artwork as a "libidinal apparatus" productive of "intensities" which circulate within a larger "libidinal economy."[18] The artwork's critical function will now be seen to reside in its capacity to short-circuit interpretation and to destroy the distinction between desire and the unconscious, thereby contesting the entire intellectual superstructure required for the operation of capitalist political economy. In *Économie libidinale*, Lyotard's next book-length work, he will go one step further and envision theoretical discourse itself as simply yet another means of producing intensities, with the entire critique of capitalism now designated as "the desire named Marx."

Although Freud had been a valuable ally in *Discours, Figure*, in order to develop a fully coherent "libidinal aesthetic" Lyotard will now have to mount a critique of several key assumptions in Freudian theory: first, Freud's notion that works of art have a substitutive or vicarious function ("They are there only in place of a missing object, as the accepted formula has it; and they are there only *because* the object is missing"); and second, "the continuing power of the theatrical schema in Freud's unconscious epistemological assumptions."[19] At the heart of the problem is Freud's unquestioning reliance upon the classical notion of representation (even though Freud theorizes the artwork as the representation of a lost object), and more generally his failure to demonstrate the intrinsic necessity of deducing theatrical schema from the economy of drives.

Lyotard points out that Freud's account of his grandchild's game of *fort-da* in *Beyond the Pleasure Principle* presupposes precisely what must be theorized: "To say that the child acts out in his suffering the pain caused by his mother's absence is to take suddenly as given all the components of the theatrical space: an actor-spectator (the child for himself), an object-sign (the spool), a memory (the presence of an absence), a final cause or goal (catharsis)" (BR, 497). As a consequence, Freud fails to pose what for Lyotard are the fundamental questions:

> How [can] the libidinal surface, swept by the drives of Eros and Thanatos, . . . give rise to an illusion of volume, a three-dimensional space, divided into stage and house, allurement and reality? How can the film on which move the drives of the primary process (which, as Freud has taught us, know no limit, no negation) turn back on itself and become a space of disjunction, uniting inside and outside: that is to say, a space that is both conceptual and representational? (BR, 497)

Lyotard maintains that Freud's analysis is governed by the demands of a secondary order (that of representation), when what is clearly at issue in the child's behavior is still the primary process. Consequently, if the primary processes know no negation, "then in the economy of drives there is not, nor can there ever be, an absence of *the mother*, or especially an absence of *mother* (as absent object)." Pleasure and pain, accordingly, must be conceived as purely affirmative, with no recourse to the "easy epistemological solution of 'the lack,'" as Lyotard describes Freud's concession to "Judeo-Platonic theology." Furthermore, the place and role of drive-representations (Freud's *Vorstellungsreprä-sentanz*) must be conceived differently: "not as substitutes concealing objects or the goals of drives, but as concentrations of libidinal energy on the surfaces of the visible and articulable surfaces that are themselves part of the endless and anonymous film of primary drives" (BR, 497).

The device by which this libidinal energy is guided, blocked, freed, exhausted, stored up or channeled into extreme intensities Lyotard calls the "libidinal apparatus" [*dispositif pulsionnel*]. If we consider the work of art as simply one kind of libidinal apparatus, we need no longer treat it as an image, or distinguish between its form and libidinal content; we only have to understand that its power to please resides "wholly in the formal labour that produces [it] on the one hand and in the work of various kinds that [it] stimulates on the other" [BR, 497]. In this sense, art is merely one kind of surface inscription and investment of libido, and can no longer be set apart in the cultural ghetto of unreality. It is no more or less true, real, pleasurable, or beautiful a priori than any other libidinal apparatus; what matters are the precise transformations of libidinal energy and the devices governing these transformations that it brings into play. In other words, one does not "interpret" a libidinal apparatus—whether it be serial music, photorealist painting, or psychoanalysis itself — one can only describe how it works by identifying the devices by which this libidinal content is made to flow, becomes dammed up, or is transformed.

This abandonment of a hermeneutic approach does not however entail a loss of historical perspective. Reversing the relationship between psychoanalysis and art, Lyotard will examine "Freud According to Cézanne," whose painting reveals a mutation within the very position of desire in modern Western society.[20] Positioning himself on the other side of this mutation in "Adorno come diavolo," Lyotard can now measure the distance separating Schoenberg's music, the tragedy-politics of Mann's *Doktor Faustus* and Adorno's *Aesthetic Theory* from his own "intensity-politics," which resonates instead with John Cage's art and Morton Felman's sound machines.[21] Lyotard finds that such categories as the intentional subject, alienation, and the negative dialectic retain a theological status in Adorno's theory, forcing him to assume a tragic, repressive stance blind to ways in which the new affects and intensities, set into circulation by modern capitalism, erode the basis for a rational critique. Here and elsewhere in the essays of the period, Lyotard argues for the superiority of an affirmative and creative Nietzschean perspectivism.

Yet, curiously, Lyotard's commitment to libidinal aesthetics will not outlast the 1970s. In 1979, in the dialogue-interview with Jean-Loup Thébaud entitled *Au juste*, he declared that the search for intensities could not "donner matière à la politique," mainly because it could not address the problem of injustice.[22] In *Au juste*, in fact, we witness what amounts to a linguistic turn in Lyotard's thinking: Marx and Freud drop out, to be replaced by Kant and Wittgenstein, as his interest shifts from libidinal economy to language games within which discourse and narrative are conceptualized as different kinds of "moves." Nowhere is this shift more explicitly evident than in *The Postmodern Condition*, published the same year.

The Postmodern Condition

This remarkable little book takes its point of departure from a simple question: how has the status of knowledge (*savoir*) changed in today's computerized society? The immediate answer — both Lyotard's hypothesis and an observable reality — is that knowledge has become an "informational commodity." Moreover, it has become increasingly clear that if knowledge is to survive as knowledge, it must be translatable into information. Hence: "We can predict that anything in the constituted body of knowledge that is not translatable in this way will be abandoned and that the direction of new research will be dictated by the possibility of its eventual results being translatable into computer language."[23] As a consequence of this transformation: "Knowledge is and will be produced in order to be sold, it is and will be consumed in order to be valorized in a new production: in both cases, the goal is exchange. Knowledge ceases to be an end in itself, it loses its 'use-value'" (PC, 4–5).

Given this new situation, one can imagine any number of directions along which to proceed. Lyotard himself is less interested in knowledge per se than in the rules for establishing what counts as knowledge, which is to say, the language games deployed in the legitimization of knowledge.[24] Furthermore, by knowledge Lyotard means not only scientific knowledge but also what he calls ("in the interests of simplicity") narrative knowledge. But however we define the latter (and its many different forms), in modern Western culture since the Enlightenment, scientific knowledge has always assumed priority, displacing traditional or nonscientific knowledge into a position of rivalry, competition, and/or supplementarity. This split or opposition has been the source of a long and familiar cultural debate, into which Lyotard now introduces both an original perspective and a bold claim. For when it comes to legitimation, Lyotard will argue, scientific knowledge no longer enjoys any special privilege. Although not itself a form of narrative knowledge, in the past it has always depended on one or another of the great narratives [grands récits] for its own legitimation. More specifically, modern science has always legitimated itself in a metadiscourse that appealed explicitly to some larger, overarching narrative like "the dialectics of Spirit, the hermeneutics of meaning, the emancipation of the rational or working class, or the creation of wealth" (PC, xxiii). What has changed is that Western postindustrial societies have developed a new incredulity toward precisely the narratives or rather "metanarratives" that in the past insured such legitimation. This incredulity now defines "the postmodern condition."

Thus, Lyotard's exploration of the status of knowledge is not only linked to but framed and contextualized by the crisis of narrative. This crisis leads Lyotard to some of his most striking formulations, as when he states in the opening pages:

> The narrative function is losing its functors, its great hero, its great dangers, its great voyages, its great goal. It is being dispersed in clouds of narrative language elements—narrative, but also denotative, prescriptive, descriptive, and so on. Conveyed within each cloud are pragmatic valencies specific to its kind. Each of us lives at the intersection of many of these. However, we do not necessarily establish stable language combinations, and the properties of the ones we do establish are not necessarily communicable. (PC, xxiv)

Of course we can speculate about the most immediate causes of the crisis of narrative: "[it] can be seen as an effect of the blossoming of techniques and technologies since the Second World War, which has shifted emphasis from the ends of action to its means; it can also be seen as an effect of the redeployment of advanced liberal capitalism after its retreat under the protection of Keynesianism during the period 1930−60, a renewal that has eliminated the communist alternative and valorized the individual enjoyment of goods and services" (PC, 37−38). But Lyotard quickly admits that such explanations are hardly satisfying. The crisis lies much deeper: in the slow erosion of the "grand narratives of speculation and emancipation" that has been at work in Western culture for over a century. In fact, Lyotard argues, the delegitimization of these narratives does not come about from external changes, but follows inevitably from internal contradictions already present within them.[25]

Perhaps the more pressing question is what holds the society together amidst this dispersion of narrative language and seeming dissolution of the social bond. Many social theorists—Lyotard cites Jean Baudrillard in particular—have answered with a rather obvious metaphor drawn from molecular physics: the social aggregate has disintegrated into "a mass of individual atoms thrown into the absurdity of Brownian motion" (PC, 15). But Lyotard himself finds this representation symptomatic of a nostalgia for a lost "organic" society. To analyze our current postmodern society, which is regulated by criteria of performativity and which indeed lacks any other legitimation, he proposes instead a minimalist linguistic model, according to which the social bond is constituted through participation in language games:

> A *self* does not amount to much, but no self is an island; each exists in a fabric of relations that is now more complex and mobile than ever before. Young or old, man or woman, rich or poor, a person is always located at "nodal points" of specific communication circuits, however tiny these may be. Or better: one is always located at a post through which various kinds of messages pass. No one, not even the least privileged among us, is ever entirely powerless over the messages that traverse and position him at the post of sender, addressee, or referent. One's mobility in relation to these language game effects ... is tolerable, at least within certain limits (and the limits are vague); it is even solicited by regulatory mechanisms, and in particular by the self-adjustments the system undertakes in order to improve its performance. It may even be said that the system can and must encourage such movement to the extent that it combats its own entropy; the novelty of an unexpected "move," with its correlative displacement of a partner or group of partners, can supply the system with that increased performativity it forever demands and consumes. (PC, 15)

The ambiguity of the passage is striking, especially considering Lyotard's earlier characterization of the way the dispersion of narrative language elements is "managed" by the current system's need to extend its own power:

> The decision makers ... attempt to manage these clouds of sociality [that is, our interactions within the context of the dispersion of narrative] according to input/output matrices, following a logic which implies that their elements are commensurable and that the whole is determinable. They allocate our lives for the growth of power. In matters of social justice and of scientific truth alike, the legitimization of that power is based on its optimizing the system's performance-efficiency. The application of this criterion to all of our games necessarily entails a certain level of terror, whether soft or hard: be operational (that is, commensurable) or disappear. (PC, xxiv)

These passages make it obvious that more is at stake than just the status of knowledge. However we frame the terms—and we shall return to Lyotard's choice of language games—clearly the current computerization of society transforms the status of the self and the nature of the social bond, in addition to provoking a crisis in the legitimizing of knowledge. Furthermore, in the computer era the State itself becomes vulnerable and even "outmoded" on a number of fronts. The most obvious threat comes from the existence of the new multinational corporations, over whose use and production of knowledge the State has little or no jurisdiction. The traditional Enlightenment assumption that learning and education fall within the purview of the State also comes under question, ironically as a consequence of the ideology of an "information free society," which would have it that society progresses only if the messages circulating within it are rich in information and easy to decode. As Lyotard notes, "the ideology of communicational 'transparency,' which goes hand in hand with the commercialization of knowledge, will begin to perceive the State as a factor of opacity and 'noise'" (PC, 5).

That Lyotard can subordinate these various themes to the crisis of narrative is of course made possible by his choice of methodology: to treat all discourse and all utterances as "moves" in a language game. A number of consequences follow, and Lyotard is quick to spell them out. Perhaps the most important is that discourse becomes a form of combat, and all speech acts "fall within the domain of a general agonistics" (PC, 10). Although one does not always "play the game to win"—aesthetic activities, for example, are played for the sheer pleasure of invention—the idea of language as agonistics restores or helps to maintain a political tension within what otherwise would threaten to become an abstract and reified form of analysis. To state, as Lyotard does, that "the observable social bond is composed of language 'moves'" (PC, 11) may be a fruitful hypothesis, but there is a danger that it will short-circuit an analysis of the specific material practices underlying and contextualizing such "moves."

Although theoretically sensitive to this *pragmatic* dimension of language, in practice Lyotard is really only interested in two situations: the way in which narrative positions the narrator, addressee, and referent, in contrast to the different positioning of scientific researcher and apprentice in the production and transmission of scientific knowledge.[26] However, we need not linger over the details of his comparison, since the results are just what we might expect. Popular or customary narrative knowledge (and Lyotard includes here the various kinds of know-how or *savoir-faire* that shape the culture) requires no external legitimation. Narratives in and of themselves determine criteria of competence and/or illustrate how they are to be applied. In thus defining what can be said and done in a culture, they articulate the fabric of the culture through their very transmission, certifying themselves in the process. Scientific knowledge, on the other hand, is produced and transmitted according to rules that are incommensurate with narrative. As a language game, scientific knowledge privileges the referent or denotative dimension to the exclusion of all others. Scientific knowledge thus requires neither particular competence on the part of the addressee nor does it acquire validity from the fact of being reported. The rules that determine its "verification" (or "falsification") in no way participate in the language games that combine to form the social bond. Thus scientific knowledge exists in a position of exteriority with regard to society.

Nevertheless, the fundamental incommensurability of narrative knowledge and scientific knowledge has not prevented narrative from being used to legitimate the latter. Lyotard delineates two distinct modes of narrative legitimation in the modern period, distinguished by whether or not the subject of the narrative is conceived "as cognitive or practical, as a hero of knowledge or as a hero of liberty" (PC, 31). The first, directed toward the speculative unity of all knowledge and issuing primarily from a German philosophical tradition, finds its most specific institutional embodiment in the university; the second, directed toward the liberation of humanity, with a primarily French and political genealogy, finds its most specific institutional embodiment in modern law and the democratic electorate. But whether the pursuit of scientific knowledge is justified for the sake of "pure knowledge" or because it will eventually help to liberate humanity matters very little, now that both narrative legitimations have lost their credibility in the general dispersion of narrative in the contemporary period. What presently serves to legitimate knowledge and indeed all social decisions at higher levels in the absence of any overarching larger narrative is the performativity model Lyotard introduced earlier and which now assumes a key role in his argument.

Basically, modern sociology provides two representational models of society within which information assumes a certain value. The first is the traditional "organic" model with its more modern functionalist version. In the 1950s, with Talcott Parsons's notion of society as a self-regulating system and the application of cybernetics to social theory, this model is modified, and society ceases to be viewed as a living organism, either theoretically or materially. Yet as Lyotard notes, the principle underlying the model is still optimistic, since "it corresponds to the stabilization of the growth economics and societies of abundance under the aegis of a moderate welfare state" (PC, 11). In contrast, Lyotard finds the current version of this model, found in the technocratic *Systemtheorie* of contemporary German theorists like Niklas Luhmann, to be cynical and despairing:

> [T]he harmony between the needs and hopes of individuals or groups and the functions guaranteed by the system is now only a secondary component of its functioning. The true goal of the system, the reason it programs itself like a computer, is the organization of the global relationship between input and output — in other words, performativity. Even when its rules are in the process of changing and innovations are occurring, even when its dysfunctions (such as strikes, crises, unemployment, or political revolutions) inspire hope and lead to a belief in an alternative, even then what is actually taking place is only an internal readjustment, and its result can be no more than an increase in the system's "viability." The only alternative to this kind of performance improvement is entropy, or decline. (PC, 11–12)

For Lyotard's purposes, the obvious difference between this model and the organic one is less important than their similar assumption of society as a unified whole. This assumption is opposed by the second or "critical" model — of which Marxism is the leading exponent — which sees society as divided (by class struggle and inequalities of all sorts) and which therefore remains wary of all syntheses and reconciliations. This model also has a complex history of modifications and internal differentiations, but in recent practice its totalizing and totalitarian effects have tended to deprive too many struggles of the right to exist. In short, on one side, alternatives to the status quo are recuperated in order to increase the system's "performativity," while on the other they are repressed out of existence. On both sides the effect is nearly the same: critique is used "one way or another as aids in programming the system" (PC, 13).

The role that knowledge will have is dictated by whichever of the two models we choose — thus knowledge will be either functional or critical — but the choice seems arbitrary and difficult. One tempting solution would be to distinguish between two different kinds of knowledge — positivist and instrumentalist versus reflexive and hermeneutic, but Lyotard finds this kind of modernist "oppositional" thinking to be "out of step with the most vital modes of postmodern knowledge" (PC, 14).

Postmodern science provides the most striking instance of one such new vital mode of knowledge; indeed, in Lyotard's argument it suffices as the *only* example. Its importance resides in the fact that the production of contemporary scientific knowledge does not operate according to the quest for performativity which serves as the only model of social legitimation now that the great narratives of emancipation and speculation are defunct. In its various searches for "instability," postmodern science even calls into question the basic assumptions of such a model. Theoretically, the performativity model assumes a positivistic "determinism" in order to establish parameters of efficiency and control; at the practical level, it assumes a quantifiable level of stability according to which input/output ratios can be measured. Postmodern science destroys these assumptions. Both mathematical and scientific research (Gödel's theorem and quantum physics) prove the intrinsic incompleteness and undecidability of any system. In its search for "singularities" and "incommensurabilities" — Lyotard cites examples of what is now called "chaos" or turbulence theory, Mandelbrot's fractals, Thom's catastrophe theory, the double-bind theory of the Palo Alto school — contemporary science increasingly suggests that "determinism" in the classical sense only exists in small islands, as special limited cases.[27] By searching methodically for the limits of the intelligible and the known, and thus for instances where accepted paradigms of explanation break down, postmodern science of necessity internalizes the process of self-legitimation as the very means by which its develops as a science. As Lyotard concisely states: "the discourse on the rules that validate it [postmodern science] is (explicitly) immanent to it" (PC, 54). As a consequence, postmodern science is both able to transform what knowledge is and to function according to a new model of legitimation:

> Postmodern science — by concerning itself with such things as undecidables, the limits of precise control, conflicts characterized by incomplete information, "*fracta*," catastrophes, and pragmatic paradoxes — is theorizing its own evolution as discontinuous, catastrophic, nonrectifiable, and paradoxical. It is changing the meaning of the word *knowledge*, while expressing how such a change can take place. It is producing not the known, but the unknown. And it suggests a model of legitimation that has nothing to do with maximized performance, but has as its basis difference understood as paralogy. (PC, 60)

In homelier terms, postmodern science legitimizes itself by generating new ideas. These ideas are simply "little stories" [*petits récits*] the scientist tells, even though he is duty bound to verify them. Unfortunately, Lyotard does not elaborate upon this "return of narrative" within science itself, except to give examples — open systems, local determinism, antimethod — which he groups under the general heading of "paralogy."[28]

In the book's concluding section, "Legitimation by Paralogy," Lyotard spells out why this model (or is it an antimodel?) is preferable to the model of rational consensus proffered by Jürgen Habermas, a task made somewhat easier by the fact that "paralogy," at least in Lyotard's sense, entails its exact antithesis — dissension. Actually, there are two models of consensus to consider. The first, that of Habermas, is based on an accord reached through free and open dialogue between rational minds following agreed-on rules, or what Habermas calls *Diskurs*.[29] But this model presupposes exactly what Lyotard argues is unacceptable: first, that there *can* be agreement about rules that would be universally valid for all language games; and second, that the goal of dialogue *should* be consensus. In short, Habermas's belief that "humanity as a collective (universal) subject seeks its common emancipation through the regulation of the 'moves' permitted in all language games and that the legitimacy of any statement resides in its contributing to that emancipation" (PC, 66) proves ill founded. The second model of consensus, as much presupposed as it is established in current Western society, is that of the performativity principle itself. Fundamentally terrorist, it recognizes only those innovative "moves" that can be utilized to increase its own performance. Both pragmatic and cynical, it manages "new input" in order to maintain and extend its own power, redefining in the process the norms of "life." In this sense, Lyotard notes, "the system seems to be a vanguard machine dragging humanity after it, dehumanizing it in order to rehumanize it at a different level of normative capacity" (PC, 63).

According to Lyotard's argument, what is required for knowledge is a model of legitimation that would respect both the desire for the unknown and the desire for justice. Rephrased in the terms of language games, it must be a model that recognizes the fundamental heterogeneity of language games (there are no universal rules or definitions and one game does not necessarily translate into another), and that any consensus on the rules defining a game and the permissible moves within it *must* be local, that is, defined by the present players and subject to eventual cancellation. Given these criteria, both of the consensus models outlined above fail. The pragmatics of postmodern science, on the other hand, meet both conditions, although whether or not it is "applicable to the vast clouds of language material constituting society" (PC, 64) remains an open question. On the practical level of daily life Lyotard finds that the "temporary contract" in professional, political, cultural, and family affairs is gradually supplanting the permanent institutions, but such provisional arrangements among local players is an ambiguous trend, since it also benefits the flexibility and operativity of the system. Perhaps the only true alternative in today's computerized society, at least the only one that Lyotard can envision, would be to give the public free access to the memory and data banks. But Lyotard remains silent, perhaps not surprisingly, on the kind of "dissension" such a move would most likely bring about.

Conclusion

Although *The Postmodern Condition* has enjoyed a wide appeal, in the long run it may well be superseded in importance by Lyotard's most recent major publication, *The Differend*, which appeared in 1983.[30] This dense, self-scrutinizing, difficult work of philosophy (rather than theory, Lyotard insists), bent on discovering its own rules (the rules of philosophical discourse) rather than presupposing their knowledge as a generative principle, extends, reworks and deepens Lyotard's interest in language games as part of a general "agonistics." Here, and by way of conclusion, I can only offer a few introductory comments.

At the very outset the titular concept points to discourse as an *agon* of unresolvable struggle:

> As distinguished from a litigation, a differend [*differend*] would be a case of conflict, between (at least) two parties, that cannot be equitably resolved for lack of a rule of judgment applicable to both arguments. One side's legitimacy does not imply the other's lack of legitimacy. However, applying a single rule of judgment to both in order to settle their differend as though it were merely a litigation would wrong (at least) one of them (and both of them if neither side admits this rule). Damages result from an injury which is inflicted upon the rules of a genre of discourse but which is reparable according to those rules. A wrong results from the fact that the rules of the genre of discourse by which one judges are not those of the judged genre or genres of discourse. (D, xi)

Lyotard's interest, however, extends far beyond the legal frame the above definitions suggest. The differend not only points to a conflict that has not yet found adequate expression within current discourse; it also demands that such expression be found.[31] In this sense the differend attests to a "lack" in our contemporary language that must be filled through the invention of new phrases. And, as Lyotard shows, this inevitably entails instituting new addressees, new addressors, new significations and new referents.

To do this the notion of language game itself must be reworked and refined. Lyotard introduces two new discursive categories. A "phrase regimen" (*régime de phrase*) is a class of phrases grouped according to a specific function: reasoning, knowing, describing, recounting, questioning, showing, ordering, and so forth. The set of rules defining the phrase (its "regimen") is neither grammatical nor semantic but *pragmatic*: it situates the positions of its instance (addressor, addressee, referent, sense) with regard to one another. Thus regimens are strictly heterogeneous and cannot be translated from one to another. However, they can be linked together (*enchaînés*) according to ends defined by a "genre of discourse" (*genre de discours*) such as to know, to teach, to be just, to seduce, to justify, to evaluate. Genres of discourse thus supply the rules for linking together heterogeneous phrases. For example, a dialogue can link together a definition or a description and a question, with the explicit aim of bringing the two interlocutors into agreement about the sense of a referent.

Lyotard's own examples, intended to demonstrate that "thought, cognition, ethics, politics, history or being" come into play when phrases are linked together, range from Protagoras's paradox (he wins whether his disciple wins or loses the suit against him) to the silence of the victims of the Holocaust. Interspersed throughout are "Notices" on Protagoras, Gorgias, Plato, Antisthenes, Gertrude Stein, Aristotle, Hegel, Levinas, Kant, the Cashinahau, and the Declaration of 1789. What emerges is a sense of discursive warfare, ever renewing itself and reform(ulat)ing itself in interminable clashes. Here the relentlessness of the *agon* goes well beyond the language games of *The Postmodern Condition*, where at least playing the game presupposes that the players agree provisionally about the rules. In *The Differend* the "players" are really the "phrases" in dispute, without agreed-upon rules or even the means to adjudicate differences. Of course these conflictual differences are what ultimately matter to Lyotard; he seeks to bring them forth from behind the cover of all strategies that would make them disappear, whether in the name of universal values, cultural sublimation, or political expediency; he wants the reader to bear witness to their proliferation, in all their incommensurable and provocative singularity.

Lyotard states clearly at the outset that he intends to refute the centuries-old prejudice that there is something in general called "man" and "language," that "the former makes use of the latter for his own ends, and that if he does not succeed in attaining these ends, it is for want of good control over language 'by means' of a 'better' language" (D, 13). It is by now a familiar poststructuralist argument, here renewed against two specific "adversaries": the genre of economic discourse (exchange, capital), and the genre of academic discourse (mastery). For Lyotard, these two adversaries, rather than common sense or public opinion, seem the most threatening to philosophy itself as differend. Indeed, it is the survival of philosophy that now most concerns Lyotard. Whereas in *The Postmodern Condition* he begins and ends with the recognition that the contemporary fragmentation and dispersal of the great narratives change the status of contemporary knowledge, in *The Differend* he moves toward a more radical claim: that the agonistic multiplicity of phrases in dispute is ongoing and recurrent. Our own history will determine which conflicts we attempt to resolve, but history — even the one that has brought us Auschwitz — can never have the last word. Silence itself is a phrase, and there is no last phrase (D, xii). Lyotard leaves us with the impression that philosophy — in the absence of any universal rules, narratives, or definable sense of justice — is the only reliable witness to the endless — indeed Heraclitian — strife of discourse.

Notes

1. For a historical overview of the notion of "postmodernism" that includes some discussion of Lyotard's contribution, see Hans Bertens, "The Postmodern *Weltanschauung* and its Relation with Modernism," in *Approaching Postmodernism*, eds. Douwe Fokkema and Hans Bertens (Amsterdam and Philadelphia: John Benjamins, 1986), pp. 9–51.

2. In his introduction Lyotard states that "we shall have to fix its [phenomenology's] historical signification although it is not assignable once and for all because there are at present *several* phenomenologists and because its meaning [*sens*] is in process and incomplete insofar as it is historical" (*La Phénomenologie*, p. 7). But later, in a "Note on Husserl and Hegel," Lyotard suggests that "the phenomenological enterprise is fundamentally *contradictory* as the designation by language of a pre-logical signified in being" and "forever incomplete because referred back dialectically from being to meaning through intentional analysis" (p. 44). As Lyotard will argue explicitly in *Discours, Figure*, the specific problem posed by language for philosophy is never adequately resolved by Hegel, Husserl, or Merleau-Ponty.

3. In *Peregrinations: Law, Form, Event* (New York: Columbia Univ., 1988), p. 17. Written in English with the help of David Carrol, this volume also contains the most extensive bibliography of Lyotard's writings currently available.

4. Ibid, p. 17.

5. *Dérive à partir de Marx et Freud* (Paris: Union Generale D'Editions, 1973), p. 23.

6. Ibid, p. 11.

7. Of notable mention are *Les Transformateurs Duchamp*, Lyotard's book on the art of Marcel Duchamp, and a series of books that mix aesthetic, speculative, and narrative genres: *Instructions paiennes, Récits tremblants*, and *Le Mur pacifique*.

8. *Discours, Figure* (Paris: Editions Klincksieck, 1971), p. 9. Hereafter DF.

9. For a defense of Lyotard's use of the term "deconstruction," which takes into account Jacques Derrida's more widely known method of deconstruction, see Rodolphe Gasché's "Deconstruction as Criticism," *Glyph*, 6 (1979).

10. See Gasché, p. 183.

11. As Lyotard makes clear, however, this language is not a language of expression in the phenomenological sense. See p. 291ff.

12. Cf. Lyotard: "[Saussure's] conception of structure leads him to absorb the whole of signification into cutting-up, i.e., into the system of intervals between terms, or the system of *values*. And yet he does not give up having recourse at the very same time to an idea of signification which opposes it to value as vertical is opposed to horizontal or depth to surface. What could pass for a failing in a linguist determined to limit his study to the structure of language, that is, the temptation of introducing the thickness of the sign into the transparency of the system, is, however, much more than an error or a naiveté; a fact which one could term transcendental is betrayed here, namely that all discourse constitutes its object in depth; when this discourse is that of the linguist and he takes signification as his object, he spontaneously thematizes it as something thick, he is led to posit signification as a sign. In reality this depth is an effect of object-positioning due to the current discourse: which holds signification at a distance and posits that it is a sign just as it does any object." (DF, 93—94)

13. Cf. Lyotard: "We can already distinguish three types of figure at work in the *Coup de dés*: the image, which is the figure placed in the order of language, but on the plane of the signified (comparison, metaphor); the form, a sort of figure which also has its place in language, but which works on the linguistic signifier and is not signified in the discourse; the sensory figure, which is a configuration distributing the linguistic signifiers (here graphic signifiers) according to demands which are not those of discourse strictly speaking, but those of a rhythm (here a visual rhythm). These figures are thus arrayed from the pure signified to the plastic signifier, via the linguistic signifier; they form a chain or a relay between the intelligible discursive order and the sensory spatio-temporal order, they prove the presence of forms able to cross the barriers separating the intelligible world and the sensory world, forms independent of the milieu they inform." (DF, 71)

14. Sigmund Freud, "Negation," in *General Psychological Theory* (New York: Collier, 1963), p. 214.

15. Ibid, pp. 215—16. Thus Lyotard can write: "Reality is never anything but a sector of the imaginary field that we have agreed to renounce, and from which we have agreed to disinvest the phantasms of our desire. This sector is bordered on all confines by the imaginary field where the fulfillments of desire by fantasy are perpetuated." (DF, 284)

16. A translation of "The Dream-work Does Not Think" by Mary Lydon appears in *The Oxford Literary Review*, 6:1 (1983), pp. 3—34.

17. Lyotard will often draw attention to and discuss the two meanings of *Wunsch* in Freud. See, in particular, "Sur une figure de discourse" in *Des Dispositifs pulsionnels* (Paris: Union Generale D'Editions, 1973), pp. 136—39.

18. See also Lyotard's essay "The Unconscious as Mise-en-scène" in *Performance in Postmodern Culture* (Milwaukee: Coda, 1977), pp. 87—98. This essay, which remains unpublished in French, also contains material from the analysis of "A Child Is Being Beaten."

19. "Beyond Representation" in *The Human Context*, 7:3 (Autumn 1975), p. 497. This essay appeared originally as a preface to the French translation of

Aron Ehrenzweig's *The Hidden Order of Art* published by Gallimard in 1974. Hereafter BR.

20. See "Freud selon Cézanne," in *Des Dispositifs pulsionnels*, where Lyotard emphasizes Freud's rigid adherence to the assumptions of classical aesthetics while living amidst an artistic revolution. In the latter, Lyotard writes:

> What is in question . . . is the very *position* of modern Western *desire*, the way in which objects, words, images, goods, thoughts, work, women and men, births and deaths, illnesses, wars, are put into circulation and exchanged within society. If this transposition of the anonymous desire that supports the institution in general and makes it acceptable had to be sized up in a few words, one could say that, roughly speaking, this desire formerly fulfilled itself in a system of exchanges that imposed a *symbolic* value on the object, just as the neurotic's unconscious produces and relates representatives of the repressed object according to a symbolic organization of Oedipal origin; while beginning with the mutation we were speaking of (and whose effect was best studied by Marx in the field of economics), the production and circulation of objects cease to be regulated by reference to symbolic values and to be attributed to a mysterious Donor; they obey the system's internal "logic" alone, somewhat like the products of *schizophrenia* seem to escape the regularization that neurosis owes the Oedipal structure, and to obey nothing but the "free" effervescence of psychic energy. (pp. 76–77, emphases in the original)

Lyotard goes on to demonstrate how both the desire to paint in Cézanne and the function of painting itself—to produce an "absolute object," no longer justifiable according to representational demands or answerable to received conventions of taste—can only be accounted for in terms of this mutation.

21. See Lyotard's essay "Adorno come diavolo," in *Des Dispositifs pulsionnels*. An English translation appeared in *Telos*, 19 (Spring 1974).

22. *Au juste* (Paris: Christian Bourgois, 1979), pp. 170–71. The English translation is entitled *Just Gaming*, trans. by Wlad Godzich (Minneapolis: Univ. of Minnesota, 1985).

23. Lyotard, *The Postmodern Condition*, trans. by Geoff Bennington and Brian Massumi (Minneapolis: Univ. of Minnesota, 1984), p. 4. Hereafter PC.

24. The notion of language games comes from Wittgenstein's *Philosophical Investigations*, section 23. As Lyotard explains, "each of the various categories of utterance can be defined in terms of rules specifying their properties and the uses to which they can be put—in exactly the same way as the game of chess is defined by a set of rules determining the properties of each of the pieces" (PC, p. 10). What appeals to Lyotard is not only the rule-governed nature of language but the fact that it is comprised of many such games, each one sui generis and untranslatable into any other. (In this sense the metaphor of language as chess game is limited, even misleading.) It follows that there can

be no hegemonic, totalizing discourse or "metagame" that would allow one to define "language," definition itself being simply one kind of language game. As Lyotard will later state in *The Differend*, there is no "language" in general, except as the object of an Idea (in the Kantian sense).

25. See *The Postmodern Condition*, pp. 38–41, for Lyotard's analysis of the "seeds of 'delegitimation' and nihilism" already inherent in the grand narratives of the nineteenth century.

26. A much fuller development of a pragmatics of language worked out from a poststructuralist perspective is provided by Gilles Deleuze and Félix Guattari in *A Thousand Plateaus*, trans. by Brian Massumi (Minneapolis: Univ. of Minnesota, 1980, 1987), especially ch. 4, "November 20, 1923: Postulates of Linguistics," pp. 75–110.

27. This complete reversal of the classical physics paradigm is presented with great force and clarity of theoretical exposition in *La Nouvelle Alliance*, by Ilya Prigogine and Isabelle Stengers, translated into English as *Order out of Chaos* (New York: Bantam, 1984).

28. See Lyotard's Note 211 (PC, p. 100).

29. Habermas uses the term "discourse" [*Diskurs*] in a very restricted, cognitive sense. See Habermas, *Legitimation Crisis*, trans. by Thomas McCarthy (Boston: Beacon, 1975, orig. pub. 1973), pp. 107–8.

30. Lyotard, *Le Différend* (Paris: Editions de Minuit, 1983). The English translation appears as *The Differend: Phrases in Dispute*, trans. Georges Van Den Abbeele (Minneapolis: Univ. of Minnesota, 1988). All subsequent references will be to the English edition, with page numbers inserted into the text.

31. Although many readers will perhaps look for affinities between Lyotard's "differend" and Derrida's neologism "différance," Lyotard's term is actually much closer semantically to Mikhail Bakhtin's notion of "heteroglossia" [*raznorecie*], which refers to the diversity within language of speech types that can never be resolved into or encompassed within a "monological" discourse. See Mikhail Bakhtin, *The Dialogic Imagination*, trans. Michael Holquist and Caryl Emerson (Austin: Univ. of Texas, 1981).

Hermeneutics

Introduction

George H. Jensen

Hermeneutics takes its name from the Greek myth of Hermes, the winged messenger of the gods, whose task is to interpret — in Greek, *hermeneuein* — the sayings, the text, of the Oracle of Delphi. Hermeneutics is, thus, the art — to some, the science — of the interpretation of texts. Yet this, the most frequently proffered definition, is extremely problematic. What is meant by *interpretation* quite often changes from one hermeneut to the next, as does what is meant by *text*. For example, some hermeneuts consider the understanding of a text to be a distinct experience or function from the interpretation of it;[1] some feel that hermeneutics considers only written texts, others written texts and spoken utterances, and still others feel that all of reality is a textual construction and thus open to hermeneutic investigation. Further, "the art of the interpretation of texts," even if we can agree on the terms, establishes only loose boundaries at best. Many texts that claim to be within the boundaries of hermeneutics seem indistinguishable from other texts that claim to be literary criticism, reading theory, linguistics, semiotics, historiography, theology, phenomenology, or deconstruction. In short, to say that one is participating in an intellectual dialogue that addresses the interpretation of texts says so much that it says virtually nothing.

Because it is so difficult to contain hermeneutics within a discipline or philosophical school, it is best viewed as a historical thread that may run a fairly straight line for an epochal moment, break, or swirl in clumps and knots, and then, once picked up by a new generation of hermeneuts, run another straight line for a while. When, within its irregular historical path, hermeneutics reforms itself, when its thread begins to run a straight line for a brief period, the process is less of a continuation than a fresh start: with altered assumptions, a new generation of hermeneuts examine an alternate approach to interpreting a different genre or notion of text. This is not to say that the past is entirely lost. Ideas, such as the concept of the hermeneutic circle,[2] do reemerge transformed as each new approach to hermeneutics grapples with the perplexities of interpreting texts. And the historical thread, as the following outline will illustrate, does begin to straighten out a bit after the Renaissance. Perhaps, one of the reasons the earlier historical thread does not always run so straight is that it is a construction, an interpretation that evolved from the circle of twentieth-century hermeneuts who wanted to place themselves within a long and distinguished tradition.

The Greek and Roman philosophers who touched on the issue of interpretation usually focused on the issues of ambiguity and contradiction both as an element of rhetorical style and a hermeneutical problem. In *Panathenaicus* (339 B.C.), for example, Isocrates delivers a speech in which he uses ambiguity to praise Athens without appearing to recant his praise of Sparta in an earlier speech. For Isocrates, ambiguity and the latitude it leaves for interpretation seems to be a useful rhetorical tool for dealing with complex rhetorical situations, but Aristotle and Cicero both condemn ambiguity as a vice of style that hinders interpretation.[3] It is not surprising that the interrelationship between rhetoric and hermeneutics would be perpetually rediscovered with later hermeneuts, for the rhetorical strategies or rules that drive the construction of texts could, at least in theory, be inverted to form strategies or rules of interpretation.[4]

Such references to the art of interpretation within classical rhetorical texts are scattered. Of these, the most systematic attempt to establish a theory of hermeneutics comes in Aristotle's *Peri hermeneias*, or "concerning interpretation," which is generally regarded as one of his earlier works. This work is less satisfying, and ultimately less influential, than Aristotle's *Rhetoric*, yet it intriguingly foreshadows the efforts of later hermeneuts.[5] In order to deal with hermeneutical problems such as contradictions within texts, Aristotle discusses the nature of verbal signs (*signa*) and the grammatical construction of statements. Later hermeneuts will return to and further develop semiotics and linguistic analysis as hermeneutic tools.

After the classical era, hermeneutics became more specialized. A distinction between how to construct and interpret legal versus stylistic texts in classical rhetoric and hermeneutics rigidifies; works on legal hermeneutics, literary hermeneutics, and biblical hermeneutics begin to crop up, if only periodically. In the twelfth century, Italian scholars, influenced by a renewed interest in Roman law, developed a special hermeneutics of jurisprudence. A number of importance treatises on legal hermeneutics slowly followed: Constantius Rogerius's *Treatise*

Concerning the Interpretation of Laws (1463), Franciscus Hotomanus's *Iurisconsultus* (1559), and Johannes von Felde's *Treatise on the Science of Interpretation* (1689). The interest in biblical hermeneutics, although already a concern of theologians like St. Augustine, intensified in the wake of the Protestant Reformation. Matthias Flacius Illyricus's *Clavis Scripturae Sacrae* (1567) and other works attempted to establish rules for a direct interpretation of the Bible. With biblical interpretation divorced from the authority of Rome, such rules were perceived as necessary to bring order to a movement that espoused direct access to the Word.[6]

With the eighteenth century, the history of hermeneutics began to form a tradition. In his *Introduction to the Correct Interpretation of Reasonable Discourses and Books* (1742), Johann Martin Chladenius (1710–1759) attempted to develop a system of hermeneutics (a scientific approach to interpretation) that would effect complete understanding. He viewed language as essentially rule-driven and texts as transparent conduits of meaning. To modern readers, such notions may make Chladenius seem more textually naive than he actually was. He did appreciate some of the difficulties of interpretation: the reader could lack concepts (prior knowledge) necessary for understanding, the text could be poorly written, or several historical authors could present variant views of the same event. Such problems disturbed Chladenius, for he wanted texts to possess the regularity of science. But he had unfaltering faith in the science of hermeneutics and the ability of an interpreter, armed with the proper rules of interpretation, to restore unity to understanding. Chladenius and other hermeneuts of the Enlightenment form a starting point from which modern tradition of hermeneutics departs.

Chladenius's alignment of hermeneutics with science was modified by nineteenth-century hermeneutics, which is also referred to as methodological hermeneutics. Schleiermacher, Humboldt, Droyson, and Dilthey were interested in reestablishing a general hermeneutics, as opposed to a legal or biblical hermeneutics. They wrote extensively on the methodology of history, which they felt could serve as the foundation for human sciences. The nineteenth-century hermeneuts, thus, moved away from science and a scientistic view of texts. Instead of viewing texts as transparent and rule-driven, they viewed language as a mediation. They believed that hermeneutics could lead the reader through a process that would recreate the experience between the author and his or her original audience, yet they also felt that their task was endless. Because history is fluid and dynamic, interpretation must constantly evolve.

In the extremely rich and influential body of work that the methodological hermeneuts produced, one finds glimpses of ideas that will be

central to the rhetorical turn of twentieth-century thought. For
example, Wilhelm von Humboldt comes close to saying that history is
a social construction:

> The facts of history in their particular connecting circumstances are
> little more than the results of tradition and research which have been
> accepted as true because they are the most probable in themselves
> and also fit best into the context of the whole.... The truth of all that
> has taken place depends upon the addition of that invisible part of
> each fact mentioned above, and which the historian therefore must
> contribute. Considered from this perspective, he *is* spontaneous and
> even creative; not that he brings forth that which is not present, but
> in that he forms, of his own ability, that which he could not have
> perceived in its true reality by receptivity alone. Like the poet, but in
> a different manner, he must take the scattered pieces he has gathered
> into himself and work them into a whole.[7]

Humboldt almost makes the kind of claims that Hayden White will
make in *Metahistory* and *Tropics of Discourse*, yet he still holds to a
belief that a history of some reality that exists outside the historian or
texts is achievable.

Twentieth-century hermeneutics, also called radical or ontological
hermeneutics, moved even farther from the scientism of Chladenius
while still assuming a basically modernist stance.[8] With the publication
of Heidegger's *Being and Time* (1927), the focus of hermeneutics shifts
to ontology. Earlier hermeneuts worked to interpret words on a page,
but Gadamer speaks of "the hermeneutic experience."[9] Language is no
longer the medium through which being is expressed; language *is*
Being.[10] This fundamental shift affected the nature of hermeneutics in
several ways. First, hermeneutics moves from the epistemological concerns of the nineteenth century, a search for a foundation for human
sciences, to a phenomenological investigation of ontology, which the
early Heidegger felt should serve as a foundation for all knowledge of
any kind.[11] Second, there is also a move from the nineteenth-century
hermeneuts' notion of understanding as reenactment (the re-creation
of the relationship between the author and his or her original audience)
to a belief that any attempt to recreate the original context of a text is
futile. Heidegger's theory of the historicity of Being, that history is not
something occurring in the past but something being lived in the
present, a continuing-to-be, does not tolerate a romantic notion of
recapturing the past.[12]

These points will be discussed more fully in the subsequent chapters
on Heidegger and Gadamer. What we will see is that the twentieth-
century hermeneuts, though they radicalized the notion of interpretation
and the role of language, are still among the more conservative of
philosophers who participate in the rhetorical turn of twentieth-century

philosophy.[13] They are not postmodernists; they still work within the modernist framework of seeking a foundation on which knowledge can be built. What is radical about their project is where they look for that foundation: in the text of Being.

Notes

1. For example, Chladenius wrote: "Since an interpretation only takes place if we are still lacking certain concepts necessary to the complete understanding of the book, the interpreter's duty terminates when we completely understand the work." See his "On the Concept of Interpretation," in *The Hermeneutics Reader*, ed. Kurt Mueller-Vollmer (New York: Continuum, 1985), p. 59.

2. We find an example of the hermeneutic circle in note 1: we must interpret a work to understand it, but must not we understand it before we interpret it? Schleiermacher wrote: "Complete knowledge always involves an apparent circle, that each part can be understood only out of the whole to which it belongs, and vice versa." See his "General Theory and Art of Interpretation" in *The Hermeneutic Reader*, p. 84.

3. Kathy Eden, "Hermeneutics and the Ancient Rhetorical Tradition," *Rhetorica*, 5 (1987), pp. 59–86.

4. For additional discussions of the relationship between rhetoric and hermeneutics, see Michael J. Hyde and Craig R. Smith, "Hermeneutics and Rhetoric: A Seen but Unobserved Relationship," *Quarterly Journal of Speech*, 65 (1979), 347–63, and H. P. Rickman, "Rhetoric and Hermeneutics, *Philosophy and Rhetoric*, 14 (1981), pp. 100–111.

5. This is not to say that Aristotle's corpus did not exert a profound influence on the history of hermeneutics. For articles on Aristotle's impact on later hermeneuts, see Robert Hollinger, "Practical Reason and Hermeneutics," 18 (1985), pp. 113–22; Massimo Marassi, "The Hermeneutics of Rhetoric in Heidegger," *Philosophy and Rhetoric*, 19 (1986), pp. 79–98; and Paul Schuchman, "Aristotle's Phronesis and Gadamer's Hermeneutics," *Philosophy Today*, 23 (1979), pp. 41–49.

6. Religious hermeneutics continues to be a strong tradition to this day. Paul Ricoeur, for example, holds a joint appointment as Professor of Philosophical Theology with the Divinity School of the University of Chicago. For modern examples of religious hermeneutics, in addition to much of Ricoeur's work, see Werner G. Jeanrond, *Text and Interpretation as Categories of Theological Thinking*, trans. Thomas J. Wilson (New York: Crossroads, 1988) and David Tracy, *Plurality and Ambiguity: Hermeneutics, Religion, Hope* (New York: Harper & Row, 1987).

7. "On the Task of the Historian," address to Berlin Academy of Sciences in 1821. Reprinted in *The Hermeneutics Reader*, p. 106.

8. For a discussion of modernism, see the general introduction to this volume.

9. Hans-Georg Gadamer, *Truth and Method*, ed. Gurrett Barden and John Cumming, translation copyright Sheed and Ward Ltd. (New York: Crossroad, 1988), p. xv. Gadamer's reaction to criticisms of the first edition of *Truth and Method* emphasize his conscious break with the tradition of nineteen-century hermeneutics: "My revival of the expression 'hermeneutics,' with its long tradition, has apparently led to some misunderstandings. I did not intend to produce an art or technique of understanding, in the manner of earlier hermeneutics. I did not wish to elaborate a system of rules to describe, let alone direct, the methodological procedure of the human sciences. Nor was it my aim to investigate the theoretical foundation of work in these fields in order to put my findings to practical ends" (p. xvi). In other words, Gadamer is saying, I did not wish to replicate the agenda of nineteenth-century hermeneutics.

10. See Hubert Dreyfus, "Beyond Hermeneutics," in *Hermeneutics: Questions and Prospects*, eds. Gary Shapiro and Alan Sica (Amherst: Univ. of Massachusetts, 1984), pp. 66−83.

11. *Being and Time*, trans. John Macquarrie and Edward Robinson (New York: Harper & Row, 1927, 1962), pp. 28−35.

12. For discussions of the formation of modern hermeneutics in the nineteenth and twentieth centuries, see Michael Ermarth, "The Transformation of Hermeneutics: 19th Century Ancients and 20th Century Moderns," *Monist*, 64 (1981), pp. 175−94, and Don Ihde, "Interpreting Hermeneutics: Origins, Developments and Prospects," *Man and World*, 13 (1980), pp. 325−43.

13. This is not to say that hermeneuts generally view truth as something that is easily grasped, but they are at least willing to acknowledge that interpretation, in the traditional sense of the term, is possible. See Marcelo Dascal, "Hermeneutic Interpretation and Pragmatic Interpretation," *Philosophy and Rhetoric*, 22 (1989), pp. 239−59, and David Ingram, "Hermeneutics and Truth," in *Hermeneutics and Praxis*, ed. Robert Hollinger (Notre Dame: Notre Dame Univ., 1985), pp. 32−53.

6

Heidegger
Language as the House of Being

Charles Guignon

In the later writings of Heidegger we often find such claims as: "Language is not a work of human beings: language speaks. Humans speak only insofar as they co-respond to language."[1] What these obscure sayings suggest is that language is not just a tool on hand for humans to use in referring to things or communicating their thoughts. On the contrary, Heidegger tells us that it is *in* language that we first *become* humans capable of discovering things or using signs. "We—human-kind—are a conversation," he says with Hölderlin. "The Being of humans is founded in language."[2] Because language is the medium in which reality is constituted, "language is at once the house of Being and the home of human beings."[3] This conception of language as the house of Being is the product of Heidegger's lifelong concern with understanding what makes things the things they are—the question of "the Being of beings." We can get a handle on his thoughts about language, then, only by clarifying his project of posing "the question of Being."

Heidegger's Project

Heidegger was born in Messkirch, a small town in the Black Forest, in 1889. The son of a cooper and church sexton, he followed the path of

This essay was made possible through my participation in the 1988 NEH Summer Institute on Interpretation at the University of California, Santa Cruz. Special thanks are due to H. L. Dreyfus and Charles Taylor, whose presentations sparked many of the thoughts developed here.

other poor Catholics from his region to the seminary where he entered
the Jesuit novitiate. At the age of eighteen he was given a copy of
Franz Brentano's *On the Manifold Meaning of Being According to
Aristotle* (1862), a work that had a strong impact on his thinking when
he switched from theology to philosophy at the University of Freiburg
in 1911. The question of Being was formulated initially by Heidegger
"in quite a vague manner" as follows: "If being [*Seiende*] is predicated
with manifold significances, then what is its leading, fundamental signification? What does Being [*Sein*] mean?"[4] In other words, we say
that such things as rocks, animals, constellations and numbers "exist."
The question is: What is it for anything to exist? What do various types
of things have in common so they can be said to *be*? Under the
influence of Edmund Husserl, the founder of phenomenology who
began teaching at Freiburg in 1916, this question was recast as asking
how things come to *show up for us* as existing in various ways. The
first attempt at an answer, Heidegger's masterwork *Being and Time*,
appeared in Husserl's *Yearbook for Phenomenology* in 1927.

Three key strands of influence shaped the composition of *Being
and Time*. First, Heidegger was deeply impressed by Husserl's ideal of
"phenomenological seeing" which turns directly "to the things themselves" as we encounter them before theoretical reflection. He was
especially impressed by Husserl's attempt to display the origins of
predicative judging in the temporal stream of pre-predicative "life-
experiences" (as revealed in Heidegger's 1920 lecture course, "Phenomenology of Intuition and Expression: Theory of Philosophical Concept
Formation"). Second, and more crucially, the important movement
called "life-philosophy" (then regarded as including Dilthey, Nietzsche,
and Bergson, but also associated with Jaspers's "existence-philosophy")
shifted the focus of philosophy from the Cartesian *ego cogito* or
"consciousness" to practical agency in a concrete, historical lifeworld.
Like the early Hegel, the life-philosophers sought to show that consciousness and the apprehensions of objects is not a given, but is
instead derivative from an underlying life-process that manifests itself
in action, language, and history. Finally, Heidegger's fascination with
the religious radicalism of Luther, Kierkegaard, and Dostoyevsky shaped
his understanding of Western history and philosophical method. He
became convinced that, just as Christendom over the millennia has
become remote from the concrete needs of actual life and from the
primordial meaning of early Christianity, so our Western understanding
of Being has become entangled in theoretical abstractions and has lost
touch with its origins. Philosophy therefore has a twofold task. It must
recover our most basic sense of what life is all about through an
interpretation of concrete everyday existence, a "hermeneutics of
facticity." And it must "de-structure" the history of metaphysics in

order to "retrieve" the primal sources of our civilization's understanding of Being.

What motivates the question of Being, then, is the conviction that our modern sense of reality, which was shaped by the rise of modern science and sketched out in the thought of Descartes, has lost touch with a deeper, more genuine understanding of what things are. According to the now dominant Cartesian picture, the world is seen as a vast aggregate of material objects or "extended substances" with properties of various sorts. Humans are a part of this natural order, but they are also unique insofar as they have minds and are capable of representing objects by means of the ideas presented in their fields of consciousness. This representationalist model of human existence rests on two correlative notions: an objectifying picture of the "external" world as consisting of brute physical things, and a subjectifying view of the human self as a subject or mind trying to formulate a correct representation of things by mapping ideas onto objects. The model is reinforced by a picture of language as a collection of signs at our disposal for designating objects and conveying our ideas about them to others. The subject/predicate structure of language seems to provide a confirmation for the substance/property view of reality. Since elementary propositions or assertions, the basic units of language, consist of subject-term and predicates, the facts they represent must be objects with properties. Given this representationalist account of language, "meaning" resides either in the semantic features of language or in the subjective ideas circulating in the minds of speakers. To think there is meaning *in the world* is simply a category mistake, the error of projecting peculiarly human subjective traits onto an inherently meaningless objective reality.

The outcome of this modern worldview has been a widespread sense of the ultimate "meaninglessness" of the world and of life itself. For Heidegger, however, this outlook is the result of "forgetfulness" brought on by a theoretical orientation that has lost contact with its roots in life. The project of "raising anew *the question of the meaning of Being*"[5] in *Being and Time* is an attempt to retrieve from oblivion a grasp of the inherent meaningfulness of life and the world. The distortions of the objectifying model, Heidegger suggests, are a product of concentrating on the ways things appear when we adopt the stance of being "pure spectators" merely observing things in a detached, disinterested manner. When we try to catch sight of how the world shows up for us in the midst of our pretheoretical everyday agency, however, we find that, for the most part, things are encountered as meaningful in the sense of *mattering* or *counting* for us in relation to our concerns. In our everyday dealings with equipment in familiar situations, what we find initially is not brute objects with properties (the "present-at-hand"), but significant contexts where things play a role as relevant for our projects (the "ready-to-hand"). By trying to retrieve our initial, prereflective *"vague, average understanding of Being"* (BT, 25), Heidegger hopes to show that the everyday lifeworld is, at the most basic level, a meaning-filled "dwelling" through which not only equipment but we ourselves show up on the scene as counting in determinate ways. From this standpoint, the objectifying picture of reality, the representationalist view of humans as subjects, and the "name and object" model of language all can be seen as highly refined theoretical constructs that are derivative from and parasitic on a "more primordial" way of being as agency in a meaningful lifeworld — our "Being-in-the-world."

The "phenomenology of everydayness" in *Being and Time* is aimed at clarifying how entities become intelligible to us in their Being in the course of our ordinary practical lives. But since human existence opens "the horizon within which something like Being in general becomes intelligible" (BT, 274), the attempt to characterize the meaning of Being begins with a description of humans, the beings who have some understanding of what things are. In order to avoid slipping into the traditional ways of regarding humans as organisms or as minds, Heidegger uses the term Dasein to refer to human existence. The term Dasein, etymologically derived from *da-sein*, or "being-there," is supposed to capture the "ways of being" of humans through which things can show up as intelligible in various ways. It is especially important not to think of Dasein as designating an individual consciousness of the sort that became central to Sartre's "existentialism." Heidegger explicitly rejects the temptation to portray our existence in terms of conscious "experience" or the "center of actions." In our everyday Being-in-the-world, he says, "even one's *own* Dasein [is] something that it can itself proximally 'come across' only when it *looks away* from 'experiences' and the 'center of its actions,' or does not yet 'see' them at all. Dasein finds 'itself' proximally in *what* it does ..." (BT, 155). Heidegger wants to bypass the assumptions of traditional ontology, with its distinctions of mind and matter, self and others, and so he tries to characterize our lives as we are "proximally and for the most part," that is, as we are "'manifest' in the 'with-one-another' of publicness," as we show up "for Everyman ... 'as a rule'" (BT, 422). For the most part, as agents involved in a practical lifeworld, we exist as already "outside" our "selves," caught up in equipmental contexts and participating in a communal world where "others" are generally "those from whom ... one does *not* distinguish oneself — those among whom one is too" (BT, 154). For this reason, Heidegger says that being a "Self" is "'only' ... a *way of Being* of [the] entity" whose most primordial being is Being-in-the-world (BT, 153; my emphasis).

This picture of human existence as inseparable from action in practical contexts leads to what might be called an "expressivist" view of human agency.[6] The expressivist view is best understood by contrasting it with the conception of action that naturally unfolds from the Cartesian model. From the Cartesian standpoint, human agency is to be understood by distinguishing "inner" motivations or intentions (the agent's beliefs and desires) from the "outer" bodily movements that are caused by those motivations. To say that an action is an "expression" on this view, then, would be to say that it is an external display of some inner mental events or states. In explaining the action, we must read backward to the agent's actual intentions: saying something, for example, is treated as a "speech act" to be explained in terms of the speaker's intentions. This model assumes that intentions and other mental processes exist and are identifiable quite independently of the outer bodily movements.

Heidegger's expressivist view, in contrast, rejects this way of privileging the "inner" and treating the "outer" as something secondary and derivative. To say that for the most part we *are* what we *do* is to say that our own identity as agents is something that comes to be realized and defined only in our ways of being manifest in the world. This view of expression becomes clearer when we consider the kinds of personality traits we take as being definitive of a person's identity. If a friend constantly responds to life's crises in a calm and eventempered way, we do not usually take this as merely an external "sign" of some inner state. Under ordinary circumstances, we encounter this person's mode of comportment as *constituting* her calmness — her *being as* a calm person. The subdued rhythm of response, the assured gestures, the even tone of voice — these *present* calmness; they "body it forth" in the public arena, easing tense situations and exuding steadiness and dependability. The demeanor, so to speak, "lets-calmness-be" as the mode of this person's being present in the world. It *is* her calmness, just as my wearing shabby clothes *is* my being a sloppy dresser. The distinction between the mental and the bodily has no role to play here. Significant questions about "what is *really* going on in this person's mind" can arise only when there are breaks or inconsistencies in the smooth flow of her comportment. But, even in these cases, such questions make sense only against a background in which people generally *are* what they do.

The expressivist view therefore drops the distinction between a genuine "inner" reality and the contingent, external persona one presents to the world. Agency is understood not in terms of inner representations effecting bodily motions, but in terms of "presentations" in the weave of a meaningful lifeworld. And so the traditional distinction between Being and appearance also drops out. Heidegger says that, for the pre-Platonic Greeks, "Being means appearing." What something *is* is only realized and made concrete in its "self-manifestation," its way of "showing itself." "Appearing is not something subsequent that happens

to Being. Appearing is the very essence of Being."[7] When the inner/
outer distinction is dropped, "meaning" no longer appears as something
"subjective" going on in our heads. Meaning is in the world—in our
familiar, attuned modes of comportment as these are woven into significant situations. And, as we shall see, since language is the medium
through which the lifeworld and our own identity as agents come to
be articulated and shaped, our actions and ways of speaking generally
comply with the understanding of Being embodied in language. Being
"speaks to us" through the medium of language, and we speak only to
the extent that we are in tune with the background of intelligibility
opened by language.

In the period from 1928 to 1945, when Heidegger was a full
professor at Freiburg, there was a gradual "turn" in his thought.
Instead of focusing on Dasein as the arena in which things show up,
Heidegger concentrated on how Being itself simultaneously reveals
and conceals itself to humans throughout history. Being, now called
the "mystery" or the "no-thing," is the Other to all human creating.
Nevertheless, Being presents itself to humans over the course of history
only because of the "clearing" or "opening" disclosed by Dasein, and it
"gives itself" in a nondistortive way only when humans have prepared
themselves properly for its self-manifestation. In the thirties, Heidegger
thought of this preparedness as a matter of being "authentic" in the
sense of decisively appropriating world-defining historical transformations of Being. This attitude accounts for (but hardly excuses) his
involvement with the Nazis. In 1933, he was elected rector of Freiburg
University and, as was expected, he became a member of the Nazi
party. Although he resigned as rector several months later, new evidence
indicates a protracted period of cooperation with the Nazis. He seems
to have felt that National Socialism was a world-transforming historical
event in the "destiny of Being," a new revelation of Being which would
counteract the dangers of runaway technology in the West. Intellectuals
therefore have a duty to appropriate this event in order to steer it away
from anti-Semitic racialism toward an authentic world-rejuvenation.

Heidegger's disgraceful behavior reflects a deeply troubling problem in his thought. If humans can only "listen" and respond to the
"silent Saying" of Being, and if Being's self-manifestations in history
are always ambiguous to the extent that they involve both revelation
and concealment, then we seem to lack any criterion for deciding
which historical events to embrace and which to resist. One might
argue that Heidegger's thought contained the resources for criticizing
the Nazi movement. As Heidegger's student Hans-Georg Gadamer
has shown,[8] our historical heritage contains moral ideals that make
totalitarianism and persecution intolerable to us. Thus, history itself
contains the bases for criticizing the Nazi horror. In the last decades

before his death in 1976, however, Heidegger took a different tack on this issue, becoming ever more critical of the notion of "decisiveness" in world affairs, and turning toward an ideal of "letting-be" or "release-ment" (*Gelassenheit*) in the face of "epochal" emergences of Being. Though the verdict is not yet in on the connection between Heidegger's thought and his actions, his profound influence on contemporary European thought compels us to come to terms with his way of address-ing "the question of Being" and his understanding of language as "the house of Being."

Being-in-the-World

We saw that *Being and Time* develops an expressivist view of human existence. This expressivism has important implications for our under-standing of the world and of our own identity as agents. First, if I *am* what I do in the course of living out my life — if there is no fixed human essence that defines my identity in advance — then I just *am* what I interpret myself as in my actions in the world. Heidegger develops this conception of the self as a "self-interpreting being" by proposing that we think of a human not as an object or thing of some kind, but instead as an ongoing "happening" or "event" — an unfolding life-course or life-story, "extending from birth to death." This conception of life as a temporal unfolding or "emergence-into-Being" is captured in the claim that Dasein is a being that *cares* about what it is. What I will be — what my life adds up to as a whole — is *at issue* for me, and consequently I am always taking some stand on my "ability-to-be" by taking over concrete possibilities in my current situation. "In each case Dasein has already bound itself up with a possibility of itself" (BT, 236) in the sense of having taken over specific roles, vocations, status relations, life-styles, traits of character, and so on. It is through these possible self-interpretations that I realize and define my Being as a person.

When we think of life as a temporal happening, we will see it as having two dimensions. On the one hand, humans find themselves already "thrown" into a world, confronted with concrete tasks rooted in the commitments they have undertaken in the past. This "facticity" is revealed in the "moods" that tune us in to situations and let things matter to us. As a parent, for instance, I find myself "stuck" with certain obligations and confronted with tasks that I can take up in specific ways. In this sense Dasein "has its Being as its own to be" (BT, 33): we are "already in" a world that predelineates the choices that will make sense. But, on the other hand, Dasein is also "ahead of itself" in taking some stand on the tasks it confronts. In my current actions I am "sketching out," no matter how unreflectively, some formulation of what sort of person I will be in my life as a totality. Since my *Being* as a human will be defined and finalized only at the culmination of my life, that is, since it is something impending and "not yet" realized, my identity is constituted by this "projection" toward the future—my "being-toward-the-end" or "being-toward-death." So, when I let the baby cry, for example, I am shaping my identity as a parent who is negligent or uncaring, regardless of what plans or good intentions I might have. Heidegger describes the Being of Dasein as a "bringing itself to fruition" (*sich zeitigen*). Because each of our actions contributes to the definition of who we *will be*, we are, so to speak, composing our own autobiographies in all we do.

A second consequence of the expressivist view is the recognition that our existence is always bound up with a meaningful lifeworld. Dasein's stance toward its own life—its "self-projective being toward its ownmost ability-to-be" (BT, 236)—is brought to realization and made concrete in its "concernful dealings" with familiar contexts of equipment. In our pretheoretical practical lives, we find ourselves engaged in using equipment that shows up as significant for us in relation to our undertakings. When everything is functioning smoothly, this "ready-to-hand" equipment is encountered as a holistic web of significance relations focused around our self-understanding as agents. In the course of hammering in a workshop, for instance, what shows up for me is not a "hammer-thing," but hammering which is "in order to" nail boards together, which is "for" building a bookcase, which is in turn "for the sake of," say, being a person with an attractive study. It is *through* my agency in this context that things come to appearance in the functional relationships that define their Being. My activities "make explicit" a preunderstood background of possible uses things can have, and so they let things emerge *as* being things of certain determinate sorts. Understanding myself as a craftsman, the tools are "appropriated" *as* precision instruments for doing fine work, not as toys or pieces of junk. But it is also the case that my *own* identity as an agent in this context is preshaped by the significances things have: in the workshop I can *be* an amateur or a patient craftsman, but not a sewer repairman or an ayatollah. In this picture of "worldhood," then, the Being of entities is defined by their ways of showing up as ready-to-hand in my dealings; Heidegger says that to suppose there are "at first" mere present-at-hand objects that *then* become invested with a use-value is an "illusion" (BT, 421). Yet who *I* am is also something that comes to be given shape only in the midst of my involvements with the ready-to-hand. There is no pregiven "real me" distinct from the fields of significance that provide the context for my agency. Thus, Heidegger can say, "Dasein *is* its world existingly" (BT, 416).

A third feature of the expressivist view follows from the fact that the world in the broadest sense is always a public world we have in common. My own unfolding life-story is interwoven into the wider weave of the ongoing story of my community. I am a parent by virtue of my relation to, and interchange with, children, playmates, other parents, teachers, sitters, and so forth. I can have my own "peculiar style" of realizing my identity in this role only in terms of the guidelines of standards and conventions laid out by the practices of my community. In this sense we always find ourselves "thrown" into a public world of what Heidegger calls "the They" (*das Man*). It is because we have been initiated into the common forms of life of a community that things come to stand out as relevant for us in familiar ways. The ready-to-hand speaks to me of significant projects because I have soaked up a sense of how things count that is made accessible by my culture: as Heidegger says, "the They itself articulates the referential context of significance" (BT, 167). The world, understood as a shared field of significance, is opened up and made accessible through our communal practices.

Finally, the shared world itself is something that develops and takes shape through the course of history. What I am doing now counts as *action* (as opposed to inadvertent movement) because of the way it figures into my own life-story. But that life-story makes sense only because of its place within the wider ongoing story of my historical culture. "Our fates have been guided in advance," Heidegger says, "in our being-with-one-another in the same world ..."; the happening of a person's life is always interwoven into the "co-happening ... of the community, of a people" (BT, 436). This "historicity" of human existence makes possible an authentic way of life. According to Heidegger, to be authentic is to "retrieve" the most meaningful possibilities embedded in one's "heritage" and to resolutely project them into the future, striving through one's actions to realize the "destiny" of one's community. The possibility of an "authentic happening of existence which arises from Dasein's *future*" (BT, 438) is disclosed by a recognition of our finitude and by a grasp of our communal existence as an emergence-into-Being that directs us to "become what we are" (BT, 186) through what we do.

Discourse and Language in *Being and Time*

If we abandon the objectifying model of human existence and adopt Heidegger's expressivist view, we are led to see Dasein as a "clearing" or "lighting," a field of "disclosedness," in which things come to emerge-into-presence *as* the kinds of things they are. Heidegger introduces the concept of "discourse" within his discussion of the three essential structures (or "existentialia") that constitute Dasein's being as a clearing. The first basic structure is "situatedness." We always find ourselves already caught up in a concrete context, which preshapes how things can show up and what stances can make sense. The second essential structure Heidegger calls "understanding." To be human is to have some prior mastery of what life is all about by virtue of our skillful coping in the contexts in which we find ourselves. This competence in living, embodied in the concrete stances we take, has been laid out in advance by the goal-directed patterns of activity of the "They." "As something factical," Heidegger says, "Dasein's projection of itself . . . is in each case already at home in a world. . . . From this world it takes its possibilities, and it does so first in accordance with the way things have been interpreted by the They." For the most part our choices are restricted "to what lies within the range of the familiar, the attainable, the respectable — that which is fitting and proper" (BT, 239). The interpretations by which we "appropriate" and "make explicit" ready-to-hand equipment *as* such and such (BT, 188–89) are guided by this prior, publicly defined understanding of what things add up to in relation to our lives.

Situatedness and understanding constitute the temporal dimensions of "having-been" and "futurity" of Dasein's being as an unfolding clearing. Discourse characterizes Dasein's way of being "present" in the world. It is evident, however, that the term "discourse" refers to more than just using language as this is ordinarily understood. Heidegger tells us that "discourse" (*Rede*) is the "literal translation" of the Greek world *logos*, which means "to make manifest" or "to let something be seen" (BT, 55–56). In this deeper sense, discourse seems to be the primal articulation of the meaningful lifeworld by virtue of which our ordinary interpretations become possible. Heidegger says that the background of "intelligibility" — that which *can* be understood — "has always been articulated, even before there is any appropriative interpretation of it. Discourse is the articulation of intelligibility. It therefore underlies both interpretation and assertion" (BT, 203–4). Here "discourse" seems to refer to the regularized patterns of acting — the routines, practices, customs and institutions — that open up our familiar, harmonized ways of taking things.

Discourse in this primal sense need not be linguistic. It seems to take place whenever "Dasein addresses itself to the objects of its concern" (BT, 460), and this occurs most often "without wasting words." The word "discourse" refers to the way "Dasein expresses itself . . . as a being-toward entities — a being-toward which uncovers" (BT, 266). For example, our standardized ways of using tools in the workshop lay out a field of significance according to which hammers, nails, boards, and workbench stand out as relevant for our projects, whereas the dust in the corner does not. Heidegger says that what "gets articulated as such in discursive articulation we call the 'totality of significations'" (BT, 204), that is, the entire contexture of possible functional relationships of ready-to-hand equipment in use. According to this early view (a formulation Heidegger later retracted), language appears as a way of expressing these prelinguistic articulations. "The intelligibility of Being-in-the-world ... *expresses itself as discourse*. The totality of significations of intelligibility is *put into words*" (BT, 204). But, even here, "language" does not refer to lexical items or signifiers in a sign-system. "Language *can* be broken up into word-things which are present-at-hand" (BT, 204; my emphasis) at a high level of abstraction. As "the way in which discourse is expressed," however, language must be understood in its role of making manifest and preserving the attuned understanding that articulates the world into a familiar field of significance.

Ordinary talking, then, "is the way we articulate 'significantly' the intelligibility of Being-in-the-world" (BT, 204). Talking is our way of "expressing ourselves." But "expression" is not a matter of making something "inner" accessible in the "outer" world. On the contrary, discoursing brings to realization our "being already outside" as we are caught up in the swim of things in everyday life. "In discoursing, Dasein *ex*presses itself not because it has, in the first instance, been encapsulated as something 'internal' over against something 'outside' when it understands. What is expressed is precisely this being-outside ..." (BT, 205). Discourse focuses and makes explicit our concrete being-together in the same world: "Communication is never anything like a conveying of experiences, such as opinions or wishes, from the interior of one subject into the interior of another. Our co-Dasein is already essentially manifest in a cosituatedness and a counderstanding. In discourse our co-Being becomes 'explicitly' *shared* ... as something that [is] taken hold of and appropriated" (BT, 205). Because discourse makes manifest our shared clearing, Heidegger says that disclosedness in general is "articulated by discourse," and that the temporality of discourse just *is* "Dasein in general" (BT, 400, 401).

Thus, far from being a mere nomenclature for designating pregiven objects, discourse *constitutes* the field of significance of our everyday public world and therefore preshapes the ways things in general can show up. Everyday speaking, which is focused and guided by this background sense of things, helps to transmit and transmute our common grasp of situations. When someone on a long line at the checkout counter of a supermarket says, "Isn't this annoying?" for example, the remark does not convey information or ask a question. Rather, it contributes to setting a tone in the situation—letting irritability be the mood in this context. Things now tend to emerge *as* a source of annoyance. Possibilities of response are laid out by the utterance: we can ignore the crack or concur in the atmosphere it creates. Language here serves to get things out in the open among us, making manifest a clearing and invoking significance relations so that they come to appear in specific ways. A remark of this sort does not so much represent anything as it *presents* things in a certain light, opening a space for a shared, attuned understanding. But, while disclosing the situation, the utterance also makes manifest the Being of the speaker as, say, short-tempered rather than easygoing. As ways in which we "make explicit" our being-already-outside, discursive expressions constitute our own identity as subjects and sustain the forms of life circulating in our public world. The meaning of our expressions is not reducible to the speaker's intentions plus features of the sign-system, for the reason that the form of life brought to realization by this kind of expression is a condition for the possibility of there *being* agents with these intentions or signs with these significations.

Although the early Heidegger seems to regard discourse as something nonlinguistic, he is also aware that language is the primary medium in which our attuned understanding is formulated and given shape. He says that our everyday intelligibility is made accessible by what he calls "idle talk": "In language, as a way things have been expressed, there is hidden a way in which the understanding of Dasein has been interpreted.... Proximally, and with certain limits, Dasein is constantly delivered over to this interpretedness, which controls and distributes the possibilities of average understanding and of the situatedness belonging to it" (BT, 211). All possible stances and ways of seizing on things are sketched out in advance by this public way of interpreting things.

> This everyday way in which things have been interpreted [in language] is one into which Dasein has grown in the first instance, with never a possibility of extrication. In it, out of it, and against it, all genuine understanding, interpreting, and communicating, all rediscovering and appropriating anew, are performed. In no case is a Dasein, untouched and unseduced by this way in which things have been interpreted, set before the open country of a 'world-in-itself' so that it just beholds what it encounters. (BT, 213)

Because the public language of the They "prescribes one's situatedness and determines what and how one 'sees'" (BT, 213), what we call "facts" in the everyday world are articulated by language. "Facts are artifacts of language"[9] insofar as language provides the grid or template through which things show up *as* "facts" of certain sorts.

But to say that reality shows up for us in a way that is already articulated by language is not to say that we initially encounter things through the lens of the standard subject/predicate assertions taken as paradigmatic by logicians and mainstream linguists. Heidegger tries to show that the "apophantic as" of assertion, through which we encounter things as mere objects with properties, is derived from a more original "hermeneutic as" of prereflective agency. In its most common uses, he suggests, language is used not to refer to and communicate information about objects, but rather to open and articulate a public space of meaningful concerns in which we find ourselves. When a worker, in the course of hammering, shouts "Too heavy! Hand me the other hammer!" he is not conveying information about a material object or issuing a command that has as its propositional content "the hammer is brought here." Instead, the linguistic expression has the function of making manifest how things are going in the entire context of significance of the work-world. The utterance lights up the situation of common concerns, revealing how things stand with the hammering and the project in general.

Here language reveals the ready-to-hand as counting in specific ways in relation to the holistic mesh of goals, interests, and practices of the agents involved. This way of making significance manifest *as* such and such is called the "hermeneutic as" of everyday agency. The linguistic utterance lets the situation emerge *as* one where the hammering is not going well. Heidegger's claim is that language can take the form of a mere subject/predicate assertion only when there has been a "changeover" in our ways of dealing with things. The "apophantical as" arises when we shift our stance toward the world from involved agency to detached observation of mere things disengaged from any particular context of significance relations. Through the subject/predicate assertion, things present themselves *as* discrete items with intrinsic properties, lacking any necessary relations to any background of practical affairs. As Heidegger says, in the assertion, the "as structure of interpretation has undergone a modification.... [T]he 'as' no longer reaches out into a totality of involvements" (BT, 200). When we regard the hammer as an object with a property, the utterance has severed its ties to the everyday sources of meaningfulness opened by our practices. In the bare assertion, discourse "no longer has any 'meaning'; that is to say, the entity, as we now encounter it, gives us nothing with relation to which it could be 'found' too heavy or too light" (BT, 412). The assertion can have a meaning in any sense only because of its place within a background of possible uses of things that is momentarily concealed.

Heidegger's conception of assertion as derivative from a more basic way of Being-in-the-world carries with it a transformed understanding of "truth." Truth regarded as the correspondence of propositions to facts is itself derivative from a more original sense of "truth" as the "unconcealment" or disclosedness of a world—"truth" in the original Greek sense of the word *aletheia*.[10] Only because a world has been opened up by our discursiveness can there be a clearing in which assertions are uttered, things encountered, criteria of correctness established, and evidence of correctness collected. Since truth is something that emerges in the interplay between Dasein and entities, there is no way to think of ourselves as "trapped within the prison-house of language" with no access to reality as it is in itself. For what we can think of as "reality" is something that emerges into presence only through the aletheiac truth of our discursiveness and articulacy as agents in the world.

In *Being and Time* Heidegger offers an interpretation of the distinction between "truth" and "untruth" as a distinction between authentic and inauthentic ways of existing. We are "in the untruth," he suggests, to the extent that we are "falling" or entangled in the routine preoccupations of day-to-day existence. The chief characteristic of inauthenticity is "forgetfulness." In order to be able to throw ourselves into the chores and rituals dictated by the They, we must be able to, so to speak, draw a horizon around ourselves, forgetting the wider issues at stake in life, and focusing on the work at hand. Heidegger says, "The self must forget itself if, lost in the world of equipment, it is to be able 'actually' to go to work and manipulate something" (BT, 405). This first-order forgetfulness is inevitable and unavoidable for agents in a world, and so Heidegger says Dasein is always "in untruth" (BT, 264–65). What is insidious, however, is the way this first-order forgetfulness is compounded by a second-order forgetting in which we forget that our current involvements are made possible only on the basis of forgetting. When this happens, one comes to assume that the currently accepted practices of the They are of consuming importance, the only viable ways of living and acting. This totalizing absorption in the current world, supported by endless idle chatter, curiosity and ambiguity about what is at stake in life, lets us drift off into "the unintelligibility of the trivial" (BT, 208) with no ability to grasp what is genuinely worth pursuing.

Becoming authentic frees us from this drifting into the "obviousness" of the current status quo and opens us up to a more clear-sighted grasp of what life is all about. Heidegger says that the authentic relation to language is "silence" and "hearing." Hearing can counteract our inveterate tendency toward oblivion by reminding us that our involvements in the current world have been made possible by a concealment or covering over of the deeper resources and possibilities for living embedded in our heritage. It thereby frees us from the rigidity and shortsightedness of drifting into public roles, and throws us onto our responsibility for taking over the possibilities made accessible by the past for the purposes of realizing our shared destiny. Dasein is "in the truth" to the extent that it is "critical" of the calcified common sense of the "Today," and resolute (*ent-schlossen*, literally "un-closed-off") in taking a stand on the potential embodied in the heritage of its historical culture.

Language in the Later Heidegger

The well known "turn" in the later Heidegger's thought is at least partly a shift from describing Being primarily as what is disclosed by human practices to thinking of it as what "gives itself" to humans and first makes human existence possible. Yet the expressivist outlook still pervades these later writings. In his transitional lectures, *An Introduction to Metaphysics* (1935), Heidegger tells us that the Greeks originally experienced Being as *physis*, as an emerging-into-presence that comes to abide. Being is "an *appearance* as a definite mode of emerging self-manifestation" that lets entities show forth in a "lighting" or "*truth* in the sense of unconcealment" (IM, 109). Here it is the "overpowering surge" of Being itself that is made manifest and realized in appearing. Only because beings come to presence *as* what they are in this event can *we* encounter them in determinate ways: "In appearing, [Being] gives itself an aspect" and, as a result, we come to encounter these aspects "from this or that point of view" (IM, 102, 104). This understanding of Being as always "more than" what humans can master or fully articulate leads to the later notions of "mystery" and "earth."

But Heidegger also makes it clear that Being's self-manifestation is not something that could occur without humans. Things can show up as counting or mattering in some way only because humans, responding to Being's "overpowering surge," articulate a field of significance that lets things become present with some determinate ordering and delimitations. The more-than-human "is made manifest and made to stand" through the "gathering" and "collecting collectedness" brought about by the comportment of a historical people. In its "historical, history-disclosing essence," Heidegger writes, "human-being is *logos*, the gathering and apprehending of the Being of beings" (IM, 171). Through the "capturing and subjugating that opens beings *as* sea, *as* earth, *as* animal," humans "undertake to govern and succeed in governing the power of the overpowering" (IM, 157, 172). Thus, although the emphasis in these later writings is on the way Being "gives itself" by appearing, it is also clear that the articulate order in which things show up *as* entities of familiar sorts depends on the field of intelligibility opened by the expressiveness of a historical people.

The centrality of language in opening this arena of intelligibility is made quite explicit in these later works. Words call forth beings "in

the structure of their collectedness" — their ways of mattering in relation
to the lives of a historical people — and thereby constitute the identity,
demarcations and stability of things. "The word, the name, restores
the emerging entity from the immediate overpowering surge to its
Being and maintains it in this openness, delimitation and permanence"
(IM, 172). Our ways of expressing ourselves in language let beings
become manifest *as* what they *are*. Heidegger says that "naming does
not come afterward, providing an already manifest entity with a designation" (IM, 172); rather, naming invokes or elicits the types of things
that can stand out in a clearing. Growing out of an initially inchoate
and amorphous response to the "surge" of Being, language defines and
sustains things, letting them *be* such-and-such: "Language, by naming
beings for the first time, first brings beings to word and appearance.
Only naming nominates beings *to* their Being *from out of* their Being."[11]
This invocative power of language is evident in many of our higher
level practices. Our modern understanding of ourselves as individuals,
for example, is made possible by a vocabulary including words like
"dignity," "respect," "self-esteem," "individual rights," and so on — a
vocabulary that makes possible practices, responses, and institutions
that would be unintelligible in societies based on codes of honor with
their emphasis on status, bonds of kinship, and success. Here language
does not just designate pregiven "facts." It shapes what can *count* as a
"fact" in the weave of our lives. In our modern, linguistically constituted
form of life, for instance, my blunders and handicaps can be treated as
accidental incidents and traits that need not reflect adversely on my
identity as a person or on the honor of my kin or clan. The vocabulary
constituting individualism helps to orchestrate the rhythms of gesture
and response, the skilled competence of our interactions, and the
attuned perceptions and interpretations that define our sense of reality.

   The field of significance opened by language is deposited and
preserved in what Heidegger calls "saying." Saying, as a "renunciation
of all the dim confusion in which a being veils and withdraws itself," is
a "projecting of lighting in which announcement is made of what it is
that beings come into the open *as*" (PLT, 73–74). Saying is a "showing"
that "pervades and structures the openness of the clearing" in which
anything can "show, say [and] announce itself."[12] Because saying is a
"composing" (*dichten*) of truth for a community, Heidegger calls it
"poetry [*Dichtung*] in the essential sense": "Poetry is the saying of the
unconcealedness of beings" (PLT, 74). "Poetic saying" seems to be
thought of as a primal articulation of things that originated at the dawn
of history and continues to "project" the possible types of interpretation
accessible for a people. But this original discursiveness is never separ-
able from the concrete ways it is given shape in natural languages. As
Heidegger says, "Actual language at any moment is the happening of

this saying, in which a people's world historically arises for it.... In such saying, the concepts of a historical people's essence, i.e., of its belonging to world history, are preformed for that people" (PLT, 74). In our everyday speaking, then, we are *respondents* who hear the call of the possibilities opened by the primal text of poetic saying as it is made manifest in our current language.

Saying or poetry thus constitutes aletheiac truth or "unconcealment," "the opening of the open region, and the lighting of beings" (PLT, 71). But the later Heidegger suggests that every emergence of truth is at the same time a "concealment," with the result that truth involves an "original strife" between unconcealment and concealment. The claim here seems to be that things can come to appear *as* such-and-such — that they can present an "aspect" — only by simultaneously masking or covering over other ways of encountering things. In this respect, concealment is a correlate of "forgetting" in *Being and Time* (though it is important to keep in mind that concealment is described as something that happens in the appearing of Being rather than as something done by humans). Just as forgetting was seen as necessary to the practical involvements that disclose the everyday world, concealment or "denial" is inevitable if the "overpowering surge" is to present itself to us as a context of significance for our historical agency. Thus, to cite a familiar example, the transition to our modern scientific outlook was made possible only by displacing an older, theocentric understanding of the cosmos as an expression of God's will.

Concealment is unavoidable, then, if there is to be any truth understood as a lighting or clearing. What produces "confusion" and "error," however, is a tendency toward "dissembling," a second-order concealment that conceals the fact that the current lighting has been achieved only at the cost of the initial concealment. Dissembling occurs, Heidegger says, when Being "cloaks itself *as* appearance insofar as it shows itself *as* Being" (IM, 109; my emphasis). In other words, a mode of appearance is taken as the final, all-embracing "Truth" about beings — as the only possible game in town — with the result that the current understanding of things becomes calcified and all viable alternatives are shut out. The prevailing sense of reality becomes "self-evident," "commonplace," and we are set adrift in our complacent assurance that nothing is any longer really in question or subject to challenge. In this sense, dissembling "metes out to all lighting the indefeasible severity of error" (PLT, 55).

In his essay "The Origin of the Work of Art" (1935), Heidegger describes how a crucial kind of "happening of truth," that opened by a great work of art, counteracts this tendency toward dissembling and makes manifest the "strife" involved in an emergence of truth. "The Origin of the Work of Art" introduces two important notions that were

not explicitly developed in *Being and Time*. First, by showing how a
"new" world can emerge for a people, it paves the way to the later
idea of "epochs" in the history of Being—different ways that Being has
become manifest in the course of our history. And, second, it introduces
the important notion of "earth" as a counterconcept to that of "world,"
and suggests that the emergence of truth always involves a "strife"
between the world's openness and the earth as that which resists total
clarity and mastery. Getting some grasp of what Heidegger means by
"earth" is essential to understanding Heidegger's later notion of humans
as the "shepherds of Being" (BW, 210) who can never achieve a
totalizing comprehension of Being.

Turning first to the suggestion that artworks bring about a "new
world," Heidegger tells us that a great work of art does not simply
represent some pregiven reality (whether that be thought of as actual
events or as an artist's intentions). Rather, an artwork *presents* and
makes accessible what can count as "real" in the lives of a people. The
work of art grows out of what is initially only amorphous and tacit in a
people's practices—a prearticulate background sense of things embodied
in their forms of life. By drawing these inchoate interpretations together
into a coherent form, it lets things stand out for the community in
some meaningful way. A tragedy, for instance, emerges out of the
background "saying" of a people, but it also transforms what was
implicit in this saying so as to bring to light the issues confronting a
people in their world. "In the tragedy nothing is staged or displayed
theatrically, but the battle of the new gods against the old is being
fought. The literary work, originating in the saying of the people, does
not refer to this battle; it transforms the people's saying so that now
every living word fights the battle and puts up for decision what is holy
and what unholy, what great and what small, what brave and what
cowardly, what lofty and what flighty, what master and what slave"
(PLT, 43). In the work, "what went before is refuted *in its exclusive
reality*" (PLT, 75; my emphasis), and a people faces the challenge of
taking a stand on what is yet unfamiliar and unmastered in their world.

But a work of art does not just bring about a new world. According to
"The Origin of the Work of Art," the artwork embodies in itself and
makes manifest an "opposition between world and earth," and so
brings to realization the primal strife of truth as both unconcealment
and concealment. In this essay, the term "world" still refers to the field
of significance that structures a people's practices, predelineates the
aims and standards guiding those practices, and so articulates a shared
sense of how things can show up for a community. The world "is the
lighting of the paths of the essential guiding directions with which all
decision complies" (PLT, 55). In order to emphasize the fact that the
world is not something "created" by humans, Heidegger says that "the

world worlds" and humans show up as "subject to" a world: "World is
the ever-nonobjective to which we are subject as long as the paths of
birth and death, blessing and curse keep us transported into Being"
(PLT, 44). Describing the world disclosed by a Greek temple, Heidegger
suggests that it is only in terms of this world that humans can appear
on the scene: "men and . . . things are never present and familiar as
unchangeable objects, only to represent also a fitting environment for
the temple, which one fine day is added on to what is already there. . . .
The temple, in its standing there, first gives to things their look and to
men their outlook on themselves" (PLT, 42–43). The work establishes
the orientation and context of significance through which the Greek
people become the "creators" and "preservers" they are. Standing
there in the clearing as an exemplar or emblem, it enshrines and
expresses the possibilities of understanding accessible to that community.

What is new in this essay is the suggestion that artworks have the
distinctive power of opening a world while at the same time preserving
a sense of that which defies total comprehension and control—the
"earth." Heidegger says that, in "setting up a world, the work sets
forth the earth"; it "*lets the earth be an earth*" (PLT, 46). This obscure
notion of the "earth" can be approached by considering a particular
example Heidegger discusses — the role of words in literary works. In
ordinary discourse, he says, speakers and writers who use words "use
them up"; language itself is unnoticed so long as one "gets the idea
across." By contrast, "the poet also uses the word," but "in such a way
that the word only now becomes and remains truly a word" (PLT, 48).
In literary works, "the word [comes] to say" by simultaneously bringing
forth the "earth" in the form of "the naming power of the word"
(PLT, 46). The "naming power of the word" here seems to characterize
the way words elicit or invoke beings "to their Being" only by concealing
other possibilities of understanding things. To say that the literary
word brings forth the naming power of words, then, is to say that it
calls forth an "explicit" outlook on things from the tacit background of
a people's saying, while still continuing to resonate with and evoke
what is unsaid and unsayable in this world. In "nominating beings to
their Being," it safeguards "the reservoir of the not-yet-revealed, the
un-uncovered" (PLT, 60) that lies secluded in the background of what
is now revealed.

Consider, for example, Sophocles' *Antigone*. A Heideggerian reading might treat the *Antigone* as enacting or bringing into focus a
transition that was only vaguely grasped in the "saying" of the Greeks:
the shift from a form of life centered on the *oikos* or household, with
its basis in kinship and blood-ties, to one centered on the *polis* or
city-state with its ruler and citizens. The tragedy lets this new world
emerge, but it does so by displaying how the rule of Creon has been

achieved only at the terrible cost of the renunciation of the old ways of
kinship attachments and blood bonds. By recalling a sense of the losses
involved in the dawning of the *polis* world, it evokes and preserves the
now displaced older ways as the "other" of the all-pervasive new
world. The bitter struggle between Creon and Antigone makes manifest
what is at stake in endorsing the city-state, and what risks accompany
any inflexible attachment to a totalizing standpoint. Through the naming
power of this literary work, the Greeks *become* the people for whom
the issues of tyranny, solidarity and the repudiation of older bonds are
put up for decision in all their actions. Yet, at the same time, they also
feel the rootedness of their world in a way of life that still exerts a pull
for them.

Seen in this way, great literary works call forth a new world while
continuing to evoke forms of life that now have been marginalized by
that world. The work disavows the familiar and commonplace, and
projects into the *future* the "vocation of historical Dasein itself"
(PLT, 76). By evoking those possibilities of understanding excluded in
the current world, it reveals the "dwelling" and "native ground" from
which a form of life originates, and therefore displays the gravity and
weightiness of the decisions confronting a people. The resonances of
the now inarticulate voices of the older ways make manifest the fact
that all decision "bases itself on something not mastered, something
concealed, confusing" (PLT, 55). Brought face to face with "the indefeasible severity of error," a people confronts the tenuousness of life
and the need for constantly renewed decisiveness and dedication. "The
dawning world [inaugurated by the artwork] brings out what is as yet
undecided and measureless, and thus discloses the hidden necessity of
measure and decisiveness" (PLT, 63). But through the work the
community is also given a sense of belongingness: "Upon the earth and
in it, historical humanity grounds its dwelling in the world." The
artwork discloses "that into which human being is already cast ... the
earth" (PLT, 46, 75).

Heidegger suggests that all great works of art, when they are
working, express the opposition of world and earth, and thereby articulate the choices definitive of our Being as humans. But literary works —
and especially great poetic works — have a privileged position among
the arts. For poetry (*Poesie*) in the ordinary sense is what defines and
makes possible a people's "saying" or "poetry" (*Dichtung*) in the
wider sense. Because language as "primal poetry" is "the happening in
which, for humanity, beings first disclose themselves to us *as* beings,
poesy — or poetry in the narrow sense — is the most original form of
poetry in the essential sense" (PLT, 74). For Western civilization, the
works of, say, Homer and Hesiod, or the Psalms of David, are not just
aesthetically pleasing embellishments on a previously existing, prosaic

experience of Being-in-the-world. Instead, as world-defining initial responses to the surge of Being, their primal naming power continues to articulate the invocative and evocative powers of language that resonate throughout our Western understanding of Being. The other arts, therefore, are derivative from the significances disclosed by great poems: "Building and plastic creation ... happen only in the open region of saying and naming," that is, in the interplay of revealing and concealing "that pervades and guides them" (PLT, 74).

In the picture of our human situation that emerges in "The Origin of the Work of Art," our expressiveness—our speaking and acting in general—are always a "response" to the play of lighting and concealment that is made manifest and preserved in poetic language. Art is "the origin of both creators and preservers, which is to say of a people's historical existence ..." (PLT, 78). It is because our own existence as historical beings is a response to the understanding of Being opened by poetry and sustained in language that Heidegger can say that "language speaks us," and that we speak only insofar as we "co-respond" to language. In our speaking and actions—in our understanding of Being generally—we are "listening to language," letting "its soundless voice come to us" (OWL, 124).

Consequences of Heidegger's View of Language

Heidegger's conception of language leads us to see that language is neither a tool on hand for communicating speakers' intentions nor a formal sign-system that plays with speakers, working "behind their backs." For the early Heidegger, under the influence of life-philosophy, language is the medium through which our most basic sense of life comes to articulation and expression. In this way, language *constitutes* our sense of reality and, indeed, our own identity as speakers employing sign-systems. According to this early view, our historically unfolding practices embody proto-interpretations, comparable to what I earlier called "the primal articulation of the lifeworld," that provide the resources from which literary works are composed. This conception of creative works as growing out of a public understanding of things had been formulated quite clearly by Nietzsche and Dilthey.[13] It is also the source of Gadamer's hermeneutic account of the relation of literature to life.[14] Gadamer, explicitly developing Heidegger's thought, points out that everyday "reality" is generally encountered as inchoate and open-ended, standing out into a horizon of "still undecided possibilities." The literary work provides closure for this amorphous background of experience, and thereby transforms the background into a "structure." Through the work, "what is emerges. In it is produced and brought to light what otherwise is constantly hidden and withdrawn."

Art is an "emergence of truth" to the extent that, by raising the tacit and confusing background of life into its structure, "a superior truth speaks from it."

There is, of course, an unavoidable paradox in this understanding of language and literature. For it holds *both* that expressions arise from the inchoate background of understanding of everyday life *and* that they first constitute and realize that background, letting it be for the first time what it really *is*. But this paradox is untroubling when we reflect on how it is a familiar part of ordinary life. We all know, for example, what it is like to find ourselves developing a strong but murky feeling about someone, and then coming to clarify the feeling through our linguistic formulations. I may vaguely take a dislike to someone, and only on reflection realize that what I really feel is envy. The formulation gives shape to the initial, inchoate response: it lets the feeling have a *place* in my overall life, connecting it to past responses and situating it as, for instance, an expression of a character trait I would like to overcome. Thus, the feeling only emerges into presence *as* the feeling it *is* through my formulations. Yet those formulations must be *true to* the feeling as it occurs in the course of my lived experience.

In a similar way, literary works may be thought of as bringing to presence a people's partially formulated or diffuse grasp of life, and "raising it to its truth." As Gadamer says, through the work, "everyone recognizes that this is how things are." The work of art lets a "truth" shine forth in the sense that it illuminates some region of the lifeworld and lets things "make sense" in the overall mesh of our shared existence.

If literary works are regarded as expressions of a shared background of understanding, then literary interpretation will be seen as moving laterally across a field of expressions, evocations, and life-contexts, not vertically from signifiers to author's intentions. Interpretation is an ongoing, open-ended "historical" process. It evolves through time and is subject to revision with changing interests and orientations toward life, yet it is also embedded in a concrete historical context from which it draws its possibilities of understanding and to which it must be faithful in its readings. And so, in interpreting texts, "we are always moving within [a historical] language, which means moving on shifting ground or, still better, on the billowing waters of an ocean."[15] There is no vantage point for discovering *the* authoritative or final interpretation of a text. Yet Heidegger makes it clear that this open-endedness should not be contrasted with an ideal of univocity. Speaking of the interpretation of philosophical works, he says that the

> multiplicity of possible interpretations does not discredit the strictness of the thought content [of what is being interpreted]. For all true thought remains open to more than one interpretation.... Nor is this

multiplicity of possible interpretations merely the residue of a still unachieved formal-logical univocity which we properly ought to strive for but did not attain. Rather, multiplicity of meanings is the element in which all thought must move in order to be strict thought.[16]

Thus, interpretation is caught up in a hermeneutic circle: we make sense of the text in terms of our tacit sense of what life is all about, but our sense of life in general is formulated and brought to light only by this and other texts. Even interpretations aimed at uncovering masked ideologies in texts spring from and return to the shared life-context. For this reason, the project of recovering meaning has to be taken as fundamental; it is a necessary condition for any interpretation whatsoever. Deconstructions and critiques make sense only if they are seen as pointing to a future reconstruction.

The hermeneutic outlook developed by Heidegger and Gadamer provides an alternative to both Sartrean existentialism and the various structuralisms and poststructuralisms so pervasive today. In his "Letter on Humanism," Heidegger rejected existentialism, arguing that the "lighting of Being" which makes possible different forms of intelligibility throughout the course of history could never be accounted for solely in terms of human subjectivity and its creations, since humans are themselves creations of these events of Being. We are the "shepherds of Being," not its creators. This Heideggerian "antihumanism" had a profound impact on such neo-Nietzschean poststructuralist thinkers as Foucault and Derrida. Foucault suggests at times that language consists of vast, tectonic discursive formations embodying sinister power plays that dictate texts and predetermine authorship.[17] And Derrida pictures language as an "arche writing" or "transcendental space of inscription" of overlapping, interpenetrating, and historically evolving codes that predetermine texts and undermine the author's intentions.[18] These extrapolations from Heidegger preserve his aim of "decentering the subject" and regarding interpretation as a lateral movement across a field of evocations rather than as moving vertically from sign to author's intention. But they disregard the expressivism in both the early and later Heidegger, rejecting the idea that texts express a background life-context that is not itself just one more text.

What is in question here is whether the poststructuralist image of the free play of textuality is tenable. If we understand ourselves not as detached minds but instead as agents involved in a meaningful life-world, we have every reason to think we usually have some "preunderstanding" of how things count for us in our practical affairs. Although this access to our "agent's knowledge" is, as Ricoeur has argued, always mediated by our cultural history,[19] it would be misleading to think of our historical culture as *just* a play of texts or as glacial discursive formations. It is certainly true that our historical culture shapes us and makes us the people we are. But it is also true that we have the capacity to grasp this context of meaningful possibilities and appropriate it in realizing our own identity as self-interpreting beings. For Heidegger, we have the ability to listen to what language says to us, and to rearticulate its possibilities of expression in contributing to the unfolding of our own historical culture. This process is always open-ended and subject to error. But the mere fact that Cartesian certainty and final totalization are not available here does not imply that we are utterly helpless in the face of mindless powers that buffet us about. In Heidegger's view, we are above all respondents and preservers who, hearing the invocations and evocations of our language, can bring what it says to speech, and so can dwell properly in the home it builds for us.

Notes

1. *The Piety of Thinking*, trans. J. G. Hart and J. C. Maraldo (Bloomington: Indiana Univ., 1976), p. 25. I have often revised translations for the sake of consistency and clarity. I usually translate the German *Sein* with the capitalized "Being," and *Seiendes* as "beings," "entities," or simply "things."

2. *Existence and Being*, trans. W. Brock (Chicago: Regnery, 1968), p. 227.

3. "Letter on Humanism," in *Basic Writings*, ed. D. F. Krell (New York: Harper and Row, 1977), p. 239. Hereafter BW.

4. *On Time and Being*, trans. J. Stambaugh (New York: Harper and Row, 1972), p. 74, quoted in David Krell's excellent General Introduction to BW, p. 6.

5. *Being and Time*, trans. John Macquarrie and Edward Robinson (New York: Harper and Row, 1962), p. 19. Hereafter BT.

6. The term "expressivism" comes from Charles Taylor's *Hegel* (Cambridge: Cambridge Univ., 1975). See also his "Action as Expression" in *Intention and Intentionality: Essays in Honor of G. E. M. Anscombe*, ed. C. Diamond (Ithaca, N.Y.: Cornell Univ., 1979), pp. 73–89. I am indebted to Robert Hollinger for pointing out this way of reading Heidegger in terms of Taylor's concept of expressivism.

7. *An Introduction to Metaphysics*, trans. R. Manheim (New Haven: Yale Univ., 1980), p. 101. Hereafter IM.

8. *Reason in the Age of Science*, trans. F. G. Lawrence (Cambridge: MIT, 1981).

9. The phrase comes from Frederick A. Olafson's *Heidegger and the Philosophy of Mind* (New Haven: Yale Univ., 1987), p. 233.

10. In *The Fragility of Goodness* (Cambridge: Cambridge Univ., 1986), Martha Nussbaum points out that the "Greek word for truth means, etymologi-

cally 'what is revealed,' 'what is brought out from concealment'" (p. 241), and in a note she cites some of the extensive literature backing up this derivation.

11. *Poetry, Language, Thought*, trans. A. Hofstadter (New York: Harper and Row, 1971), p. 73. Hereafter PLT.

12. *On the Way to Language*, trans P. D. Hertz (New York: Harper and Row, 1971), 126. Hereafter OWL.

13. See, for example, "On the Origin of Religions," section 353 of *The Gay Science*, trans. W. Kaufmann (New York: Random House, 1974), where Nietzsche shows how the founders of religion take a "way of life" that occurs "alongside other ways of life, and without any sense of its special value," and then provide it with an "*interpretation* that makes it appear to be illuminated by the highest value ..." (p. 296). The interpretation brings to presence what now can be seen as having been implicit in that way of life all along. Also see Dilthey's discussions of the relations of life, expression, and understanding in "The Construction of the Historical World in the Human Sciences," in *W. Dilthey: Selected Writings*, ed. H. P. Rickman (Cambridge: Cambridge Univ., 1976).

14. *Truth and Method*, trans. G. Barden and J. Cumming (New York: Seabury Press, 1975), pp. 101–2, and passim.

15. *What Is Called Thinking?*, trans. J. G. Gray and F. Wieck (New York: Harper and Row, 1972), p. 192.

16. *Ibid.*, p. 71.

17. For example, *The Archaeology of Knowledge*, trans. A. M. S. Smith (New York: Harper and Row, 1972), and "What Is an Author?" in *The Foucault Reader*, ed. P. Rabinow (New York: Pantheon, 1984).

18. See especially "Plato's Pharmacy," in *Dissemination*, trans. B. Johnson (Chicago: Univ. of Chicago, 1981).

19. *The Conflict of Interpretations*, ed. D. Ihde (Evanston: Northwestern Univ., 1974). See my "The Twofold Task: Heidegger's Foundational Historicism in *Being and Time*," *Tulane Studies in Philosophy*, 32 (1984), pp. 53–59.

7

Gadamer's Hermeneutics
Prejudice, Dialogue, and Edification

Georgia Warnke

Appealing to various philosophies of language, discourse and narrative, the critique of foundationalism in philosophy is now well under way. Richard Rorty has argued that our knowledge of ourselves and of our social and natural world is neither a representational faculty nor, therefore, in need of justification as one. The idea that knowledge can represent or mirror things as they "really" are is rather a residue of the Greek view of knowledge as a form of direct familiarity with objects and of the "ocular metaphor" this view involves. Rorty insists that both view and metaphor are optional and claims that "if this way of thinking of knowledge is optional, then so is epistemology, and so is philosophy as it has understood itself since the middle of the last century."[1] The final consequence of the "linguistic turn" in philosophy is the recognition that we need to substitute edification for epistemology and a "conversation of mankind" for narrow philosophical claims to have discovered the grounds for truth. In a similar vein, Michel Foucault has claimed that any appeal to supposedly neutral standards for truth or rational justification simply reflects the discourse supported by some institutionalized distribution of power,[2] while Jean-Francois Lyotard points to a postmodern "incredulity toward metanarratives."[3] By meta-narrative, Lyotard means the kind of philosophical metadiscourse that is supposed to justify either scientific knowledge or the moral and political practices of a society. Postmodernism, as he characterizes it, involves the recognition that there is no such legitimating discourse but only alternative, nonjustifying language games.[4]

Jürgen Habermas has drawn somewhat different consequences from the "linguistic turn" in philosophy and, in particular, from the move to replace foundationalist endeavors with philosophies of discourse. On the one hand, he agrees that we can no longer seek grounds for the justification of validity claims in "the way things are," Platonic Forms, or transcendental conditions for the possibility of knowledge. On the other hand, he uses the turn to language, conversation and discourse to find a detranscendentalized foundation for reason in the pragmatic presuppositions of argumentation. In his view, the critique of foundationalism cannot extend to a critique of reason as a whole. Rather, argumentations in which we are concerned to come to an understanding with others over disputed truth claims or norms of action have a rational framework: we must assume that the structure of our communication both excludes all force other than that of the better argument and neutralizes all motives other than the cooperative search for truth. These presuppositions can be counterfactual; any actual arguments in which we engage may involve all sorts of motives other than that of a cooperative search for truth and any social consensus we reach may reflect the exclusion of certain groups, relations of fear and power, strategies of manipulation, psychological factors or even naked coercion. Nevertheless, whereas Rorty, Foucault, and Lyotard understand a philosophy of discourse as a criticism of the Enlightenment's recourse to an idea of reason independent of the norms or power relations of any particular culture, Habermas emphasizes idealizing presuppositions of argumentation that anticipate reason.

Hans-Georg Gadamer's "philosophical hermeneutics" is of interest to this debate insofar as it can be understood as an attempt to forge a middle path between Habermas's position, on the one hand, and the views of the recent spate of anti-Enlightenment thinkers, on the other. Gadamer was born in Breslau at the turn of the century and entered the University of Marburg in 1919. There he studied with the neo-Kantians, Paul Natorp and Nicolai Hartmann and completed his dissertation in 1922. He did not begin to make philosophical progress, however, he claims, until 1923 when he began to study with the pivotal figure in his philosophical thinking, Martin Heidegger.[5] Hartmann had already observed that Gadamer was only partially satisfied as a neo-Kantian student, and upon meeting Heidegger, Gadamer quickly gave up what he considered his "abstract exercises" in philosophy for a more historical way of thinking. Gadamer habilitated in 1928 and taught in Marburg as a private *Dozent* until 1938 when he became a professor in Leipzig. He remained there during the war, moved to Frankfurt in 1947, after the Russians had replaced the Americans as the occupying force, and moved to Heidelberg two years later. Gadamer's magnum opus, *Truth and Method*, was not published until

1960, when he was already close to retirement. Against the powerful influence of positivism, then at its strongest, *Truth and Method* tries to resurrect the experience of truth in art, history and language. Its debt to Heidegger and hence its affinities with "postmodern" and "neopragmatic" attacks on the Enlightenment are clear. In this essay, however, I would also like to point to its affinity with a Habermasian defense and reassessment of the legacy of the Enlightenment. Hence I shall first consider Gadamer's objections to the Enlightenment and his emphasis on the connection between knowledge and prejudice. I shall then turn to his account of hermeneutic conversation and to his analysis of *Bildung* or self-cultivation. Despite Rorty's interest in this latter aspect of Gadamer's thought, the fundamental premise of both it and hermeneutic conversation seem to me not too distant from that of Habermasian discourse.

Gadamer's Criticism of the Enlightenment

In Gadamer's view, the naïveté of the Enlightenment's appeal to an unconditioned reason reflects an underestimation of the force of history and an overestimation of method. According to the Enlightenment, what obstructs the progress of both science and morality is prejudice, and prejudice arises from two sources: first, from an uncritical reliance on beliefs, practices, and norms simply handed down by the tradition to which one belongs and, second, from an overhasty, unmethodical approach to a subject matter. Overcoming prejudice thus requires the formulation and rigorous application of reliable methods of research, the unprejudiced or unconditioned results of which are thought to be easily contrasted to those issuing from the simple authority of tradition. As against this view, Gadamer argues that any method is only as reliable as the prejudices that already underlie it and, moreover, that what results from the application of method is as inescapably bound to a historical context as are the results of prejudice. His argument can be reconstructed in three steps.

Gadamer argues, first, that prejudice is part of any attempt to understand meaning. Following F. D. E. Schleiermacher, Wilhelm Dilthey, and others in the hermeneutic tradition, he claims that any attempt to understand the meaning of a text or of such text-analogues as actions, social practices, or norms must have a context. We never come upon the objects we are trying to understand without some orientation, but instead grasp them as part of some framework, as part of a field of relations and contrasts with which we are familiar, as an answer to some range of questions and concerns we can recognize. We must fit the meanings we are trying to understand within some familiar context and thus have some assumptions and expectations with regard to them in order to be able to understand them *as* anything at all. In approaching a text we suppose that it is a book of some kind, that it falls within some tradition or genre or writing, that it seeks to articulate some sort of experience or argument and so on. Without some such framework of assumptions and expectations we can have no situation for the meaning we are trying to understand and hence no foothold in terms of which to begin to understand it.

The hermeneutic tradition conceived of such a foothold as the basis for a circular approach to understanding. We project an initial meaning for the objects we are trying to understand in light of the prejudices we bring to them. We then revise this initial understanding in line with the meaning further analysis discovers and use our revised understanding as the context for projecting a new understanding of meaning. On the basis of our understanding of the title of a book, for instance, we suppose that the text we are reading has a certain point, will try to articulate a certain experience or develop a certain sort of argument. We use this supposition as a guide for our interpretation of its individual parts or aspects but the supposition can "come to nothing."[6] Our understanding of the very first chapter of a book may require us to revise our understanding of the title. Still, our procedure then is to use our new understanding of title and first chapter as a guide to the meaning of additional parts of the text and to use these additional parts as ways of correcting our understanding of title and first chapter.

In the view of the hermeneutic tradition, this circle of interpretive anticipations and reassessments comes to an end with a final understanding that is meant to be "objective" in the sense that all conflicts in the meanings of the various parts of the text have been resolved. By reviewing one's projection of the meaning of a text in light of one's interpretation of its various parts and, conversely, by assessing one's interpretation of individual parts in light of the unity of meaning they compose for the whole, one is meant to be ultimately led to a complete understanding that need not be resubmitted to the hermeneutic circle. For the hermeneutic tradition, then, acknowledging the necessity of interpretive projections or prejudices in the understanding of meaning does not preclude the possibility of objectivity. One projects onto the whole of one's text or text-analogue an interpretation based only on a part of it, such as its title or first chapter, and this projection necessarily goes beyond the evidence that is initially available to one. Nevertheless, what such a projection provides is a preview of possible meaning that opens the way to a more adequate understanding of the text or text-analogue at issue. Indeed, as Gadamer himself notes, literally a prejudice (*Vorurteil*) is simply a prejudgment (*vor-Urteil*), a judgment offered tentatively before all the necessary evidence is available in order to provide a basis for more penetrating interpretation and judgment

(MW, 255; TM, 240). The Enlightenment's wholesale rejection of prejudice in favor of method thus leaves no basis for the "objective" analysis that it seeks to promote.

Gadamer's analysis of prejudice parts company with the hermeneutic tradition at just this point, however. In his view, although the hermeneutic circle indicates how our provisional understandings of meaning can be revised, it cannot be used to support the idea of moving from a thoroughly conditioned and prejudiced understanding to an objective analysis. Rather, in a second step of his argument, Gadamer contends that both our anticipatory projections and our attempts to revise them remain rooted in the concerns and practical involvements we bring to the project of understanding from the start. At issue here is what Heidegger calls the "forestructure" of understanding and what Gadamer refers to as a "horizon" (WM, 258 ff.; TM, 269 ff.). Meaning is always the product of, first, a specific context within which it is understood; Heidegger calls the process here a fore-having (*Vorhabe*) of understanding. Second, it is a result of the specific perspective from which it is approached. Heidegger refers here to a fore-sight (*Vorsicht*). Finally, it is a result of the specific way it is conceived (a preconception or *Vorgriff*).[7] These conditions of understanding are not transcended in our revisions of the original meaning we project. Gadamer holds to the hermeneutic claim that we can revise our initial assumptions about a text or text-analogue in light of a criterion of coherence according to which the various parts or aspects of our text or text-analogue must be fitted together as parts of a comprehensive whole. Still, he argues that what we ultimately take as the comprehensive whole remains itself conditioned by the horizon of our interpretive efforts, by the concerns, assumptions, purposes and life-contexts we bring to the project of understanding. We thus move not to an objective or canonical judgment of meaning but rather to one that confers upon our object a meaning that makes sense to us, given these concerns, assumptions, context and purposes.

In this context, Gadamer talks of a "fusion [*Verschmelzung*] of horizons" (WM, 289; TM, 273). We necessarily interpret our object from the prejudiced position afforded by the nexus of our concerns, projects, general background knowledge, and involvements. We cannot step out of this horizon of assumptions any more than we can step out of our skin; rather what we take as the possible parameters for an interpretation of the object is already a horizon determined by our perspective. Hence, by a "fusion of horizons," Gadamer means that our concerns are so integrated with the text or text-analogue at issue that this integration constitutes the meaning of the object for us. For this reason, Gadamer stresses not only the connection the hermeneutic tradition suggests between prejudice and prejudgment but also the radical contrast between prejudice (*Vorurteil*) and judgment (*Urteil*). "The prejudices of the individual," he claims "are, far more than his judgments, the historical reality of his being" (WM, 261; TM, 245; translation altered). No understanding achieves the objectivity the hermeneutic tradition once sought; all rather remain particular *interpretations* and arise out of particular interpretive horizons.

We have seen that Gadamer follows Heidegger in locating understanding in the practical concerns and involvements of interpreters. The claim just cited indicates that Gadamer also, more explicitly than Heidegger, locates this nexus of involvements in history. Hence, the third step in his argument is the claim that the particular "forestructure" or "horizon" we bring to the process of interpretation is not ours alone but rather that of the historical tradition to which we belong. Central here is the notion of "effective history" (*Wirkungsgeschichte*) or the idea that the concerns, practical involvements, and attendent assumptions we bring to the project of understanding are not the products of an individual self-determination or choice; they are rather the products of history. We grow up in specific families and societies and participate in specific aesthetic, moral-political, and scientific cultures. Through our participation in these cultures and societies we learn to speak a certain language, to adopt certain standards of cogency and intelligibility and to adopt a certain orientation and perspective on various events, literatures, and the like.

Gadamer does not deny the possibility of modifying the conceptual language, orientation, and standards one has inherited. As we have already seen, we can revise our initial understanding of a text or text-analogue and if this initial understanding is one bequeathed to us by the traditions to which we belong, the possibility of interpretive revisions means that we can also revise the traditions to which we belong. Nonetheless, in revising them, we remain not only within a hermeneutic circle, as noted above, but within a *historically situated* hermeneutic circle, within the province of an effective history that continues to influence the lines and terms of our modifications as well as the standards to which they adhere.

We necessarily bring to a study of Shakespeare's work, for example, certain expectations as to the standards it will uphold. These expectations are not an idiosyncratic creation, but a result of traditional assumptions about Shakespeare that we simply inherit. We may of course be disappointed; still, in Gadamer's view this disappointment only highlights our participation in the tradition of Shakespeare-understanding we now find in need of modification. Moreover, in seeing the need to modify our culture's evaluation of Shakespeare, we are appealing to its standards of excellence, standards in part created by the history of Shakespeare scholarship and evaluation itself. We thus necessarily retain certain features of our traditions (in this case its standards of excellence) even as we reject others (here, its assessment of Shakespeare's work). Certainly we could argue against these standards as well, but we do so as historically situated members of a culture and tradition with the insights and experiences it has afforded us. Gadamer's own example of this process is the idea of the classical (WM, 269 ff.; TM, 253 ff.).

This idea, he argues, is significant for two reasons. First, it is a preeminently historical concept. The aesthetic works and concepts we call classical are those that remain meaningful despite the progress of history; this phenomenon does not mean that what we term classical *transcends* history; rather it testifies to a certain historical continuity, for *through* history the classical acquires a certain weight and normative force. Second, the classical retains this normative force despite historicist attempts to reduce it to the concept of a specifically ancient style. If a work is considered classical, this does not primarily mean that it belongs to the artistic and architectural style of a certain period *in* history; it means rather that it exerts a hold over all subsequent periods of history and indeed over us. As exemplified in such ideas as that of a classical education, for instance, it embodies a standard to which it is thought we *ought* to aspire. Moreover, it retains this hold even against our attempts to escape or rebel against it, for the standard it establishes remains the standard against which we measure the success of our alternatives. New developments in art or literature pose the question of whether and how they stand up to, even as they criticize or reflect on, that which we consider classical.

For Gadamer, this standard established by the idea of the classical exemplifies the standards established by the effective history of tradition in general. It is important to see that this argument for the strength of traditions is neither naive nor methodological. In situating the expectations we bring to the project of understanding in tradition, Gadamer does not mean that we always belong to a single and conceptual tradition, the assumptions and expectations of which we could learn to enumerate. Traditions include practices and forms of life and thus involve a practical as well as a theoretical orientation. Neither is Gadamer's point that we ought always to be conscious of tradition in attempting to understand our texts and text-analogues. Understanding, he claims, always rests on some orientation and this orientation does not come out of nowhere; it is based rather, as we have seen, on assumptions, expectations, purposes, and life-contexts, rooted for their part in a history. We are socialized and educated into cultures, disciplines, and practices with a history, and hence, into traditions. Even when we try to break with these traditions and to approach a given subject matter without the prejudices they involve, they retain their power as that which serves as the background for our new efforts, conditioning both the force and the lines of our rejection as well as the focus for our present concerns. As Gadamer writes:

> We are always standing within tradition and this "standing-in" is no objectifying relation so that what tradition says might be thought of as something other or alien. It is always already our own, a model or exemplar, a self-recognition in which later historical hindsight will see not really knowledge but the most simple stability of tradition. (WM, 266; TM, 250; translation altered)

Given the discussion thus far, the consequence of Gadamer's criticism of the Enlightenment would seem to issue in a simple capitulation to the force of tradition. Not only are our traditions the foundations of our initial approaches to meaning; in addition, they retain their authority over our attempts to change our lives, form independent judgments and achieve an unconditioned point of view. The trajectory Kant projected in his essay "What Is Enlightenment" from a dependence on authority to independence and reasoned self-reliance becomes, in Gadamer's hermeneutics, simply the appropriation and modification *of* authority. Maturity and responsibility (*Mündigkeit*) must now be interpreted not as the ability to use one's own reason against the prejudices of one's age; they rather reflect the capacity to acknowledge the connection between tradition and what one takes as reason, to recognize one's historical finitude and the decisiveness of the knowledge and practical orientations made possible by the traditions to which one belongs.

But what can this new form of maturity leave of the Enlightenment? Is reason now nothing more than the motor that moves us around the circle of our historically conditioned prejudices, allowing license to some even as we reject others? Habermas has argued against Gadamer that he cedes too much to the authority of traditions. Habermas admits that the "objectivistic" self-understanding of the "methodical" sciences stemming from the Enlightenment leads them to overlook their hermeneutic bases. Scientific disciplines are themselves traditions, with their own languages, assumptions and forms of socialization; moreover, they belong to cultures with inherited concerns and purposes. Indeed, revolutions within sciences are made possible by the accumulated force of the problems and anomalies that the tradition of the science makes possible. As Habermas therefore quotes Gadamer, "The moment of historical influence is and remains effective in all understanding of tradition even where the method of the modern historical sciences has gained ground."[8]

But Habermas still insists on the difference between "everyday communicative experience" and "self-reflective understanding." In his view, Gadamer both neglects the reflective power reason can achieve if allied with methodical science and overlooks the dangers of what Habermas calls a "linguistic idealism." Traditions, Habermas insists, are not only the locus of shared understandings, concerns and projects. They also reflect relations of power and domination. To reject the partial independence of reason for the simple acceptance of tradition — or, at best, for its traditionally directed reform — is to allow these relations of power and domination an unimpeded power not only over the objects of interpretation but over the understanding of them. In remaining within the circumference of tradition, we give up any possibility of assessing the rationality of its direction:

> The happening of tradition appears as an absolute power only to a self-sufficient hermeneutics; in fact it is relative to systems of labor and domination. Sociology cannot, therefore, be reduced to interpretive sociology. It requires a reference system that, on the one hand, does not suppress the symbolic mediation of social action in favor of a naturalistic view of behavior ... but that, on the other hand, also does not ... sublimate social processes entirely to cultural tradition.[9]

But Gadamer has what appears to be an easy response to Habermas, for systems of labor and domination cannot be thought to be outside the traditions whose rationality they are supposed to affect. If the economic and social factors that allegedly distort the transmission of various traditions can be articulated in language, they are also necessarily part of a tradition. Their specific articulation as distortions is an interpretation of a certain phenomenon, embedded itself in a certain orientation and therefore also prejudiced.[10] If we cannot get outside a tradition to a reference system for ascertaining its rationality, however, is there any room for the kind of critical standpoint Habermas wants to secure? Gadamer's accounts of hermeneutic conversation and self-cultivation or *Bildung* seem to me to suggest that there is.

Hermeneutic Conversation

The implication that Gadamer draws from his account of prejudice and tradition is not that we are enclosed within the hermeneutic circle, but that our critical reflection upon our own prejudices and traditions requires dialogue. At issue here is what he calls the *docia ignorantia*. If we are prejudiced this is because we are finite creatures. We are situated in history and can attain only the inevitably partial perspective that this situation in history allows us. The knowledge we can have, then, is not the absolute knowledge for which historicists such as Ludwig von Ranke and Johann Gustav Droysen already criticized Hegel, a knowledge which presupposes that history ends and, hence, that we can have a comprehensive understanding of it. Rather, the knowledge we can have is that of Socrates: the knowledge that we do not know.

In Gadamer's hermeneutics, this kind of knowledge is reflected in what he calls an "anticipation of completeness" (*der Vorgriff der Vollkommenheit*) (WM, 278; TM, 262). On one level, this idea is simply that of the hermeneutic circle. If we can revise our prejudices about meaning by seeing the way in which the parts of a text or text-analogue cohere to form a comprehensive whole, then this ideal of unity or completeness also provides a criterion of understanding. In interpreting a text or text-analogue we must suppose, at least pro-visionally, that it forms a coherent or self-consistent whole, for other-wise we can have no standard for questioning our initial projections of the meaning of any given part or section of them. During a debate between Gadamer and Jacques Derrida, in a series of lectures in Paris in 1981, Derrida claimed that what Gadamer called a "good will" towards one's text—the assumption of its internal coherence and meaningfulness—was simply a return to metaphysics. Derrida asked: Why not assume that the condition of understanding lies in ruptures with the text, that we need not to assume a continuity of meaning but rather to explode discontinuities?[11]

In his reply, Gadamer claimed that even the assumption of dis-continuity presupposes continuity. Unless we assume that a text is a meaningful whole we have no criterion for determining when we have misunderstood it or parts of it. Our presumption must be that the various parts of a text can be integrated into a unitary whole so that when we find a section of the text that deviates from this unitary meaning, we can see the need to revise some part of our understanding of either whole or part. Of course, it may ultimately be necessary to give up the idea that a particular text or text-analogue we are studying composes a unity of meaning; but this is so only if our attempts to discover it in a given text or text-analogue continually falter. Con-versely, if we assume only disruptions and discontinuities from the start, we have no standard for distinguishing between failings of the text and failures of our own ability to understand.

Gadamer adds a second dimension to his account of anticipating completeness. The idea includes not only the assumption that the text or text-analogues we study compose a unity of meaning; it also includes the assumption that this meaning is true. We can test the adequacy of a given textual interpretation only by assuming that the text at issue possesses a unified meaning, that if our interpretation of one chapter conflicts with our interpretation of another, we need to revise our understanding of one or the other or both. But we also need to assume that we can learn from the text, that it can teach us something and hence that the claims it makes might be true. Otherwise, we can have no standard for testing the truth of our own assumptions. If we begin by assuming that a given practice or work is irrelevant to our concerns, then we can have no basis for questioning those concerns.

In his interpretation of Zande witchcraft practices, Peter Winch offers an instance of Gadamer's point.[12] Winch argues that accounts of these practices that can conceive of them only as poor cousins to Western technology, as superstitious attempts to control natural processes, fail to learn what the Azande can teach us precisely about our own concerns. He suggests that if, conversely, one were to approach Zande witchcraft as a practice to be taken seriously, with, in other words, the expectation of learning from the Azande, it might be possible to find in the practice an effort to deal with problems and issues with which we are still concerned. The appropriate framework or set of prejudices for understanding Zande witchcraft, Winch contends, are *not* those surrounding questions of technology, in fact, but rather those surrounding prayer. Despite our reliance on an eventual technological solution to all our problems, we share with the Azande a sense of our ultimate vulnerability and cosmic contingency, and it is in terms of responding to this sense that their practice of witchcraft can offer provocative suggestions for our own way of life. In Winch's view, it can teach us about being part of the universe, about acknowledging its vastness and, hence, about the place of technology within it.

Along similar lines, Gadamer suggests that if we want to understand a text or text-analogue, we must expect or hope it to tell us something true, to illuminate a subject matter for us and hence offer us a way of revising our knowledge and even, perhaps, our way of life. Certainly, we always come already prejudiced to the project of understanding and these prejudices both effect and affect our understanding of the text or text-analogue under study. At the same time, the condition of being prejudiced requires an openness to the text or text-analogue, a recognition that one may be wrong and therefore ought to be willing to learn. One has to take seriously the claims of one's object of study so as to be able to define and test one's own prejudices against them.

For Gadamer such testing is, in fact, the point of hermeneutics: if we study ancient cultures, read new books or try to understand others, it is because we need to assess the validity of our presumptions, views and form of life. Given the force of effective history, we can do so only by assuming the cogency and power of alternatives. Hermeneutic understanding is a form of conversation in which we participate with the object of our study in an effort to come to an understanding over issues of mutual concern. Each participant in this process of coming to an understanding must be seen as an equal dialogue partner, as equally capable of illuminating the subject matter at hand. The result of such a hermeneutic conversation is a new understanding of the subject matter at issue, one arrived at through the conversation and reflecting the education the interplay with text or text-analogue promotes.

Of course, the illumination and examination of beliefs and prejudices that dialogue effects does not render our new understanding free of prejudice. Our encounter with alternative interpretive horizons itself takes place within the hermeneutic circle. Still, the result, for Gadamer, is necessarily a development of our initial views. In confronting opposing views and assumptions, we are obliged to reconsider or, at the very least, reconfirm them in light of the alternatives we have encountered. The fusion of horizons that occurs here need not signal substantive agreement. It may not be an option for us to adopt Zande beliefs in witchcraft, for example, and we may decide to reject the argument or perspective of a particular text. But Gadamer's contention is that whatever the outcome of conversation — whether we finally agree or disagree with what we have understood — the result is an achievement of understanding in which our own initial position is clarified and modified in connection with the other and thereby enriched. The process here is one of integration and appropriation: our initial expectations and assumptions are changed by the encounter with other perspectives, even if we have finally to reject them for ourselves. In rejecting them, we affirm our own perspective in a new way, a way more differentiated, aware of its own difficulties and able to defend itself. This is what Gadamer seems to mean, then, in claiming that understanding is in fact equivalent to reaching an understanding with others or, as he puts the point, "Understanding (*Verständnis*) is primarily agreement (*Einverständnis*)" (WM, 168; TM, 158).

On the reading offered above, coming to an understanding with others over a subject matter does not preclude disagreeing with them. Our agreement with them consists in the fact that we can articulate and justify our own perspective only by coming to terms with the counterview offered by our text or text-analogue and by being able to define precisely the way we do disagree with it. Hence, the possibility of distinguishing our own position on a given subject matter from either that of a text or even that of the tradition as a whole is not eradicated. Gadamer's point is rather that we can develop, refine and rationally justify our own beliefs and practices only if we are willing to appropriate others (and even those of the tradition) in the sense that we are willing to articulate and test our beliefs and practices in their light. To this extent, Gadamer's point is a Hegelian one: achieving an understanding of a given subject matter involves synthesizing different views, forging a consensus in which even disagreement reflects the attainment of a "higher" stage of knowledge, if only because it is more differentiated, better articulated and hence more sophisticated.

Nevertheless, there seems to be a significant ambiguity in Gadamer's analysis of coming to an understanding. In particular, the Hegelian sense in which he equates understanding and agreement oscillates with a more substantive sense. Earlier, I indicated that the concept of the classical serves him as a paradigm for the normative hold of a tradition. As we saw, the concept includes more than the artistic style of a certain period in history and encompasses a general ideal of excellence. Despite historicist efforts to reduce the concept to the former definition alone, the ideals associated with it are preserved in such notions as that of a classical education and in the question of whether certain forms of art are "classical" regardless of the period of their creation. In this way, the legacy of the classical continues to exert a force, whether it is acknowledged or not, and thus provides a clear instance of what Gadamer calls effective history. But in his analysis of the concept of the classical Gadamer makes another point as well. The classical is not simply a notion that orients our aesthetic responses, it is also "a special way of being historical, the historical achievement of preservation that, in a continually renewed proof lets something true exist" (WM, 271; TM, 255).

Here the Hegelian sense of synthesis or consensus that includes both the appropriation of one's text or text-analogue and its "sublation" in a more sophisticated and differentiated understanding seems to give way to a notion of synthesis that emphasizes simple preservation. The hermeneutic interpretation of the classical seems not to have the character of a mediation or education in which one's encounter with a text or other symbolic structure allows one to arrive at a better understanding of a given subject matter even if one disagrees with the text or text-analogue itself. Instead, hermeneutics simply rescues classical truths.[13] This implication of Gadamer's analysis of the classical seems to me to describe a tendency within his philosophy as a whole and may be the source of many of the complaints about its conservative character. On the one hand, the hermeneutic consensus with one's text or other aspect of the tradition indicates the dialogic achievement of a richer understanding of matters in question; on the other, this consensus means the capacity to see the substantive truth of one's object and, in general, of the tradition to which one belongs. Here, agreement is not a critical synthesis of views but instead a capitulation to the validity of what one takes one's text or text-analogue to say. This account of consensus allows Gadamer to end *Truth and Method* with an astonishing claim:

> When we understand a text, its meaningfulness charms us just as the beautiful charms us. It brings itself to validity and has always already charmed us before we come to ourselves, so to speak, and are able to test the claim to meaning that emerges from it. What confronts us in

the experience of the beautiful and in understanding the meaning of the tradition really has something of the truth of a game. In understanding, we are drawn into a happening of truth and come, as it were, too late if we want to know what we should believe (WM, 465; TM, 446).

For the most part, however, Gadamer's analysis does not support this view. Because we are prejudiced, there is a sense in which we always "agree" with the tradition of which we are a part. Our orientation toward an object of study is affected by it and even our ideas of what modifications are necessary in its outlook and practices are influenced by it. Still, we can test the claims of this tradition, entering into a dialogue or virtual dialogue in which we confront it with other perspectives and become educated in the sense that those perspectives become an integral part of our own self-understanding, whether we agree substantively with them or not.

Two points bear emphasizing here. First, as I have already implied, this process of coming to an understanding through dialogue serves a justificatory function: it is the way we both acknowledge our prejudices and test them. Hence, despite the apparent affinities between Gadamer and anti-Enlightenment thinkers, his critique of the Enlightenment is directed not at dissolving the concept of reason into discourse; instead, discourse has the rational function of allowing us to clarify, test and either confirm or reject our prejudices. Second, this process of hermeneutic justification is, for Gadamer, the process of tradition itself. Traditions do not embody simply the dead weight of history; rather, to the extent that they remain vital, it is because they are continually deepened in line with the insights achieved in interpretive encounters with different perspectives and indeed different aspects of themselves. Gadamer goes so far as to call this process an "act of reason"; as he writes, "Even the most genuine and solid tradition does not persevere by nature, thanks to the force of the inertia of what once existed. Rather, it needs to be affirmed, embraced and nurtured" (WM, 266; TM, 250; translation altered).

This analysis of tradition as a dialogically produced and even justificatory enterprise is further clarified, it seems to me, in Gadamer's account of *Bildung* or, as Richard Rorty translates the term, "edification."

Bildung and Practical Philosophy

Rorty uses Gadamer's account of *Bildung* to distinguish between one kind of education that leads to a new appreciation of diversity and another kind limited to the concerns of rational justification. The aim of the former, edification, is not to discover foundations for either legitimating or criticizing our beliefs but, rather, to foster an awareness of different ways of coping with the world, of different life-options and of different forms of self- and world-description. To be edified is to know that our beliefs and convictions form one world of discourse within a universe of possibilities and therefore to be aware that they do not derive from *the* truth or *the* moral law but represent instead a workable way of speaking and acting. It is a way that our history has bestowed upon us for historically contingent reasons and a way that we therefore need not try to justify except as one that still works for us.

Gadamer's analysis of the dialogic character of understanding provides some support for this contrast between edification and an epistemological interest in the foundations of our beliefs and practices. As we have seen, Gadamer places the possibility of being educated or edified in the *docta ignorantia* or in the capacity to acknowledge one's ignorance and historical finitude; the *telos* of such education, then, is not as much certainty as the recognition of the value of diverse perspectives. Moreover, Rorty's use of the idea of *Bildung* is also supported by Gadamer's analysis of experience. Experienced people are those who have been able to learn from events in their lives and have learned because they were aware of their fallibility. That is, they have learned because they were open to the dialogic possibility that their beliefs and prejudices might be refuted and were willing to revise or supplement them when they were. Hence, despite the emphasis in the sciences on confirming experimental results through the *repetition* of the experience, Gadamer claims that experience is primarily "an experience of negation" (WM, 357; TM, 318), a discovery that one's analysis is inadequate to the subject matter at issue and must be revised.

In describing this kind of experience Gadamer turns explicitly to Hegel's account of dialectic and particularly to the moment of sublation (*Aufhebung*) in which one recognizes the prejudiced and one-sided character of one's knowledge and moves to a more differentiated perspective. In Hegel's work, this dialectical process culminates in "absolute knowledge." This is essentially what Gadamer sees as the final synthesis projected by the hermeneutic tradition: thought is supposed to be finally reconciled to its object and therefore requires no further transformations or modifications. For both Gadamer and Rorty, however, experience and edification lead in the opposite direction, not to absolute knowledge, but, as Gadamer puts it, "to that openness to experience that is set free by experience itself" (WM, 339; TM, 320). In studying other cultures, performing scientific experiments and questioning one's own tradition, what one primarily acquires is not rationally grounded truth but a capacity for future learning. One learns that one's own historical horizon incorporates only one set of perspectives for self- and world-understanding and that this set of perspectives is itself subject to historical change.

Still, Gadamer's account of *Bildung* differs from Rorty's in including a connection to capacities for tact, judgment, and taste. To be sure, because of modern science's supposed monopoly on the proper dimensions of rational knowledge, precisely such capacities as tact, taste and judgment are viewed as untestable, unrepeatable and as purely subjective phenomena. Gadamer, however, argues that this is a mistake, that although tact, taste and judgment cannot be reduced to methods and although they adhere to no clear rules, they nevertheless remain forms of insight. If someone is tactful, this means that he or she knows what to say and what not to say. Similarly, if someone has taste, this means that he or she knows what is beautiful or appropriate and what is not. Gadamer insists that taste goes beyond an eye for fashion or a conformity to the stylistic concepts of a particular group and rather involves "real normative power" insofar as "it knows itself to be certain of the agreement of an ideal community" (WM, 35; TM, 36). The person with taste, then, may be ahead or behind contemporary notions of style. Still, that he or she has taste is manifest in the ability to see how things go together and where lines are to be drawn. The same holds of judgment; again, it involves an ability to select and discriminate, to see how general laws and rules are to be applied to particular cases and so on. The capacity to judge well, as the capacities for taste and tact, cannot be learned by following procedures laid down in advance, nor can it be formulated as a set of rules. Gadamer's suggestion is rather that tact, taste and judgment comprise simply the content of what is learned in becoming *gebildete* or edified.

Bildung, for Gadamer, is thus a "genuine historical idea" (WM, 9; TM, 12), in that the *gebildete* person is one who has acquired *insight* from his or her global interests. Insofar as *Bildung* involves the development of the capacities for taste, judgment and tact, it is more than a simple recognition of historical diversity; it rather involves the ability to see how historically diverse perspectives and horizons of concern are to be appropriately integrated into one's life and understanding. For this reason, *Bildung* does not as much replace "knowledge as the goal of thinking"[14] as, instead, reveal the limits of a certain kind of knowledge, namely, an objective knowledge of facts modeled on the natural sciences. Tact, taste, judgment, and the *Bildung* that forms them are part of what Gadamer sees as *practical* knowledge, a knowledge of how to understand oneself and one's history and, indeed, of how best to live.

This account of *Bildung* seems to indicate how far Gadamer's position is from the approaches of either postmodernism, in general, or neopragmatism, in particular. In Gadamer's view, the problem with a philosophical concern with foundations is not its concern with rational justification or with what he also calls a "giving of accounts" (*Rechenschaftsgabe*).[15] Rather, problems arise when this "giving of accounts" is limited to the legitimation of scientific knowledge and thus when the connection between reason and action or social practice is severed. For Gadamer, as for Habermas, the danger here is that of restricting the possibilities for a rationalization of social life.

As Gadamer describes it, the modern world is characterized by a faith in science that defines all problems as technical problems that are, sooner or later, to be solved by scientific and technical means. The "expert" has replaced the "man of practical wisdom" so that social policy is not the result of a practical reason informed by hermeneutic insight but instead the result of decisions by specialized groups of experts. Gadamer argues that such a society of experts is also a "society of functionaries." What is important is not the sensitivity and insight into issues that Gadamer thinks can be developed in the dialogic self-cultivation made possible by an encounter with other traditions and with differing aspects of one's own; instead, social decisions more often follow the logic of a technological imperative. The course of techno-logical and scientific advance is thus no longer guided by practical insight; rather, the reverse is far truer. Social goals and purposes are themselves dictated by technological demands and possibilities. The effect of this reversal of the roles of practical-moral deliberation and scientific-technical reason, however, is, Gadamer thinks, an increase in "social irrationality."[16]

As he sees it, then, the present task of philosophy is to counter these tendencies by retaining some of its traditional prerogatives. Post-modernism and neopragmatism are right to criticize philosophy's incar-nation as epistemological judge, the ultimate arbiter of truth and meaning. Against postmodernism and neopragmatism, however, Gadamer argues that a task remains for philosophy: the integration of our knowledge within a cohesive whole, the articulation of a public consensus on common aims and purposes and thereby the establishment of a direction for the scientific and technological apparatus.

If Gadamer thus differs from contemporary forms of anti-Enlightenment, his differences with Habermas's defense of Enlighten-ment should not be ignored. As Habermas does, Gadamer turns to discourse and dialogue as the ground for a detranscendentalized conception of reason. At the same time, he denies that the problems of modernity and, specifically, of the modern collapse of reason into the instrumental reason of science and technology are to be overcome by transcending the content of discourse and dialogue for their universal-pragmatic structure. In abstracting from the substantive content of our dialogue with others, Habermas's strategy also abstracts from the historical traditions that in Gadamer's view give motivational force to questions of how we ought to live. On the social and political level, hermeneutics thus argues for a collective and dialogic encounter with tradition in which we are able to revise the versions of the good life it contains in accordance with the level of *Bildung* we have managed to attain. Gadamer asks whether it is "so perverse to think that in reality the irrational cannot hold out in the long run" and, explicitly acknowledging his debt to Hegel, points to specific historical advances such as the recognition, if not realization, of the freedom of all.[17] Reason, Gadamer thinks, develops historically and does so through the dialogic attempts of communities to form a collective conception of "the good."[18]

This analysis, however, remains unsatisfying in an important respect. Earlier I pointed to Habermas's critique of the potential irrationality of tradition, an irrationality he thought could be criticized by pointing to the conditions of labor and domination that affect the tradition. Gadamer rejects this solution as a restriction upon the scope of tradition, which, in his view, encompasses labor and domination as well as the linguistic tradition, narrowly conceived. But it remains the case that Hegel can rely upon the historical advance of reason with more justification than Gadamer since he connects it to the ultimate reconciliation of world-spirit with itself. If we give up both on Hegel's teleological conception of history and on Marxian attempts to find a critical standpoint independent of tradition, how can we guarantee that the dialogic attempts of communities to form a collective conception of the good will move in a rational direction? If the conversation through which we attempt to educate ourselves is constrained by relations of power, will our education not itself be constrained? Hermeneutics teaches us to rely on our capacities for tact, taste, and judgment. But what we take as tact, taste, and judgment will reflect our prejudices and traditions. If these are Orwellian, then what we take as our collective *Bildung* may well represent a collective decay.

Notes

1. Richard Rorty, *Philosophy and the Mirror of Nature* (Princeton: Princeton Univ., 1979).

2. See Michel Foucault, *Power/Knowledge*, ed. Colin Gordon (New York: Pantheon, 1980), chs. 5 and 6.

3. Jean-Francois Lyotard, *The Postmodern Condition: A Report on Knowledge*, trans. Geoff Bennington and Brian Massumi (Minneapolis: Univ. of Minnesota, 1984), p. xxiv.

4. Ibid., see pp. 39ff.

5. Gadamer, *Philosophical Apprenticeships*, trans. Robert R. Sullivan (Cambridge: MIT, 1985).

6. Hans-Georg Gadamer. *Wahrheit und Methode*, 4th ed. (Tubingen: J. C. B. Mohr, 1975), p. 252. Hereafter WM. Translated as *Truth and Method*, translation copyright Shead and Ward Ltd. (New York: Seabury, 1975), p. 237. Hereafter TM.

7. An interpretation of paragraph 32 of Heidegger's *Being and Time*, trans. John Macquame and Edward Robinson (New York: Harper and Row, 1963).

8. "A Review of Gadamer's *Truth and Method*" in *Understanding and Social Inquiry*, eds. Fred Dallmayr and Thomas McCarthy (Notre Dame: Notre Dame Univ., 1977), p. 361.

9. Ibid.

10. See the essays by Habermas, Karl-Otto Apel, and Gadamer in Karl-Otto Apel et al., *Hermeneutik und Ideologiekritik* (Frankfurt: Suhrkamp, 1977). See also Paul Ricouer, "Ethics and Culture, Habermas and Gadamer in Dialogue," *Philosophy Today*, 17 (1973); Jack Mendelson, "The Habermas-Gadamer Debate," *New German Critique*, 18 (1979); and Dieter Misgeld, "Discourse and Conversation: The Theory of Communicative Competence and Hermeneutics in Light of the Debate between Habermas and Gadamer," *Cultural Hermeneutics*, 4 (1977).

11. "Gutes Wille zum Macht," in *Text und Interpretation: Deutsch-Französische Debatte*, ed. Philippe Furget (München: Wilhelm Fink Verlag, 1984).

12. Peter Winch, "Understanding a Primitive Society," in *Understanding and Social Inquiry*, eds. Fred Dallmayr and Thomas McCarthy (Notre Dame: Notre Dame Univ., 1977), pp. 159–88.

13. See also criticisms by Peter Christian Lang in *Hermeneutik, Ideologiekritik, Aesthetik* (Konigstein: Forum Academicum, 1981) and Hans Robert Jauss in *Toward an Aesthetic of Reception*, trans. Timothy Bahti (Minneapolis: Univ. of Minnesota, 1982). Both consider Gadamer's account of the classical dogmatic and claim that it overlooks the historicity of understanding that Gadamer stresses. The classical cannot be reduced to a purely historical concept because it speaks immediately to each age. As Gadamer writes, it "does not first require the overcoming of historical distance for, in its constant communication, it does overcome it" (WM, p. 274; TM, p. 257). Lang argues that this depiction of the classical has already decided on its "superior truth" (Lang, p. 24) and hence works against the supposedly "open" character of hermeneutics. Jauss claims that Gadamer's account of the classical neglects the distance between the present and a text of the past. A classical text does not speak immediately to each age; rather, as with any text, we must be conscious of the classical text's own historicity. Both of these criticisms miss an important aspect of Gadamer's analysis, however. For Gadamer, the "superior truth" of the classical is not decided in advance, nor does it transcend the text's historicity exactly. The classical is classical rather because it continues to *prove* its superiority to each new generation of interpreters. It is thus a "notable mode of

being historical, the historical process of preservation that through the constant proving of itself sets before us something that is true" (WM, p. 271; TM, p. 255). It seems to me that what is odd about this conception is that it ignores the moment of historical change that Gadamer writes into preservation. Although the classical preserves its truth in *some* sense, this sense is the Hegelian one in which it becomes part of a new synthesis and does not remain the concept it was.

14. Rorty, p. 359.

15. Gadamer, "Philosophie oder Wissenschaftstheorie?" in *Vernunft im Zeitalter der Wissenschaft* (Frankfurt: Suhrkamp, 1976), p. 138; translated as "Philosophy or Theory of Science?" in *Reason in the Age of Science*, trans. Frederick C. Lawrence (Cambridge, Mass.: MIT, 1981), p. 162.

16. See Gadamer, "Was ist Praxis? Die Bedingungen gesellschaftlicher Vernunft," In *Vernunft im Zeitalter der Wissenschaft*, pp. 59–60; translated as "What Is Practice? The Condition of Social Reason," in *Reason in the Age of Science*, pp. 73–74.

17. Gadamer, "Hegel's Philosophie und ihre Nachwirkungen bis heute," in *Vernunft im Zietalter der Wissenschaft*, p. 51; translated as "Hegel's Philosophy and its Aftereffects until Today," in *Reason in the Age of Science*, p. 36.

18. Gadamer, "Philosophie oder Wissenschaftstheorie?" p. 135; "Philosophy or Theory of Science?" p. 159.

Myth, History, and Discourse

Introduction

George H. Jensen

Susanne K. Langer, one of Ernst Cassirer's most important disciples, wrote that one of his "first startling discoveries" was that "myth and language appeared as genuine twin creations, born of the same phase of human mentality, exhibiting analogous formal traits, despite their obvious diversities of content."[1] And, she continued, Cassirer believed that both myth and language play a role in the apprehension of values, which precedes even the perception of facts. It is this attention to myth, language, and values as well as their affect on the construction of reality that makes Cassirer an important figure in the rhetorical turn of twentieth-century thought. What sets him apart from other transitional figures is his attention to myth.

Before Cassirer, few philosophers felt that the study of myth was proper or fruitful.[2] The rising importance of empiricism since the Enlightenment fostered the view that myth was mere superstition, a primitive form of thought that should be explained away or delegated to anthropologists for study. Myth and science, as well as myth and history, were considered clear dichotomies. In Cassirer's revolutionary theory, myth is thought of as a historical stage, preceding science but still influencing it. If science is to understand itself, it must, he contended, understand myth as well.[3] Cassirer devoted an entire volume of *Philosophy of Symbolic Forms* to mythic thought, thus sending an important message to those who followed: the study of myth is an important part of the study of human thought and human discourse. In his last work, *The Myth of the State*, he explored the rhetorical use of myth, which he perceived to be one of the great dangers of modern life.[4]

Although it is difficult to trace a clear developmental line from Cassirer's work and what came later, he certainly opened the field for those who followed, including Carl Jung. It is odd, however, that Cassirer and Jung, whose projects are so similar, worked in such apparent independence. Perhaps this is because they were working against different traditions. Although both initiated neo-Kantian and phenomenological investigations of the symbolic forms of mythic thought, Cassirer was, in part, working against Kant's ahistoricism, while Jung was, in part, working against Freud's focus on the individual. Jung's theory of the collective unconscious moves beyond the individual subconscious to the transpersonal as it interacts with culture and history. His archetypes, like Cassirer's symbolic forms, supply a general structure for reality, but they are never, Jung cautions, fully developed until they emerge into and merge with a cultural context. Contrary to popular notions of his theory, Jung believed that the fully developed archetypes (as opposed to the bare archetypal form) of one culture cannot be transplanted into another culture.[5] Although one can speak of the presence of an archetype (say, the trickster) across cultures, the trickster of Western Europe is not the trickster of China or India. The archetypal form of the trickster is primordial, but its development occurred — and continues to occur — within the context of language and culture. Jung wrote:

> The forms we use for assigning meaning are historical categories that reach back into the mists of time — a fact we do not take sufficiently into account. Interpretations make use of certain linguistic matrices that are themselves derived from primordial images. From whatever side we approach this question, everywhere *we find ourselves confronted with the history of language*, with images and motifs that lead straight back to the primitive wonder-world.[6]

For both Cassirer and Jung, myth should not only be viewed as a historical phenomenon, it should also be viewed as a historical agent. Like Cassirer, Jung commented on the appropriation of myth in the Nazis' rise to power in the 1930s.[7] Unlike Cassirer, however, he emphasized the positive changes that myth could effect in both the individual and society.

Roland Barthes, although he draws his theoretical inspiration from the semiotics of Saussure, also sees myth as emerging from the history of language and then rhetorically effecting social and historical change. In *Mythologies*, he wrote:

> It is human history which converts reality into speech, and it alone rules the life and the death of mythic language. Ancient or not, mythology can only have a historical foundation, for myth is a type of speech chosen by history: it cannot possibly evolve from the "nature" of things.[8]

Barthes feels that mythology is a semiotic field because it deals with forms, and it is a historical field because it deals with ideology. Mythology, thus, "studies ideas-in-forms."[9]

To explain the operation of myth, Barthes uses the example of a photograph on the cover of *Paris-Match*. The image is both simple and powerful: a black, who is wearing a French uniform, salutes. The mythic image, Barthes explains, emerges from ideology as it evolved within a linguistic history. The black man and his uniform are historically situated signifiers that fluidly operate within the "shapeless associations" of a linguistic tradition. The signified, within the context of language, is a concept (French imperialism) that operates as part of a fluid ideological tradition. Myth, which Barthes calls a "second-order semiological system," is a distortion of language that renders it static and reduces it to a gesture. The gesture is a "tamed richness," a moment of history that is frozen into a form. Myth, thus, creates meaning and "imposes it on us." It is a historical phenomenon that emerges from a linguistic history and returns to it for revitalization, but it is also a historical agent that imposes rhetorical meaning on us and effects historical change.[10]

Although Cassirer, Jung, and Barthes did not use the word "rhetoric" in association with myth, they all to some degree held that myth lived rhetorically in the modern world. More recent theorists on myth have discussed its rhetorical function more dramatically and overtly. They have also recognized that myth and history, once viewed from a rhetorical perspective, are not the distinct categories we once thought they were. For example, in writing *The Sacred Remains: Myth, History, and Polity in Belau*, Richard J. Parmentier chose to use the term "history" in lieu of "ethnohistory." He explains:

> I would rather rehabilitate the term "history" and stress that the inclusion of the intentions and intentionality of people who create and interpret their own past is essential, rather than supplementary, to adequate ethnographic study. And the fact that "history" would then label a cultural category as well as an established scholarly discipline should be an indication both that our own historical discourse participates in broader cultural principles and assumptions, and that the historical study of other cultures is always the study of historicizing activities within their cultures.[11]

Like myth, history, even the history of professionals, serves a rhetorical function. The historical record is, as Parmentier concludes in his research, created or destroyed and reinterpreted "to served specific ideological ends."[12] This is what Bruce Lincoln calls "the instrumentality of the past."[13] Within the pragmatics of rhetoric, myth and history are not so distinct: both of these narratives of the past are canonized when rhetors wish to preserve the status quo and reinterpreted when rhetors wish to effect social change.

Notes

1. "On Cassirer's Theory of Language and Myth," in *The Philosophy of Ernst Cassirer*, ed. Paul Arthur Schilpp (New York: Tudor, 1949), p. 387.

2. Prior to Cassirer, most important among the few philosophers who investigated myth were Giambattista Vico and F. W. Schelling, both of whom influenced Cassirer's work.

3. Cassirer, pp. xvii, 14. The presence of mythic thought in scientific discourse is a theme also explored by Hans Blumenberg, *Work on Myth*, trans. Robert M. Wallace (Cambridge: MIT, 1979, 1985) and William Irwin Thompson, *The Time Falling Bodies Take to Light: Mythology, Sexuality, and the Origins of Culture* (New York: St. Martin's, 1981).

4. *The Myth of the State* (New Haven: Yale Univ., 1946).

5. Jung, "Archetypes of the Collective Unconscious," in *The Archetypes and the Collective Unconscious*, trans. R. F. C. Hull (Princeton: Princeton Univ., 1959), especially pp. 6, 14–15, 25, 30, 36.

6. Ibid., pp. 32–33. Emphasis added.

7. See Jung's "The Concept of the Collective Unconscious," in *The Archetypes and the Collective Unconscious*, pp. 47–48.

8. Barthes, *Mythologies*, trans. Annette Lavers (New York: Hill and Wang, 1957, 1972), p. 110.

9. Ibid., pp. 111–12.

10. Ibid., pp. 114, 117, 118, 121, 123.

11. Parmentier, *The Sacred Remains: Myth, History, and Polity in Belau* (Chicago: Chicago Univ., 1987), p. 7. Recent work that expresses a similar rhetorical perspective of myth includes Robert Borofsky, *Making History: Pukapukan Anthropological Constructions of Knowledge* (Cambridge: Cambridge Univ., 1987); Stephen O'Leary and Michael McFarland, "The Political Use of Mythic Discourse: Prophetic Interpretation in Pat Robertson's Presidential Campaign," *Quarterly Journal of Speech*, 75 (1989), pp. 433–52; Marshall Sahlins, *Historical Metaphors and Mythic Realities: Structure in the Early History of the Sandwich Islands Kingdom* (Ann Arbor: Univ. of Michigan, 1981); Bradd Shore, "Human Ambivalence and the Structuring of Moral Values," submitted to *Ethos*; and Gary A. Wright and Jane D. Dirks, "Myth as Environmental Message," *Ethnos*, 48 (1983), pp. 160–272.

12. Parmentier, p. 5.

13. Lincoln, *Discourse and the Construction of Society: Comparative Studies of Myth, Ritual, and Classification* (New York: Oxford Univ., 1989), pp. 15–50.

8

Ernst Cassirer and the Philosophy of Symbolic Forms

C. H. Knoblauch

Along with the sign theory of C. S. Peirce, the structural linguistics of Ferdinand de Saussure, and the modern logics of Gottlob Frege and Charles Morris, Ernst Cassirer's "philosophy of symbolic forms" is a primary source for the ideas and arguments of contemporary semiotics. There are, in fact, some noteworthy points of contact among these lines of reasoning, albeit peripheral ones. Saussure, Frege, and Morris occasionally appear in Cassirer's work, voices to be reckoned with even if often in disagreement. Cassirer shares with Saussure a common regard for the language theory of Wilhelm von Humboldt and the sociological theory of Emile Durkheim. He is much indebted to the structuralist methodology of Saussure and Roman Jakobson, although also opposed to Saussure's view of a merely dyadic relationship between "signifier" and "signified." While he seems to have been unaware of similarities to Peirce, his thinking about symbols intriguingly parallels Peirce's view of the sign, notably a shared understanding of triadicity, which retrieves the mediating concept of "interpretation" that is missing in Saussure's argument.[1] At the same time, however, Cassirer was neither a logician like Frege nor a linguist like Saussure, and his contribution, unlike theirs, lies neither in a formal description of the "sign" nor in a grammatical analysis of one or another sign system. More important, his intellectual sympathies lie fundamentally outside the traditions of realism and pragmatism that dominate early twentieth-century semiotics, particularly the blend of pragmatics and positivism introduced by Morris. Whatever the conceptual overlaps with struc-

215

turalist and pragmatist lines of reasoning, Cassirer's thought is distinctive, not derivative, and shaped by the specific intellectual and historical contexts of his life.

Cassirer's philosophical values are rooted in the liberal tradition of German humanism, powerfully influenced by the neo-Kantian idealism of late nineteenth-century Marburg, and importantly affected by the moral catastrophe of Nazi Germany, whose national socialism he fled in 1933. The context of his concern for the problem of "meaning" is defined by broader questions about the relationship between knowledge and freedom, where "culture" — the embodiment of knowledge and the supreme achievement of symbolic action — entails a continuing process of human self-realization, a perpetual liberating of the "Spirit." Cassirer seeks to understand the interpretive nature of knowing; the concrete processes by which human beings make meaning; the various, historically situated, and coequal modes of symbolization by which knowledge is created; the domains of knowledge that, together, make up our historical, social, and cultural life; and above all the power of expressivity to actualize human potential — to realize human freedom. Cassirer's focus is epistemological, hermeneutic, and — in the technical sense — idealist, not metaphysical or positivistic. His interest is process (or "function"), not object (or "substance"); mind, not cognition; meaning, not signification; expressivity, not reference; symbol, not signal. In *Language and Myth* (LM), *An Essay on Man* (EM), and the monumental *The Philosophy of Symbolic Forms* (PSF), among other original philosophic as well as historical studies,[2] Cassirer offers a systematic representation of symbolic action by appeal to its concrete workings in particular domains of thought and feeling, including myth, language, science, and art. Throughout, he pursues a central thesis, that "human knowledge is by its very nature symbolic knowledge" (EM, 57), that symbolization is the species-specific human capacity to make meaning and thereby produce the coherence of culture. This distinctive human ability is found in palpable, historical life; it is a phenomenon, not a metaphysical abstraction. Its various manifestations are similarly conceived in history, changing according to altered conditions of life, evolving through use, fundamentally different in their manners of operation but equally valid, equally valuable, in constituting — and reconstituting — cultural practices and forms of social reality.

Echoes of Cassirer's line of reasoning may be heard through a remarkable range of contemporary disciplines, from anthropology to literary criticism, as has been amply demonstrated elsewhere.[3] The point can be quickly made by surveying his importance in the relatively new field of "rhetoric and composition," where some distinguishing themes of the past twenty years include "the composing process," "writing as a mode of learning," "the making of meaning," "expressive writing," and "the forming power of language," conceptions that all evidently reflect Cassirer's influence. Janet Emig includes him as a charter member of the "tacit tradition" of modern rhetoric, explaining that Cassirer's voice joins those of Dewey, Langer, Luria, Vygotsky, Kelly, and Kuhn in articulating the "web" of statements in which she situates her own views of writing and knowing.[4] Ann Berthoff points to Cassirer also as a powerful influence on her idea of creative imagination — "the active mind, the mind in action making meaning." Her book *The Making of Meaning* is full of explicit and implicit debts to Cassirer's philosophy, including him, along with Peirce, Whitehead, Langer, I. A. Richards, and Burke, among the "semioticists" who have recognized "that knowing is integral to all symbol systems."[5] Cassirer figures too in James Britton's theory of discourse, according to which, through modes of symbolization, "man represents to himself, cumulatively, what his world is like, and his responses are thereafter mediated by that world-representation."[6] Britton's concept of "expressive writing" derives as much from Cassirer, particularly his view of the prerational substratum of language, as it does from Vygotsky or Sapir. The philosophy of Ernst Cassirer permeates the writings of Emig, Berthoff, and Britton, all of whom are identified in composition theory with a certain way of thinking about conception, expression, and the nature of meaning — all of whom agree with the judgment that "human knowledge is by its very nature symbolic knowledge."

Intellectual Context

In 1896, at age twenty two, Cassirer began a course of study with Hermann Cohen, founder of the Marburg school of neo-Kantianism and one of the great later nineteenth-century authorities on Kant's philosophy. Not surprisingly, the influence of Marburg and the tradition of German idealism is unmistakable throughout Cassirer's work, albeit modified by his more comprehensive treatment of the problem of meaning — specifically his rejection of Marburg's tendency to reduce knowledge to the domain of mathematical reasoning.[7] Idealism supposes in general that a priori intellectual principles and operations account for the comprehensibility of "things." Hence, it opposes, on one hand, the metaphysical ground of meaningfulness, where reality is presumed to be intrinsically coherent apart from human apprehension, and, on the other hand, the experiential ground of meaningfulness, where sensory information is the source and test of true understanding. Idealism grounds meaningfulness in consciousness, Berthoff's "active mind," as it relates dialectically to the materials of sensory awareness. Cassirer argues, in line with the idealist position, that no reality exists independent of the symbolic representations by which human imagination creates

the variegated meaningfulness that is understood as "real" and articulated — objectified — as culture. He further insists, as Kant did, that
"sensory" experience, conceived as prior to consciousness, is as illusory a
conception as the inherently ordered reality of classical metaphysics.
Phenomenal experience is itself a product of human understanding,
derived from the constitutive action of mind. Kant writes in his introduction to *The Critique of Pure Reason* that "experience is without
doubt the first product which our understanding brings forth." Coleridge,
the great English exponent of Kant, makes the same point in the
Biographia Literaria: "We learn all things indeed by occasion of experience; but the very facts so learnt force us inward on the antecedents,
that must be pre-supposed in order to render experience itself possible"
(Ch. IX). Cassirer presents this classic idealist case as well: the processes
of symbolic action, which are the source of culture, "provide the
building-stones from which the world of 'reality' is constructed for us,
as well as that of the human spirit, in sum the World-of-the-I. Like
scientific cognition, they are not simple *structures* which we can insert
into a given world, we must understand them as *functions* by means of
which a particular form is given to reality" (PSF, 1, 91).

   Cassirer is at greatest pains to make this argument in connection
with empirical science, in the process challenging a primary contention
of the objectivist tradition that has informed the natural sciences since
the emergence of empiricism in the seventeenth century. Lockean
positivism had articulated a position, still influential if not dominant
today, that recognizes science as the only source of real knowledge,
the supremely truthful discourse, because it "begins" supposedly from
sensory "data" and then offers a rigorously dispassionate analysis leading
to stable, indeed timeless, axiomatic understanding. But even science
remains a human artifact from Kant's perspective, offering a knowledge
inevitably conditioned by the ways in which human beings see and
interpret. Cassirer, whose earliest work was in the philosophy of science,
begins from, and eventually goes beyond, the Kantian point of view.
Science, he insists, must renounce "its aspiration and its claim to
an 'immediate' grasp and communication of reality. It realizes that
the only objectivization of which it is capable is, and must remain,
mediation" (PSF, 1, 76). "The facts of science," he explains, "always
imply a theoretical, which means a symbolic, element. Many, if not
most, of those scientific facts which have changed the whole course
of the history of science have been hypothetical facts before they
became observable facts" (EM, 59). In science, the "interpretation of
experimental facts" always depends on "certain fundamental concepts
which have to be clarified before the empirical material can bear its
fruit" (EM, 28). In physics, for instance, notions such as mass and
force, atom or ether, are "free 'fictions,'" which cognition devises "in

order to dominate the world of sensory experience and survey it as a world ordered by law." Such concepts are the words of a scientific language "meaningful in itself and ordered according to fixed rules" (PSF, 1, 85). Finally, for even the most "determined empiricists," the "interpretation of ... empirical evidence contains from the very outset an arbitrary assumption" — a "theory" which becomes "a Procrustean bed on which the empirical facts are stretched to fit a preconceived pattern" (EM, 21).

Consistent with his apprenticeship at Marburg, where the pure rationality of mathematical science was a central tenet, Cassirer devotes much of his writing to the "discourse" of science, from the early *Substance and Function* (1910), to lengthy portions of Volume 3 of *The Philosophy of Symbolic Forms* (1929), to a chapter in *An Essay on Man* (1944), published shortly before his death, where he speaks of science as "the highest and most characteristic attainment of human culture" (207). This emphasis is hardly surprising given Kant's own original commitment to scientific reasoning as the ultimate model for philosophic inquiry, provided that it is construed in idealist rather than positivist terms. Cassirer furthers Kant's critique of scientific knowledge, incorporating the implications of post-Euclidean geometry, relativity, and quantum mechanics, and depicts the interpretive character of empirical method — the peculiar features of its symbolic mode. But he also modifies Kant's emphasis, and that of the Marburg school as well, on the authoritativeness of mathematical knowing, retrieving a larger conception of "science" — the practices of discursive reasoning (including philosophy) — while also investigating the variety of symbolic modes, each with its own constitutive principles, its own legitimacy as an impulse of the human spirit, that finally comprise culture. As Langer explains in her essay "On Cassirer's Theory of Language and Myth," Cassirer rejects the idea of one "categorical scheme" — in which the laws of discursive logic are equated with thinking itself — "as the absolute way of experiencing reality," instead distinguishing a range of "alternative symbolic forms" that produce "alternative phenomenal 'worlds.'" With this expansion of perspective, "the Kantian doctrine that identified all conception with discursive reason, making reason appear as an aboriginal human gift, is saved from its most serious fallacy, an unhistorical view of mind."[8] What replaces that doctrine for Cassirer is an understanding that "myth, art, language, and science" appear equally as symbols, "not in the sense of mere figures which refer to some given reality by means of suggestion and allegorical renderings, but in the sense of forces each of which produces and posits a world of its own." By these expressive vehicles, situated in history, "the spirit exhibits itself in that inwardly determined dialectic by virtue of which alone there is any reality, any organized and definite Being at all" (LM, 8).

Themes and Methods

Throughout his work, Cassirer is chiefly preoccupied with the nature of knowledge as a cultural artifact and the nature of culture as a semiotic artifact. He seeks to reveal and illustrate the diverse modes of symbolic action by which knowledge and culture are constituted. "Man lives in a symbolic universe," he writes in *An Essay on Man*. "Language, myth, art, and religion are parts of this universe. They are the varied threads which weave the symbolic net, the tangled web of human experience" (EM, 25). That "symbolic net" *is* culture, a product of human imaginative energies, a range of prerational, commonsense, practical, and theoretical knowledge in terms of which human beings construct their "everyday lives" as well as their intellectual, moral, and spiritual consciousness. Cassirer aims to develop what, in *An Essay on Man*, he calls "anthropological philosophy," where Kant's "critique of reason" necessarily becomes a "critique of culture" — because to constitute knowledge, through the mediation of symbolic form, is, effectively, to produce culture. Anthropological philosophy "seeks to understand ... how every content of culture ... in so far as it is grounded in a universal principle of form, presupposes an original act of the human spirit" (PSF, 1, 80).

For Cassirer, borrowing in some respects from Hegel's notion of the reciprocity of the Ideal and the Actual,[9] "spirit" refers to that distinctively human agency that is ever dialectically opposed to the material other. Culture is an "objective" artifact but more than a stark materiality: it is an expression of the human spirit, articulated by means of the modes of symbolic action. "Spirit" defines a collective consciousness, not to be associated with subjectivism (which Cassirer opposed)[10] or, still less, confused with a solipsistic notion of radical individuality. To be sure, he writes, "every organism is ... a monadic being. It has a world of its own because it has an experience of its own" (EM, 23). But at the same time, "Man is to be studied not in his individual life but in his political and social life" (EM, 63). Humankind exists in and through its individuals; but it is comprehensible only conceived as a whole — conceived, that is, as intersubjectivity. Since language, for instance, according to Cassirer "arises not in isolated but in communal action, it possesses from the start a truly common, 'universal' sense." Had it been otherwise, had the linguistic sign "merely expressed an individual representation produced in the individual consciousness, it would have remained imprisoned in the individual consciousness, without power to pass beyond it." For Cassirer, language, no less than the other symbolic forms, "as a *sensorum commune* could only grow out of the sympathy of activity" (PSF, 1, 286): it is, at once, the product and the producer of the spiritual life of a people. To study the substance of culture, in all its forms, is to seek understanding of the social — but also more than merely material — the "spiritual" or distinctively *human* construction of knowledge.

Cassirer undertakes that study not through speculative, metaphysical definition but through the concrete analysis of symbolic practices. The "content of culture," he insists, "cannot be detached from the fundamental forms and directions of human activity" — "'being' can be apprehended only in 'action.'" Therefore, while it is proper for the "philosophical critique of knowledge" to assume a "unified, ideal center" amidst the various manifestations of cultural expression, this center "can never lie in a given essence but only in a common *project*." In other words, *functions* rather than objects are the focus of attention. The various products of culture, including myth, art, religion, and science, "become parts of a single great problem-complex: they become multiple efforts, all directed toward the one goal of transforming the passive world of mere *impressions*, in which the spirit seems at first imprisoned, into a world that is pure *expression* of the human spirit" (PSF, 1, 80–81). Cassirer's tactic is to characterize and richly exemplify alternative symbolic forms as concrete traces of the workings of the spirit. His method, as he himself represents it, is "transcendental," aimed specifically at a phenomenology of consciousness. In transcendental method what is investigated is not some object of knowledge conceived as pure "essence" — in this case, culture or symbolic form "in itself" — but the manner in which an object comes to be known or constituted in consciousness. Culture as "object" is only an intuited "center" presented to the understanding through awareness, including philosophical analysis, of the practices that comprise it. Symbolic form is to be known by depicting the orderly ways in which people experience the world, not by conceiving form as a metaphysical abstraction. "It is, as it were, the fundamental principle of cognition that the universal can be perceived only in the particular, while the particular can be thought only in reference to the universal" (PSF, 1, 86).

Language, Myth, and Science

The *Philosophy of Symbolic Forms* devotes a volume to language and a volume to myth, two of the three symbolic modes that Cassirer regards as, historically, the most significant enacters of cultural reality. A significant portion of Volume 3 concerns science, the mode to which he gives so much attention in his early work. *An Essay on Man* goes further, recapitulating much of the thinking in *Symbolic Forms* but extending its analysis to religion, art, and history, in order more adequately to fulfill the promise of its subtitle: "An Introduction to a Philosophy of Human Culture." Cassirer's position remains generally consistent throughout. The symbolic forms "are not imitations, but *organs* of reality, since it is solely by their agency that anything real becomes an object for intellectual apprehension, and as such is made visible to us" (LM, 8). Perhaps the clearest statement of Cassirer's central point is this passage from Volume 1 of *Symbolic Forms*:

> Every authentic function of the human spirit has this decisive charac-teristic in common with cognition: it does not merely copy but rather embodies an original, formative power. It does not express passively the mere fact that something is present but contains an independent energy of the human spirit through which the simple presence of the phenomenon assumes a definite 'meaning,' a particular ideational content. This is as true of art as it is of cognition; it is as true of myth as of religion. All live in particular image-worlds, which do not merely reflect the empirically given, but which rather produce it in accordance with an independent principle. Each of these functions creates its own symbolic forms which, if not similar to the intellectual symbols, enjoy equal rank as products of the human spirit. None of these forms can simply be reduced to, or derived from, the others; each of them designates a particular approach in which and through which it constitutes its own aspect of 'reality.' They are not different modes in which an independent reality manifests itself to the human spirit but roads by which the spirit proceeds towards its objectivization, i.e., its self-revelation. If we consider art and language, myth and cognition in this light, they present a common problem which opens up new access to a universal philosophy of the cultural sciences (78).

The "formative power" of myth consists in its "expressive" func-tion, while that of language lies in its "intuitional" function and that of science in its "conceptual" function. Myth articulates an animate, passionate world in which human feelings, desires, and fears are objec-tified, through symbols, as responsive agencies, gods, demons, and other personifications, in nature itself. Language articulates the world of everyday life, of "common-sense" experience with its palpable images and ordinary ideas of "things" and their properties, the connec-tions among things in space and time, the ways in which one thing is attributed to or predicated of another. Science articulates an austerely rational world of pure relationships detached from the sensory and the emotive, a world preeminently conveyed through mathematical reasoning. These modes, and others, "function organically together in the construction of spiritual reality, yet each of these organs has its individual assignment." It remains for a philosophy of culture to seek "their mutual limitation and supplementation," which Cassirer sets out to do by calling upon a wealth of detail from contemporary psychology, anthropology, linguistics, history, religious theory, and physical as well as social science. He cycles repeatedly back and forth through the different modes, making juxtapositions, finding interconnections, explaining significant differences. "In discursive thought, the particular phenomenon is related to the whole pattern of being and of process; with ever tightening, ever more elaborate bonds it is held to that totality. In mythic conception, however, things are not taken for what they mean indirectly, but for their immediate appearance; they are taken as pure presentations, and embodied in the imagination" (LM, 56). "Language and myth stand in an original and indissoluble correlation . . . from which they both emerge but gradually as independent elements. . . . In the vocables of speech and in primitive mythic figurations, the same inner process finds its consummation: they are both resolutions of an inner tension, the representation of subjective impulses and excitations in definite objective forms and figures" (LM, 88).

If there is a distinctive mode of meaningfulness for each symbolic function, there is also, according to Cassirer, an evolutionary, historical progression from the mythic to the scientific imagination. Cassirer leaves no doubt about his attitude toward science as the most fully evolved form of consciousness: "There is no second power in our modern world which may be compared to that of scientific thought. It is held to be the summit and consummation of all our human activities, the last chapter in the history of mankind . . ." (EM, 207). His evolutionary perspective leads him, as a result, to frame the emergence of symbolic modes in terms of originations, the primordial links between myth and art, the primitive moment in which language erupted, the gradual development from imagistic to conceptual thinking. "That myth and language are subject to the same, or at least closely analogous, laws of evolution can really be seen and understood only in so far as we can uncover the common root from which both of them spring" (LM, 84). "Before man thinks in terms of logical concepts, he holds his experiences by means of clear, separate, mythical images" (LM, 37). As a result, Cassirer's appreciation for modes of symbolization other than science includes a characteristically romantic recollection of the now compromised "original creative power" of the Word: "If language is to grow into a vehicle of thought, an expression of concepts and judgments, this evolution can be achieved only at the price of forgoing the wealth and fullness of immediate experience. In the end, what is left of the concrete sense and feeling content it once possessed is little more than a bare skeleton." But the loss is restored in modern culture (as Coleridge and Keats had argued as well) through the power of artistic expression to reclaim the emotional content of language: "Here it recovers the fullness of life; but it is no longer a life mythically bound and fettered, but an aesthetically liberated life." Poetry in particular maintains the "mythic power of insight" although what it expresses is neither "the mythic word-picture of gods and daemons, nor the logical truth of abstract determinations and relations." Instead, it depicts self-consciously a world of "illusion and fantasy," where "the realm of pure feeling can find utterance" in a "full and concrete actualization" (LM, 98–99).

This evolutionary-historical conception of the symbolic modes notwithstanding, Cassirer shows an essential generosity toward each mode as an authentic medium of understanding—all "enjoy equal rank as products of the human spirit." He does not patronize the mythic imagination as "primitive" and delusional; it is rather primordial, the deepest root from which other forms of meaningfulness have grown and to which those forms still, in varying degrees, retain a subterranean attachment.[11] It also produces a legitimate knowledge, a text, as it were, of "mythic ideas" that, "no matter how manifold, how varied, how heterogeneous they may appear at first sight, have their own inner lawfulness; they do not arise from a boundless caprice of the imagination, but move in definite avenues of feeling and creative thought" (LM, 15). Myth is an account of life, though one unbounded by the conventions of discursive logic; it is an enactment of the human condition, of the ways in which human beings are situated in the world. The account is dramatic rather than theoretical, grounded in unselfconscious belief rather than skepticism, and formed from perceptions that are always "impregnated with ... emotional qualities." What is depicted is "a world of actions, of forces, of conflicting powers," in which objects are always "benignant or malignant, friendly or inimical, familiar or uncanny, alluring and fascinating or repellant and threatening" (EM, 76–77). In myth, dreams and desires become projected as reality; there is no "clear division between mere 'imagining' and 'real' perception, between wish and fulfillment, between image and object" (PSF, 2, 48–49). The mythic imagination focuses on the "sensible present," the immediate, palpable experience of nature, without concern for categorizing or systematizing its objects: it is "captivated and enthralled by the intuition which suddenly confronts it" (LM, 32). As that intuition acquires symbolic form, it *becomes* reality, for there is no distinction between name and thing, no space between symbol and meaning: the name "is merged with its object in an indissoluble unity" (LM, 58). Finally, the mythic world view is "synthetic" rather than analytic, possessing a "fluidity" of substance and form in which objects are distinct but not separate and may freely re-form themselves even into their opposites. "To mythical ... feeling nature becomes one great society, the *society of life*. Man is not endowed with outstanding rank in this society.... Men and animals, animals and plants are all on the same level" (EM, 81–83). If one law characterizes the world of mythic thought, it is the law of metamorphosis.

Language shares with myth a "noteworthy indifference" to distinctions between inward and outward reality, since the ground of language is expressivity, a fusing of subject and object (PSF, 1, 177ff.). According to Cassirer, language "never denotes simply objects, things as such, but always conceptions arising from the autonomous activity of the mind. The nature of concepts, therefore, depends on the way this active viewing is directed" (LM, 31). Language, then, like myth, has "a productive and constructive rather than a merely reproductive function" (EM, 131). Furthermore, language does not form itself, any more than myth does, "by any sort of reflective contemplation," such as that of discursive thought, "the calm and clear-headed comparison of given sense impressions and the abstraction of definite attributes." Language emerges out of dynamic, phenomenal immediacy, where expression and denotation coalesce, only gradually objectifying itself, "through progressive organization and ever more definite articulation," as a structured logic of "ordinary" experience (LM, 36). But there are important distinctions as well. The relationship between language and reality is construed in a fundamentally different way, where "the magic function of the word" in mythic thinking is "eclipsed and replaced by its semantic function." The word is no longer identical to its object, as in mythic thought, nor does it possess mysterious powers: "It cannot change the nature of things and it cannot compel the will of gods or demons." Its power now consists in its capacity to name and sort, relate and differentiate, attribute and predicate — in short, to constitute the world according to the logic of grammar (EM, 111).

Where myth encourages synthesis and metamorphosis, language enables and sustains difference, distributing (in accordance with what Humboldt calls its "inward form") a structured universe of objects, meaningful as such through their oppositions and antitheses, in order to make possible at once a complex expression of intuited "reality" and a practical orientation to the environment (PSF, 1, 120). Through their "everyday terms and names" people derive their most fundamental "objective or theoretical view of the world," a view which is not simply given but which results from the unending "constructive intellectual effort" that language enables (EM, 135). What is named depends on the "teleological perspective," the concentrated (but not altogether conscious) attention of the namers: only what is related to "the focus point of willing and doing," only "what proves to be essential to the whole scheme of life and activity," is "noticed" amidst "the uniform flux of sense impressions" and named (LM, 38). Human speech fulfills both a "universal logical task," in which spatial, temporal, and other conceptualizations are composed as a substratum for understanding, and also "a social task which depends on the specific social conditions of the speaking community," objectifying the consciousness of that community, conceiving its self-identity, articulating its institutions and values, determining and assisting its modes of practical cooperation.

And, of course, since there are many languages in the world, there are also multiple worldviews, and multiple social realities, supported by the action of alternative grammars (PSF, 1, 159).

Scientific thinking, finally, and the concepts of theoretical knowledge generally, "constitute merely an upper stratum of logic which is founded upon a lower stratum, that of the logic of language.... All theoretical cognition takes its departure from a world already preformed by language; the scientist, the historian, even the philosopher, lives with his objects only as language presents them to him" (LM, 28). But at the same time, science offers more than merely "an enlargement or enrichment of our ordinary experience. It demands a new principle of order, a new form of intellectual interpretation" (EM, 209). What distinguishes discursive reason from the action of ordinary language is its essential indifference to describing a world of things and its concern for the general expression of logical relationships. In his *Philosophy of the Enlightenment* Cassirer observes that the real achievement of science lies not in the "new objective content" it makes available "but in the new *function* which it attributes to the mind of man." Scientific knowledge does not lead "out into the world of objects"; it serves rather "as a medium in which the mind develops its own self-knowledge" (PE, 37). Science seeks to articulate universal principles and laws, which may then order — rationalize — "the great spectacle of the world" in accordance with the highest abstractive capacities of human intellect. "Universal law, which is discovered and formulated in thought, forms the necessary correlate of the intuitively experienced boundlessness of the universe" (PE, 38).

To be sure, science cannot fulfill its ambition without scrupulous attention to the facts of nature. But those facts serve (initially) stimulative and (finally) corroborative functions: they assist in the posing of problems and in the verifying of solutions within a given context. "The object cannot be regarded as a naked thing in itself, independent of the essential categories of natural science; for only within these categories which are required to constitute its form can it be described at all" (PSF, 1, 76). So, what lies at the center of scientific reasoning is the characteristic interpretive practices of discursive symbolization, which precede and enable the accumulating of "facts." That reasoning aims to "deliver the contents of sensory or intuitive experience" from the "isolation" of their concreteness: "it causes these contents to transcend their narrow limits, combines them with others, compares them, and concatenates them in a definite order, in an all-inclusive context." The end is a model, an equation, a law, a "closed system" of some sort, in which "there are no more isolated points; all its members are reciprocally related, refer to one another, illuminate and explain each other." The significance of any "separate event" derives from the fact that "it is stamped with the character of this totality" (LM, 32). This system is, of course, altogether "artificial," a human construct. "Nature as such only contains individual and diversified phenomena": science does not "describe facts of nature" when it constructs its general laws and models; it simply constitutes a particular form of knowledge. "Every system is a work of art — a result of conscious creative activity" (EM, 209).

Symbolic Form

Given Cassirer's transcendental method, the general question (what exactly is "symbolic form"?) receives the only kind of answer of which it admits: an oblique one, because it is to be understood through its manifestations and not as an object in itself. Symbolic form lies implicit in symbolic function: it is the "shape" of knowing, as knowing is enabled by a mode of symbolization. "In the symbolic function of consciousness — as it operates in language, in art, in myth — certain unchanging fundamental forms, some of a conceptual and some of a purely sensory nature, disengage themselves from the stream of consciousness; the flux of contents is replaced by a self-contained and enduring unity of form" (PSF, 1, 89). Cassirer depends importantly here on Humboldt's concept of *innere Sprachform* — the grammatico-semantic structure of a natural language that constitutes its formal identity and distinguishes it from other languages. "A similar 'inner form' may be sought in religion and myth, in art and scientific cognition." This form can only be found "through the phenomena themselves from which we 'abstract' it," but at the same time "this very abstraction shows that the law is a necessary constituent factor of the content and existence of the particular" (PSF, 1, 81). Natural language offers Cassirer the best available analogy for characterizing other symbolic forms, though he also concedes the limitations of analogy. Any such form may be likened to a "language" — an articulation of the spirit — insofar as it includes some material aspect, a "phonetic" content, which is informed by a principle of organization, an organic structure. Symbolic form is, then, so to speak, a "grammar of the symbolic function," where any given "symbol" is equivalent to a word in that particular "language," sharing the structural features of the system as a whole while representing with some degree and kind of specificity. Symbolization, finally, is the species-specific action of human consciousness, consisting in the production of meaning through the coalescence of subject and object, perceptual matter and conceptual structure, that is enabled by the mediation of signs.

Critical Appraisals

The most interesting critiques of Cassirer's philosophy, as might be expected, come from positions that are adjacent to his or that emerge from the same or related sources. Plainly, traditional empiricist or positivist views of discourse, whether the discourse of science or some other mode, conflict irreconcilably with the arguments that Cassirer seeks to advance. Just as plainly, the assumptions of classical metaphysics, including those that inform the dominant tradition of ancient rhetoric, have few, if any, substantive points of agreement with the neo-Kantian perspective. But starkly opposed views rarely offer interesting appraisals of each other, tending instead to ignore, dismiss, or simplify as a means of managing incomprehensibility. In the case of Cassirer's theory, as perhaps with any philosophical argument, the challenges that provoke further thinking come from closer to home — specifically out of the great debate between Kant and Hegel that echoes throughout neo-Kantianism (including but not limited to the Marburg tradition), modern phenomenology, and certain Marxist schools of thought.

The phenomenologist Hans-Georg Gadamer, for instance, offers some characteristic reflections on the limits of Cassirer's position in a collection of essays titled *Philosophical Hermeneutics*.[12] The philosophical break with neo-Kantianism initiated by Heidegger, among others, and the subsequent "dissolution" of the Marburg school, centers, as Gadamer sees it, on the failure of Marburg generally to confront "the problem of language." Neo-Kantianism is committed to the privileging of science as the evolved and dominant ideal of knowledge, so that the comprehensive, enveloping phenomenal world that language articulates is subordinated to the technological world evoked by utilitarian, scientific signs. More seriously, it also presumes a self-contained and, to that extent, alienated "consciousness" that subordinates language to a merely instrumental status as the expressive vehicles of mind, a means of objectifying experience. Gadamer acknowledges that Cassirer "brought the phenomenon of language into the program of Marburg . . . idealism," placing it alongside myth in a challenge to the hegemony of science. But he adds that, in doing so, Cassirer did not break with "the methodological principle of objectification," where what is assumed is the primacy of "transcendental consciousness," Cassirer's "human spirit," which acts upon experience through the mediation of language, or some other symbolic form, conceived as an instrumentality (199).

The trouble, according to Gadamer, is that this view fails to account for "the uniqueness of the phenomenon of language," which does not merely stand alongside myth, art, or science, in a relationship of equivalency but which "represents the sustaining medium of all of these manifestations of the spirit." It would not even be proper to give language a "special distinction" among symbolic forms, since it is not finally a "formal" power at all but rather an encompassing reality, which constitutes not only the world of everyday life that Cassirer ascribes to it but also the other realms of meaningfulness he explores — and one more that he does not — namely, the experience of consciousness itself, which Cassirer had located outside the web of meaning.[13] For Gadamer the true pursuit of philosophy is not a phenomenology of consciousness, as Cassirer sought, but rather a phenomenology of language. He takes no note of the fact, and would surely have remained unpersuaded in any case, that Cassirer had substantially responded to this critique in his famous debate with Heidegger, where he insisted that the distinction of modes of symbolic action, including myth and science, represents possibilities of meaningfulness that lie properly beyond the domain of "ordinary language." For Heidegger and Gadamer, language constitutes the boundaries of objective reality. For Cassirer, "objective mind is not exhausted by . . . the structure of everydayness."[14]

Marxist philosophers of language, the most thoroughgoing of whom is perhaps Voloshinov, have challenged the idealist tradition in similar ways, although extending the critique on materialist grounds. Voloshinov was a member of the Bakhtin Circle, and the issue that most preoccupied the early members of the circle, during the late teens and early twenties of this century, was German philosophy, particularly the thinking of the Marburg neo-Kantians. Although Voloshinov does not criticize Cassirer directly in *Marxism and the Philosophy of Language*,[15] he does challenge neo-Kantian idealism in some detail in a depiction of Humboldtian language theory, which he characterizes as an instance of "individualistic subjectivism." According to Voloshinov, Humboldt's tradition regards language as "an unceasing process of creation realized in individual speech acts," while the laws that govern linguistic creativity "are the laws of individual psychology" (48). For him, the virtue of Humboldt's position is its opposition to the structural abstractions of objectivist linguistics, its regard instead for the stream of speech, where the true phenomenal and historical reality of language is to be found. But its principal limitation is its positing of individual consciousness as an autonomous realm, apart from and prior to the materiality of language. Voloshinov concedes that Cassirer's neo-Kantianism offers a "change of outlook" compared to Humboldt, one rooted in dialectical relationships between form and matter, community and individual (11n.). Language is necessarily a social phenomenon, though individual speakers constitute its palpable reality. Language has form, though its form changes in the historical stream of speech. But he faults Cassirer no less than Humboldt for a false privileging of consciousness, which, in the light of his own materialist views, necessarily entails not only the subordinating of language to an instrumental capacity as Gadamer had suggested, but also a mentalistic conception of the symbol.

For Voloshinov, language is a system of signs, residing in the materiality of speech. "A sign is a phenomenon of the external world. Both the sign itself and all the effects it produces . . . in the surrounding social milieu . . . occur in outer experience." The material reality of language constitutes the ideological conditions of social life, including the domain of "consciousness," which is itself an ideological artifact: "consciousness can arise and become a viable fact only in the material embodiment of signs" (11). Cassirer had distinguished sharply between the symbol and the "signal," insisting that the two belong to different universes of discourse: "a signal is a part of the physical world of being; a symbol is a part of the human world of meaning" (EM, 32). In Voloshinov's work the notion of "sign" is explored in detail, but the notion of "symbol" is conspicuously absent. "Signification" displaces "meaning." On this issue the idealist Cassirer and the materialist Voloshinov can only be at loggerheads.

Notes

1. For a discussion of dyadic versus triadic views of the sign, together with mention of Cassirer's links to both Peirce and Saussure, see John Michael Krois, *Cassirer: Symbolic Forms and History* (New Haven: Yale Univ., 1987), pp. 50–52. For Peirce's views in particular, see also Ann E. Berthoff, ed., *Reclaiming the Imagination* (Portsmouth, N.H.: Boynton/Cook, 1984), pp. 167–72.

2. Cassirer wrote prolifically, as both an original philosopher and a historian of philosophy, but the majority of his major works appeared originally in German, becoming only gradually accessible to English-speaking audiences. This circumstance, together with the fact that the arguments in Cassirer's major books demand considerable effort from the lay reader, have no doubt affected the character and quality of his impact on American discourse theory. The earliest of Cassirer's works to be translated were contributions to the philosophy of science, *Substance and Function*, originally published in Berlin in 1910, and *Einstein's Theory of Relativity*, Berlin, 1921; both books were translated by William Curtis Swabey and Mary Collins Swabey and published in a single volume in 1921, by Open Court Publishing Company, Chicago. These studies contain many anticipations of Cassirer's later thought, reveal his Marburg neo-Kantian origins, and attest to the range of his ideas, but they are more demanding than a casual reader will prefer and more useful for the historian of Cassirer's philosophy than for those whose primary interest is discourse theory. The shortest and most accessible of Cassirer's studies in symbolic form is Susanne K. Langer's translation of *Language and Myth*, Dover Publications,

1946, still readily available in paperback and a stimulating introduction to his mature thought. (This is abbreviated in the text as LM.) *An Essay on Man*, published in English by Yale University Press in 1944 and abbreviated in the text as EM, is the next best available source, also in paperback, more demanding than *Language and Myth* but entirely readable and perhaps the fullest account of his "anthropological philosophy." By all accounts the centerpiece of Cassirer's achievement in discourse theory is *The Philosophy of Symbolic Forms*, originally published in Berlin between 1923 and 1929. It did not appear in English until ten years after his death, translated by Ralph Manheim and published in three volumes by Yale University Press, 1953, 1955, and 1957. (This work is abbreviated in the text as PSF.) Both lengthy and complex, it is as difficult, particularly for nonphilosophers, as it is rewarding. A fourth volume, which Cassirer projected but did not complete, is promised from Yale Press, edited by Donald Verene and John M. Krois. Several of Cassirer's studies in the history of philosophy are also available in English and should not be overlooked because of the light they shed on theories of knowledge and discourse, which Cassirer rejected but nonetheless knew how to explain in cogent, sympathetic detail. Foremost among them is *The Philosophy of the Enlightenment* (PE in the text), translated by Fritz C. A. Koelln and James P. Pettegrove, published by Princeton University Press, 1951, and later as a Beacon Press (Boston) paperback in 1955. It remains one of the clearest introductions to the rationalist and empiricist philosophical traditions. Two other worthy historical accounts are *The Individual and the Cosmos in Renaissance Philosophy*, translated by Mario Domandi, New York, 1964, and *The Platonic Renaissance in England*, translated by Koelln and Pettegrove, Austin, Texas, 1953. Though not specifically relevant to the issue of discourse theory, *The Myth of the State*, published by Yale Press in 1946, is important reading for anyone who wishes to understand the critical link in Cassirer's thought between the question of meaning and the domain of ethics, specifically the value of freedom, a human entitlement profoundly jeopardized by the Nazi perversion of the German state. A similar theme is explored in *Symbol, Myth, and Culture*, edited by Verene, Yale Press, 1987, a collection of previously unpublished papers from the last decade of Cassirer's life.

3. Among a great many secondary sources, the most comprehensive review available of Cassirer's philosophical achievement remains *The Philosophy of Ernst Cassirer*, edited by Paul Arthur Schilpp and published by Tudor (The Library of Living Philosophers), New York, 1949. The contributors to that volume had all been endorsed by Cassirer himself as best qualified to represent his thinking, and they include Susanne Langer, whose *Philosophy in a New Key* might equally be counted as a thorough analysis, though also an extension, of Cassirer's ideas. Useful, too, is *Philosophy and History: Essays Presented to Ernst Cassirer*, edited by H. J. Paton and Raymond Klibansky, New York, 1964. John Michael Krois's *Cassirer: Symbolic Forms and History*, Yale Press, 1987, is a significant, and more contemporary, study which includes, not just a challenge to traditional views of Cassirer's neo-Kantianism, but a broad rereading of his work. Two articles by Donald Verene are noteworthy for their contextualizing of Cassirer's thought: "Kant, Hegel, and Cassirer: The Origins of the Philosophy of Symbolic Forms," *Journal of the History of Ideas*, 30

(1969), 33–46; and "Cassirer's Philosophy of Culture," *International Philosophical Quarterly*, 22 (1982), 133–44. Finally, the Introduction by Charles W. Hendel to the English translation of *Symbolic Forms* provides an excellent overview of the intellectual relationship between Cassirer and Kant.

4. See Janet Emig, *The Web of Meaning*, eds. Dixie Goswami and Maureen Butler (Portsmouth, N.H.: Boynton/Cook, 1983), pp. 38, 42, 146–56.

5. Berthoff, *The Making of Meaning* (Portsmouth, N.H.: Boynton/Cook, 1981), p. 103.

6. James Britton, Tony Burgess, Nancy Martin, Alex McLeod, and Harold Rosen, *The Development of Writing Abilities* (London: MacMillan Education Ltd., 1975), p. 78.

7. Biographical sketches of Cassirer are available in Krois, pp. 13–32, and in Dimitry Gawronsky, "Ernst Cassirer: His Life and His Work," in *The Philosophy of Ernst Cassirer*, 3–37. The influence of Marburg neo-Kantian idealism is discussed in Fritz Kaufmann, "Cassirer, Neo-Kantianism, and Phenomenology," and William H. Werkmeister, "Cassirer's Advance Beyond Neo-Kantianism," both in *The Philosophy of Ernst Cassirer*, pp. 801–54. 759–98. A central thesis of Krois's argument, however, is that this influence has been exaggerated in earlier studies.

8. Susanne Langer, "On Cassirer's Theory of Language and Myth," in *The Philosophy of Ernst Cassirer*, p. 392.

9. Hegel's influence on Cassirer, and the differences between their views, is discussed in Charles Hendel's Introduction to Cassirer's *Philosophy of Symbolic Forms*, 1 (New Haven: Yale Univ., 1955), pp. 32–35.

10. Cassirer emphasizes his antisubjectivist position in the debate with Heidegger. See John M. Krois, "Cassirer's Unpublished Critique of Heidegger," *Philosophy and Rhetoric*, 16 (1983), pp. 147–59, and Ernst Cassirer, "'Mind' and 'Life': Heidegger," which Krois translates on pp. 160–66 of *Cassirer: Symbolic Forms and History*.

11. Hans Blumenberg has suggested, however, that Cassirer's evolutionary view implies the obsolescence of myth once scientific reasoning achieves cultural priority. This criticism becomes important in connection with Cassirer's examination of the mythic contours of the Nazi state (*The Myth of the State*, 1946), where he can only stand aghast at Germany's "incomprehensible reversion" to mythic thinking. See Blumenberg, *Work on Myth*, trans. Robert M. Wallace (Cambridge: MIT, 1985), including the "Translator's Introduction," viii–ix, and passim.

12. Trans. David E. Linge (Berkeley: Univ. of California, 1976).

13. Here Gadamer is evidently replicating Hegel's views of language and consciousness. See ch. 1 of Hegel's *Phenomenology of Mind*, and elsewhere.

14. Cassirer, "'Mind' and 'Life': Heidegger," translated on p. 161 of *Cassirer: Symbolic Forms and History*.

15. Trans. Ladislav Matejka and I. R. Titunik (Cambridge: Harvard Univ., 1986). The debate continues over whether Bakhtin himself authored or coauthored this work, along with other texts of his "Circle."

Feminism

9

The Woman Question — And Some Answers

Angelika Bammer

man 1. An adult male human being. 2. Human beings collectively; the human race; mankind — to be one's own man
woman 1. An adult human female. 2. The female part of the human race; women collectively — the little woman

*Funk & Wagnall's Standard
College Dictionary* (1968)

A living language must keep pace with improvements in knowledge and with the multiplication of ideas.

Noah Webster (1817)[1]

> I am a woman committed to
> a politics
> of transliteration, the methodology
>
> of a mind
> stunned at the suddenly
> possible shifts of meaning — for which
> like amnesiacs
>
> in a ward on fire, we must
> find words
> or burn.

Olga Broumas (1977)[2]

It is widely recognized by now, certainly within feminist circles, that one can really only talk about feminism in the plural. There is no

235

feminism and no women's movement. There are, rather, feminisms and women's movements with differing issues and differing emphases in response to differing needs. Yet despite these differences some issues have been held to be so central to women's struggles for emancipation that they can be posited as characteristics of contemporary feminism in general. One of these issues is language.

Obviously, the degree to which language was identified as an issue differs from case to case. In some cases, in France, for example, where feminism developed and articulated itself within the context of the intellectual (i.e., university-based) Left of the late 1960s, the emphasis on language as a tool with which power could both be constructed and deconstructed was particularly strong. In other cases, such as the feminism of Black American women and women of the colonized world, language was generally not perceived to be the main site of struggle,[3] even though its role as a means of oppression or, conversely, liberation, was readily acknowledged. Yet in all of these movements language was an issue, and a critical one at that. The purpose of this essay is to show some of the differing ways in which this issue has been framed within different feminist contexts and discuss the strategies that resulted from these divergent theoretical and political starting points.

I will begin with a premise, common to these varieties of feminism, that, as the British historian Sheila Rowbotham put it, "Language is part of the political and ideological power of the rulers."[4] As another British feminist, the linguist Dale Spender, explained in the introductory chapter of her book *Man Made Language* (1980): "One of the basic principles of feminism is that society has been constructed with a bias which favours males; one of the basic principles of feminists who are concerned with language is that this bias can be located in the language."[5]

In the most general terms, as Spender puts it, the feminist position on language is based on two historical premises: that the English "language has been literally man made and that it is still primarily under male control," and that this "monopoly over language is one of the means by which males have ensured their own primacy." In other words, the language we have learned is an essential means by which patriarchal power constructs and legitimates itself. Therefore, as feminists were quick to point out, from the perspective of women the language "we" were using was not "ours" but "theirs." Indeed, the text in which the basic principles of contemporary feminism were first put forth in theoretical terms and historically documented, Simone de Beauvoir's *The Second Sex* (1949), begins with precisely this observation: as women we don't even know what the very terms that define us really mean. Therefore, de Beauvoir's groundbreaking study of the social construction of gender and its role in the historical oppression of women was launched by a simple question about the meaning of the basic term with which feminism inevitably begins: "what is a woman?"[6]

Given the premise that language was a primary source and instrument of male domination, what kind of options did women have? They could remain silent and refuse to use what the American poet and feminist theorist Adrienne Rich called "the oppressor's language"; they could enter the language and claim it as, by rights at least, equally theirs; or they could create an alternative, woman-made language of their own. These were the positions with which the feminist debate over language began in the early 1970s.

As I have already mentioned, it was in France that this debate was waged with particular intensity. Nor is this surprising. For the context in which a given feminism develops and articulates itself necessarily determines the terms and the character of its struggle. In contrast to American feminism that grew, for the most part, out of the activist politics and social movements of the 1960s, French feminism largely developed within the professional context of the university and other institutions of high culture, a world in which mastery of language provided access to institutional power. In a very real (i.e., material) sense, language in this context *was* power. And since men were actuallly wielding the power, the equation "language = power = phallus" was not at all far-fetched. From this vantage point, language was regarded as quintessentially male, the symbolic embodiment of what Jacques Lacan defined as the law of the father or, in a word, Culture. For feminist intellectuals in this context, language presented an obvious dilemma: for the very mastery of language with which a woman was able to establish her credentials as a professional prohibited—or, at least, inhibited—her identification as a woman, as one who speaks in a woman's voice. As a result of this dilemma the importance of language both as a site of struggle and a means of intervention in that struggle was so foregrounded that French feminism often appeared to be virtually defined (if not confined) by this issue.

The insistence on the politics of language has, no doubt, been one of the most significant contributions of French feminism to contemporary feminist thought. However, other feminisms also reflected on this issue in equally important ways. The American women's movement identified language as a feminist issue from the outset. However, within the American context this issue was framed and approached very differently than it was in France. In line with the pragmatic, affirmative-action approach that characterized the main current of American feminism, particularly in the first decade from the early to late 1970s, language was seen as something to which women had equal rights and should thus have equal access. This "equal rights" approach that American feminists employed to demand legal and economic reforms[7] was applied as well to language. As battles were fought over terms like "chairman" or "mankind," the unequal treatment of women in language was combatted through consciousness raising as well as through administrative and legislative means.[8] The terms of the battle seemed self-evidently clear: it was "us" versus "them." The "us," of course, were women; the "them," equally obviously, were men.

The obviousness of this paradigm, however, was soon challenged from within the movement itself. For no sooner had women begun to analyze languages as a form and means of oppression than it became evident that the problem with language was not just a question of gender. As the power dynamics between and among women came under scrutiny and finally attack, it became apparent that language was a problem between women and among feminists as well. For in the relationships between different groups of women — white women and women of color, heterosexual and lesbian women, bourgeois and working class women, Gentile and Jewish women — there was also an "us" and a "them." The fact that language was a tool of patriarchy and thereby institutionally oppressive to women was only one side of the issue. Equally problematic, indeed much more disturbing in its implications for feminism, was the fact that women were themselves active participants in the construction and use of this language.

What became clear in this difficult and often painful process of dealing with the fact of difference *within* (within, among other things, what had initially been assumed to be a clear and simple "us") was that the language issue was neither clear nor simple. Affirmative action and consciousness raising were not only insufficient, but failed to address the fundamental problem of complicity inherent in the lack of clear boundaries between "us" and "them." Changing language meant that language itself, in its complex sociopsychological dynamics, had to be probed and understood. This recognition had a significant impact on the politics of language among American feminists. In the course of the 1980s a noticeable shift took place from the predominantly quantitative approach to language that had characterized the previous decade, an approach informed methodologically by the social sciences and politically by "equal rights" premises, to an intense involvement with what were initially identified as "French" feminist theories, in which issues of language and gender were explored on the basis of philosophical and psychoanalytic paradigms.[9]

In the course of this inquiry into language from both American and French perspectives, certain facts about language were established that have since formed the basis for feminist work in the field. Primary among these was the fact that, unlike other institutions with which we can choose to affiliate, language is a cultural institution to which our affiliation is not optional. Its shaping influence extends from our most conscious minds to the deepest levels of our unconscious psyches. Indeed, we are unthinkable without language: our very sense of self — our identity as individuals and as members of whatever communities with whom we choose, or are assigned, affiliation—is constructed and experienced through language.

Both in theory and in practice, then, a feminist politics of language was, from the beginning, predicated upon two axioms with different methodological and political implications. The first axiom, that language is part of the "system" (an apparatus that is separate from and imposed on us and that we can, therefore, always reject or cast off), conceived of language in the political terms of an oppression/liberation model. The second axiom, that language is not something separate, but rather part of who we essentially are, approached language on the basis of principles derived from fields that studied the formation of social and personal identity, such as anthropology and psychoanalysis.

In light of these axioms, which positioned women both within and outside the language structures of patriarchy, options like the ones that had initially been envisaged in the abstract—retreat into silence, integrate into the existing language, or invent a new one—proved to be both conceptually and tactically unsound. In relation to language, there were no obvious, certainly no simple, solutions. The strategies, almost inevitably, had to be contradictory.

The remainder of this essay will be a discussion of different feminist strategies in relation to language. For purposes of presentation, I have ordered the material into different sections, each of which focuses on one particular approach. Through this ordering, I hope to give a sense of the breadth and complexity of responses within contemporary feminism to what I have called the politics of language, while at the same time developing in some detail positions that I consider to be—or to have been—both important to and representative of feminist work in this area. Thus, with the caveat that they are not isolated, but rather contingent and overlapping, I will focus on three different positions feminists have taken in relation to language.

The first position is that women have an equal right to the power of language and should be treated as equals within it. Tactically, this means that whatever changes in the structure and use of language are necessary to ensure this equality must be identified and enforced. As exemplary of this position I will discuss the work of two feminist linguists, Dale Spender and Luise Pusch. The second position takes the antithetical view, namely that male domination is so deeply inscribed into the very structures of the existing language that women neither have a place there nor should they try to make one. Instead, they should take refuge either in the oppositional space of silence or the countersphere of a woman's language. The work of Mary Daly, Verena Stefan, and Hélène Cixous illustrates this position from three different perspectives. Using Luce Irigaray as a mediating term, I will move to the third position, which takes what I would call a deconstructive approach and transforms the polarity of the previous two into the dynamics of a dialectic. Standing at the nexus of poststructuralist and feminist theories, this is the position that from the early 1980s gained ascendence in the academy and now constitutes the conceptual starting point for most feminist analyses of texts. Positing that ultimately neither appropriation nor refusal are viable, or even desirable moves, the deconstructive position proposes disruption and play as maneuvers that most effectively and, in the end, most radically destabilize the hegemonic structures of the status quo. To illustrate this approach I will briefly mention Jane Gallop and then go on to discuss Monique Wittig in more detail.

Appropriations

By the time Dale Spender wrote *Man Made Language*, the groundwork for a feminist politics of language had been laid. Within the preceding five years, beginning with the virtual explosion of work in the field in 1975,[10] a number of linguistic and sociolinguistic studies in the United States and Great Britain, with a specific focus on gender, had set the stage and defined the basic parameters for an activist feminist approach to language. There was agreement on the premise that change was necessary. What was not clear was the relationship between social inequalities between women and men and gender disparities in language. Which came first? How were they connected? How could they be made to change? These are precisely the questions Spender takes up in *Man Made Language*. Building on the substantial body of work that had already been done ("That there is sexism in the English language is now well substantiated and generally accepted," 15), she sets out to draw conclusions and make a case of her own.

As is already evident from her title, Spender approaches the issue of language from a "we" (women)/"they" (men) position. Positing that the semantic derogation of women first constructs and then confirms their subordinate status, Spender decidedly rejects the idea of women's complicity in this process: it "is unlikely that women were instrumental in achieving this end" (24). However, she does believe that women should take an active and responsible role in changing this deplorable state of things, even though they did not cause it. The unfairness of this proposal, not to mention the contradictory nature of her own position (namely that women are not responsible, but then again they are) goes without comment.

As a firm believer in the possibility — and necessity — of change in the status and representation of women, whether it be in grammatical structures, personal relationships, or society at large, Spender envisions nothing short of a transformation of the patriarchal order by challenging, linguistically and socially, its basic concept that "women are negative because they are minus male" (32). Her goal is to change the established order whereby women are spoken for long before they can speak for themselves. Yet her goal is not that women become like men. Rather, she demands that they be free to realize themselves as women. Language, she posits, can and will play a crucial role in this process.

Strategies toward this end evolve from the gender polarity of her premises. Spender proposes what amounts to a three-step program. In the first place, women must speak up for themselves and not allow men to continue to dominate them. Secondly — and this is the political core of Spender's program for change — women must speak *as women*. The last step, finally, follows from the preceding one: language itself must be changed so that women and men can speak in a language that is true to their differences.

Spender argues that for women to simply speak, to merely occupy space in language, is inadequate. The critical move is becoming conscious of and giving voice to the historically gendered place from which they are speaking. This insistence on the importance of a gendered positionality in language is what characterizes Spender's position on the question of women, language, and change. For women to not only speak, but speak as women in their own language, she suggests, undermines the very premises of a "man-made" language. The potential effects could be revolutionary. For not only would such a move change who speaks and what is spoken of, language itself and discursive practices, public and private, would be transformed. In the end, therefore, Spender proposes a revolution in language. As she attempts to show in *Man Made Language*, it is only by breaking the rules of a language game in which women have historically been situated as the losers that they will ever be able "to establish their own autonomy as *women*" (216).

The West German linguist Luise Pusch has set herself the task of putting such a vision into practice. This task, and her work toward it, put an end to what had begun as a remarkably successful and promising university career: a full professor of linguistics in her early thirties, recipient of the prestigious Heisenberg award in 1979, Pusch had published over forty essays and two books when, in 1980, her essay "German as Men's Language: Diagnosis and Suggestions for Therapy" appeared in a special issue of the professional journal *Linguistische Berichte* [Linguistic Reports]. This publication and the ensuing controversy cost Pusch her job at the University of Konstanz. Undaunted, however, she has continued her work, both as a researcher and as an activist in behalf of a feminist transformation of culture.

Das Deutsche als Männersprache [German as Men's Language][11] is an anthology of Pusch's studies of language, in particular the German

language, from her perspective as a feminist and a linguist. In addition
to scholarly essays this anthology includes a selection of the work with
which she has been earning not only a living, but a reputation as one of
the most sharp-eyed and sharp-tongued commentators on the sexual
politics of culture: short, satiric glosses on gender bias and sexism in
language written for a popular audience.[12] Starting with the observation
that while her mother tongue is "comfortable and clear" when men use
it, it is "difficult, complicated and confusing" for women (7–8), Pusch
sets out to examine why this is so, how it happened, what the consequences are, and what can be done to change it.

Positing that, like sexual violence, language is an instrument of
male domination by which women are either disempowered or over-
powered, she, as did Spender, calls for nothing short of a linguistic
revolution. Women should not just enter language, but take it over
completely. Taking to its most radical extreme Spender's suggestion
that, if women are to establish their autonomy, the rules of the patriarchal
language game must be broken, Pusch advocates a systematic and
categorical overthrow of one of the cardinal rules of language, the rule
that establishes the normative status of the masculine gender. As a
countermove, Pusch proposes an equally systematic "feministization"
of language in which the feminine becomes normative and dominant
while the masculine is subordinated and muted. For languages like
German that, in contrast to English, are bound by the rules of grammatical gender, this solution is simple and practical: instead of forming
the feminine by adding an ending, she proposes having only one
form—the feminine—that encompasses both. The masculine, then,
would be formed by simply cutting off the superfluous ending.[13]

Fantasies of Flight

The American feminist theologian Mary Daly certainly agrees that the
rules should be broken.[14] Daly, however, takes a qualitative leap
beyond even such radical rule breakers as Pusch by rejecting the entire
system of patriarchal culture—institutions, customs, language—as so
fundamentally misogynist that it can never be made serviceable for
women. Addressing herself specifically to women who, like herself, are
attempting to bring their feminism to bear on their work as academics,
she raises the question of the political implications of conventional
scholarly practices, in particular those that engage language. Positing
that traditionally scholarship, far from being objective and neutral,
has, in fact, functioned as an instrument of oppression and even violence
in the service of patriarchy, she documents how the conventions of
scholarly discourse—its construction of authority as masculine and
its refusal to disclose whose interests it serves by speaking in a de-

personalized voice—have effected not only the textual, but actual, erasure of woman. Appropriation of such a deadly language is, therefore, in Daly's view, not a feminist option.

In her earlier works, *Beyond God the Father: Toward a Philosophy of Women's Liberation* (1973) and *The Church and the Second Sex: With a New Postchristian Introduction by the Author* (1975), Daly still grappled with the question of the relationship of women to the Christian tradition and their place within the institutions of Christian religions in the contemporary world. *Gyn/Ecology: The Metaethics of Radical Feminism* (1978)[15] marked her attempt to break, once and for all, with this tradition.

Positing that the power of patriarchy pervades everything from the institutions around us to the thoughts and feelings we carry within, she concludes that women must "spring into free space" and undertake the "discovery and creation of a world other than patriarchy" (2). The first step is a step out of language. For deception about reality "is embedded in the very texture of the words we use" (3).[16] The only way out, in her view, is to strip words and concepts of the meanings patriarchal culture has assigned them—that is, cut them loose to become free-floating signifiers. Like the rubble of a house that has been dismantled, those pieces that might be useful in the construction of new meanings can then be taken up, retooled, and attached to new signifieds.[17] What Daly proposes is a fundamental reconstruction of culture. In terms of language this means creating what Daly calls "gynocentric writing" through a wild and furious process of inventing, reshaping, and, when necessary, excising words. In short, Daly exhorts women to play with language in a game, the acknowledged stakes of which are nothing short of life and death.[18] Positing that once patriarchal language has been stripped of its authority and divested of its meaning, women will be free to "invent, dis-cover, re-member" (24) their own female meaning, Daly ends with a utopian vision of female wholeness and authenticity embedded in a language in which women speak for and as themselves: "we name our Truth ... we find our Original Be-ing ... we spin our Original Integrity" (423).

The problematic nature of this final vision—its essentialism, its imperialist appropriation of the experience of nonwhite, non-Western women under the rubric of a global sisterhood[19]—merely compounds a problem that is evident in Daly's analysis from the very outset: her own thinking is still deeply embedded in the same metaphysical paradigm she so emphatically rejects. The categorical opposition between the binary poles of Good and Evil has been recast in gender terms; the belief in the possibility of salvation through spiritual transcendence reappears in the form of a feminist utopia. Some are right, others wrong; some are worthy, others not. The principles and assumptions on which the dogmas of the very Christianity she rejects are ultimately founded, recur in a new, but no less dogmatic, form.

This was the very dilemma that the German writer Verena Stefan encountered when she set out to write about "life among women" from a woman's point of view.[20] Coming to writing as an activist in the initial, radically separatist phase of the West German women's movement in the early 1970s,[21] Stefan published *Shedding* in 1975. In this slim, pocket-sized paperback, which the subtitle characterizes generically as *Autobiographical Sketches Poems Dreams Analyses*, Stefan portrays the "everyday treatment of a woman colonized in a city of the first world." She takes herself as her own exemplary persona. Response to its publication documents the degree to which this persona was indeed seen as exemplary: despite the fact that there was almost no publicity, the first edition was sold out immediately; within a year, *Shedding* had sold over 80,000 copies, made a completely unknown author a celebrity and established "women's literature" as a promising new field in the German publishing market.

The irony of this success was that it is precisely this notion of a "women's literature" that *Shedding* explicitly problematizes. Writing as a woman, Stefan finds, is virtually impossible, because from the moment she attempts to write from the perspective of a woman, language fails her: "I kept bumping into the language at hand, word upon word, concept upon concept" (Foreword). Trying first to juxtapose two versions of a heterosexual encounter (the man's in one column, the woman's in another) she concludes that the two experiences are so fundamentally incompatible that they cannot be put together. Thus, she decides to put men and their ways behind her in search of new ways that are more true to herself. The break is radical: "I lead a different life, speak a different language" (54).

Positing that language and experience are inextricably bound up with one another, she realizes that for a woman to write authentically about her "self," particularly her sexuality—to even experience her "self" authentically, in an unalienated way—she must have a language with which to do so. And since language, as Spender was to put it, is "man-made," "brutal and misogynist," as Stefan sees it, in relation to women and their bodies, she must start at point zero. She must start by finding basic words for basic things, such as the sexual parts of her body. Instead of the pejorative terms in which women's bodies and female sexual experience are commonly described, she searches for a different language.

But how would a woman's language be different? This is the question *Shedding* sets out to answer. Stefan's premise is that what men's language has degraded, women's language would dignify. Rejecting both popular slang words ("cunt") and clinical terms ("vulva") as equally foreign to what she feels, she reaches for metaphors. What she comes up with is a language of plants and flowers. Yet the solution merely highlights the problem. For this language, too, has already been occupied. Stefan acknowledges her problem from the outset: "woman as nature seems such a hackneyed cliché — overused and abused by men. Nature itself seems to have become a cliché; patriarchy has destroyed it" (Foreword). Nevertheless, for lack of another option, Stefan uses this "hackneyed" language and, in so doing, recasts woman in much the same terms in which patriarchal culture has already cast her. With her hair like moss, her breasts like gourds, and her vulva like snapdragons, she, once again, em-bodies nature. The female difference that Stefan sought to affirm in terms of autonomy and separation thus circles back — in the image of woman as nature — to rejoin one of the oldest stereotypes of female difference constructed within patriarchal culture.

Within French feminism this dilemma was identified from the outset as the place where feminist theory and practice had to start and to which it inevitably had to return. Intellectually and politically shaped by the debates around questions of language, sexuality, and power that raged in French intellectual circles through the 1960s and 1970s (which continue to this day),[22] and drawing on work in areas as diverse as linguistics, structural anthropology, psychoanalysis, and philosophy, French feminists held that the issue of sexuality could not be separated from the issue of textuality. Moreover both, they insisted, had to be seen in terms of gender. "Let the priests tremble," warned Hélène Cixous, "we're going to show them our sexts!"[23]

One of the first texts to lay out the parameters of such an analysis was *The Newly Born Woman* (1975), coauthored by Hélène Cixous and Catherine Clément.[24] Cixous's essay, "The Laugh of the Medusa," which appeared that same year and is a variation on the themes explored in the book, was immediately recognized as a landmark text in the field of feminist theory.[25] Cixous begins, manifesto-like, with the declaration that the "future must no longer be determined by the past" ("Medusa," 245). Against a history of oppression and repression which has rendered women silent, she calls upon women to revolt and to stage this revolt in writing: "Woman must write her self: must write about women and bring women to writing ... Woman must put herself into the text — as into the world and into history — by her own movement" ("Medusa," 245). Yet even as she calls for a "writing that inscribes femininity," she recognizes that a woman's language does not yet exist: "At the present time, *defining* a feminine practice of writing is impossible *with an impossibility that will continue*" (*Woman*, 92; second emphasis mine).

Nevertheless, Cixous writes not against, but *into*, this impossibility. For it is in process, she maintains, in the act of *using* language that "*the very possibility of change*" ("Medusa," 249) is created: "It is in writing, from woman and toward women, and in accepting the challenge of the discourse controlled by the phallus, that woman will affirm woman somewhere other than in silence" (*Woman*, 93). Unlike Stefan, therefore, Cixous does not set out to discover or invent a different language for woman. Her call for change is at once less ambitious and considerably more radical. She calls for a complete destruction of the codes and conventions that have heretofore governed language and subjected those who used it to its terms. Concurring, at least in this respect, with the Lacanian premise that in a language that represents the symbolic field of the Law of the Father there is no space for women except as absence or lack, she uses this same psychoanalytic paradigm to suggest a solution. Invoking and, in the process, conflating two different paradigms of repression—one in psychoanalytic terms, the other in terms of a liberation movement: "we the repressed of culture ... we are black and we are beautiful" ("Medusa," 248), Cixous maps out the imaginary scenario of a women's revolution: "When the 'repressed' of their culture and their society returns, it's an explosive, *utterly* destructive, staggering return, with a force never yet unleashed and equal to the most forbidding of suppressions" ("Medusa," 256). Ultimately, Cixous imagines, the master's house—the culture of patriarchy and its languages—will not be dismantled, bit by bit, but exploded by the volcanic force of woman's irrepressible desire to write her "self" as a subject into history.

What this history, this subject "woman," or this new language will look like, neither she nor anyone else can yet know. All we can do, suggests Cixous, is begin to move in that direction: "For us [women] the point is not to take possession in order to internalize or manipulate, but rather to dash through and 'fly'" ("Medusa," 258).[26] As we break away from the old and open ourselves up to the anticipation of the as yet unforeseeable, space is cleared "that can serve as a springboard." And in this free space—this "beginning of a new history"—"the precursory movement of a transformation of social and cultural structures" can at least begin ("Medusa," 252, 249).

Luce Irigaray begins, as did Cixous, with the premise that within the logic of conventional discursive structures, "there is no possible place for the 'feminine,' except the traditional place of the repressed, the censured."[27] In *Speculum of the Other Woman* (1974)[28] she presented massive evidence to this effect, documenting how within the Western tradition, knowledge, whether philosophically or psychoanalytically defined, has been cast in terms that exclude the possibility of authentic knowledge about women. This book, with its systematic and global attack on such hallowed concepts as Truth and Logic, provoked such controversy, particularly among Lacanians, who were stung by her sharp critique of their treatment of female sexuality, that Irigaray was expelled from her teaching position at Vincennes, where she had been a colleague of Cixous's and Clément's.[29] In a number of essays, collected in 1977 under the title of one of the most provocative and influential essays, *This Sex Which Is Not One*,[30] Irigaray takes up and pursues the central questions raised by the premises of *Speculum*: If there is no place for the feminine in traditional discursive and epistemological structures, where is it? And, even more basically, *what* is this "feminine" we are looking for?

Clearly, according to Irigaray, the feminine is not what male images and fantasies have thought it to be; it is not to be found on "the screen of their projections." There, woman has either had no "self," or she has had a "multitude of 'selves' appropriated by them [men], for them, according to their needs or desires" (*Sex*, 17). In particular, Irigaray targets philosophy as a central repository of such representations of women fashioned by men "according to their needs." In "The Power of Discourse and the Subordination of the Feminine," written the same year as Cixous's "The Laugh of the Medusa," she spells out her reason for doing so: "inasmuch as this discourse sets forth the law on all others, inasmuch as it constitutes the discourse on discourse ... it is indeed precisely philosophical discourse that we have to challenge" (*Sex*, 74). Yet in contrast to the solution proposed by Daly, Irigaray insists that it "is not a matter of toppling that order so as to replace it — that amounts to the same thing in the end — but of disrupting and modifying it. In other words, the issue is not one of elaborating a new theory of which woman would be the *subject* or the *object*, but of jamming the theoretical machinery itself, of suspending its pretension to the production of a truth and of a meaning that are excessively univocal" (*Sex*, 68, 78).

Toward this end, Irigaray elaborates a multistage strategy. The first step is exposing the coherence and systematicity of philosophical discourse as a trick with mirrors, the effect of an endlessly self-referential, specular economy in which the subject, the logos, is able to continuously reflect itself by itself. As a means of intervention, Irigaray proposes applying principles derived from the practice of psychoanalysis to philosophical critique in a process of what she calls "interpretive rereading," i.e., probing the text for its unconscious — "its procedures of repression ... its imaginary configurations ... and also, of course, what it does not articulate at the level of utterance: *its silences*" (*Sex*, 75).

The second, interim, stage is what she describes as "mimicry," in which a woman deliberately takes on the prescribed guise of femininity, thereby exposing this role as precisely that, a role to which she has been assigned, and at the same time, showing that she is not identical with this role, because her real self *"remain[s] elsewhere."* Where it remains, where the real feminine is, is a question to which Irigaray has no more definitive an answer than does Cixous. However, she has clear ideas about where and how to start looking. Instead of seeing themselves as images constructed within a phallomorphic paradigm, women must find a language with which to "speak themselves," a language based on their own sexual "imaginary."[31] Positing a basic homology between cultural systems of representation and libidinal systems of desire, Irigaray insists that woman's language would not be the same as man's because her desire is also fundamentally different. The masculine sexual economy, she argues, is linear and teleological and perceives difference in hierarchical terms; the female sexual economy is polymorphous, open-ended and plural with difference and sameness coexisting side by side. In the end her argument rests on biological bedrock, on the fact that because woman's "genitals are formed of two lips in continuous contact . . . [she is], within herself, . . . already two—but not divisible into one(s)" (*Sex*, 24). Woman's language, or what Irigaray refers to as "parler-femme" [speaking (as) woman], would, so she speculates, be based on this same principle.

Deconstructions

In the last chapter of *The Daughter's Seduction: Feminism and Psychoanalysis* (1982) the American feminist theorist Jane Gallop takes up the issue of a feminist cultural counterpractice raised by Cixous and Clément in *The Newly Born Woman*.[32] There, Clément had argued that effective resistance and genuine selfhood are only possible in the realm of what Lacan calls the Symbolic—the realm in which subjectivity, constructed in and through language, simultaneously becomes conscious and socially inscribed.[33] Countering that the symbolic order as we know it is so fundamentally patriarchal that it does not allow women to become subjects, much less agents of change, Cixous argued that female subjectivity can only exist by either taking refuge in those spaces outside the Symbolic that Lacan calls the Imaginary[34] or by traversing the symbolic order and producing a new, unregulated space of dis-order.

This polarization between Cixous and Clément is a false one, says Gallop. To choose between these two positions would merely leave us with a nonsolution to an already false dilemma. Instead, she argues, we need to engage both positions in dialogue, a process that Cixous and Clément themselves model in the third and final section of *The Newly Born Woman*.[35] What emerges through dialogue, then, is an open space in which opposing positions are recognized as equally valid and necessary. As Gallop puts it in the discussion of Cixous and

Clément with which she concludes *The Daughter's Seduction*, by refusing
to choose between them we not only reject "traditional notions of
opposition," but, more importantly, we practice a new mode of thinking
in which the pleasure of difference replaces the traditional, illusory
comfort of unity-as-sameness. What we need, maintains Gallop, is a
thinking in which "both the imaginary and the symbolic, both theory
and flesh" (150) are affirmed in an approach that acknowledges desire
in language as well as in the body.[36]

This conclusion to *The Daughter's Seduction* is where her next
book begins. In *Thinking Through the Body* (1988)[37] Gallop takes up
centrally the question of the relationship between culture (the realm of
language, writing, textuality) and the body, in particular the female
body (the realm of desire and sexuality). Like Cixous and Clément,
with whose work she had ended her previous book, or like Adrienne
Rich and Roland Barthes with whom she engages in dialogue here,
Gallop posits the need for a living connection between these two
realms. The violent sundering of this connection in patriarchal civilization, a state commonly referred to as the "mind-body split," is what
she challenges and sets out to mend. The idea, indeed ideal, of the
intellectual as a disembodied mind, she argues, is not only undesirable,
but ultimately untenable, because thinking is always mediated through
the subjective agency of concrete persons. Thinking, in other words, is
always embedded in the materiality of life. This means that it is both
historical and embodied. On the basis of this premise, Gallop explores
the potential of embodied thinking, or as she puts it, "thinking through
the body," through simultaneously careful and irreverent readings of
texts in which the complex relationships between concepts and signifieds,
signs and referents, are analysed and contextualized.

Cixous and Clément end *The Newly Born Woman by* foregrounding
the question of feminist political practice: what means of intervention
are possible and what forms of counterhegemonic practice feminism
might evolve. Clément takes issue with Cixous's concept that women
must take or steal what they need from the culture and then take off,
steal away. Such stealing, in either sense of the word, whether taking
what does not belong to us or taking something away, is not really
possible, she points out: "we [women] don't steal anything at all — we
are within the same cultural system [as men]" (137).

The idea that there is nowhere to steal to because we are all
"within the same ... system," is a premise held in common by most
critical theories developed in the poststructuralist context. Nowhere,
however, has this assumption and its consequences been developed
more consistently than in the field of deconstruction. According to the
model of deconstruction as elaborated by Derrida and his followers,
meaning is inherently unstable and plural because it is always contingent

and thus "constantly deferred in the never-ending webs of textuality in which all texts are located."[38] As a result, the boundaries between inside and outside, self and other, no longer hold. "Flight," in the sense of escape to another, culturally separate, realm is consequently not possible. Meaning is neither singular nor given, but rather exists as a plurality of possible meanings circulating between text, ideology and reader.[39] The task of the critic, therefore, is not to *give* meaning, but to *intervene* in the circulation of meanings that are already given. In the process, particular meanings are released toward particular ends. This act of intervention or disruption, even if not by intent political, is decidedly so in practice. The more various critical theories probed the ideological and psychoanalytic dimensions of our/their interpretive acts, the more it became evident that there was no such thing as a neutral or disinterested reading.

This concept of disruption on the level of meaning as a political act, the belief in and practice of a politics that was avowedly textual, characterized the brief period of cultural revolution in Western Europe that came to be known as May 1968. It was in this context that, particularly in France, both deconstruction as an academic practice and women's liberation as a political movement took shape.[40] In the conjunction of these movements the political and intellectual foundation of texts like Cixous and Clement's *The Newly Born Woman* was laid. And it was in this context of radical inquiry into the relationship between politics and culture — an inquiry based on the recognition that culture was not only inherently political, but that, conversely, the most insistent articulations of politics were cultural — that a young writer, intellectual and activist, Monique Wittig,[41] wrote a text, at once experimental fiction, philosophical inquiry, and political treatise, that still stands as one of the most passionate and probing investigations of this relationship from a feminist perspective: *Les Guérillères*.

Central among the questions Wittig investigates in this text is one that in the context of May 1968 as well as in subsequent literary theories has all too often been reduced to a mere slogan, namely the question of revolution on the level of the text. In *Les Guérillères*, revolution is also metaphorized as writing. Yet, as a banner-like sequence of slogans covering an entire page of the text proclaims, this is a writing that is radically different, a writing dedicated to the destruction of its own former identity: "AGAINST TEXTS/AGAINST MEANING/WHICH IS TO WRITE VIOLENCE/OUTSIDE THE TEXT/IN ANOTHER WRITING."[42]

Already the title, *Les Guérillères*, a neologism that simultaneously evokes both the image of warrior and guerilla fighter and then transfers this composite into a newly invented female form,[43] signals the fact that this text is about a war on, and within, language. Moreover, it tells us that this war is being fought from a female perspective. Yet this is not a war in which men are the main enemy.[44] It is a struggle of women's liberation from bondage within the confines of a system that denies people—women and many men as well—consciousness of their role as shapers of history. Thus, it is a war waged by a "species that seeks a new language" (131).

Initially, it is women who band together and form an army (the "guérillères") so that they can destroy that which will otherwise destroy them: the system of symbols and codes by which the world is ordered and by which they are defined: "The women say, the language you speak poisons your glottis tongue palate lips. They say, the language you speak is made up of words that are killing you. They say, the language you speak is made up of signs that rightly speaking designate what men have appropriated" (144).

However, unlike Mary Daly, Wittig does not define this murderous language as men's language, and unlike Verena Stefan, she does not suggest that women seek a language of their own. In fact, *Les Guérillères* deliberately works against such notions through the structure of its narrative. The narrative begins in an idyllic, pastoral world of only women at one with themselves in a state of nature; time is suspended in a seemingly perpetual present. This is a female utopia in which Cixous's concept of "writing the body" seems to have been realized: there is no mind-body split, no alienation, no oppression. Cixous wrote: "Woman must write her self: must write about women and bring women to writing, from which they have been driven away as violently as from their bodies—for the same reasons, by the same law, with the same fatal goal." ("Medusa," 245)

Yet there is also no history: "there is no future, there is no past" (50). This utopia is undesirable; even if it were desirable, it would be untenable. The women are prisoners in a closed and static paradise in which what has always been done is repeated, and what has always been known in rewritten. Thus, Wittig insists from the very beginning that alienation from language and culture in terms of the oppressor/oppressed model used by feminist theorists like Rowbotham or Spender is not the only form of oppression. Equally oppressive, if not worse, is the condition of being so completely and contentedly embedded in an established cultural system that critical reflection, much less resistance, has become impossible. The liberation movement of the guérillères thus begins with their recognition that they have become "prisoners of the mirror" and must break out.

Elsewhere, in an essay whose title ("One is Not Born a Woman")[45] evokes and pays tribute to Simone de Beauvoir, Wittig warned against the consequences of forgetting that gender is not "natural" but social, constructed in and through language. To accept language as given or

natural is, as Wittig argues, the first and decisive step into one's own
voluntary emprisonment in the categories ("woman," for example, or
"man") by which we are defined and to which an oppressive culture
confines us. Taking a radically materialist position ("there is no nature
in society"),[46] she maintains that we are not who we *are*, but rather
who we *become* in the process of acting.

Repeatedly invoking throughout *Les Guérillères* Mao's concept of
revolution as a permanent and perpetual state of cultural transformation
("Let a hundred flowers blossom, a hundred schools compete," 76),[47]
Wittig challenges and attempts to overthrow[48] fixed notions of everything
from who "woman" or what "utopia" is to what "revolution" might
mean. Even the hallowed feminist notion of man as the enemy is
challenged in this text. As the narrative moves us from a female utopia
to the scene of historical struggle in which women and men grapple
together — sometimes in conflict, sometimes as allies — against a reifying
system which makes us all into objects and denies us historical agency,
Wittig suggests that it is this system, not each other, that we must fight.
Utopia, therefore, is not the niche within which we fit ourselves *into*
the system, but rather the refusal to be thus confined. Empowerment is
to claim one's place in history, not to attempt to step out of it; it is the
ability to shape reality in accordance with one's needs and desires.
Such empowerment, according to Wittig, means having a language in
which we are not already inscribed and defined in terms set by others,
but are free to express ourselves as we see ourselves and as we are in
the process of changing: "They say, we must disregard the statements
we have been compelled to deliver contrary to our opinion and in
conformity with the codes and conventions of the cultures that have
"domesticated us . . . They say that in the first place the vocabulary of
every language is to be examined, turned upside down, that every
word must be screened" (134).

Other Voices

This agenda of the guérillères sums up a radical feminist position on
the politics of language. Embedded within it is the programmatic
premise on which feminist work on language was initially founded,
which was that since language has functioned as a means of women's
oppression ("the codes and conventions that have domesticated us"),
their basic attitude toward it should be relentlessly critical ("every
word must be screened"). At the same time, another assumption,
equally basic to feminist cultural activism, is operative in the statement
of the guérillères. For implicit in their call for a vigilant screening of
language, a rejection of all forms of language by which a hegemonic,

patriarchal culture effects domination over those it has designated Other, is the suggestion that another language, a different and better one, be developed in its stead. Consistent with her historical materialist stance, Wittig stops short of proposing what such a language actually might or should be. At the end of the narrative, *Les Guérillères* leaves us at the historical threshold of this task.

"The war is over," one of the guérillères proclaims in the final passage. Weary of battle, the women and men stand and sing the Internationale together. When they are finished, they remain standing "in a kind of embarrassed silence" (144). This silence with which the struggle of the guérillères comes to a temporary end symbolically summarizes yet another position most feminist work on language holds in common: namely, that while there is agreement on the fact that change is needed, there is no shared vision of what the nature of this change might be. As the guérillères put it, "they are starting from zero. They say that a new world is beginning" (85).

The problem, of course, is precisely that they/we are not starting from zero, but are rather engaged in the much more painstaking task of dismantling the house of the master's language at the same time that new structures are being created. The problem, in other words, is that the materials we use in the work of cultural (re)construction—words, concepts, narrative structures—are rarely in themselves new, but come laden with the historical baggage of their previous and currently operative existence.

In the process, the question of authority—who authorizes this new construction, whose work is it and for whom?—again raises an issue that has been central to feminist work on language from the outset: the question of voice, and even more particularly, of authorial voice. Indeed, the contention with which I began this essay, that there is no feminism as such, only feminisms, has often been framed as a problematic of the pronoun: Who is this "we" we are speaking as and whom are "we" speaking for? Wittig ends *Les Guérillères* with an image of unity and sisterhood-in-struggle: "Moved by a common impulse, we all stood to seek gropingly the even flow, the exultant unity of the Internationale" (144). Yet, in light of the vast differences among women, this image, the evocation of a "common impulse" and "exultant unity," is more on the order of a utopian projection than a description of historical feminist reality. Thus, the injunction to examine language with relentless care and precision, to "screen every word," as the guérillères exhort us, might well begin with the simple word "we." As the Black American poet, Lorraine Bethel, put it provocatively in the title of a poem "dedicated to the proposition that all women are not equal, i.e., identical/ly oppressed": "WHAT CHOU MEAN *WE*, WHITE GIRL?"[49]

As discussions within feminist circles shifted from a focus on commonality and sameness *as* women (or what had been referred to as "sisterhood") to a focus on differences *between* women, sisterhood was seen less as a given, an automatic bond based on the simple fact of sex and gender, and more as a matter of commitment. From this perspective, sisterhood meant not just *being* women together, but, more importantly, *working* together to actualize "strategic coalitions across class, race, and national boundaries."[50] Again, the politics of language were at issue. Yet now the issue was not what "their" (i.e., men's) language was doing to "us," but rather how "we," as women whose relationships to one another were marked by the complex history of differences that had divided and sown enmity and distrust among us, were dealing with the issue of language and/as power among ourselves.

This, then, is the junction at which feminist discussions of language currently stand: an acutely self-conscious and self-critical awareness of our use of language, especially when we claim to speak as feminists. As the feminist writer and filmmaker Trinh T. Minh-ha notes, "Wo− appended to man in sexist contexts is not unlike Third World, Third, Minority, or Color affixed to woman in pseudo-feminist contexts. Yearning for universality, the generic woman, like its counterpart, the generic man, tends to efface difference within itself."[51] Increasingly at issue in much feminist writing since around the mid-1980s is the question of how "we," in the name of feminism, have constructed an identity of self—of woman—defined not only in terms of gender, but also in terms of class and race and global power hegemonies. As some of the most challenging work in the field of recent feminist critical theory has compellingly shown, Gayatri Chakravorty Spivak's contention that "Western intellectual production is, in many ways, complicit with Western international economic interests," applies to the production of feminist theory and critical practice as well.[52] In "Under Western Eyes: Feminist Scholarship and Colonial Discourses," Chandra Talpade Mohanty makes this point explicit by documenting historically how "feminist writings . . . discursively colonize the material and historical heterogeneities of the lives of women in the third world."[53] What is at issue, then, for feminism "is the place/s of postcolonial woman as writing and written subject." What is called into question is nothing less than the status of Western culture as a whole: "What is at stake is not only the hegemony of Western cultures, but also their identities as unified cultures: in other words, the realization that there is a Third World in every First world, and vice-versa."[54]

What does this mean in practice? It means, in the first place, that we recognize the fact that we are not only users, but authors of language—that is, that we are coresponsible for what is done to and with language, and must answer for the consequences. This means that we acknowledge our own positionality within language, where it benefits and protects us (e.g., as whites or heterosexuals) and where it oppresses and threatens us (e.g., as people of color or of the working class). Above all, a feminist politics of language means resisting the use of language as a means of appropriating the right of others to speak for themselves, in their own voices.[55] As Trinh T. Minh-ha puts it, this means shifting from the authoritative stance of a universalizing monologue ("speaking for and about") to the interactive space created by dialogue ("speaking near by or together").[56]

It means, furthermore, that we be conscious not only *for* whom but also *as* whom and in whose name and interests we are speaking. As Christine Delphy documents in a provocative essay entitled "Patriarchy, Feminism and Their Intellectuals," this is a particularly vexed issue for academic feminists. For they can either use the learned discourse in which academic knowledge is conventionally produced and legitimated, or they can speak a common tongue that deliberately seeks to include nonacademic feminists. In the first case, they end up allying themselves, through a kind of discursive complicity, with the very institution they as feminists criticize; in the second case, their critique loses credibility with the people to whom it most directly addresses itself (fellow academicians) because the language in which it is cast can be dismissed as unprofessional. Delphy has no ready solution to this dilemma. However, she warns feminist intellectuals not to buy into the legitimating myth of academic discourse as "Pure, Neutral, Universal." "This passionless approach," she cautions, "is a devil's trap."[57] Instead, she insists, our language must reflect the fact that far from being disinterested analysts, we are involved participants: the "only guarantee that we will not, as intellectuals, be traitors to our class, is our awareness of being, ourselves, women, of being among those whose oppression we analyse."

Consequences

In theoretical terms, feminism presents itself as a radical critique of language, which it sees, on the one hand, as an emblem and tool of power and, on the other hand, as a means of social and self-transformation. What does this mean in practical terms? On the whole, I would say, at least in regard to societies such as ours (i.e., the 1990s in America) in which feminism has secured a place in the domain of public discourse, feminist insistence on the importance of language as a political reality has had a measurable, even if not yet revolutionary, impact on the general consciousness about and use of language.

Obviously, the power of cultural conservatives like E. D. Hirsch, who staunchly refuse to acknowledge the changes that have taken place in the last decade in response to feminist cultural activism, should not be underestimated.[58] Nevertheless, the commitment to eliminating sexism in language, even if not in as remotely radical a program as that envisioned by Wittig's guérillères, has made its effect felt in places as diverse as children's literature, newspaper editorials, job descriptions, and the teaching of college ("freshperson") composition. As early as the mid-1970s professional organizations, as well as private and public institutions from the local to the national level, were responding to feminists' call to review the degree to which the language they used exhibited and perpetuated sexist biases.[59] These developments in the field of women and language were recorded and disseminated in the form of a newsletter (*Women and Language News*) started in 1976 by Cheris Kramarae and Paula Treichler at the University of Illinois; by 1984 this newsletter had become a regular scholarly journal, *Women and Language*.

By now many of the changes proposed and discussed within the past two decades have become standard practice. Even though some authorities on writing and language, like *The Chicago Manual of Style*, in its 13th edition (1982) still dismiss the politics of language rather cavalierly,[60] others, like the *MLA Handbook for Writers of Research Papers* (3d edition, 1988) treat it with respect and seriousness. Having posited, in the section entitled "Language and Style," that "the key to successful communication is using the right language," the authors of the *MLA Handbook* go on to substantially expand the traditional notion of linguistic rightness and wrongness by including as criteria not just questions of grammar and semantics, but also of "social connotations." Their position, as a result, is strong and unequivocal: "Your language ... should not suggest bias or prejudice toward any group."[61]

Not surprisingly, the most serious treatment of the issue of women and language is to be found in the work of feminist scholars. *The Handbook of Nonsexist Writing*, originally compiled by Casey Miller and Kate Swift in 1980, is now in its updated second edition.[62] Moreover, with the publication of *Language, Gender, and Professional Writing: Theoretical Approaches and Guidelines for Nonsexist Usage*, edited by Francine Wattman Frank and Paula A. Treichler (Modern Language Association, 1989), a text now exists that will undoubtedly stand as the standard reference work in the field for some time to come. By combining essays discussing the theoretical issues as well as the historical developments in the field of women and language with practical "guidelines for nonsexist usage," and concluding with a comprehensive bibliographical apparatus, the editors have provided a useful text for anyone for whom the gender politics of language still poses questions calling for answers.

Obviously, feminist research and activism in the field of language have focused consistently on what in the parlance of the nineteenth century has often been referred to as the "woman question": the question of who "woman" is, how a biological person becomes socially en-gendered, what the consequences are, and what to do about this state of things. For feminism, regardless of its different emphases at different times and in different contexts, is always about two things: women and sexism. On the basis of the premise that the concept of "woman" and the codes and conventions of the cultures we call "patriarchal" are social, not biological, in origin, feminists have insistently focused attention on the need for the cultural change that the woman question raises. Long before Lacan or Derrida, feminists had established the connection between patriarchy and culture, pointing out that the subordination of women is inscribed as much in "our" literature as in "our" laws.[63] The feminist agenda, therefore, is necessarily "committed to a politics of transliteration," as the poet Olga Broumas puts it. If, as a deconstructionist might say, woman has always already been written (or if, as Gertrude Stein put it, somewhat more cryptically, "patriarchal poetry is the same"), then the steps to be taken follow logically and implacably. First, she must refuse to be written[64] in the terms that have already been set. "Let her try," writes Stein, "Let her try./Just let her try./Let her try./Never to be what he said./Never to be what he said./Never to be what he said."[65] Then new ways of thinking, of constructing reality in language, must be found: "Like amnesiacs/in a ward on fire, we must/find words/or burn."[66]

It is here that the radical potential of feminist analyses of language becomes most evident. As feminist inquiries into the politics of language soon revealed, it was not just a few words and some concepts — "chairman" or "girl" — that needed changing. The entire language and the ideological assumptions informing its structure and use, not only in relation to gender, but also in relation to class, race, age, sexual orientation, national, ethnic, and religious affiliations, needed to be fundamentally reexamined: "the vocabulary of every language is to be examined, modified, turned upside down."[67] As is richly documented by the work of feminist writers like Monique Wittig or Trinh T. Minh-ha, or feminist scholars like Chandra Mohanty, Mary Poovey, or Elizabeth Fox-Genovese, who, from a perspective at once materialist and historical, analyse how constructs like gender, race, class, and national identity are ideologically constructed in and through language, this process is well underway.[68] It goes without saying that much more remains to be done. For, as the entry on "Language" in *A Feminist Dictionary* reminds us, language is "a symbol system which is a basic problem and a brilliant possibility."

Notes

1. Found in Cheris Kramarae and Paula Treichler, *A Feminist Dictionary* (London: Pandora, 1985), p. vii.

2. Olga Broumas, "Artemis," in *Beginning With O* (New Haven: Yale Univ., 1977), pp. 23–24.

3. I am indebted for this term to Bell Hooks, who discussed its centrality to a feminist theory informed by a consciousness of race and of class in a lecture at Emory University in 1988. For an elaboration of the political, personal, and theoretical meanings of this term from the perspective of a black American feminist academic and cultural activist, see Hooks, *Talking Back: Thinking Feminist, Thinking Black* (Boston: South End, 1989).

4. Sheila Rowbotham, *Woman's Consciousness, Man's World* (Harmondsworth, England: Penguin, 1973), p. 33.

5. Dale Spender, *Man Made Language* (London: Routledge & Kegan Paul, 1980), pp. 14, 12.

6. Simone de Beauvoir, *The Second Sex*, trans. H. M. Parshley (New York: Vintage, 1974), p. xv.

7. For an excellent comparative analysis of the differences in approach between American and European women's movements, see Mary Fainsod Katzenstein and Carol McClug Mueller, eds., *The Women's Movement of the United States and Western Europe* (Philadelphia: Temple Univ., 1987).

8. Early studies, such as Robin Lakoff's *Language and Woman's Place* (New York: Harper and Row, 1975), conducted, for the most part, by social scientists, reflect the predominance of this approach. In France, by contrast, the discursive and conceptual parameters of the work on language were from the outset set by the fact that the participants in the debate were mostly in the so-called "human sciences" (*sciences humaines*), i.e., trained in philosophy and literature.

9. Historical markers of this shift were the publication, in 1980, of two key texts: *New French Feminisms: An Anthology*, ed. Elaine Marks and Isabelle de Courtivron (Amherst: Univ. of Massachusetts), provided American feminists with a broad and thorough introduction to the "new" French feminist theories; *The Future of Difference*, eds. Hester Eisenstein and Alice Jardine (Boston: G. K. Hall), not only foregrounded "difference" as a focus within feminism, but opened up the exploration of its consequences. A year later, *Signs*, which had by then established itself as the leading journal of feminist theory and scholarship, devoted a special issue [*Signs*, 7 (Fall 1981)] to "French Feminist Theory"; in 1982 *Diacritics* followed with its special issue, "Cherchez la Femme: Feminist Critique/Feminine Text" [12:2 (Summer 1982)], while Jane Gallop's *The Daughter's Seduction: Feminism and Psychoanalysis* (Ithaca: Cornell Univ., 1982) brought Lacan and French Lacanian feminists into the orbit of American feminist theorists and critics.

10. The year 1975 saw the publication of Robin Lakoff, *Language and Woman's Place* (New York: Harper and Row), Mary Ritchie Key, *Male/Female Language* (Metuchen, N.J.: Scarecrow), Barrie Thorne and Nancy

Henley, eds. *Language and Sex: Difference and Dominance* (Rowley, Mass.: Newbury House), and Shirley Ardener, ed. *Perceiving Women* (London: Malaby). The following year Cora Kaplan's theoretical analyses of "Language and Gender" appeared in *Papers on Patriarchy* (London: Women's Publishing Collective); Casey Miller and Kate Swift mapped out some of the practical consequences of these analyses in *Words and Women: New Language in New Times* (New York: Anchor Books/Doubleday). In 1977 Alleen Pace Nilsen, whose Ph.D. thesis on "Grammatical gender and its relationship to the unequal treatment of males and females in children's books" (Univ. of Iowa, 1973) was one of the earliest scholarly studies of the relationship between the structures of language and the construction of gender and its social consequences, coedited (along with Julia Stanley, Haif Mosmajian and H. Lee Gershuny) *Sexism and Language* (Urbana, IL: NCTE).

11. Luise Pusch, *Das Deutsche als Männersprache: Aufsätze und Glossen zur feministischen Linguistik* (Frankfurt am Main: Suhrkamp, 1984). See also Pusch, *Feminismus — Inspektion der Herrenkultur: Ein Handbuch* [Feminism — Inspection of Patriarchal Culture: A Handbook (Frankfurt am Main: Suhrkamp, 1983)] and, since 1988, her annual pocket calendars, "Berühmte Frauen" ["Famous Women"], also published by Suhrkamp.

12. Most of these glosses were published, through a good part of the 1980s, in the West German feminist journal *Courage*. Three glosses and an essay ("Total Feminisation: Thoughts on the Feminine as a Comprehensive Gender") ["Totale Feminisierung: Überlegungen zum umfassenden Femininum"] can be found in the fourth edition of the *Women in German Yearbook: Feminist Studies and German Culture*, ed. Marianne Burkhard and Jeanette Clausen (Lanham, MD: Univ. Press of America, 1988).

13. Most German nouns, for example, are cast in the feminine form by adding the ending −in (−innen in the plural) similar to the archaic English −ess suffix, as in poetess. Containing as it does both masculine ("Dichter") and feminine ("Dichterin"), Pusch quite logically points out, "Dichterin" is the most encompassing form and thus should stand as the universal.

14. Daly holds doctorates in both theology and philosophy from the University of Fribourg, Switzerland, and teaches theology at Boston College.

15. Mary Daly, *Gyn/Ecology: The Metaethics of Radical Feminism* (Boston: Beacon, 1978).

16. One of the examples Daly gives is the word "spinster": for while "it is commonly used as a deprecating term," its real meaning, according to Daly, is a woman "who defines her Self, by choice, neither in relation to children nor to men, who is Self-identified" (Daly, p. 3).

17. My reference is, of course, to Audre Lorde's influential essay, "The Master's Tools Will Never Dismantle the Master's House," in *Sister Outsider: Essays and Speeches* (Trumansburg, NY: Crossing, 1984), pp. 110−14.

18. Daly's most powerful illustration of this point, namely that the games of language affect the lives of real people, is her discussion of suttee and its rendering in the language of male scholars. See chapter three, "Indian *Suttee*: The Ultimate Consummation of Marriage" (pp. 113−33). For a critical discussion

of these scholars and their language as not just male, but Western and white, see Gayatri Chakrvorty Spivak, "Can the Subaltern Speak?" in Cary Nelson and Lawrence Grossberg, eds. *Marxism and the Interpretation of Culture* (Urbana: Univ. of Illinois, 1988), pp. 271–317.

19. See Audre Lorde's "An Open Letter to Mary Daly" in *Sister Outsider*, pp. 66–72. See also the final section of this essay. "Other Voices."

20. Verena Stefan, *Shedding*, trans. Johanna Moore and Beth Weckmueller (New York: Daughters, 1978). [Original: *Häutungen: Autobiografische Aufzeichnungen Gedichte Träume Analysen* (Munich: Frauenoffensive, 1975)]. The unpaginated foreword, from which I am quoting here, was not included in the published version of the American translation.

21. The Swiss-born Stefan went to Berlin in 1968 where, after completing her training as a physical therapist, studied sociology at the Free University. She was a founding member of the feminist group "Bread ♀ Roses," which focused particularly on issues involving women's reproductive rights and health care. Stefan also became an active member of the women artists' community in Berlin, participating in the planning and production or a major exhibition on women artists in 1976. She makes her living through her work as a physical therapist.

22. To do much more than mention the major (and, no doubt, obvious) names would surpass the limits of an essay such as this, which is intended and designed as a survey. Therefore, I will merely recall to memory key figures and texts in this debate such as Jacques Lacan (first seminar, 1953–54; published 1975; *Écrits* 1966), Jacques Derrida (*L'Écriture at la différance*, 1967; *Eperons. Les styles de Nietzsche*, 1976), Michel Foucault (*L'Ordre du discours*, 1971; *Histoire de la sexualité*, vol. 1: *La volonté de savoir*, 1976).

23. Hélène Cixous, "The Laugh of the Medusa," trans. Keith and Paula Cohen, in Elaine Marks and Isabelle de Courtivron, eds. *New French Feminisms: An Anthology* (Amherst, Mass.: Univ. of Massachusetts, 1980), pp. 245–65. [Original: "Le rire de la Méduse," *L'Arc* (1975).]

24. Hélène Cixous and Catherine Clément, *The Newly Born Woman*, trans. Betsy Wing (Minneapolis: Univ. of Minnesota, 1986); hereafter abbreviated as *Woman*. [Original: *La jeune née* (1975).] (The fact that this important text was not made available to English-language readers until a decade after its original publication is an interesting item of reception history.) Born in Algeria to Franco-German Jewish parents, Cixous went to France to study English shortly after the outbreak of the Algerian War. An active participant in the student uprisings of May 1968, she began teaching experimental literature and feminist courses at the University of Paris VIII (Vincennes) and became head of the Center of Research in Women's Studies, which she cofounded. She has written and published voluminously in all genres: scholarly studies, novels, plays, and essays. Catherine Clément has taught philosophy at the University of Paris I and VIII and written several books on the politics of psychoanalysis from a Marxist and feminist perspective. She is cultural editor of the socialist weekly *Le Matin*.

25. Its publication in the very first issue of the newly founded American scholarly feminist journal *Signs* (Summer 1976) was a touchstone for the incipient Franco-American feminist theory debate.

26. In the French original, Cixous plays on the double meaning of the verb voler, which means both "to steal" and "to fly." Women, she argues, need to free themselves from the bondage of respect to established authorities; they must take (voler = steal) what they need and take off (voler = fly) with it to do with as they will.

27. "Power," p. 68.

28. Originally published in 1974, *Speculum of the Other Woman* was not published in English (trans. Gillian C. Gill) until 1985 by Cornell University Press.

29. Trained as a psychoanalyst and with doctorates in linguistics and philosophy, Irigaray, even after her expulsion from the Freudian School at the behest of the Lacanian faction, continues to practice as an analyst and do research, particularly on issues of language and psychology, at the Centre Nationale de la Recherche Scientifique. She has published several books, each of which is an inquiry into the nature and effects of philosophical and psychoanalytic methods and/or principles from a feminist perspective.

30. *This Sex Which Is Not One*, trans. Catherine Porter with Carolyn Burke (Ithaca, N.Y.: Cornell Univ., 1985).

31. "This Sex Which Is Not One" and "When Our Lips Speak Together" are the two essays in which this concept and its implications for language are spelled out most clearly.

32. After having taught in the French Department of Miami University in Oxford, Ohio, for a number of years, Jane Gallop is now professor of humanities at Rice University, where she also chairs the Women's Studies program.

33. I refer here to the useful definition provided by Chris Weedon in *Feminist Practice and Poststructuralist Theory* (Oxford: Basil Blackwell, 1987): "The symbolic order in Lacanian theory is the social and cultural order in which we live our lives as conscious, gendered subjects. It is structured by language and the laws and social institutions which language guarantees" (p. 52).

34. I refer again to Weedon: "The imaginary is a term used to describe the pre-Oedipal identification of the infant with its mirror image ... At this stage in its development, the child is neither feminine nor masculine, and has yet to acquire language" (p. 51).

35. The degree to which the dialogic constitutes a recurrent structural principle of recent feminist theory is, in itself, noteworthy. *La jeune née*, for example, is structured in the form of a dialogue: first, Clément speaks (part 1: "The Guilty One"), then Cixous (part 2: "Sorties: Out and Out: Attacks/Ways Out/Forays"), until finally, they argue it out (part 3: "Exchange"). A number of Irigaray's essays (among them, "When Our Lips Speak Together") are also written as silent dialogues, addressed to a "you" with a "we" implied.

36. A number of essays by the French semiotician and avant-garde theorist Julia Kristeva have been collected under this title, *Desire in Language: A Semiotic Approach to Literature and Art* (New York: Columbia Univ., 1980). However, while gender questions are repeatedly broached in these essays, gender remains more or less a marginal issue.

37. Jane Gallop, *Thinking Through the Body* (New York: Columbia Univ., 1988).

38. Weedon, p. 163.

39. For a particularly clear and useful discussion of both the theoretical premises and practical consequences of a deconstructive method, see Catherine Belsey, *Critical Practice* (London: Methuen, 1980). I am drawing here most specifically on her last chapter, "Towards a Productive Critical Practice."

40. The doubled reference in the title of Toril Moi's *Textual/Sexual Politics: Feminist Literary Theory* (London: Methuen, 1985) to both the deconstructive concept of textual politics and the feminist concept of sexual politics explicitly acknowledges this convergence.

41. Monique Wittig's first novel, *L'Opoponax* [*The Opoponax*] (1964) had only recently been awarded one of France's most prestigious literary prizes, the Prix Médicis, and Wittig was being hailed as one of the most promising and brilliant new writers by the likes of Alain Robbe-Grillet and Marguerite Duras. After having completed her literary studies in Paris, she worked as a proofreader for the publisher, Editions de Minuit. At the same time, she took an active part in radical politics, both as a member of the "Red Dykes" and as a founder of a separatist group, "Revolutionary feminists." She has written several books of feminist experimental fiction, and numerous political and theoretical essays. In 1977, along with Simone de Beauvoir and Christine Delphy, she cofounded a new French journal of feminist theory, *Questions féministes* (an English-language edition of which, *Feminist Issues*, has been appearing since 1980). Wittig now lives in California.

42. Monique Wittig, *Les Guérillères*, trans. David LeVay (New York: Avon, 1973), p. 143. [Original: *Les Guérillères*, 1969.] This proclamation with which the text begins is echoed just before the end. See fn. 49.

43. "Guerrier," in French, means warrior; "guerilla" means guerilla fighter; these terms, however, are grammatically masculine; a female form does not technically exist.

44. As the French sociologist and feminist theorist, Christine Delphy, outlined in a landmark essay published a year after *Les Guérillères* appeared, the "main enemy" is "the patriarchal mode of production of domestic services (i.e., the unpaid performance of these services by women)." ["The Main Enemy," in *Close to Home: A Materialist Analysis of Women's Oppression*, ed. Diana Leonhard (Amherst: Univ. of Massachusetts, 1984), p. 73.] Delphy, one of the cofounders of *Questions féministes*, has argued for a theory and practice of what she calls a "materialist feminism" ("a radical feminist analysis based on marxist principles"). See "The Main Enemy," p. 59.

45. Monique Witting, "One Is Not Born a Woman," *Feminist Issues*, 1:2 (Winter 1981), pp. 47–55.

46. Wittig, "One Is Not Born a Woman," p. 449.

47. Mao's concept of revolution as a permanent, ongoing state of cultural transformation was particularly popular during the events of May 1968 in Western Europe, especially in France. The Chinese cultural revolution was a historical reference point for many Left French intellectuals (Kristeva, Barthes, et al.) until well into the 1970s.

48. The text of *Les Guérillères* opens onto a full page of word sequences that, both in form (bold print and capital letters) and imagistic density, have the quality at once of a chant, a manifesto, and a prose poem. This page ends with a proclamation—"THE WOMEN AFFIRM IN TRIUMPH THAT/ALL ACTION IS OVERTHROW"—and then, interspersed by a blank page with an empty circle, the narrative "begins."

49. Lorraine Bethel, "WHAT CHOU MEAN *WE*, WHITE GIRL? or, the culled lesbian feminist declaration of independence (dedicated to the proposition that all women are not equal, i.e., identical/ly oppressed)," in Lorraine Bethel and Barbara Smith, eds. *Conditions: Five* [*The Black Women's Issue*], 2:2 (Autumn 1979), pp. 86—93.

50. Chandra Talpade Mohanty, "Under Western Eyes: Feminist Scholarship and Colonial Discourses," *boundary 2*, pp. 333—59.

51. Trinh T. Minh-ha, "Difference: 'A Special Third World Women Issue," in Trinh T. Minh-ha, ed., *She, The Inappropriate/d Other*, special issue of *Discourse*, 8 (Fall/Winter 1986/87), p. 31.

52. Spivak, "Can the Subaltern Speak?," p. 271. See also Gayatri Chakravorty Spivak, *In Other Worlds: Essays in Cultural Politics* (London: Methuen, 1987), especially "French Feminism in an International Frame" and "A Literary Representation of the Subaltern: A Woman's Text from the Third World." For other work that takes up the issue of feminism, language, and the colonizing gesture of intellectural discourse, see Barbara Christian, "The Race for Theory," *Cultural Critique*, 6 (Spring 1987), especially pp. 59—60; Trinh T. Minh-ha *Woman, Native, Other: Writing Postcoloniality & Feminism* (Univ. of Indiana, 1989) and Donna Haraway, *Primate Visions: Gender, Race, and Nature in the World of Modern Science* (London: Routledge, 1989).

53. Mohanty, "Under Western Eyes," p. 334.

54. Trinh T. Minh-ha, "Introduction," *She, The Inappropriate/d Other*, p. 3.

55. I am paraphrasing from a talk by Hélène Cixous, "Poetry is/and (the) Political." Given as a presentation at a conference held in New York in 1979 to commemorate the 30th anniversary of the publication of Simone de Beauvoir's *The Second Sex*, it has not been published in English.

56. Trinh T. Minh-ha, "Difference," p. 33.

57. Christine Delphy, "Patriarchy, Feminism and Their Intellectuals" in *Close to Home: A Materialist Analysis of Women's Oppression*, trans. and ed. by Diana Leonard (Amherst: Univ. of Massachusetts, 1984). I am referring in particular to the end of this essay (pp. 151—53).

58. In his *Cultural Literacy: What Every American Needs to Know* (New York: Vintage, 1988), E. D. Hirsch, Jr., not only has no reference to sexism, he leaves out feminism entirely.

59. In 1977, for example, both the American Psychological Association and the International Association of Business Communicators issued their own guidelines for nonsexist language use: Charles N. Cofer, Robert S. Daniels, Frances Y. Dunham, and Walter Heimer, eds., "Guidelines for Nonsexist Language in APA Journals," *American Psychologist*, 32 (1977), pp. 486–94; J. E. Pickens, P. W. Rao, L. C. Roberts, eds. *Without Bias: A Guidebook for Nondiscriminatory Communication* (San Francisco: International Association of Business Communicators, 1977).

60. There is a single, very brief, reference to avoiding "racist or sexist connotations" under the rubric "Watching for lapses." These lapses include "racism and sexism," as well as (and apparently on the same order) "dangling modifiers, split infinitives" or "overuse of an author's pet word" (p. 61).

61. *MLA Handbook for Writers of Research Papers*, 3d edition, eds. Joseph Gibaldi and Walter S. Achtert (New York: Modern Language Association of America, 1988), p. 34.

62. Casey Miller and Kate Swift, *The Handbook of Nonsexist Writing*, 2d edition (New York: Harper and Row, 1988).

63. Among the most lucid and eloquent demonstrations of this connection are Virginia Woolf's *A Room of One's Own* (1929) and *Three Guineas* (1938).

64. In "'The Blank Page' and the Issues of Female Creativity" [in Elizabeth Abel, ed. *Writing and Sexual Difference* (Chicago: Univ. of Chicago, 1982), pp. 73–95], the literary critic Susan Gubar discusses the implications of such a stance for women writers and, by implication, feminist critics.

65. Gertrude Stein, "Patriarchal Poetry" (1927); excerpts in Louise Bernikow, ed. *The World Split Open: Four Centuries of Women Poets in England and America, 1552–1950* (New York: Random House, 1974), p. 236.

66. Broumas, "Artemis," p. 24.

67. Wittig, *Les Guérillères*, p. 134.

68. An excellent example of such an approach is Elizabeth Fox-Genovese's reading of Harriet Jacobs's *Incidents in the Life of a Slave Girl*, positioned as the epilogue to her book, *Within the Plantation Household: Black and White Women of the Old South* (Chapel Hill: Univ. of North Carolina, 1988). Mary Poovey's work, from her first book, *The Proper Lady and the Woman Writer: Ideology as Style in the Works of Mary Wollstonecraft, Mary Shelley, and Jane Austen* (Chicago: Univ. of Chicago, 1984), to her most recent, *Uneven Developments: The Ideological Work of Gender in Mid-Victorian England* (Chicago: Univ. of Chicago, 1988), illustrates this approach throughout, as does the work of Trinh T. Minh-ha, both in its "creative" and its "critical" manifestations.

Contributors

Angelika Bammer, Assistant Professor of German and Institute of Women's Studies, Emory University, is the author of *Partial Visions: Feminism and Utopianism in the 1970s* (Methuen, forthcoming) and numerous articles on contemporary women's literature, film, and the politics of theory. She is currently working on *Mother Tongue and Other Strangers: Discourses of Foreignness in Twentieth-Century Literature*, a study of the work of authors who have been displaced from their native cultures.

James A. Boon, Professor of Anthropology, Princeton University, is the author of *The Anthropological Romance of Bali, 1597–1972* (Cambridge University Press, 1977); *Other Tribes, Other Scribes: Symbolic Anthropology in the Comparative Study of Cultures, Histories, Religions, and Texts* (Cambridge University Press, 1982); and, most recently, *Affinities and Extremes: The Bittersweet Ethnology of East Indies History, Hindu-Balinese Culture, and Indo-European Allure* (University of Chicago Press, 1990).

Thomas DiPiero, Assistant Professor of French and Comparative Literature, University of Rochester, is the author of *Formidable Masters: Aesthetics and Ideology in Early French Fiction* (Stanford University Press, forthcoming), and has edited a special issue of *Diacritics* (Winter 1988) on money. He is currently working on a book dealing with ideology and masculinity.

Martin Donougho, Associate Professor of Philosophy, University of South Carolina, has written on German philosophy, especially Hegel, and on the philosophy of art, where his interests lie in literary theory, the visual arts, and music. In 1991 he held an NEH fellowship to work on a book on Hegel's *Aesthetics*, and he is also completing a translation of Hegel's 1823 lectures on aesthetics.

Charles Guignon, Associate Professor of Philosophy, University of Vermont, is the author of *Heidegger and the Problem of Knowledge* (Hackett, 1983) as well as articles on hermeneutics, psychotherapy theory, Wittgenstein, and Rorty. Currently he is editing a volume of essays, *The Cambridge Companion to Heidegger*, and coauthoring a book, *Understanding and Moral Values in Psychotherapy*.

John Johnston, Associate Professor of English, Emory University, is the author of *Carnival of Repetition: Gaddis's "The Recognitions" and Postmodern Theory* (University of Philadelphia Press, 1989), as well as articles on contemporary fiction and literary theory.

265

C. H. Knoblauch, Associate Professor of English and Director of Graduate Studies at State University of New York in Albany, is the coauthor, with Lil Brannon, of *Rhetorical Traditions and the Teaching of Writing* (Boynton/Cook, 1984). He has also published numerous articles on rhetoric, composition theory, and literacy theory.

Michael S. Roth, Hartley Burr Alexander Professor of Humanities at Scripps College, is the author of *Psycho-Analysis as History: Negation and Freedom in Freud* (Cornell University Press, 1987) and *Knowing and History: Appropriations of Hegel in Twentieth-Century France* (Cornell University Press, 1988). He is currently working on a book on the conceptualization of memory disorders in nineteenth-century Europe.

Georgia Warnke, Assistant Professor of Philosophy, Yale University, is author of *Gadamer: Hermeneutics, Tradition and Reason* (Stanford University Press, 1987) and numerous articles.